HISTORY

IN EXILE

Pamela Ballinger

HISTORY
IN EXILE

Memory and Identity at the Borders of the Balkans

PRINCETON UNIVERSITY PRESS · PRINCETON AND OXFORD

Library of Congress Cataloging-in-Publication Data

Ballinger, Pamela, 1968–
History in exile : memory and identity at the borders of the Balkans
/ Pamela Ballinger.
p.   cm.
Includes bibliographical references and index.
ISBN 0-691-08696-6 (cloth: alk. paper)—
ISBN 0-619-08697-4 (pbk.: alk. paper)
1. Italians—Istria (Croatia and Slovenia)—Ethnic identiy.
2. Refugees—Italy.   3. Istria (Croatia and Slovenia)—Ethnic relations.
4. Julian March—History.   5. Italy—Boundaries—Yugoslovia.
6. Yugoslavia—Boundaries—Italy.   I. Title.
DR1350.I78 B35   2003
305.85104972—dc21   2002020056

British Library Cataloging-in-Publication Data is available
This book has been composed in

www.pup.princeton.edu
Printed in the United States of America
1   2   3   4   5   6   7   8   9   10

For my parents

CONTENTS

LIST OF ILLUSTRATIONS

THE RESEARCH and writing of this book took place along many shores: those of the Italian port city of Trieste and the adjacent Istrian peninsula (the subjects of this work), the Northern Californian coastline, the rocky beaches of my native Puget Sound, and the shingled stretches of my adoptive Maine. In my trajectory from North America to Europe, as well as from Trieste to Istria, I undertook a journey in reverse from that of many of my informants; displaced from Istria after World War II, many of them permanently relocated to the nearby city of Trieste or transited through its refugee camps on their way to resettlement in Italy, the New World, and Australia. But like these Istrian exiles, or *esuli,* I came to construct my own sentimental cartography based on those places—really, the "limens" of seas—which have been the sites of my emotional and intellectual engagement.

In mapping out this personal cartography, I was guided and helped at every turn by both individuals and institutions, whom I can only begin to acknowledge here. I am particularly grateful to the staffs at the Slovene Ministry of Technology in Ljubljana, Slovene Cultural and Economic Union in Trieste (SKGZ), the Slovene Students' Dormitory in Trieste, the Slovene Research Institute, the Institute for Ethnic Studies in Ljubljana, and the European Center for Ethnic and Regional Studies in Maribor for assistance during my first summers (1992, 1993) of preliminary investigation. Aleksej Kalc, Dušan and Anna Maria Kalc, Majda Kodrić, Vera Klopčić, Doriza Pečar and family, and Marta Verginella were among those who gave generously of their time and made the prospect of returning for an extended fieldwork period less daunting. The first two summers of fieldwork were made possible by a National Science Foundation Travel Grant, a Singleton Grant (from Johns Hopkins's Department of Italian and Spanish), and a Pre-Dissertation Fellowship from the Council for European Studies.

The extended fieldwork project I carried out between January 1995 and September 1996 was funded at various stages by Fulbright, Institute for the Study of World Politics, SSRC-MacArthur, SSRC-Western Europe, and Wenner-Gren. I am grateful to all these agencies for making my research possible. My MacArthur Peace and Security Fellowship also enabled me to spend a term at the School of Slavonic and East European Studies (SSEES) in London before heading to the field. During my time in London, I learned much about (former) Yugoslavia from Wendy Bracewell, Cathy Carmichael, James Gow, and Dušan Puvačić. I also benefited from working with the documentation of the Allied Military Government / Free Territory of Trieste at the U.S. National Archives and express my gratitude to the staff there.

Upon arriving in Trieste, the Istituto Regionale per la Cultura Istriana (IRCI) provided me with an invaluable institutional base for my work. I could never adequately thank IRCI for the generous support given to me throughout my stay and beyond. IRCI's current president Silvio Delbello and former president Arturo Vigini, Director Piero Delbello, and Secretary Chiara Vigini offered advice (scholarly and practical), access to archives, and a working space. The Centro di Ricerche Storiche di Rovigno similarly hosted me during my time in Croatia and generously offered access to its library. Director Giovanni Radossi, librarian Marisa Ferrara, Donald Schiozzi, and researchers Elvio Baccarini, Sabrina Benussi, Orietta Moscarda, Nicò Sponza, and Fulvio Šuran merit special mention for their help and kindness.

The associations of the exiles in Trieste and the Italian minority in Istria also welcomed me, allowing me to participate in diverse events and providing me with various publications. Warm thanks are owed to the Associazione delle Comunità Istriane, Associazione Nazionale Venezia Giulia e Dalmazia, Circolo di Istria, Unione degli Istriani, and Università Popolare di Trieste. I am similarly grateful to the Unione Italiana and its constituent Comunità degli Italiani (particularly Rovigno's Comunità degli Italiani) in Istria. While space does not permit me to thank all those individuals in these organizations who helped me, I single out the following: Roberto Batelli, Marcello Bogneri, Silvio Cattalini, Giorgio Damiani, Mario Dassovich, Livio Dorigo, Anna Maria Muiesan Gasparin, Gianni Giuricin, Fritz Grimm, Liana Martinč iDomenica Malusa, Karmen Medica, Giuliano Orel, Anita Parovel, Antonio Pellizzer, Ruggero Rovatti, Anita Slatti, Maurizio Tremul, Marucci Vascon, Pietro Vascotto, Marino Vocci, Denis Zigante, and Silvano Zilli. I also appreciate the help given me by Padre Flaminio Rocchi and his Foundation in Rome, as well as that proffered by Marino Micich of the Museo Fiumano in Rome. Warm thanks are also owed to the approximately one hundred individuals in Italy, Croatia, and Slovenia with whom I conducted life histories, as well as to the many individuals from the New World and Australia who sent me letters, life histories, and photos.

The Istituto Regionale per la Storia del Movimento di Resistenza nel Friuli–Venezia Giulia also opened its collections to me. At the Istituto, Tullia Catalan, Tristano Matta, Giampaolo Valdevit, and Sergio Zucca all offered valuable scholarly advice. Other scholars in Trieste who gave of their time include Elio Apih, Gloria Nemec, Raoul Pupo, and Roberto Spazzali. Fellow students of the region, Bojan Basker, Sabrina Benussi, Maria Grazia Kuris, Lidija Nikočević, Laura Oretti, and Marta Verginella, proved unflagging in their support and became dear friends.

The Oretti family in Trieste adopted me, and I found myself with a *mamma Italiana,* as well as a sister. In Rovigno, the Benussi family similarly offered me a haven where I could always drop in for a chat or a laugh. Thanks also to the Burić and Činić families for making me feel so welcome. As a result of these

friendships, Trieste and Rovigno remain places to which I feel that I am returning "home" each time I visit again.

Carrying out fieldwork was just one aspect of completing this project. The
actual write-up was made possible by funding from the Center for International
Security and Cooperation (CISAC) at Stanford University and the Newcombe
Foundation. CISAC provided me with an institutional base throughout the
writing period. I could not have asked for a more wonderful and intellectually
stimulating place in which to translate my fieldwork experience into prose.
Lynn Eden and David Holloway helped push my thinking in new directions at
the same time that their interest in my project gave me confidence that the topic
had interdisciplinary significance. My advisors and readers at Johns Hopkins—
JoAnne Brown, Nancy Struever, Michel-Rolph Trouillot, and Katherine Verdery—deserve special thanks for their input and advice at all stages of the dissertation. I also appreciate the useful suggestions given by Gillian Feeley-Harnik
during the project's initial formulation. Katherine Verdery merits particular
praise for reading multiple drafts and providing extensive criticism; her comments were crucial in helping me focus a large amount of material around key
themes. Other individuals who read chapters at various stages include Joe
Bandy, Wendy Bracewell, Thomas Emmert, Orietta Moscarda, Marilyn Reiz-
baum, Roberto Spazzali, Giampaolo Valdevit, and Marta Verginella. The "Culture of Insecurity" group at the University of Minnesota and Kent State endured
multiple drafts of the paper that became chapter 3; I appreciate the close readings offered by Hugh Gusterson, Mark Laffey, and Jutta Weldes. My reviewers
at Princeton University Press—Donald Carter, Michael Herzfeld, and Douglas
Holmes—offered invaluable critical input as I revised the original manuscript.
Mary Murrell did an exceptional job as editor, guiding the transformation from
a dissertation to a finished book. Anna Rein must also be acknowledged for her
careful correction of my translations from Italian to English and Dalia Geffen
for her excellent copy editing. While this study has benefited from the input of
various readers, I remain solely responsible for its defects.

I reserve my final thanks for those who vicariously lived this project with me.
Nikolai Ssorin-Chaikov read countless drafts throughout the write-up period
and proved an unfailing and invaluable intellectual interlocutor, as well as
friend. My parents, Sandra and Richard Ballinger, provided support—financial,
practical, and moral—during seven long years of graduate school. They worried about my working in "danger zones" like Croatia (as well as Baltimore),
looked after my affairs while I was in the field for two years, and listened to my
doubts and fears about the project. They remained the cardinal point on a "sentimental cartography" ranging from the Mediterranean to the Puget Sound, and
I dedicate this book to them.

A version of chapter 3 appeared in the volume *Cultures of Insecurity: States,
Communities, and the Production of Danger,* edited by Raymond Duvall, Hugh

Gusterson, Mark Laffey, and Jutta Weldes (Minneapolis: University of Minnesota Press, 1999). Sections of chapters 4 and 8 derive from the essay "*Convivenza e Civilta:* Visions of Europe at the Edge of the Balkans," contained in *The Yugoslav Conflict and its Implication for International Relations,* edited by Stefano Bianchini and Robert Craig Nation (Ravenna: Longo Editore, 1998). Portions of the arguments detailed in chapters 1 and 6 make up the article, "The Istrian Esodo: Silences and Presences in the Construction of Exodus," published in *War, Exile, Everyday Life,* edited by Renata Jambresiæ Kirin and Maja Povrzanoviæ (Zagreb: Institute of Ethnology and Folklore Research, 1996).

AMG	Allied Military Government
AN	Alleanza Nazionale
ANVGD	Associazione Nazionale Venezia Giulia e Dalmazia
BETFOR	British Element Trieste Force
CADDY	Committee to Aid Democratic Dissidents in Yugoslavia
CLN	Comitato di Liberazione Nazionale
CLNI	Comitato di Liberazione Nazionale dell'Istria
DC	Democrazia Cristiana
DDI-IDS	Istrian Democratic Assembly
EU	European Union
FFA	Women's Antifascist Front
FTT	Free Territory of Trieste
GNI	Gruppo Nazionale Italiano
HDZ	Croatian Democratic Union
IRCI	Istituto Regionale per la Cultura Istriana
IRO	International Refugee Organization
LpT	Lista per Trieste
MSI	Movimento Sociale Italiano
OF	Front for the Liberation of the Slovene Nation
PCI	Partito Comunista Italiano
PDS	Partito Democratico della Sinistra
PPI	Partito Popolare Italiano
PSI	Partito Socialista Italiano
RSI	Repubblica Sociale Italiano
SKGZ	Slovene Cultural and Economic Union
SLORI	Slovene Research Institutes
UI	Unione Italiana
UIIF	Unione degli Italiani dell'Istria e di Fiume
UNRRA	United Nations Refugee and Relief Administration
UpT	Università Popolare di Trieste

HISTORY

IN EXILE

In the Shadow of the Balkans, on the Shores of the Mediterranean

IN the border zone between Italy, Slovenia, and Croatia known as the Julian March reside members of families who were divided and scattered at the conclusion of the Second World War when Italy and Yugoslavia partitioned the region. These separated kin live on the fringes of the Gulf of Venice, an inner body of water making up part of the Adriatic Sea, which today divides populations as much as it once united them. Triestine writer Claudio Magris's description of the forests in this region hold equally true for its seas: "The woods are at once the glorification and the nullification of borders: a plurality of differing, opposing worlds, though still within the great unity that embraces and dissolves them" (1999, 107).

Though the fluidity of the sea would appear to defy any attempt at sovereignty, political borders cut through them. Indeed, the Adriatic's waters have witnessed the struggles of diverse powers—in more distant epochs, Venice, Austria, and the Ottomans and in the last century, Italy and Yugoslavia—to secure and police the adjacent territories. The most recent example involves the dispute between Slovenia and Croatia over precisely where, in the tiny Gulf of Piran, to draw the maritime frontier between those two states, which declared independence from Yugoslavia in 1991. This border contest, though seemingly in comical miniature, reflects the dramatic transformations that have reshaped the political geographies of the Julian March, as well as former Yugoslavia and the Balkans, in the last decade. The story I tell in this book traces the reconfigurations of memory and identity in relation to both political and symbolic boundaries.

In particular, I explore contemporary political debates surrounding the contentious post–World War II partition of the Julian March, memories of which the 1991 division of the Istrian Peninsula between Slovenia and Croatia echoed and renewed. The rearrangement of political borders after the Second World War provoked the Istrian exodus (l'esodo istriano), entailing the migration of between 200,000 and 350,000 ethnic Italians (as well as Slovenes and Croats).[1] My account here of the consequences of this displacement for those ethnic Italians who left (the andati or esuli) and those who remained (the rimasti) reflects the recent impulse on the part of scholars to study what many see as representative of the contemporary condition: the exiled, the refugee, the boundary crossers of various sorts. In her book on the Appalachian coal-mining region of West Virginia, Kathleen Stewart encourages us to "[i]magine a place grown intensely local in the face of loss, displacement, exile, and a perpetually deferred desire to return to what was always already lost or still ahead, just beyond reach" (1996, 16).

Closer at hand, in the field of Mediterranean anthropology, studies of Greek refugees—those of the 1922 population exchange between Greece and Turkey, of the Cyprus conflict, and of the Greek-Macedonian dispute (Brown 2002; Danforth 1995; Hirschon 1998; Karakasidou 1997; and Loizos 1981)—have challenged once-prevalent assumptions of either stable identities or (putative) cultures. As in the case of the Istrians I examine, the Greek and Macedonian examples deal with former refugees for whom the condition of exile has become permanent and for whom the moment of displacement proves central to historical consciousness. My analysis offers an innovation, however, in its attention to the experiences of those who undergo actual displacement together with those who suffer interior displacement, losing their homeland without ever physically moving. In heeding Malkki's fruitful suggestion (1995) to broaden our understanding of what the unit of analysis ("exile") consists of, I demonstrate how examining only one group misses the crucial dialogues (implicit and explicit), as well as shared histories, uniting these populations.

Considering diverse victims of displacement in tandem further helps link the work on forced migration with that on economic and so-called voluntary migration. Scholars in the latter field have begun to question the old dichotomies of sending and receiving communities, instead noting the multidirectional and often long-standing flows of migrants (Glick Schiller 1999; Kearney 1986; Stack 1996). Just as the example of massive Italian emigration to the New World has informed the thinking and rethinking about "classic" patterns of economic migration (Baily 1990; Glick Schiller 1999), so does the case of Italians from Istria help us reexamine our theoretical models of displacement. As I demonstrate, an analysis of the forms of identification forged through violence in the Istrian case proves productive for a critical interrogation of related topics of theoretical debate such as hybrid and borderland identities.

Though in a very different context from that of Stewart, who reports from a liminal part of the United States, my work also illuminates the (always unstable) constitution of locality and peripherality in a region profoundly shaped by displacement. At the same time, I do not just imagine such a space but also explore the imaginings of those who inhabit it and thereby render space meaningful as *place* (Carter, Donald, and Squires 1993, xii). Central to these understandings are interwoven images of both nature and culture: land and sea, churches and cemeteries. Ultimately, it is the sea—its beauty, as well as its association with coastal cities and "civilization"—that esuli and rimasti alike recall with both affection and sadness. As a song in Istrian dialect puts it, "I hear the voice of your sea, which sighs for my return" (*Del tuo mar la vose sento; che sospira el mio ritorno* [Sizzi in Bogneri 1994, 224]).

The sea that inspires esuli's longings has also animated a rich body of anthropological scholarship. In studying the consequences of partition for ethnic Italians from Istria, I address many of the concerns—including violence, symbolic group boundaries, political patronage—that informed the classic texts of what has come to be called Mediterranean anthropology, even as the methodological and theoretical framing of the project reflects shifts in both the object of study itself and how contemporary scholars conceptualize it. Whereas traditional Mediterraneanist studies typically focused on rural or marginal communities, often treated as isolated from or hostile to larger state structures, my analysis firmly situates the experience of the esuli and their kin, the rimasti, within the moving interstices of state centers and peripheries. Traversing the boundaries of states and ethno-national groups, as well as the disciplines of anthropology, history, and political science, this book is a product of the ongoing reconceptualizations of the very notion of what constitutes the anthropological field.

The theoretical musings of Marcus (1998), as well as the Europeanist ethnographies of Carter (1997) and Holmes (2000), offered important reference points for undertaking a "multi-sited" ethnographic project in which I based myself in two primary locales (Italian Trieste/Trst,[2] from January to October 1995, and Istrian Rovigno/Rovinj, from November 1995 to September 1996) while visiting and conducting interviews throughout the broader region known as the Julian March. My methods included formal interviewing and life histories (with approximately fifty conducted among the esuli and fifty among the rimasti), participant observation in various events and rituals, archival work, and close readings of the extensive literature of local scholarship, memoirs, prose, and poetry exploring the exodus.[3]

At the same time, my research took inspiration from older studies that had innovated within the confines of the Mediterraneanist framework. Herzfeld's (1985) work on Cretan sheep thieves and his demonstration of the ways in which marginality within the state is continually reproduced, for example, and Cole and Wolf's (1974) classic account of competing ethnic identities in the Italian Tyrol (an area that, like the Julian March, has a long history of competing irredentisms) raised early on the problem of symbolic (ethnic) group boundaries within the context of complex, modern states.

This issue of boundaries proves inherent to the very vision of a Mediterraneanist discourse laid out and endlessly debated by social historians (most notably Fernand Braudel) and anthropologists, even if the borders in question are usually those of the region and "culture area" itself. Echoing the words of Braudel, whose magisterial work on the "inner sea" any scholar of the Mediterranean must acknowledge, Predrag Matvejević writes of this body of water:

Getting to know the length and breadth of the Mediterranean is no easy task. We are
never certain how far it extends, that is, how much of the coast it occupies and where
it ends, on either land or sea. (1999, 7)

In his attempt to unlock the riddle of what, if anything, defines the Mediterranean, Matvejević paradoxically admits:

Its boundaries are drawn in neither space nor time. There is in fact no way of drawing them: they are neither ethnic nor historical, state nor national; they are like a chalk
circle that is constantly traced and erased, that the winds and waves, that obligations
and inspirations expand or reduce. (Ibid., 10)

Matvejević's vision of the ultimate indeterminacy of the sea nonetheless
shares certain assumptions with definitions of the Mediterranean as a "homogeneous environment" (Braudel 1972a, 1972b; Gilmore 1982), although Matvejević's ecological markers include such intangibles as sea smells, waves, and
nets. Matvejević's conceptualization of the sea contrasts sharply with other
widely circulating views in, and of, the region that rigidly map populations onto
territory. Examples of the latter include late-nineteenth- and twentieth-century
Italian nationalist and irredentist claims to the eastern Adriatic; again, however,
these competing accounts rest on similarly "ecological" notions. Indeed, in their
beliefs about peoples' "belonging" to or being rooted in particular territories and
environments, many of the ethnic Italians with whom I worked refracted the
scholarly debates about the broader region. Informants continually spoke of
Italian *civiltà,* or civilization, as simultaneously derived from (in the sense of
ecological adaptation) and having profoundly shaped (tamed, that is, civilized)
the landscape of the Julian March.

   The fundamental ambiguity around the question of "cultural ecology" in
Matvejević's book, appropriately titled *Mediterranean: A Cultural Landscape,*
does not prove coincidental and undoubtedly reflects, at least in part, his own
location as a Slav hailing from those territories once contested by Italy and Yugoslavia. Envisioning the sea from the perspective of a South Slav born in
Mostar, fifty kilometers inland from the Adriatic Sea, Matvejević's only partial
claim to a Mediterranean identity points to the long (albeit always incomplete)
hegemony exercised by Latinate culture in the Adriatic. Braudel goes so far as
to argue, "The Adriatic is perhaps the most unified of all the regions of the sea"
(1972a, 125), owing to centuries of influence by the Italian peninsula on the
eastern Adriatic. The question of which culture is most authentic and autochthonous or "indigenous" to the Adriatic littoral lies at the heart of the contests over territory that form the backdrop to the exodus of Italians from Istria.
Throughout this book, I examine the history and legacies of this powerful mapping of a space (terrestrial and maritime) onto populations, in particular those
groups labeled Italians, Slovenes, and Croats. My account of these processes
proves historical in two senses: I explore the ways in which understandings of

the past inform these contests over identity, as well as over territory, and I examine these identity claims over time.

In doing this, I bring an anthropological focus on localized identities in the Mediterranean—the subject of so many monographs that if they recognized the relationship of the local to the broader context at all, they tended to do so within a framework of modernization (or integration into the capitalist world system) that either idealized or pathologized a folk past—into a productive dialogue with the Europeanist discussion in other disciplines about the problematics of modernity. More precisely, I address perhaps the central issue at the heart of Europe's vexed modernist projects: the legacies of violence and victimhood generated by the "dual traumas" of fascism and communism in the twentieth century. The "timeless" Mediterranean thus acquires an all-too-real historical specificity as a site of bloodshed, ethnic violence, and suffering. An older focus on tradition, understood as local rituals and practices, converges with the extensive literature on the politics of the past, yielding an account that illuminates both the (re)configurations of broad landscapes of memory shaped by war and other state-sponsored violence and the "microphysics" of such violence as refracted through individual and family narratives.

The image of the Mediterranean as a site of state-sponsored violence does not altogether accord with the stereotypical passions and romance associated with that realm. The region has, of course, not only challenged scholars who have sought to map its boundaries and capture its essence but also seduced countless writers, artists, and travelers. From the outset of his book, Braudel confesses: "I have loved the Mediterranean with passion, no doubt because I am a northerner like so many others in whose footsteps I have followed" (Braudel 1972a, 17). As an anthropologist and a young American woman, I too followed in the footsteps of my many predecessors. The seduction to which I was prone was not, however, what one might expect (for example, that of Henry James's naive heroine Daisy Miller) but rather that of *complicity* in a fieldwork encounter centered on what Robben (1995) has deemed the "politics of truth and emotion among victims and perpetrators of violence."

From the first days of my fieldwork stay in Trieste, I found myself drawn into a sphere of mutual recriminations and competing, often exclusive, claims to victimhood. Because I sought to analyze the common landscape within which these memories competed, I necessarily had to enter several different communities: those of the Istrian exiles, of the Italian minority in Istria, of the Slovene minority in Italy, and of academics in the regional circuit. Despite my repeated explanations that I wanted to study the operation of memory, rather than produce an "objective" history of events in the Julian March in the immediate postwar period, many informants in Trieste and later in Istria expressed their satisfaction that at last their story (the "real story") would be known in the English-speaking world.

Each group viewed me as an instrument for *its* history, and, predictably, various factions promoting diverse histories existed within those respective communities. I heard exiles' accounts of "Slavic barbarity" and "ethnic cleansing," suffered in Istria between 1943 and 1954, as well as Slovene and Croat narratives of the persecution experienced under the fascist state and at the hands of neofascists in the postwar period. Admittedly, I could not forget—as many exiles seemed to do—that the exodus from Istria followed on twenty years of the fascistization and Italianization of Istria, as well as a bloody Italian military campaign in Yugoslavia between 1941 and 1943. Nor could I countenance some exiles' frequent expressions of anti-Slav chauvinism. At the same time, however, I could not accept at face value the claim by some that the violence the Slavs suffered under fascism justified subsequent events in Istria or that all those who left Istria were compromised by fascism. Similarly, I came to reject the argument that ethno-national antagonism had not entered into the equation, as well as the counterview that the exodus represented simply an act of "ethnic cleansing." Thus, like Robben, working with both perpetrators and victims of the Argentine "generals' war," I eventually learned that "[e]ach group was seductive in its own way, and it was only after months of interviewing that I succeeded in recognizing the prevalent defenses and strategies" (ibid, 83).

Despite this recognition, I felt conflicted throughout the fieldwork and writing processes, as if I were betraying one or the other group by consorting with the "enemy." My knowledge (however limited) of Serbo-Croatian[4] and my sojourn in Istria aroused suspicion among some esuli (although some saw my multi-sited work as important and much needed). As often occurs during fieldwork (see Herzfeld 1991, 47–54), informants even joked nervously about my being a spy. Sometimes they trotted out the old Italian tag line about "antropoloCIA" (a play on the words *antropologia* [anthropology] and *CIA*), and one esule even asked, quite seriously, "Are you sure you're not a Mata Hari?" before agreeing to let me participate in an exile event. Given contemporaneous U.S. diplomatic and military engagement in former Yugoslavia, the possibility that I was a spy apparently did not seem altogether impossible. This fear also suggests that some esuli thought their cause was so politically sensitive and important as to merit CIA surveillance. All too frequently, I did not know how to respond to such suspicions and experienced discomfort about my "duplicitous" activities.

This awkwardness and insecurity about my own location in the field points to the anthropological expectation of empathetic rapport with the informants (an assumption that often leads to disappointment; see Keiser 1991 for a dramatic example). The traditional anthropological relationship usually entails championing the oppressed and celebrating the margins at the expense of the center, history and experience from below over that from on high. The relationship of the esuli and rimasti to centers of state power, however, cannot be categorized in such simple black-and-white terms. Indeed, the complicated flows between the center and the periphery put into question some of our very notions of place, as well as the distinction between (authentic, popular) memory/oral history and official historiography; this reveals considerable fluidity and fluctuation, depending on time and level, between what Holmes (1993) deems licit and illicit discourse.

In light of this, my account here of my time in the field reflects not so much a standard "ethnography of empathy" but rather what Marcus (1998) and Holmes (1993) have begun to sketch out as an "ethnography of complicity." This approach offers a more nuanced response to the insidious nature of informants' discourses than that proposed by Robben, who merely "learned to distinguish seduction from good rapport" (1995, 83), thereby leaving in place his faith in "the interplay of empathy and detachment that sound fieldwork ordains" (ibid., 99). Robben frames the issue of ethnographic complicity in largely moral terms, which replicates the discourse of informants expressing their (the "one") truth. Such a replication becomes particularly problematic in a situation like that of the Julian March, where individuals or groups may in different moments or contexts have been both victimized and victimizer; similarly, such groups may variously inhabit either the (relative) margins or the centers of power.

More productive is the model of licit and illicit discourse that Holmes offers. Fittingly, Holmes first came to this notion in his research in the rural districts of Italian Friuli, to the north of Trieste, and then elaborated it in his interviews with various members of the European Right. Holmes deems "illicit" a political discourse that

> aims at reestablishing the boundaries, terms, and idioms of political struggle. The resulting political practice is deconstructive. Its authority is often parasitic, drawing strength from the corruption, ineptitude, obsolescence, and lost relevance of established political dogmas and agendas. Its practitioners negotiate and map the points of contradiction and fatigue of partisan positions. They scavenge the detritus of decaying politics, probing areas of deceit and deception. By doing so they invoke displaced histories and reveal deformed moralities. They strive to introduce the unvoiced and unspeakable into public debate. Established political forces resist these "illicitudes," defining those who articulate them as racists, terrorists, bigots, or as some other form of essentialized pariah. (Holmes 1993, 258)

As I detail in subsequent chapters, the discourse of the Istrian exiles revolves around a sense of having been politically exploited and subsequently forgotten. It is not coincidental, of course, that the exiles succeeded (to varying degrees) in finding new audiences for their histories at precisely that moment (the 1990s) when the "deformed moralities" and corruptions of the Italian First Republic (the postfascist reconstruction state) and socialist Yugoslavia led to the respective implosion of both entities. In the exiles' case, the boundary between licit and illicit discourse remains porous and reflects a complex history whereby

Italians in the eastern Adriatic have contested territorial borders mapped out by diplomats and treaty makers.

At certain points, the alternative symbolic borders constructed by these exiles in opposition reflect the state-making projects of an earlier epoch (particularly those of Italian and Slavic irredentism), suggesting that flows between the center and the periphery are not unidirectional; nor are groups that reside literally on the margins merely the passive victims of state elites. Despite their oft-stated hostility to the state, the esuli in fact enjoy an ambivalent relationship with representatives of the Italian state. One example: Different exile associations have found patrons within Italian political parties, both those in power and those in the opposition. Furthermore, contemporary exile accounts often demonstrate remarkable continuity with irredentist narratives dating from the period of Italian unification until the First World War (the term *irredentism* derives from the struggle for an Italian state and the desire to redeem the unredeemed lands, the *irredenta;* for more on narratives associated with this struggle, see chapter 2). These irredentist demands initially enjoyed the support of the Italian state formed in 1861, then became a nuisance when Italy formed an alliance with Germany and Austria in 1882; they received state endorsement again during World War I when Italy joined the Allied side against the Hapsburg Empire, found legitimacy in the eyes of *some* Italian leaders during the post–World War II dispute over Istria (see chapter 3), and finally returned to their original status as an oppositional discourse challenging the state (see chapters 4 and 5). Taking analytical account of this shifting terrain demands work in "discontinuous spaces," both in temporal and spatial terms. As Marcus argues, "This version of complicity tries to get at a form of local knowledge that is about the kind of difference that is not accessible by working out internal cultural logics. . . . In effect, subjects are participating in discourses that are thoroughly localized but that are not their own" (1998, 119).

The slippery nature of such a discourse therefore renders it particularly challenging—in intellectual as well as moral terms—for the anthropologist trained in the notion of holism, as well as in the expectation of rapport and identification with informants who typically "resist" the powerful or hegemonic. Both Holmes and Robben comment on the frequent frames of reference shared between themselves and their interlocutors (European neofascists and members of the Argentine military, respectively [see Crapanzano 1986 for his discussion of a troubling identification with whites in apartheid-era South Africa]). Informants whose actions neither anthropologist could countenance morally (and with whom the typical fieldwork "identification" did not occur) nonetheless refused to submit to the expectation of exotic Otherness typically ascribed to those labeled as racist or violent. For while "[t]he idea of complicity forces the recognition of ethnographers as ever-present markers of 'outsideness,'" (Marcus 1998, 118), there paradoxically exists an increasing lack of distance between the observers and the observed.

The individuals whose experiences animate these pages, for example, do little that is exotic in the ethnographic realist sense. When the authors or speakers noted here are not attending events at exile or Italian minority centers, they are doing what many of us do in our daily lives: they go to work, if retired they may look after grandchildren, they finish their shopping before the stores close and prepare meals, and they spend evenings in front of the television. This is not to imply that the increasingly shared structures of material, everyday life are understood or lived in exactly the same ways everywhere but rather to highlight the relative and deliberate scarcity of "classic" ethnographic descriptions in this book. This signals an abandonment of the anthropological effort to fully get inside a (putative) culture and associated holistic assumptions about cultural process whereby understanding one set of practices (such as activism in exile centers) demands rooting them in other activities carried out by the same actors.

By consciously choosing not to privilege exclusively (though I do use it) one of anthropology's classic modes of both research design and exposition—the experiential aspect of "being there" (Clifford and Marcus 1986), observing what Malinowski called "the imponderabilia of daily life" (1984)—I further underscore and thereby bracket the claims to privileged knowledge made by exiles (and other survivors) who experience displacement and other traumas in the first person. Just as anthropologists have derived their scholarly and moral authority from "bearing witness" through firsthand observations, so too do survivors claim a special knowledge and moral authority. The constitution of this experiential authority, and the il/licit forms it assumes, is less the basis for my identification or nonidentification with the subjects of my research than itself the question to be investigated. I do not wish to imply that all such claims should be denied as illegitimate but rather to signal my own interest in the process whereby such discourses are legitimated or authorized precisely in *moral* terms. By not taking all such claims at face value, I also underscore the question of complicity in its most literal sense, that of possible collaboration by individuals with fascist and state socialist regimes. Like the effects of displacement, the potential of such complicity lurks within and shapes many of the narratives explored in this book.

I first learned of the violent recent history of Istria at the moment when those who had lived through it were responding to larger geopolitical transformations—notably the end of the Cold War and the breakup of Yugoslavia—and seeking to reposition their group histories. Discouraged in my plans to work in Dalmatia by the Serb-Croat war, I spent the summers of 1992 and 1993 traveling through the Julian March. At that time, I encountered self-described ethnic Italians who were born and raised in the Istrian Peninsula and who conceived of their identities in extremely divergent ways.

One Istrian Italian esule, a sixty-year-old retired schoolteacher born in the Istrian town of Parenzo/Poreč and today residing in the Italian port city of Trieste, insisted on her *italianità,* or pure Italian-ness. Eleonora noted that Istria historically had been under Venetian rule for many centuries before becoming a part of the Hapsburg Empire (in 1797), the Italian state (in 1920), and, later, the Yugoslav federation (after World War II).[5] In Eleonora's opinion, after the Second World War the "Slavs" had stolen an Italian land and driven out its original residents, many of whom—including Eleonora—had settled in nearby Trieste, from which on a clear day they could gaze on the lost homeland. As Eleonora put it, "We were victims of 'ethnic cleansing' in Yugoslavia before the term had even been invented."

Eleonora and her parents had abandoned Istria in 1948, when she was thirteen, after the family home was nationalized by the local communist authorities. In Trieste they joined Eleonora's older brother, Gigi, who in 1945 had first fled to Pola/Pula (a naval port at the base of the Istrian Peninsula) and eventually to Trieste; at that time, both cities were under the Anglo-American Allied Military Government. Gigi had left in the face of partisan threats to *"finire nelle foibe,"* that is, to meet his end in the karstic pits *(foibe)* in which partisans executed several thousand persons in 1943 in Istria and in 1945 around Trieste. In contrast to Gigi's clandestine nighttime flight on foot, Eleonora and her parents legally "opted" for Italian citizenship three years later by the terms of the Italo-Yugoslav Peace Treaty of 1947 and spent four years living in cramped conditions in a refugee camp. They eventually obtained an apartment in a housing complex on the outskirts of Trieste, which was built for Istrian refugees by the Italian state in the 1950s.

Reflecting on her experiences, Eleonora contended that "genuine Istrians" (*istriani veraci,* or in istro-veneto dialect, *istriani patocchi*) are to be found only outside Istria's territorial confines. An active participant in the exile association Unione degli Istriani (Union of the Istrians), Eleonora located the spirit of Istrian culture in the exile community of Trieste. Members of this community reconstructed various aspects of traditional Istrian life (such as saints' days celebrations and local festivals) together with more newly minted traditions commemorating the violence of the foibe and the exodus.

Eleonora's cousin Gino (the son of her paternal uncle) still lives in the Istrian town of Rovigno and tells a different tale. Too young to be called up for military service during World War II, Gino (born in 1928) nonetheless joined the Istrian Italian partisans *nel bosco* ("in the woods") during the final months of the war. He soon became an activist in the Unione degli Italiani dell'Istria Fiume, the Italian minority organization sponsored by the Tito regime, and found steady work in Rovigno's cigarette factory, or *fabbrica tabacchi.* His two children attended the Italian-language schools in Rovigno. One subsequently became a teacher at the Italian school, and the other a journalist. Although some townspeople, or *rovignesi,* remember Gino as a strong adherent of the party line, he claims to have been an ardent antifascist but not a committed socialist. Indeed, he contends that Yugoslav partisans (and later the regime) manipulated Italian antifascists, taking advantage of (*sfruttando*) their ingenuity and enthusiasm.

Like Eleonora, Gino expressed a sense of being both Italian and Istrian. Whereas for Eleonora "Istrian" signifies Italian, for Gino "Istrian" represents a hybrid of Italian and Slavic languages, cultures, and populations. In line with this, Gino enthusiastically supports the regionalist movement that arose in Istria in the early 1990s promoting a vision of a multiethnic and multicultural Istrian identity. According to Gino, the regionalist movement represents an important opportunity to mend the torn fabric (*ricucire il tessuto*) of Istrian life and to heal the wound (*il ferito aperto*) left open by the Istrian exodus. Even as their political commitments and beliefs differed dramatically, Gino and Eleonora agreed that for too long the story of the exodus and its victims had remained forgotten, canceled, and buried (*una storia dimenticata, cancellata, sepolta*).

With their competing visions of Istrian identity, these cousins do not constitute an anomalous case but rather give voice to two pervasive and competing views of identity that divide the population of ethnic Italians who once lived in or still inhabit Istria. One model of identity envisions Istria as a "pure" Italian land "stolen" by Slavs, and the other understands Istria as historically characterized by ethnic and linguistic hybridity. In the first view, *Istrian* becomes synonymous with *Italian,* in the second *Istrian* represents a Latin-Slav hybrid. The former belief tends to be advocated by the vocal community of Istrian Italian *esuli* who settled in nearby Trieste; the latter is heard among Italians who chose to remain in Istria after World War II.

Understanding the puzzle that Eleonora and Gino presented led me to this book. The personal histories of Gino, Eleonora, and their relatives and friends intersect major currents of twentieth-century European experience: nationalism and state building, the two world wars, the confrontation between fascism and socialism, the Cold War and its end, the resurgence of large-scale violence in late-twentieth-century Europe, and troubling questions about where Eastern Europe and the Balkans belong in a union of European states. My analysis centers on the question of how populations situated at the borders of state systems lived through dramatic processes of state formation and dissolution and subsequently recall and narrate the violence (physical and symbolic) attendant to the ultimately impossible project of rendering state and nation congruent. Examining the narrative space between those who became exiles and those who remained behind, I trace the symbolic and material effects of multiple moments of violence and erasure, which together may be said to constitute a "wound culture" (Seltzer 1998),[6] a phrase that accords with the constant discussion in the region of *un ferito ancora aperto,* or "a wound that remains open." In particular, I focus on the rituals—semantic and otherwise—through which the violence of the first half of the twentieth century informs the present experience of those who inhabit the partitioned territory of the Julian March.

Those who suffered the consequences of living at the margins of hostile state systems often, as in the case of the esuli and rimasti of the Julian March, cast themselves as unambiguous victims of violence (particularly by the state). In reality, however, the relationship of such groups to state bureaucracies and systems of patronage—particularly in the realm of historical production and state-sponsored research institutes and/or organizations associated with political parties—proves much more complex. Such local and regional actors possess not only certain forms of agency but also, quite obviously, various degrees of complicity in relation to state power, past and present. The relationships of Eleonora's brother, Gigi, to the Italian fascist regime and of Gino to the socialist Yugoslavia regime offer just two examples of possible complicity usually excised from self-narratives of victimization. In the case of the Julian March, such issues become particularly charged, bound up as they are with the legacies of the authoritarian regimes of fascist Italy and socialist Yugoslavia and the apportioning of blame for the violence committed in the name of those states.

With the radical transformation of those postwar regimes which dominated Italy and Yugoslavia from 1945 to 1991—in Italy, the corruption scandal known as Tangentopoli facilitated the demise of the Christian Democratic political machine, whereas Tito's socialist federation in Yugoslavia violently dissolved into ethnically defined states—previous verities about the partisan war against the fascists have come into question. The storytelling practices of groups like the esuli and rimasti have proven significant for these recastings of national history. At times, though, the Istrian Italians' black-and-white accounts of victimization go against efforts to explore the nuances of the civil wars that occurred within the broader conflict of the Second World War. Various actors in the region necessarily obscured such complexities in their accounts of World War II and the exodus, deploying memories as a form of what I call a "politics of submersion."

Informants such as Gino and Eleonora continually spoke of history as something to be exhumed, as having been submerged or sent underground (echoing the subterranean horror of the foibe) and only now being brought into the light. The imagery of both light and underground darkness refers to a complex tangle of associations: the foibe and the region's elaborate speleological topography, a rejection of the long-standing idea that the esuli were merely chasing shadows or ghosts, the notion of a light (or lamp) of civilization extinguished in Istria by the exodus, and possibly even a symbolic inversion of the darkness (blackness) commonly paired with fascism. The metaphors of submersion and disinterment also point to participants' view of memory as an indelible imprint whose experiential truth counters the falsities of official historiography (recalling the Platonic allegory of the cave and the shadows on its walls which can only approximate the ideal, true forms). Such a vision underwrites esuli and rimasti efforts to deploy meanings of the past as truth claims centered around narratives of victimization. These narratives are, in turn, underwritten by references to those material traces of history which "testify" to the rootedness and autochthony of the Italian populations of Istria, whose genealogies the exodus sought to erase; as Cascardi (1984) has suggested, the common sense notion of a "recuperation" of the past (what we might call the storage model) makes questions of authenticity central to those practices of remembrance labeled "memory" and "history." Similarly, Starn deems authenticity "memory's Siamese twin" (1999, 193).

Istrians' alternate and complementary usage of archaeological and illuminist imagery when talking about the past highlights the Julian March's interstitial location and the ways in which both contemporary Istrians and exiles who settled in Trieste continue to live in the long historical shadow cast by the postwar exodus. Just as surely as the state borders demarcating Italy, Slovenia, and Croatia divide a territory with a certain historical, cultural, and architectural integrity, the exodus continues to dominate local and regional politics in an obsessive manner. (Some readers will no doubt be reminded of other political circumstances shaped by exile politics, such as those of Miami.) On a more micro level, the children of those who lived through the exodus grew up in the nebulous half-light of this difficult experience.

Descendants testify to the powerful effects—self-censure, framing personal identities, and shaping interfamilial relationships—exercised by memory in families whose lives unfolded within the space of exodus. One woman, born in 1958 to a father who had fled Istria as a teenager, struggled with her parent's virulent rejection of the former territory. Maddalena grew up in a household filled with rancor against Slavs and the rimasti. Indeed, her father refused to even admit that some Italians remained in Istria, as I discovered one day when my comment about rimasti unleashed his angry retort: "If you haven't understood that there are no Italians left in Istria, you haven't understood anything!" The father's refusal to return to his hometown, a forty-five-minute drive from Trieste, piqued in his daughter a curiosity that led to the latter's discovery and love of Istria. Maddalena's frequent visits to Istria thus created a certain tension and even anxiety in the family (particularly when her car broke down and she asked her father to pick her up in Istria). Visiting the site of her father's former home, Maddalena eventually learned from her father's former neighbor that immediate members of the family—who, she had been told, were long dead— had instead lived out their lives in Istria, dying in the 1980s; she confirmed this fact by examining their death certificates at the town registry. She never confronted her father with this shocking and unsettling knowledge, reasoning, "Clearly something happened to divide the family during the exodus which was so painful and traumatic that my father had to negate the existence, for me but also for *himself,* of those members of the family who chose to stay." For Maddalena, filling the lacuna excised in memory suddenly illuminated what for her had seemed irrational or exaggerated aspects of her father's behavior.

Other children I met experienced similar revelations that helped explain their parents' often puzzling responses and that shed light on the shadows cast by the exodus over parent-child relations. I was present one day at the Centro di

Ricerche Storiche di Rovigno, the Istrian institute dedicated to the Italian minority, or rimasti, when a woman stopped in to request information about her grandmother. Having grown up in Tuscany, far removed from the continual polemics and history making of Trieste, Romana knew only what her esuli parents had recounted about their departure from Istria and the wartime execution of her maternal grandmother. She was shocked to learn that her slain grandmother was widely recognized as a great antifascist partisan and that numerous streets, monuments, and cultural circles in Istria bore her name in recognition of her heroism.

Raised on bitter invectives about Slavs and communists, Romana marveled that her own grandmother numbered among the heroic figures appropriated by the Tito regime and the Italian minority, a fact her mother had never communicated to her. When the staff of the research center showed Romana a photograph of her grandmother's house (honored as the birthplace of the antifascist "martyr"), she burst into tears. Whereas the Istrian account of her grandmother's life and political identity differed dramatically from her mother's narrative, the house matched the mental picture Romana formed from her mother's descriptions—"Yes, that's the courtyard my mother always talked about." Romana's experience, like Maddalena's, reveals the silences and selectiveness of memory that figure not only in public history making about the exodus but also within families and between generations. As E. Valentine Daniel notes, "Regardless of who the witness is—the villain, the surviving victim, or you and I—the violent event persists like crushed glass in one's eyes. The light it generates, rather than helping us see, is blinding" (1996, 208).

Despite the nontransparency of such violence, in the following chapters I take up the challenge of analyzing the identity politics centered on exhuming the past in the border area between Italy and ex-Yugoslavia. I demonstrate how marginalized groups on both sides of the former Cold War divide employ the metaphor of "raising up buried histories" in order to authorize contemporary moral and political claims. In Italy and former Yugoslavia, these uses of the past reflect and refract much broader projects of national redefinition centered on issues of ethnicity and race, and hence of those questions of purity and hybridity highlighted by the cousins Eleonora and Gino. The ongoing projects of national reconfiguration in Italy, Slovenia, and Croatia in which these themes of purity and hybridity come to the fore intersect dramatically in the border area of the Julian March, just as they did at key points during the twentieth century. I discuss these earlier moments at length in part 1. Part 2 focuses on the means (semantic and otherwise) by which the esuli and rimasti attempt to "bring into the light" their stories, as well as to use the associated moral capital for various political ends.

CHAPTER ONE

Mapping the Terrain of Memory

HAVING sketched out broad theoretical issues that frame this project, I now lay out the landscape of memory in the Julian March, that is, the terrain shaped by historical processes and, in turn, the field in which the production of memory and history occurs. Some anthropological accounts of displacement, loss, and nostalgia have offered superb microstudies focusing on individual houses and neighborhoods as sites of remembrance and social architecture (Bahloul, 1996; Hirschon 1998). By contrast, in dealing with an entire region (and in keeping my eye on states), my canvas remains necessarily broad, although I try to sharpen the focus on various points that make up this *paesaggio* or landscape. My principal field sites, the city of Trieste and the Istrian town of Rovigno, offer two such locales in a landscape whose sum is greater than its parts.

At first glance, these sites do not appear commensurable, given that Trieste is a city (with a population of approximately 200,000) and Rovigno a small town (with just over 12,000 residents). In contrast to Trieste, for instance, the more intimate setting of Rovigno facilitated for me a much more profound integration into the daily life of the rimasti and other rovignesi, whereas my contacts with esuli in Trieste often occurred in more institutional contexts (though I did befriend a number of younger people there with whom I had more informal encounters). At the physical or architectural level, as well, the two places do not greatly resemble one another, a reflection of their different historical trajectories. Mirroring other Hapsburg cities in the region, such as Zagreb or Fiume/Rijeka, Trieste presents a resolutely Central European face, its architecture a mix of neoclassicism, art nouveau, and baroque (with some Italian fascist monumentalism thrown in for good measure). This mix reflects the city's peculiar history as an imperial free port developed to provide the Hapsburgs with an outlet to the sea from which they could combat their maritime rivals, the Venetians. Only in the nearby town of Muggia, which today sits on the border between Italy and Slovenia, do the architectural signs or traces of Venice become apparent.

Like Muggia and in contrast to Trieste, Rovigno reveals itself as a typical Venetian town, its elevated church of Saint Euphemia and bell tower visible from miles away at sea. Venetian windows and balconies grace buildings in the Cittàvecchia, or Old Town, whose entrance consists of an archway featuring the lion of Saint Mark (the preeminent symbol of Venice). Signs of Austria also

Figure 1.
Traces of Venice

a. *(above)* Lion of St. Mark, bell tower of Rovigno

c. *(right)* Venetian arch leading to Rovigno's Old Town

result of
rivalry
(appropriation)

b. (*above*) Venetian windows in Istria

d. (*left*) Comunità Italiana, Dignano, Istria (note the Italian and Croatian flags)

prove abundant, however, as in the cigarette factory and fish-canning plant or in the former villa of Baroness Hutterött on the nearby island of Saint Andrea. In 1797, after several centuries of separation, Istria and Trieste were united under the Hapsburg Empire (followed by a brief Napoleonic interlude); in 1849 the Hapsburgs divided the administrative district of the Littoral (*Küstenland*), which included Trieste and Istria, into the Province of Trieste and the Margravate of Istria (Rusinow 1969, 11).

Following the Venetian Republic's demise in 1797, some of the Italian-speaking peoples of Trieste and Istria began to identify with the project of building a unified Italian state. Ironically, it was in Trieste's quintessentially Central European cafés such as Caffè San Marco and Caffè Tommaseo (still in operation today) that irredentist Italian intellectuals met to plot the fall of the Hapsburg Empire. The economic history of Trieste since its triumphant "redemption" by the Italian *madrepatria* (motherland) in 1918 has been one of slow but inexorable decline. The once-lively port remains largely moribund, despite various attempts to revive traffic and make Trieste the "gateway to the East." The city now subsists to a large degree on small commerce, fueled in the 1970s by the relative prosperity of Yugoslavs eager to buy Western goods and sustained by Croats who find it less expensive to shop in Italy than in their own country. One of the few thriving import-export industries is coffee, out of which the local Illy family has built a thriving international business. The city's social composition mirrors this decline; Trieste is one of Italy's oldest centers in demographic terms. A significant part of this elderly population consists of Istrian exiles, most of them pensioners with ample time for participating in exile activities.

Unlike Trieste, Istrian coastal towns such as Rovigno grew from the 1960s on, thanks in large part to the development of mass tourism. This situation contrasts with the abandonment of the Istrian interior, whose desolation dramatically testifies to the massive postwar exodus. With its charming Old Town and kilometers of National Park in which to walk, bike, or relax on the beach, Rovigno quickly became one of the champions of Yugoslav tourism. (Although tourism declined precipitously during the years of the Yugoslav Wars, the industry shows signs of recovery.) Thanks to the help of governmental housing projects and easy credits for building large villas with attached tourist rental apartments, much of the population of Rovigno (including the rimasti) abandoned the Old Town in the 1960s and 1970s for the new suburbs. Many rovignesi confessed to me that they missed the intimacy and vitality of Cittàvecchia, the ritual promenades, or *passeggiate,* even though the houses in the new area are much more comfortable, prestigious, and private (see Herzfeld 1991 for a similar case of tourism-induced wealth and nostalgia for the Old Town).

During my stay in Rovigno, for instance, I rented an apartment in the New Town from a typical Istrian couple: the wife was a self-identified Italian, the husband a Croat, and their children usually spoke Italian with the mother and Croatian with the father. This family occupied half of a large structure, with the

culturally mingled families

husband's brother and his family living on the other side and the two brothers' elderly parents living upstairs. I occupied one of the small attached apartments rented out to tourists in the summer. Given this, I had the opportunity to get to know the family and to observe firsthand the Istrian "hybridity" celebrated in the region and embodied by mixed marriages between Italians and Slavs.

As these brief descriptions suggest, Rovigno and Trieste offered quite different settings in which to conduct fieldwork. These differences should not, however, be overdrawn. Rather, the expected contrast between the cosmopolitanism associated with cities and the provincialism inherent in small towns requires critical examination. In addition, Trieste and Rovigno do mirror one another in the sense that each represents the stronghold (*roccaforte*), respectively, of the esuli and rimasti. Trieste's public face, for instance, is dominated by certain narratives associated with Italian irredentism and nationalism; fittingly, the city's symbolic heart remains the massive Piazza Unità d'Italia (Square of Italian Unity), whose Central European facades were appropriated by a nationalist project celebrating the lost territories' "redemption." Piazza Unità serves as the site of the city's major rallies and protests, particularly those associated with the Italo-Yugoslav territorial dispute after World War II (see chapter 3).

Rovigno, in contrast, asserts a long-standing socialist tradition, whose vitality earned the city the appellation Red Rovigno (Rovigno la Rossa).[1] Though this political identity dates from the Hapsburg period, it came to the fore during the era of Italian fascist control. Townspeople proudly contributed volunteers to the antifascist cause in the Spanish civil war and, later, in the fight against the Italian and German militaries. Those Italians who remained after the exodus often adopted an aggressively pro-Yugoslav stance (at least publicly), and the leaders of the rimasti there were known among other Italians in Istria for their toughness (*durezza*). Because of this, the Italian community has remained a vital and tangible presence in Rovigno, a fact reflected by the creation in 1968 of a research center for the Italian minority. Given these intertwined but distinct histories and their roles as respective reference points for the esuli and rimasti, Trieste and Rovigno offer two particularly appropriate spaces from which to investigate the broader politics of memory in the Julian March.

Geographies of Violence

In its social and physical geographies, the Julian March—like the Balkans and Eastern Europe more generally—has been read as either a bitterly contested borderland or a fruitful meeting place of cultures, languages, and ethnic groups ("a bridge culture" characterized by cross-fertilizations in art and literature [Mucci and Chiarini 1999]). Within European symbolic geography, Eastern Europe has been imagined as a demimonde poised between light and darkness (Wolff 1994), whereas Balkan peoples have appeared to abide "'in a _east/west d√_

twilight zone illuminated neither by the radiance of the West nor by the exotic glow of the East'" (Todorova 1997, 78). More specifically for the Eastern Adriatic, Wolff has characterized the attitude of imperial Venetian administrators toward their Dalmatian territories as a "demi-Oriental" perspective (2001, 15). In the eighteenth century, Venetian writers and politicians alike demonstrated intense interest about the linguistically and ethnically distinct peoples of Dalmatia known as the Morlacchi. "The ideological importance of the Morlacchi pointed toward an anthropological classification of the Slavic peoples, based on new Venetian knowledge of Dalmatia, in the context of the Enlightenment's contemporary articulation of the idea of Eastern Europe; the philosophical reconception of Europe, as divided between more and less civilized western and eastern domains, perfectly fit the evolution of Venice's imperial perspective on its eastern Adriatic province" (ibid., 7).

Eighteenth-century Venetian classifications of the Morlacchi saw this population as part of a Dalmatian nation that included Italians and whose most relevant divisions were those between "civilized" residents of coastal cities and backward rural dwellers, rather than those between ethnic or racial groups (ibid., 11). (Admittedly, however, by the end of Venetian independence, various writers had increasingly moved toward understanding the Morlacchi as appertaining to a larger Slavic world.) By the nineteenth and twentieth centuries, however, Dalmatia, as well as the Balkans / Eastern Europe, was increasingly figured as a site of racial and cultural mixture or hybridity. Such images also operate on a smaller scale for the Julian March, variously depicted as "the one area where the three great European racial groups—Mediterranean, Germanic, and Slav—meet" (Moodie 1945, 57), as a crossroads and historic "frontier region," and as the site of "unabated tension" (American Military Government 1950, 2; see also Sluga 2001 for an extended review of scholarship on Trieste as a boundary space).

The latter view of the Julian March as an area of conflict and contrast, rather than coexistence, emphasizes the experience of its inhabitants during much of the twentieth century, when the region witnessed considerable violence and demographic change in the periods during, between, and after the two world wars. The passage of Trieste and the Istrian Peninsula to Italy after World War I and the collapse of the Austro-Hungarian Empire, for example, led to the emigration of most of the area's Germans, as well as the subsequent exodus of thousands of ethnic Slovenes and Croats (together with some Italian antifascists) who refused to abide by the fascist regime's Italianization policies (Kalc 1983–84). Dalmatia's 1919 incorporation into the neophyte Yugoslav state occasioned a similar movement of Italians out of the region, although some merely transferred within Dalmatia to the Italian enclave at Zara, officially annexed to the Italian state after World War I.

The subsequent flight of Italians from Dalmatian Zara and Istria between 1943 and 1954 constituted perhaps the most dramatic population transfer in the region during the twentieth century. This, in tandem with a policy to resettle Istria with South Slavs, reduced ethnic Italians from a formerly sizable population to a tiny minority in the Yugoslav state at the same time that it further Italianized the city of Trieste. Approximately one-third of all Istrian refugees permanently settled in Trieste, significantly altering the city's composition and rendering it in some ways an Istrian city; housing complexes built by the Italian state in the 1950s and 1960s for these refugees also extended the physical boundaries of the city. The coastline near Trieste became more Italian as the result of such resettlement policies, with the Italian state expropriating land owned by ethnic Slovenes in order to build exile housing.

The region's physical landscape makes manifest in myriad ways these geographies of multiple violence and displacement. Trenches and gun emplacements from the Great War are still visible in some areas. Every so often the earth disgorges the occasional bomb or mine from one of the world wars; numerous war memorials (great and small) dot the territory; pits (or foibe) in the rocky, karstic terrain stand as ghastly tombs for those whose encounters with "partisan justice" finished there; the abandoned ghost towns of the Istrian interior still make painfully evident the effects of the post-1945 exodus; the faint traces of slogans visible on buildings in Istria proclaim "The People's Power!" or "Long Live Stalin! Long Live Tito!"; and neofascist graffiti in Trieste demand "Schiavi fora!" (Slavs Out!, *schiavi* being a derogatory epithet that plays on a historic association between *slavi,* Slavs, and *schiavi,* or slaves).

This landscape not only recalls past violence, however, but also becomes the contemporary site of contestation. Indeed, the territory itself—today divided between the Italian, Slovene, and Croatian states and referred to by different names, depending on the speaker's linguistic and political preferences—appears to mirror what some have deemed the "divided memory" (Rusconi 1995) of World War II. As Alessandro Portelli notes, "The brilliant definition, 'divided memory,' must be enlarged and radicalized to define not simply the dichotomy (and implied hierarchy) between the institutional memory of the Resistance and the collective memory of the community, but also a fragmented plurality of different memories" (1997, 158).

In the course of conducting research in different parts of the region I came to realize, following Portelli, that the divided memory of the territory did not consist of a simple contrast between either official, state history and "authentic" collective memory, on the one hand, or between those who left and those who stayed, on the other. Groups such as the esuli and rimasti have complicated relationships to the centers of power, particularly in the realm of historical production. In addition, differences such as political affiliation, class, and gender at times divide ostensibly united communities such as those of the esuli and rimasti from within as much as from each other. When I refer to "collective memory," then, I do not mean that Istrians share some sort of common *mentalité* or that collective memory consists merely of the aggregation of numerous individual memories. Rather, I use the term *collective memory* because actors do.

Figure 2.
The scars of exodus, Istria

a. *(above)* Slogan on an Istrian house dating from the early postwar period, "W il Potere Popolare" (Long live the people's power)

b. *(right)* Abandoned and decaying structures in the Istrian interior "bear witness" to the events of the exodus

This language reflects, even as it obscures, the power dynamics inherent in speaking for a group identity, as well as in contrasting collective memory to history. In seeking to constitute putative communities, the discourses of the esuli and rimasti (particularly those of their leaders) thus play upon and derive authority from what Portelli calls the implied hierarchy between history and memory, as well as the contrast between those who left and those who remained. At the same time, individual memory may write against or fragment these unitary narratives, an issue explored in chapters 6 and 7.

Monuments both express and attempt to contain these tensions between individual and collective memories, as well as those between competing group memories. A rich body of scholarly work has explored contests over the meanings surrounding memorials, especially those dedicated to war, and associated ritual commemorations.[2] Even when the designers of monuments seek to impose unitary meanings, thereby silencing "contrary interpretations of the past" (Middleton and Edwards 1990, 8), they can never completely control the reception of the messages conveyed, reflecting the inherent tension contained within such memorials (see Young 1993 for one example).

In the Julian March, the construction of monuments to the Second World War and the exodus reflects the always contested efforts (whether by the state or other groups, such as the exiles) to narrate "a highly selective story, focussed on what is basic for the community and turning away from everything else. . . . An event is given a memory-place (lieu de mémoire) in the form of statue, museum or concentration camp site, and annually repeated day" (Hartman 1994, 15–16). Together with Emilia-Romagna, the region of Friuli–Venezia Giulia possesses the largest number of World War II monuments in Italy when reckoned in relation to the overall population (see Dogliani 1999, 21) and the second-highest number of antifascist memorials (Sluga 1999, 186).

Some memorials (and the public rituals associated with them), such as the tablet at Basovizza/Basovica honoring four Slovene antifascists executed by the Italian regime in 1929, prove modest. Like the autochthonous Slovene community in Trieste, the monument is tucked away on the Karst, the rocky plateau above the urban center, and attracts little attention from those not already aware of its presence. Much more prominent is the nearby memorial to the foibe of Basovizza, one of many such pits in which civilians and military personnel were executed during the brief period of Yugoslav administration of the zone in May and June 1945. This site has been adopted as a gathering place by Italian nationalists and Istrian exiles and in some sense serves as a counterpoint to Trieste's other national monument commemorating the horrors of the Second World War: Risiera di San Sabba, the only Nazi extermination camp in Italy.

Risiera di San Sabba served not only as a center for the transit of Italian and Yugoslav Jews to camps deep within the Reich but also as a site for the interrogation, torture, and execution of partisans, both Italian and Slav. Slovenes in the Julian March were among the first to organize armed resistance against Italian fascism beginning in the 1920s, and a good part of the estimated three thousand persons killed at San Sabba were Slavs (Bon Gherardi 1972; Fölkel 1979). Given this, some have seen the camp as a monument to Slavic heroism.[3] This (Yugo)Slav tradition of antifascist resistance is also recalled in the myriad memorials in the small, predominantly Slovene villages around Trieste, as well as in local places of remembrance throughout the towns of Istria; the red star of communism (and of the Yugoslav flag) typically adorns such markers, regardless of within which national boundaries they fall. These monuments partake of a broader narrative celebrating communist partisans in ex-Yugoslavia and Italy, narratives subject to revisionist tendencies in both contexts since the 1980s. The extensive and varied commemoration of the Second World War in Trieste and its surrounding territory thus embodied and made explicit what was silenced or submerged in the broader national contexts of Italy and Yugoslavia: deeply divided memories of fascism, the Second World War, and communist atrocities.

Alongside these dramatic reminders of violent ethno-national and political conflicts, however, exist other, more subtle markers of memory and identity that bear testimony to a past (the *longue durée?*) marked by peaceful linguistic and cultural exchange between groups. The linguistic varieties of the region, both Slavic and Italian, for example, are heavily inflected with, respectively, Italian and Slavic words and expressions, as well as Austro-Germanic terms. Similarly, the cuisines of Trieste and Istria reveal a literal melting pot of culinary traditions, as typified by the Istrian dish of fusi/fuzj (a conelike handmade pasta served with a goulash meat sauce, usually wild boar or chicken), the ubiquitous Austrian kraut and wurst, and desserts such as strudel and local variants like *presnitz* (invented on the occasion of Austrian empress Elizabeth's visit to Trieste). Though not as dramatic or as obvious as war monuments, such markers of memory nonetheless prove equally important to local understandings of identity, for it is through aspects such as language, food, and dress that "tradition" becomes literally embodied (Benson 2000; Turner 1993).

It does not appear coincidental that throughout the region, particularly in Trieste, an enormous local market for books and journals is dedicated to such local customs, as well as to regional history. The readership for these books is not restricted to scholars or self-described intellectuals but rather finds a wide and varied public. Examples of such works include dictionaries of local dialects, as well as volumes of poetry and prose written in those dialects. In contrast to many other contexts where the use of linguistic varieties deemed dialects (in opposition to "standard" languages) reflects class particularities, in the Julian March dialects remain widely diffused and cherished as symbols of local identities.[4] In both Trieste and Istria, I heard dialects spoken in academic institutes as well as in humble trattorias. As an university-educated researcher of things Istrian stated, "Dialect is the language of the heart, of the sentiment"; she herself spoke Triestine dialect exclusively at home, though she used standard Italian with me. Admittedly, this ability or inability to switch to standard Italian for the ignorant anthropologist did to some degree signal a speaker's class and educational attainments.

Dialects and related expressions such as traditional songs distinguish *nostri istriani, naši istrijani,* or "our Istrians" (whether Italians, Croatian, or Slovene) from others at the same time that dialects may also mark more localized identities within Istria. While drinking coffee in the main piazza of Rovigno/Rovinj one day, an Istrian Italian friend and I marveled at a noisy and exuberant post-wedding procession. Cars festooned with decorations circled the fountain in the tiny piazza as members of the wedding party honked horns and let out whoops. Residents of the town seated in cafés looked on with interest and amusement as the bride and groom emerged from the cars to promenade along the waterfront and pose for photos. "Guarda quelli" (Look at those guys), muttered my friend with contempt. "Sono veri balcanici; noi rovignesi non facciamo così" (These are real Balkan peoples; we rovignesi don't do such things), she added, referring to stereotypes of non-Istrian Slavs as vocal and ostentatious, concerned with putting on an expensive spectacle, in contrast to the self-described stingy *(tirchi, avari)* Istrians and rovignesi.

In my friend's estimation, these Slavs were neither rovignesi nor Istrian. As the band accompanying the wedding party struck up the chords of "La Mula di Parenzo," a popular song in Istrian dialect (and one frequently trotted out for tourists during the summer season), two elderly Italian women in their sixties at the neighboring table commented with some surprise, "Ah, ma questi sono nostri!" (Ah, but these are ours!). Although willing to admit that these Slavs spoke Istrian dialect, my friend, however, remained unconvinced that these raucous celebrants were genuine Istrians and most certainly rejected the possibility that they were authentic rovignesi. I would hazard to guess, though, that if she encountered these Slavs in Zagreb or Belgrade, my friend would recognize them as "nostri" (ours). Like the town bell towers, or *campanili,* which symbolize local affiliations in Italy (Silverman 1975) and Istria alike, dialect reinforces a sense of *campanilismo* which may compete and/or coexist with notions of pan-Istrian identity on the part of both exiles and rimasti. As in Istria, dialect in Trieste serves as an important situational marker of who is authentic to a particular community, at various points distinguishing Istrian exiles from other Italians, Italians from Slovenes, or Slovenes in Italy (*nostri sloveni,* or "our Slovenes") from those in Slovenia proper. Although I detail such debates over autochthony and authenticity in part 2, I note here that dialect often appears to serve as a necessary but perhaps insufficient indicator of identity.

In certain moments, then, dialects may come to represent cultural intermixture, and in other contexts they appear to divide populations. Similarly, other features of the memory landscape—such as architecture—may be and have been read as signs of either hybridity or division. Istria's towns, with their characteristic Venetian churches and bell towers (as well as the occasional Austrian building or factory), are variously cited as signs of either cultural fusion or an unmistakable italianità.[5] By referring to material traces of the past, members of each group underscore their claims to bring to light a history—the *true history*—that has been silenced for too long.

Although members of these groups typically fail to recognize the reconstructive nature of their histories, their insistence on history's concreteness forces us to take theoretical account of this materiality. As Trouillot notes of the past, "What happened leaves traces, some of which are quite concrete—*buildings, dead bodies, censuses, monuments, diaries, political boundaries*—that limit the range and significance of any historical narrative. This is one of the many reasons why not any fiction can pass for history: the materiality of the socio-historical process (historicity 1) sets the stage for future historical narratives (historicity 2)" (1995, 29; my italics). The material traces—buildings, dead bodies, borders—that prove so central to various claims about autochthony in the Julian March reflect an ongoing history of contestation over territory that continues to shape historical narratives and political claims to both purity and hybridity put forward in the region—like those voiced by the cousins Eleonora and Gino.

Architectonic language pervades that of local actors, who frequently complain about being strangers in their homes (*stranieri a casa nostra*) and who root semantic memory in a landscape, at once both concrete and poetic in its evocation, of various architectural monuments: houses, cemeteries, and churches. In his discussion of historic conservation and tourism in the Cretan town of Rethemnos, Herzfeld has contrasted social time as "the grist of everyday experience" (1991, 10) with that of "monumental time," which "encounters events as realizations of some supreme destiny, and it reduces social experience to collective predictability" (ibid.). Herzfeld argues, "Between social and monumental time lies a discursive chasm, separating popular from official understandings of history" (ibid.). In the Julian March, and particularly in Trieste, this clear-cut opposition does not hold, as the monumental time of other eras and regimes (the irredentist struggle and fascism for the esuli and the socialist struggle for the rimasti) comes to inflect the very experience of social time of those individuals who contest the states whose shadows they live(d) in. In place of a discursive chasm, there exist numerous discursive conjunctures between the state-sponsored histories of past epochs—now transformed into oppositional discourses—and the narration of individual life histories and experiences. This inflection is further revealed by the deep interpenetrations of oral and written memory in the Julian March.

Although all individual and personal memories are ultimately products of the social and cultural matrixes in which they are embedded (Halbwachs 1992; Portelli 1997), the local terrains in which "Italian" narratives are made indicate an especially close relationship between spoken and written accounts, as well as public and private memories. This proves particularly true for the esuli in Trieste, who have been nurtured in a local political environment characterized by an obsessive outpouring of memoirs and studies of the war and the exodus;

the situation was somewhat different for Istria until recently, although the ha-giographic literature on the partisan war and its "martyrs" also exerted a pow-erful influence over what could be said publicly and the form such statements took. These contemporary local terrains of historical production refract the rel-atively recent emphasis in Italian historiography on the experience of the com-mon person, particularly in relation to the events of World War II. They also draw on a pamphlet tradition dating from the irredentist struggle (see chapter 2), as well as a rich regional literary tradition. Many of the region's most cele-brated authors—figures such as Italo Svevo, Umberto Saba, Scipio Slataper, and the contemporary writers Fulvio Tomizza and Claudio Magris—were associ-ated with this irredentist cause or have devoted considerable space to the "na-tional question" and the peculiarities of the area as a border zone.

Svevo seems especially relevant here, since he articulates local and long-standing interests in issues of memory and identity. Though praised by observers like Karl Marx and the futurist Filippo Tommaso Marinetti as a new and mod-ern city, early-twentieth-century Trieste was home to many intellectuals obsessed with memory, aging, and decline. The center for the psychoanalytic movement in the Italian peninsula, Trieste's intellectual climate proved receptive to devel-opments in Vienna and received a direct stimulus through the psychoanalytic practice of Edward Weiss, one of Freud's pupils. A literary tradition thus grew up around figures like Svevo, who reflected the contemporary interest in mem-ory (particularly the Freudian focus on the individual mechanisms of memory, dreams, and repression). Svevo also wrote extensively on the theme of age. His novels *Senility (When a Man Grows Older)* and *Confessions of Zeno* reveal this ob-session with aging, as well as memory, as do his short stories, for example, "The Old Old Man."

At various points in this book, I draw on literary figures such as Svevo in order to highlight, rather than downplay, the textuality of my own discussion and that of my informants (particularly in part 1). Whereas this textuality re-flects the specificity of the Julian March case, literary products more generally retain wide currency in Italian culture and society even in an era dominated by visual communication. Many of the Italians I knew in both Trieste and Istria thought of the Romans and Dante, as well as homegrown figures like Svevo, as their ancestors. Informants often cited the poetic authority of these figures in order to illustrate their point.

In his role as progenitor of the standardized Italian language (the Tuscan di-alect) and thus as national poet, for example, Dante stands as the embodiment of that Italian urban high culture or civilization (*civiltà*) often invoked by esuli and rimasti alike as distinguishing them from "Balkanic" peoples.[6] Dante also refers to Istria in *Inferno,* describing Pola as the natural terminus of Italy. Many esuli take this as irrefutable proof of their historical right to Istria (for details, consult Bogneri's *Il culto di Dante a Pola nell'ultimo secolo*). The work of literary figures such as Dante or Svevo not only provides further poetic "evidence" for certain claims made by the esuli or rimasti, however, but also actively shapes the rhetorics of purity and hybridity which inform the history-making practices of these two groups.

Landscapes of Identity: Discourses of Purity and Hybridity

Although the Yugoslav breakup has reconfigured the debate over ethno-national purity and hybridity in the Julian March, the broad outlines of this contest date back at least as far as the late Hapsburg period when national and irredentist claims challenged cosmopolitan, "imperial" ideologies. In the course of the twentieth century, the struggle between these competing visions radically transformed Trieste and its hinterland. At the end of the nineteenth century, Trieste presented itself as a Hapsburg cosmopolis with a lively linguistic and confessional mix of peoples that included Greek, Armenian, Serbian, German-Austrian, Jewish, Italian, and Slovene communities. With a topography distinguished by a diversity of houses of worship and cemeteries claimed by these respective communities, Trieste also suggested the appearance of a modern urban center.

In an 1857 article written for the *New York Daily Tribune,* Karl Marx had favorably compared Trieste with its historic rival, Venice. Pondering Venice's economic eclipse by the Hapsburg port, Marx declared, "Venice was a city of memories; Trieste on the other hand like the United States had the advantage of not having any past" (in Cary 1993, 39). Nearly four decades later, the English travel writer Robert Howard Russell echoed Marx in his judgment: "Trieste is a very modern, new, and smart-looking city, and is one of the busiest-looking places you come across on the continent" (1896, 5). Desiring to get off the beaten tourist track and seek out picturesque peoples, Russell followed the advice of an Austrian official to take the Lloyd Triestino steamer down the Adriatic coastline to Dalmatia and Montenegro. Russell perceived Trieste as the geographic terminus of a modern European order, as the switch point of an extensive railway and shipping network linking the imperial center, Vienna, with romantic and vaguely Oriental locales in the Balkans and beyond.

Less than a century has passed since the demise of that imperial order, and yet the contemporary visitor to Trieste would likely find herself puzzled (as I initially did) by the descriptions of the port as bustling and new, as a rootless urban space that attracted an unknown Irish writer by the name of James Joyce (who from 1904 to 1915 gave English lessons for the Berlitz branches in Trieste and Pola/Pula) or that inspired the urbane penning of Joyce's pupil and friend Italo Svevo. Today Trieste seems a quiet Italian backwater, a city whose obsession with the past—both its glories and its traumas—mirrors its economic stagnation and political isolation, imparting a melancholy, almost oppressive, air. Writer Joseph Cary, an admirer of Joyce and Svevo, expressed his disappointment when he confronted the contemporary reality of a city that he had long known and loved only in its literary evocations: "Dead for years. A ghost town. Triste [sad] Trieste" (1993, 7).

The story I tell in this book helps explain how Trieste went from being the cosmopolitan entrepôt of a Hapsburg imperial center at the end of the nineteenth century to the provincial, nationalist periphery of an Italian center at the end of the twentieth century. In the context of the late Hapsburg Empire, areas like the Julian March (after 1867 incorporated into the Austrian half of the Dual Monarchy) increasingly came to figure as zones of a hopeless admixture in contrast to a central Austrian or German core. Such group identifications acquired new, unsettling political meanings in the latter half of the nineteenth century. Pieter Judson argues that the 1880s witnessed an increasing shift away from a liberal-integrationist, assimilationist "Austro-German" identity toward a more narrow ethno-nationalist understanding of German-ness as various groups coalesced to demand or defend their collective rights.

> This transformation of identity would be accomplished by relocating national identity in the geographic spaces people occupied, by redefining those spaces according to their particular nationalist significance. To continue with the example of Iglau, the town became known in the 1880s primarily as an *island* of Germans surrounded by a sea of hostile Czechs. Provinces like Moravia, where many such islands were to be found, became known as *frontiers*, where Germans and Slavs met on imagined borders. (Judson 1996, 383; on the well-established notion of linguistic islands, see also Todorova 1997, 48)

As Hapsburg Germans did, Italian speakers from Istria and Dalmatia spoke (and continue to do so today) of Latinate linguistic islands stranded within a sea of menacing Slavs. (For a similar rhetoric in Romania, see Verdery 1991, 121–29.) This language crystallizes fears of being overwhelmed, of the inability to draw borders of containment or stem inundations (whether understood as those of culture or of blood). Linke compares the metaphoric use of such submersion by water with that of subversion by blood.

> The concept of *subversion by blood* locates the transgression of racial boundaries in a sphere that is spatially below and at once inside. In contrast, the image of *submersion by water* points to the realm above and outside as the source of danger. The focus on blood served to interiorize the source of racial contagion: the flow of blood, regarded as dangerous and threatening, issued from inside the nation's body. Contact with the contaminating substance was rendered inevitable by its proximity: since one could not escape or flee from the contagion, it had to be eradicated. In contrast, the focus on water acts to exteriorize the locus of contamination. It is displaced from the body to the natural environment. But inundation by water likewise poses a threat to the center—not from within (as in the case of blood) but from its outermost margins. The social goal is to establish as great a separation as possible from it, without being engulfed or overwhelmed. (1999, xii)

The anxiety of inundation from the margins, one shared by many of the self-identified Italian and Germanic peoples of the Hapsburg Empire, points to parallel processes by which notions of frontiers—"the idea of the *frontier*, the border, the geographic place where opposing nations met and confronted each other, the setting for the colossal and daily struggle between nations" (Judson 1996, 394–95)—were created in the Julian March, with "peoples" (qua ethnic groups) mapped onto specific territories. Like Germans in Bohemia (see Cohen 1981), Italian speakers in the mixed areas of Istria and Dalmatia found their hold on local politics threatened by the growing national consciousness and political organization of Slavic groups (notably the Slovenes and the Croats). Italians opposed not only Slavs, however, but also their German masters, whom Italians accused of privileging Slavs in classic divide-and-conquer manner.

Despite this Italian antagonism toward their Austrian overlords, "ethnic" Germans and Italians nonetheless occupied similar structural positions in their local/regional domains of power within the empire. Both groups, for example, grew increasingly defensive over language rights, organizing private "national language" schools (the German School Association, or Deutscher Schulverein, and the National League, or Lega Nazionale, respectively) where the imperial government was unwilling to provide them.[7] Nationalist understandings of both Italian and German identity within the Austrian context rested on similar notions of superior civilizations given expression in their languages. Such understandings did not oppose earlier liberal formulations of identity (even as they competed with them) but rather followed out of the endorsement of hierarchy implicit in Austrian liberalism. "According to these liberal nationalists, neither geographic location nor the sheer number of people who spoke a given language was as decisive in determining a group's relative status or power in the monarchy as was quality, defined by the group's cultural and financial achievement," writes Judson. "As one nationalist author pointed out [in 1887], '*With the exception of Italian,* German is the only one of all the languages spoken in the Austrian Monarchy that has an absolute value; the others have only a relative, local value" (1996, 386; my italics). The German language was thus regarded as an expression of a superior civilization in a manner that recognized similar Italian assertions about civiltà along the eastern Adriatic. Such statements indicate how prior notions of civilizational and linguistic complexes became mapped onto geographic sites, thereby making claims for territorial and political borders that required certain kinds of policing and control.

At the same time, ethno-national identities ostensibly corresponding to places were in fact highly class specific (Sluga 2001, 14–15). In Prague, for example, German identity pivoted on a self-image of a propertied elite that precluded a more popular base (Cohen 1981, 282), whereas in the Julian March a strident Italian identity held only a limited appeal for the mercantile elite, usually described as "cosmopolitan" in outlook. The content and scope of Italian irredentism, as well as its countercosmopolitan discourse, has often been exaggerated or romanticized.

A competing set of local historiographical narratives and political orientations view Trieste and its hinterland as inherently and continuously Italian from their days as a Roman colony or, alternatively, as hybrid spaces with a unique, local, or regional aspect characterized by the intermingling of diverse peoples. Trieste and the Julian March prove in this sense akin to Kathmandu, described by Liechty as a space overdetermined by places. Following Liechty, we may investigate for Trieste "how one space becomes the site for a host of places, each claiming the same ground for its own configuration of meanings, or with how layers of signification (multiple places) come to envelope the same referent (a particular space)" (1996, 99; on spaces with many places, see also Carter 1997; Herzfeld 1991). More precisely, we may ask how one configuration of meanings— in this case, privileging Italian-ness—comes to dominate (at least in some contexts) and to subordinate alternative understandings of place.

Trieste's multiple determination as a place was brought home to me quite forcefully in the final days of my fieldwork when I participated in a summer school organized by a group of anthropologists based at the University of Ljubljana and held in the Istrian town of Pirano/Piran (Slovenia). Those in attendance included various anthropologists coming mainly from Europe (Germany, Slovenia, Italy, Croatia, and Norway), their students, and anthropology undergraduates from Ljubljana. At this field school, I gave an hour-long lecture in which I focused on political and symbolic contests to interpret and shape the memory of the Istrian exodus. I discussed the strategies whereby exiles present both Istria and Trieste as historically Italian spaces, in both cultural and linguistic terms, and thus silence other interpretations of postwar events like those of the rimasti or the Slovenes.

After my talk, a German professor insisted that I had inadvertently "bought into" the exiles' representation of Trieste and Istria, conflating their ideological representations of Italian-ness with life on the ground. Even after I reiterated, in response to one of his questions, that very few Italians in Trieste can speak Slovene or that Italians in preexodus Istria (with some exceptions) rarely spoke more than a few words of Slovene or Serbo-Croatian, this academic continued to argue ("on principle") that I must be mistaken, that the reality of interwar Trieste and Istria must have been one of Italian-Slav intermixture, in contrast to contemporary ideological representations of exclusivity. Another professor then asked about what he called the Austrian movement in Trieste and its imperial nostalgia, a query that again pointed to alternative understandings of the region's historical character.

Later that afternoon, the group of conference participants traveled to Trieste, a forty-five-minute car ride from Pirano/Piran, whose promontory is visible on a clear day from the urban center. In Trieste we were given a guided walking tour by Tullia Catalan, a historian specializing in the region's Jewish history, including the tragic episode of Risiera di San Sabba. Catalan described and pointed out various marks of the city's cosmopolitan past, such as the synagogue and the Serbian Orthodox church. At this the German scholar smiled and nodded; his thesis that I had exaggerated the city's stridently Italian public face apparently was confirmed. As we continued our trek through the small downtown, however, the signs of the city's transformation became evident, and our guide narrated the changes wrought by the irredentist period and the city's passage to Italian control after World War I. My German colleague then quizzed Marta Verginella, professor of social history at the University of Ljubljana and member of the city's Slovene minority, about bilingualism in the city. Verginella reiterated my earlier statements, noting that the only bilingualism is to be found among the city's minorities rather than its self-identified Italian inhabitants. Feeling somewhat vindicated, at that time I still viewed Trieste's transformation in largely chronological terms, an Italianized city having supplanted a more diverse and cosmopolitan one.

In a sense, this view accurately represents the ways in which Italian fascism, the post–World War II territorial dispute, the subsequent partition of the Julian March, and the Istrian exodus reinforced a defensive and hyperorthodox discourse of italianità at the same time that these events altered the social geographies of the city and region. In another sense, though, my German interlocutor proved correct: I had taken certain aspects of the city's present Italianness for granted. More important, and contrary to what he had intended, I had too readily accepted ideological statements about the cosmopolitan past—of the city, as well as of the region and the empire—as factual descriptions. In juxtaposing cosmopolitanism and localism in the manner of Appadurai, who writes of localized worlds being inflected by "cosmopolitan scripts" (1996, 63), I had failed to consider the possibility that in the Julian March local cosmopolitanisms might instead be inflected by regional and imperial politics. Since then, I have subsequently come to view both cosmopolitanism and Italianism (or irredentism) as long-standing discursive configurations shaped in tandem; their relative prominence in the conduct and outward shape of public life in the Julian March has shifted over time but still exerts considerable weight.

I came to this understanding in part as the result of extended conversations with Maria Grazia Kuris, a freelance journalist. Born to a Greek sailor who married a Triestine, Kuris remains fascinated with her native city at the same time that its political and economic closure deeply frustrates her. Yet the Trieste that fascinates Kuris the most—the Trieste of the port, where as a young child she would talk to her father's maritime companions, and the Trieste of the Greek community—is one that I remain largely ignorant of. In a series of newspaper articles and an extended essay (1999), Kuris explores those little-known and publicly invisible or semivisible communities (Greeks, Armenians, Albanians,

Germans, Anglicans, Serbs, and so on) with a historical presence in the city dating back to the imperial period. Despite their low profile today, these groups have their own organizations and, in a certain sense, their own Trieste(s). When Kuris asked about the Slovene-Italian tensions that dominate local politics as reported in newspapers such as *Il Piccolo,* for example, a member of the Greek community evinced little or no interest, articulating a worldview focused not on territory and land but rather, in Braudelian fashion, on ports of call, seas, and islands.

Although I had been long aware of the presence of diverse populations in contemporary Trieste, I had neither seriously interrogated the image of imperial cosmopolitanism (which led me to see such groups as remnants or "pockets" of a once-widespread diversity) nor considered the way in which regional discourses of both cosmopolitanism and irredentism were jointly forged in the context of a multiethnic empire increasingly riven with nationalistic demands. Marina Cattaruzza's 1995 book, *Trieste nell'ottocento: Le trasformazioni di una società civile* (Trieste in the nineteenth century: The transformations of a civil society) suggests that in the nineteenth and early twentieth centuries Trieste was economically and culturally controlled by a class-bound, politically restrictive bourgeois mercantile elite that was considerably less cosmopolitan than late-twentieth- and early-twenty-first-century nostalgia would make out. Lois Dubin's (1999) work on Hapsburg Trieste's Jewish population similarly details this mercantile ethos, as well as the influence of a centralized state that offered legal corporate standing to groups, based on their "productive service."

Cosmopolitanism in this context signaled a validation of an imperial context that favored the fortunes of Trieste's elite rather than the universalistic outlook and celebration of diversity often implied by the term. Though Jews were not excluded from the city's financial or political structures in the nineteenth century, for example, associations of the urban elite, like the Casino Vecchio, remained marked by "an anti-Semitic prejudice of cultural origins [that] was a common patrimony of the high-level state functionaries" (Cattaruzza 1995, 48). Furthermore, Marina Cattaruzza argues that the years before the Great War witnessed not only the city's most impressive economic-industrial growth but also "a profound disintegration and dis-aggregation of its social fabric, whose components came to find themselves in a relationship of reciprocal and irreconcilable contraposition" (ibid., 6). These conflictual relationships were drawn along not only ethno-national lines (Slovene, Italian) but also class ones.

The extent of this conflict and the degree of support for irredentist ethno-national identities (whether those of Italians or of Slovenes/South Slavs) should not, however, be exaggerated. To do so would merely exchange assumptions about a lost cosmopolitan idyll for nationalist perspectives that see the Austro-Hungarian Empire in general, and the Julian March in particular, as inherently riven by dissent. Rather than counterpoise one narrative to another as a more

accurate version of events, I consider the two as expressions of competing ideologies that have, in their dialectical relationship, powerfully shaped identities
and interpretations of the past in both Trieste and Istria.[8]

Angelo Vivante's classic *Irredentismo Adriatico* (1912) highlights the key terms
and debates of the cosmopolitan/irredentist dialectic. Guided by a political
agenda of autonomy and socialism, Vivante constructs a powerful counternar-
rative to irredentist theses and one that remains influential today for scholarship on the region, as well as for those articulating alternative visions to those
of Trieste Italiana or Istria Italiana. His account also reveals how an older "autonomist" tradition associated with the mercantile class within Hapsburg Trieste eventually became wedded, at least in some circles, to socialist ideas. This
convergence was facilitated by the Austro-Marxist approach to the specific challenges of the Hapsburg monarchy. Thinkers such as Otto Bauer and Karl Ren-
ner "proposed a socialist federal state that would discard the idea that national
groups could only be politically represented by exercising sovereignty over nationally homogeneous territory" (Sluga 2001, 19). As filtered through the Triestine autonomist tradition, this line of thinking has direct continuities with local
articulations of communism during the interwar period and World War II.

In his account, Vivante takes on the irredentist tenets that Trieste (in its past,
present, and future) remains irrefutably Italian and that this italianità has
proven to be the guiding thread of the city's history. Rather, according to Vivante, the incompatibility of economic factors with the "national question"—a
theme that reappears time and again in debates over the city's future (in 1918,
1945, and the 1990s)—constitutes a guiding principle in Trieste's history. In
support of claims made for the city's Italian character, for instance, Italian irredentists frequently noted that modern Trieste had grown up on the ruins of the
early Roman settlement of Tergeste while they downplayed the fact that from
1382 until the conclusion of the First World War, the city played an integral
economic role within the Hapsburg Empire. Notwithstanding Trieste's prosperity and growth as a function of its development as an imperial port, irredentist historiography portrays the 1382 "dedication," which ended a period of
communal autonomy ("Italian" in character), as an act of usurpation by the
Hapsburgs (Godoli 1984, 20–23). Vivante thus reclaims this local tradition of
autonomy from irredentists.

Whereas some irredentist writers interpret demands for unification with Italy
as evidencing Trieste's Italian soul, Vivante posits these claims as reflecting the
desire of a very small, if vocal, minority. He refutes an irredentist narrative that
sees 1829 and 1848 as key moments in the development of "national consciousness" in Venezia Giulia. The founding of the association known as the
Gabinetto di Minerva and the journal *Favilla* by a nucleus of Triestine intellectuals in 1829, for example, often figures as an important act by early Italian patriots; valorizing the region's Roman and Latin traditions, such associations
stimulated local interest in the classical past. Vivante counters that intellectuals

such as Pietro Kandler, member of the Gabinetto di Minerva, argued for a return to a Triestine tradition of communal autonomy *within* the empire.

Similarly, in Vivante's account 1848 does not represent the beginning of strong anti-Austrian sentiment in the region, contrary to Italian nationalist interpretations (for example, Scocchi 1949) that take the events of that year as the crucial "spark" for the awakening of Italian political consciousness in the region. The crushing of the Venetian Republic, formed in 1848 under the leadership of Daniele Manin, as well as the death or exile suffered by many of its supporters, occupies a prominent place in accounts of Istria's historic ties to Venice (and, by extension, Italy). The 1930 volume *Figure del Risorgimento in Istria* (Figures of the Risorgimento in Istria) typifies such narratives, which posit Istria's inherent italianità and its long struggle with reunion with Venice and Italy. The author describes Istria in 1848 as both burning with a "desire for free representation and national independence" (Quarantotto 1930, 17) and providing Venice and Rome with courageous volunteers (for a more modern and nuanced version of this thesis, see Apollonio 1998). This tract reflects, even as it works to construct, a tradition of patriotic volunteers from the irredentist lands and, hence, of suffering and exile. The hagiography of irredentist "martyrs" continues to be invoked in the narratives of Italian exiles from Istria, within which (Yugo)Slavs were easily fitted into the structural space of enemy that Austrians had occupied until World War I.

Vivante rejects the contention, central to this irredentist martyrology, that the empire's Italian populations were ruthlessly oppressed by Austrian "tyrants" and their Slavic foot soldiers. Whereas Italian nationalists claim that the Austrian regime increasingly privileged Slavs in economic and political positions in classic divide-and-conquer fashion, Vivante maintains that Italian landlords oppressed Slavic peasants in Istria. Furthermore, he notes that even Italian firms in Trieste often preferred Slovene employees to ethnic Italians for reasons that had to do with business rather than national sentiments. Noting the hybridity that results from urbanization, Vivante nonetheless views this as a largely superficial process whereby an Italian varnishing (*verniciatura*) is added to the exterior of an essentially Slavic whole. The thin overlay of Italian-ness follows out of, in Vivante's estimation, the economic predominance of Italians in Istria and Trieste, as well as the privileging of Italian dialect as the lingua franca of business.

Throughout *Irredentismo Adriatico,* then, Vivante emphasizes the primacy of economics, rather than culture or nationalist conflict, as having determined the region's history. As an alternative to the irredentist project, Vivante posits a "separatist solution" (within the bounds of the empire) that would recognize the Julian March's natural, economic ties to its Slavic hinterland. Although Vivante links this up to a socialist tradition opposing irredentist nationalism, the terms of the debate remain largely captive to a nationalist imaginary, challenging neither the assumption of essential "ethno-national" wholes that may meet and produce hybrids nor the notion that populations belong to a specific territory.

Vivante never questions, for example, the fact that these "Italians" and "Slovenes" come from distinct cultural complexes. Sluga notes more generally that though "[t]he views of nationalists and socialists were separated not only by their respective opinions of the existing economic hierarchy, but the political meaning each attributed to Trieste's diversity . . . [nonetheless] there were aspects of the nationalist view that most socialists accepted, including the naturalness and significance of national allegiance, and the salience of national-cultural identities" (2001, 24). The territorial unity that Vivante envisioned thus reinscribes, albeit in a new manner, the notion of the region as a "transitional zone" between culture areas. The irredentist and cosmopolitan/autonomist arguments rehearsed in Vivante's account reveal the way that both discursive configurations reflected, even as they were delimited by, the internal politics of the Hapsburg Empire.

Writing on the eve of the world war that would dramatically alter Trieste's destiny, Vivante undervalues the degree to which members of the city's "cosmopolitan" elite could also endorse a national identity (Italian) that would contradict their economic interests. We need only think, for example, of the Jewish writer Ettore Schmitz and his literary evocations of a Central European world in which the Hapsburg port of Trieste represented a cosmopolitan crossroads of Latin, Slavic, and Austrian cultures. Yet, we must also remember that Schmitz assumed the pen name *Italo* Svevo and became a supporter of the Italian irredentist cause.[9] In one of his short stories, Svevo voices the contradictory attitudes of these Austrian businessmen–*cum*–Italian patriots: "But I hadn't realised the far-reaching changes that had taken place. Finding that my native city was at last emerging from a kind of middle-ages, I cheered the Italian troops down in the streets; but then I went off to my office and conducted business as usual, as though Austrian soldiers and short rations were still the rule" (1969, 113).

Svevo's love of his city's "hybrid" nature in tandem with his support for the Italian cause was shared by a generation of Triestine intellectuals who, in the decade before the Great War, hotly debated the city's character. Young writers such as Scipio Slataper denounced the city's "spiritual emptiness" while drawing inspiration from its contradictions and contrasts, its "tripartite soul" (German, Slovene, and Italian). Slataper, whose Italian first name and Slovene surname symbolized the city's "hybridity," deemed Trieste "a place of transition, which means a place of struggle. Everything in Trieste is double and triple, beginning with its flora and ending with its ethnicity" (in Cary 1993, 46). Slataper's intellectual colleagues and friends at the Florentine weekly *La Voce,* to which the young Triestine contributed his "Lettere triestine," inviting Italians to discover the unredeemed city, considered Slataper "the perfect symbol, in short, of that Trieste of his where three races mingle" (Prezzolini in Cary 1993, 139). Yet *La Voce*'s intellectual and political project, like Slataper's, was a firmly Italian one. The space for ambiguity and contrast offered to Slataper and other Triestine intellectuals was severely restricted by the beginning of World War I, which forced such "nationalist cosmopolites" to take sides. The war instead made popular a vocabulary of *autochtoni* (autochthonous, indigenous) and *invasori* (invaders, occupiers) (Sluga 2001, 28), which already had currency in the nineteenth century among Italian irredentists writing about Dalmatia.

Although Italy had been allied with Austria-Hungary and Germany in the Triple Alliance since 1882, the Great War prompted Italy to proclaim neutrality and to eventually enter the conflict on the side of the Allies in 1915. That Triestine youths like Slataper or the Trentine socialist Cesare Battisti joined the Italian forces as volunteers, thereby committing an act of treason from the point of view of the Austrian state whose citizens they remained, suggests the limits of such cosmopolitan hybridity. The cosmopolitan ethos in Hapsburg Trieste seems, then, to have been associated variously with the mercantile class discussed by Cattaruzza and Dubin, the socialist tradition embodied by Vivante's work, and a regional literary tradition given expression by figures such as Slataper and Svevo. Although intellectuals working within this literary tradition moved along a Prague-Trieste-Florence ambit that traversed Italy and Austria-Hungary (Marchi et al. 1983; Pellegrini 1987), this tradition nonetheless remains strongly Italian in flavor (not least in its language of expression). The ambiguous space occupied by such intellectuals in whose works and lives discourses of cosmopolitanism and irredentism intersected further underscores the need to treat these terms not as bipolarities but rather as derived from a common history. This common history must be remembered when examining the contemporary invocation and reworkings of these discourses.

The Cartographies of Historical Production in the Julian March

Having sketched out the broad contours of the Julian March as a landscape marked by state making (and state breaking), as well as literary production, let us ask, what is the precise terrain from which contemporary historical accounts in the region—specifically those concerning Istria's partition and the exodus—issue? Answering this question entails mapping the institutional frameworks within which history making occurs and in which I conducted fieldwork.

In Trieste the events of the war and exodus dominate the city's "memoryscapes" (Yoneyama 1999). The Second World War also proved an important site for the performance of identity in nearby Istria, though the narrative possibilities under the Titoist regime were much more restricted. The history of this period remains an intensely public topic of discussion in Trieste, a debate in which individuals feel authorized by their personal experiences to participate. Any given week in the city will undoubtedly feature several events that touch on the region's "traumatic" recent history: book presentations, meetings sponsored by the exile associations, lectures by professors affiliated with the University of Trieste and/or various historical institutes, films, and gatherings of former war veterans or partisans. In spite of the general high regard displayed throughout Italy for academic authority and titles, conferences and talks given by scholars in Trieste are often met by impassioned personal testimonies and, at times, loud and angry denunciations from audience members.

I discovered this within days of my arrival. In February 1995, along with several hundred persons, I attended a special public screening in Trieste of Slovene documentaries dating from the immediate postwar years. Organized by the Istituto Regionale per la Storia del Movimento di Liberazione nel Friuli–Venezia Giulia and the cinema group La Cappella Underground, the program featured films only recently available from the Archives of the Republic of Slovenia. These included actual footage shot by Yugoslav partisans in the course of their guerrilla war, together with short pieces dating from the period of the "Trieste Crisis," when the Italian and Yugoslav states engaged in the propaganda war over Venezia Giulia within which the Istrian exodus unfolded. Such clips showed manifestations of support for the Yugoslav "liberators," with enthusiastic demonstrators carrying signs, written in both Italian and Slovene, proclaiming "Long Live Tito!" "Long Live the Red Army!" "We Are a Part of Yugoslavia!" and so on. Most of these films dated from 1945–47, the period in which the Anglo-American occupiers of Trieste identified Yugoslav state socialism as an instrument of the Soviet Union.

The series of shorts concluded, however, with a breezy film from 1950 that presented a reconciliatory vision of life in the frontier zone. Set to the beat of jazzy xylophone music, the film featured both Trieste and Capodistria/Koper (a port just across the border in what is today Slovenia) and showed the movement of peoples and goods between the two. The footage played up the similarity of life on both sides of the frontier and showed friendly guards happily waving people across the border. This film elicited audible murmurs and comments from the public. Indeed, a number of audience members seemed particularly disturbed or offended by this seemingly light film, given that its vision of coexistence along the border appeared to embody the hypocrisy of both the Italian and the Yugoslav state after the formal resolution of the Trieste Crisis. In the question-and-answer session following the program, several members of the audience asked on what basis the films were selected. One man complained that the films needed more contextualization, arguing that in order to understand the postwar climate in the region one must first know the history of the "Forty Days" of Yugoslav "occupation" of Trieste (May–June 1945) and events in the adjacent Istrian Peninsula. Others came forward to offer their own testimonies about these events. Such scenes, which appeared to contrast personal experience to "official" or scholarly accounts, were repeated at most of the programs I subsequently attended in the region. These frequent performances of

personal and collective identity offer a primary means by which a "wound culture" reproduces itself in the Julian March.

Presentations I made in different forums in Trieste often prompted comments
that began, "With due respect to the *dottoressa americana,* who is too young to
have lived through such events, I personally saw [or heard, or lived through], . . ."
after which would come a long monologue about the individual's own experience. The respect shown me as a "doctor" (in Italy, the *laurea,* or first degree,
entitles one to the title of *dottore* or *dottoressa*) alternated with a familiar and fa-
milial (as demonstrated by the invocation of kinship terms and analogies, for
example, "like a daughter for us" or "honorary Istrian") address due to my gender and relative youth. At times, however, resentment replaced such affection.

My status as a representative of "lamerica" evoked, for instance, sometimes
ambivalent responses that mirrored divided opinions over the United States'
historic and contemporary role in regional politics. Many locals in Trieste
shared fond memories of the Americans (in contrast to the "cold" British) who
"liberated" and occupied the city after World War II. Others expressed gratitude to the United States for the Marshall Plan and a tough Cold War stance on
communism. Other exiles, however, maintained that Trieste's Anglo-American
occupiers had ultimately sold them out by sanctioning the "sacrifice" of Istria
in exchange for Italian control of Trieste. Indeed, at times I worried that I might
be seen as yet the latest in a line of U.S. representatives who had betrayed the
Italians from Istria. Some exiles played on my fears, chiding me, "*You* Americans did not behave well" (during the Trieste Crisis, with the bombardment of
Zara in 1943, and so on).

Painfully aware of my precarious status as a young outsider, I tried to listen
respectfully to such comments. The arrival of an American anthropologist with
no family ties to the region to study the Istrian question evinced considerable
interest, particularly since it was widely recounted that I had studied Native
American groups like the Apache and the Kiowa during my undergraduate
years. Some observers (particularly professional historians who often endured
long outbursts from esuli at conferences and presentations) found this connection to the "exotic" amusing. That I would presumably train on the Istrians the
lens I had previously turned on indigenous peoples confirmed in a comic way
what some of these scholars "knew all along": the esuli were yet another "primitive" and irrational population. Some exiles rejected any possible analogies.

At one talk I gave in Trieste in 1997, I discussed the semantics of exile and
mentioned similarities between the narratives of the esuli and the Hutu refugees
studied by anthropologist Liisa Malkki (1996); I saw pained or puzzled expressions on the faces of some of the esuli in attendance. During the question-
and-answer session, a man who had resettled in Trieste asked me which historical case I found most similar to that of the Istrian exiles. When I began to
talk about the Cubans in Miami, he blanched. Clearly, he had wanted either a
confirmation that the Istrian exodus was unique (*un esodo unico,* a line that many

exiles repeat) or perhaps some reference to the classic people of exodus, the Jews; certainly, he expected the exiles' narratives of suffering to be located within a Western or European history of persecution. Instead, a historian laughingly congratulated me afterward on the presentation, "Great! The exiles like Hutus and the Cubans!" (*"Grande! Gli esuli come gli Hutu e i Cubani!"*).

Indeed, at many presentations attended by professional historians who were locally born, I often noted either a weary resignation to the long (and at times, rambling) testimonies typically offered by audience members or the somewhat smug bemusement of academics who "knew better." Triestine scholars who considered themselves serious historians (in contradistinction to the autodidactic historians in the city) complained to me about living in a city where the past "refused to die" and thereby prevented the ostensibly dispassionate and distanced examination known as the "historian's craft." Yet attending public events dedicated to Trieste's recent history (a kind of "interactive history") usefully revealed the lively contestation locally of broader narratives about the immediate postwar period. At the same time, these locally dominant accounts worked to efface other experiences and perspectives within the city, such as those of the Slovene minority and of Italian communists. Thus although Istrian esuli may rightly argue that their memories counteract official (national) historiographies, at the local level their narratives are in no way marginalized.

Within Trieste, the organizations formed by the Istrian exiles have played a key role in setting the tone for and terms of this powerful local discourse. The three principal exile associations in Trieste—Associazione delle Comunità Istriane, Associazione Nazionale Venezia Giulia e Dalmazia (ANVGD), and Unione degli Istriani—all sponsor public events and publish a variety of books and pamphlets dedicated to the exodus, as well as Istrian history, traditions, and dialects. The various esuli organizations are grouped together under the Federazione degli Esuli, or Federation of the Esuli. In Trieste, there also exists the Associazione dei Giuliani nel Mondo, a club for émigrés of all sorts (not just Istrian exiles) from Venezia Giulia. Set apart from these large associations is the small Circolo di Istria, formed by a group of leftist intellectuals interested in dialogue with contemporary Istrians.

Until political transformations in the early 1990s broke down the traditional political alliances that defined Italian public life in the postwar period, these exile associations generally coincided with the major battle lines in the Italian political scene. From 1945 to 1990, the primary actors in Italian electoral politics were the ruling Christian Democrats (Democrazia Cristiana, or DC), the opposition Italian communists (Partito Comunista Italiano, or PCI), and the independent socialists (Partito Socialista Italiano, or PSI), who at times allied themselves with the PCI and at times with the DC. The neofascist Movimento Sociale Italiano (MSI) proved small in its numbers but nonetheless played a significant role as—depending on one's viewpoint—either the heir of the fascist legacy or the guardian of the national(ist) dream. The primary political cleavage between the church/DC and the PCI created competing symbolic and social universes; individuals often negotiated these two alternative worlds in seemingly contradictory ways, as Kertzer (1980) discusses in his ethnography of daily life in a PCI stronghold in Bologna. In the radicalized youth culture of post-1968, the primary polarity was instead between "black" (neofascists) and "red" (communists or groups advocating violent tactics, like the Red Brigades).

The end of the Cold War and the massive corruption scandal known as Tangentopoli saw the disbanding of the Christian Democrats and their regrouping in the Popular Party (Partito Popolare Italiano, PPI). The PCI faithful instead fractured into the left-wing Party of the Democratic Left (Partito Democratico della Sinistra, PDS) and the small, secessionist Communist Refoundation (Rifondazione Comunista) (see Kertzer 1996 on these changes). Just as the PCI leadership sought to distance the party from its specifically communist past, MSI leaders also refashioned a more generically right-wing party, the Alleanza Nazionale (which some hard-core *missini* rejected). In coalition with the Forza Italia Party founded by television magnate Silvio Berlusconi and the secessionist Lega Nord (Northern Leagues) of Umberto Bossi, Alleanza Nazionale briefly came to national power in 1994–95. As of this writing, this coalition has returned to power with the national elections of spring 2001.

In chapter 4, I discuss the impact these political transformations have had on understandings of the Istrian question. These party reorganizations have not, however, fundamentally altered the structure of the exile associations in Trieste, which reflected the old political map of Italy. During and immediately after the exodus, there came into being two organizations competing to speak as the voice of the Italians from Istria: the Comitato di Liberazione Nazionale dell'Istria (CLNI) and the ANVGD. The ANVGD leadership drew on Istria's traditional ruling class, some of whose members were compromised with the fascist regime and sought to relegitimize themselves. The CLNI, by contrast, was made up of young antifascists, a number of them with links to the church and its political wing, Azione Cattolica (Catholic Action) (Volk 1999, 274). Though both organizations agreed on the need to preserve Istrian culture and identity, particularly through a compact resettlement of refugees in Trieste, they disagreed fundamentally in their judgments of fascism. Keeping alive the hope of Istria's "redemption" and celebrating rituals associated with both the irredentist and the fascist era, the ANVGD proved to be more closely linked with the irredentist tradition. The CLNI instead associated *la patria,* or the nation, with democracy and, not surprisingly, became the privileged representative of the esuli vis-à-vis the government (ibid., 274–77). These divisions underscore the shifting nature and multiple moments of center and periphery, state and nonstate.

The structure of the exile organizations in Trieste further blurs the lines, especially those between the irredentist/fascist and antifascist traditions represented by the ANVGD and CLNI, respectively. The Unione degli Istriani, the most prominent of these associations in Trieste, has long been associated with the political Right (the MSI and today the Alleanza Nazionale and Forza Italia), whereas the Comunità Istriane has generally been seen as closer to the political Center (formerly the Christian Democrats). The Circolo di Istria instead has a leftist image. Though the pronouncements of the organizations' leaders often do reflect these general political allegiances, the membership of these organizations proves fluid; many individuals who adhered to the DC, for example, frequent the Unione degli Istriani and/or the Comunità Istriane, and Marino Vocci, one of the Circolo di Istria's founders, later headed the regional political committee for Romano Prodi and the Popular Party (heir to the DC).

Although these various organizations in Trieste often share personnel and publications, they also compete with one another to speak as the voice of the exile and play similar roles for their members, organizing events and publishing books and journals. These journals and bulletins both supplement and stand in for face-to-face socializing, often publishing local news such as births, weddings, and deaths. In addition to the pan-Istrian journals—including the official organs of the Comunità Istriane, Unione degli Istriani, and Associazione Nazionale Venezia Giulia e Dalmazia—there exist numerous bulletins for clubs composed of members of the same village or town; the Unione and the Comunità serve as umbrella groups for many of these smaller, locale-specific clubs.

The Istituto Regionale per la Cultura Istriana (IRCI), established in 1983, represents the scholarly center for the study of Istria and the exodus. Constituting the esuli's scientific and scholarly base, IRCI's board has representatives from each of the various exile associations (which at times provokes bitter controversy and factionalism). Proposed projects include the creation of a library of oral histories, a study of the social composition of the esuli, the editing of an archive of documents from the Istrian CLN (Comitato di Liberazione Nazionale), and the creation of an exodus museum. The museum initiative grew out of the recovery of unclaimed personal possessions transferred to Trieste by esuli and placed for several decades in a storage hangar; by displaying these personal effects, the museum will emphasize the historic and material presence of Italians in Istria, as well as convey the physical loss experienced by the exiles (Delbello 1992).

In line with these architectonics of memory, the walls of IRCI display numerous old maps of Istria and the Julian March, as well as posters and advertisements from the period of Italian administration. In their literal mapping of memory, these cartographies make manifest the esuli's challenge to current state borders through claims to autochthony and moral authority. In a mirroring effect, the Centro di Ricerche Storiche di Rovigno, the Italian minority center in Istria, also offers a literal gallery of old maps, a prominent feature since the institute's remodeling and expansion two years ago. (Admittedly, this cartographic emphasis reflects not only the visioning of alternative geographies but also the more prosaic fact that the directors of both institutions are avid collectors of antique maps, books, and postcards.) IRCI maintains contacts with the Centro di Ricerche Storiche through direct collaboration among researchers and more indirectly through the Università Popolare di Trieste (UpT). Established in the struggle for an Italian-language university during the period of Austrian rule, today the UpT channels intellectual goods and services from Italy to the Italian minority in Istria. The Italian minority in Istria has its own set of associations, the local Comunità degli Italiani, overseen by the Unione Italiana based in Fiume; I describe these in detail in chapter 7.

The autochthonous Slovene minority in Italy similarly possesses a state-sponsored organizational apparatus centered on the Slovene Cultural and Economic Union. Slovenes can claim their own newspaper (*Primorski Dnevnik*), publishing house, library, and archives. The Slovene Research Institutes (SLORI) in Trieste/Trst and Gorizia/Gorica publish histories detailing the fascist and neofascist persecution of the Slovenes; scholars at these associations often collaborate with colleagues in Slovenia and actively contribute to a national historiographical tradition there. Historians in Slovenia, such as Milica Kacin-Wohinz, have published extensively, for example, on Slovenes' persecution under fascism and their resistance struggle. Slovene historians instead tended to gloss over or ignore the Istrian exodus until just a few years ago (Giuricin 1997; Verginella 1997).[10]

In Croatia, researchers at historical institutes and universities similarly made little or no mention of the exodus in the decades following this population transfer. One of the first frank discussions of these events is found in publications put out by the Centro di Ricerche Storiche di Rovigno. Established in 1968, the Centro di Ricerche Storiche represents the principal research center for the Italian minority in Istria. Many scholars from Italy also utilize the collections there. Although Centro scholars have been able to fully take up the topic of the exodus only since 1990, one author published a memoir as early as 1973, in which he rejected the common assumption that all those who left Istria were fascists (Giuricin 1997, 1). Following this example and that of publications in Trieste, in the 1980s various other Croatian authors began to mention the exodus, unleashing lively polemics in Yugoslav papers and magazines. Historian Luciano Giuricin singles out the 1990 publication by respected ethnographer Vladimir Žerjavić as particularly significant, since this work offered the results of archival research on the "option" of Italian citizenship. Despite the interest shown by a serious "Croatian" scholar in this topic, however, the most sustained research in Croatia on the exodus has been carried out by scholars who are members of the Italian minority—including Marino Budicin, Luciano Giuricin, Nelida Milani-Kruljac, Orietta Moscarda, and Antonio Pauletich—affiliated with the Centro di Ricerche Storiche.

Many of the centro's scholars have also conducted research at or collaborated with the Istituto Regionale per la Storia del Movimento di Liberazione nel Friuli–Venezia Giulia in Trieste. One in a network of regional institutes in Italy associated with the political Center-Left and promoting the study of the Resistance and liberation, this is perhaps the institute in Trieste most engaged with broader Italian historiographical currents. Historians such as Tullia Catalan, Silva Bon Gherardi, Tristano Matta, Raoul Pupo, Giampaolo Valdevit, and Marta Verginella—some of Trieste's most capable and rigorous scholars of recent regional history—are or have been associated with the institute. The work of such scholars appears in *Qualestoria*, a journal published by the instituto featuring articles, book reviews, and edited documents. The istituto also puts out various books.

Four of the istituto's associates collaborated on the 650-page *Storia di un esodo: Istria, 1945–1956* (History of an exodus: Istria, 1945–1956), published in 1980. Apart from Padre Flaminio Rocchi's *L'esodo dei 350 mila Giuliani Fiumani e Dalmati* (The exodus of 350,000 Julians, Fiumans, and Dalmatians), the volume that exiles often refer to as their standard reference work, *Storia* represents one of the few attempts to provide a comprehensive account of the exodus. Many exiles disagree strongly with the volume's tone and interpretations, which they see as reflective of the Istituto's leftist bent. (The scholars themselves also admit to the incompleteness of their archival sources, some of which have become available since Yugoslavia's collapse.) When I mentioned to an esule that I was going to the istituto in order to speak with one of the book's collaborators, I was warned, "There are still Stalinists in Trieste." The book's leftist orientation (as evidenced by its "necessary preamble" about how fascism precipitated postwar events in Istria) and the presentation of the problem of the esuli in the past tense (as one that "remained open for many years" [Colummi et al. 1980, 497]) contrasts sharply with histories sponsored by the exile associations.

The intense engagement of regional institutes, associations, and scholars in historical debates whose terms have been largely set by local politics (or, more precisely, by the conjunction of local and international politics) helps explain why the extensive literature devoted to the problems of Italy's eastern border largely remained confined ("forgotten") to a closed regional circuit until relatively recently. The field of historical production in the Julian March (and in my cursory description here I have focused on Trieste and Istria, the sites of my fieldwork) thus proves intensely politicized, as well as fragmented. As a result, scholars often remain ghettoized to a certain degree by their own identities: Slovenes tend to work on Slovene history in Slovene institutes, Italians in Istria do likewise, and those in Italy with political orientations leaning to the Left or the Right find homes in appropriate environments; for example, the Istituto Regionale per la Storia del Movimento di Liberazione nel Friuli–Venezia Giulia is said to have a left-wing (or center-left) orientation. Scholars I knew frequently complained about this ghettoization. I do not mean to denigrate the considerable amount of high-quality and interesting work produced in the Julian March. Rather, I want to underline the way that a system of institutes and minority associations tied directly to state patronage and occupying a landscape historically marked by both ideological and ethno-national conflict constitutes a particular terrain of historical production, into which I ventured as a novice anthropologist.

This terrain bears the mark of state-making and state-breaking processes by which the center and the periphery, as well as their particular relationship, have been repeatedly reconfigured and the Julian March (whether envisioned in terms of national purity or hybrid impurity) constituted *as a region*. Although my analysis complicates uncritical celebrations of "history from below," from another direction it contributes to the critical rethinking (see Sahlins [1989] and Herzfeld [1997]) of the stato-centric and top-down assumptions that have dominated theorizing about the inculcation of ethno-national identities. Examining large-scale processes of identity formation from the margins of states reveals the multidirectionality (if unevenness) of their operation, with understandings from the periphery refracting and acting back on those of the ostensible center. A more decentered perspective that takes into account liminal groups like refugees—impure boundary transgressors who nonetheless symbolize the nation in exile—further underscores the tremendous and continual ideological labor required to secure and police various boundaries between states, ethnic groups, and center/periphery. In chapters 2, 3, and 4, I explore crucial moments in this boundary (re)drawing for the Julian March.

Part I

MAKING AND BREAKING STATES

CHAPTER TWO

Geographies of Violence:
Remembering War

IN PART I, I explore how actors in the Julian March have forged narratives of memory and identity within the intersection of regional, national, and international politics and at three key moments of boundary collapse and construction: World War I, World War II, and the end of the Cold War and the breakup of Yugoslavia. Examining these historical junctures not only grounds current processes of identity formation in prior experience but also breaks down rigid dichotomies between center and periphery, top and bottom. This highlights the ways in which the "state" actually consists in multiple moments, layers, and agents. Herzfeld suggests that in addition to being wary of reifying the state, anthropologists should make this process itself—one in which both scholars and state subjects collude—the object of analysis. He argues, "An anthropology of nationalisms and nation-states must get inside this ongoing production of static truths. To do so means looking for it among all segments of the population, for all are implicated" (1997, 10). Herzfeld also advocates viewing "'top' and 'bottom' as but two out of a host of refractions of a broadly shared *cultural engagement* (a more processual term than the static *culture*)" (ibid., 3).

Analyzing the production of historical narratives offers a key entry point into these processes of cultural engagement and the agencies (literal and figurative) involved. Furthermore, "such narratives and plots are a rich source of connections, associations, and suggested relationships for shaping multi-sited objects of research" (Marcus 1995, 109). Rather than referring strictly to a particular literary device, I use the term *narrative* here to signify descriptions (written and spoken) that tell a story. A narrative by definition possesses a teleological structure: it has a clear beginning, a middle, and an end toward which it inexorably moves. Although most of the accounts I examine are, in fact, roughly chronological, I use the term *narrative* loosely while retaining its essential defining characteristics (its tripartite structure), without insisting on strict chronological movement.

Whether oral or written, narratives that describe lives dramatically shaped by displacement not only display the more specific tripartite structure associated with liminal encounters (see chapter 6) but also highlight moments of drama and intensity, even as the very drama of those moments may be produced largely through their telling *after* the act of loss. Italo Svevo puts it nicely in his

Further Confessions of Zeno when he comments, "Life in practice is diluted, and therefore obfuscated, by many things which, when one is describing it, never get mentioned. One does not mention breathing until it becomes panting, neither does one mention one's many holidays, meals, sleep, until some tragedy deprives one of such things" (1969, 16–17). This prompts Svevo to conclude, "For this reason the descriptions of lives—of which a considerable part is omitted: the things everyone experiences but no one ever mentions—become more intense than the lives themselves" (ibid.).

In focusing on the moment of exile, probably one of the most intense experiences in the lives of the individuals subjected to it, Istrian esuli not only elaborate their experiences after the fact but also frequently pattern their understandings on earlier narratives detailing the struggles of irredentists against the Austrians and their Slavic "allies." These older understandings of exile and martyrdom may have even encouraged Italians to abandon Istria, influencing the way that events were interpreted and constructed at the time, as well as ex post facto. Notions of sacrifice and ultimate redemption may have led Istrians to hope (and to continue to do so) that they would ultimately return to their homes in Istria. The Istrian case thus illustrates the power of deep narratives to structure and mediate the unfolding of events, as well as their later recollection.

As James Young has suggested, even an apparently unprecedented event like the Holocaust in fact drew on various discourses about Jewish persecution, those of victims and perpetrators.[1]

> This is to suggest that the events of the Holocaust are not only shaped *post factum* in their narration, but that they were initially determined as they unfolded by the schematic ways in which they were apprehended, expressed, and then acted upon. In this way, what might once have been considered merely a matter of cultural, religious, or national perspective of the Holocaust assumes the force of agency in these events: world views may have both generated the catastrophe and narrated it afterward. Thus perceived, history never unfolds independently of the ways we have understood it; and in the case of the Holocaust, the interpretation and structural organization of historical events as they occurred may ultimately have determined the horrific course they eventually took. (Young 1988, 5)

Young's comments temper the frequent description of the Holocaust as unprecedented and, to a large degree, ineffable. In his influential book on Holocaust memory, Langer contends that oral testimonies in particular make manifest the ultimate impossibility of describing the Holocaust experience. Langer contrasts oral histories with literary renderings, noting that the former constitute narratives beyond analogy, metaphor, and mythic associations. "Oral testimony is a living commentary on the limits of autobiographical narrative, when the theme is such unprecedented atrocity. It also reveals the limits of memory's ability to re-create that past" (1991, 61).

Even if the Holocaust may be a unique case in its indescribability (though much evidence exists to the contrary), in both Trieste and Istria (to different degrees) written and oral memories, as well as public and private ones, intertwine and intersect (see also the critique of Langer in Davis 1999, 123). In the previous chapter, I noted the continued salience for esuli of a literary tradition associated with figures such as Svevo. In this chapter, I detail the ongoing significance of Christian narratives of martyrdom and redemption. Though accounts of displacement typically refer to the story of the Jews' Exodus from Israel—which constitutes the metanarrative of exile (Gilroy 1996, 207)—the images of martyrdom and redemption favored by the esuli refer to precise Christian readings of their experience. They also draw on a well-established genre of specifically "Italian" writings about exile dating from the medieval and Renaissance periods; "contrasts between center and margin, fertility and barrenness, community and wilderness were repeated and renewed again and again" (Starn 1982, 10) in the work of exiles such as Dante, whose experience many banished nineteenth-century Risorgimento patriots subsequently invoked (Ciccarelli 2001).

Within both Christian and nationalist traditions of writing "sacred lives," the relationship between orality and textuality often remains porous and flexible (Coon 1997, 7–9). This suggests that although useful (particularly in underscoring issues of power and access), the oral/written dichotomy should not be overstated. In places like the Julian March, reifying this distinction proves one of the means by which we further the "ongoing production of static truths" (Herzfeld 1997, 10). Monuments provide one prominent site at which such "truths" are negotiated. Writing of the memorializations of Christian martyrs, Abou-El-Haj remarks, "Central to these efforts was the range of art and architecture, the visual and spatial topography generated for the cult of saints" (1994, 1). These comments also hold for the various "sacred" topographies constructed (and contested) in the Julian March during the nineteenth and twentieth centuries.

Remembering the "War that We Won"

Crucial to contemporary articulations of the experience of exile from Istria are older narrative structures derived from the irredentist struggle and the Great War. As one female activist and a retired schoolteacher put it: "We need to remember the war that Italy *won*." Situating understandings of the Istrian exodus within these more extensive narratives cautions us against seeing "memory politics" in exclusively presentist terms. Although the dream of redemption seemingly realized after World War I dissolved two decades later with the brutal sacrifice of the Istrian Italian "homeland" to Tito's Yugoslavia, irredentism and the Great War's religio-nationalistic language of sacrifice nonetheless retains currency for the Istrian exile associations in Trieste. The seat of the

Unione degli Istriani, located in Piazza Goldoni in downtown Trieste, resembles a living museum to irredentism. Having written an undergraduate thesis on the poet Gabriele D'Annunzio, who in 1919 led a band of Italian ex-soldiers and nationalists in occupying the Yugoslav port of Fiume/Rijeka, I had initially viewed the rhetoric of irredentism as a relic of the past. Imagine my surprise, then, when I first visited the Unione degli Istriani in the summer of 1992; crossing the threshold, I saw D'Annunzian mottoes inscribed on the walls, Italian flags, and maps of Istria. What I had previously studied as a historical phenomenon in relation to D'Annunzio suddenly, startlingly, came to life.

Later that summer, I again found myself struck by the way in which irredentist rhetoric, specifically that associated with D'Annunzio, remained a living tradition in Trieste. In the first year following Yugoslavia's breakup, various Italian nationalist groups inside and outside Trieste revived questions of Italy's "historic right" to Istria. Neofascist leader Gianfranco Fini (together with Mirko Tremaglia and Triestine senator Roberto Menia) traveled to Belgrade in 1991 for a series of talks with Serbian officials about the divvying up of the Adriatic between Serbia and Italy (Fubini 1996). In Trieste demonstrators (many, but not all, of them esuli) demanded the renegotiation of border treaties with ex-Yugoslavia and the restitution of esuli property. The neofascist Movimento Sociale Italiano inundated the city with campaign posters calling for a "New Irredentism."

In November of that year, local MSI leader Roberto Menia organized a "D'Annunzian Sunday" (domenica dannunziana), for which ten thousand people gathered. Menia invoked one of the poet's most celebrated Great War exploits, the "Trick (or Joke) of Buccari" (Beffa di Buccari). At the head of three small navy motorboats that slipped into the narrow Bay of Buccari near Fiume, D'Annunzio and his men had allegedly eluded the Austrian navy, narrowly escaping the harbor under a heavy fog cover. The enemy found only a mocking message in a bottle. In the D'Annunzian spirit of the beau geste (in Italian, the desire to fare la bella figura), Menia stood aboard a similar speedboat and tossed into the sea 350 bottles containing messages demanding the return of Istria to Italy.

In the renewed (if marginal and brief) territorial debate over Istria that followed Yugoslavia's collapse, other nationalist groups in Trieste, such as the Lega Nazionale (National League), similarly invoked D'Annunzio but distanced themselves from the fascist tradition with which the poet is often associated. For some Italian nationalists, including the Fiuman "government-in-exile," which donated a marker on the seventieth anniversary of the March of Ronchi (leading to Fiume's occupation), D'Annunzio represents not the Saint John the Baptist of fascism, as is commonly supposed, but the incarnation of patriotism associated with Risorgimento hero Giuseppe Garibaldi (Host-Venturi 1976, 11–12). The different interpretations of D'Annunzio and his legacy crystallize in miniature the tensions in the Italian nationalist tradition, whose co-optation by the fascist regime discredited a range of alternative understandings of the patria. In a sense, then, what usually constitutes a source of nationalist rhetoric's strength—its ability to accommodate divergent visions and to provide a consensus of sentiment even where a consensus of meaning is lacking—led to the sometimes indiscriminate rejection of older nationalist discourses after the disaster of World War II.

Given the lack of a unified narrative (of either victory or defeat) of that conflict, it would prove exceedingly difficult to create a single, overriding monument to the Second World War in the Italian territory of the Julian March. Indeed, it is hard to imagine an Italian memorialization of World War II akin to that of Redipuglia, the massive national shrine just to the east of Trieste honoring the dead of Italy's World War I (for a similar divergence in French memories of the two world wars, see Farmer 1999, 5–6). Although explicitly a monument to the First World War or the War of Redemption, as some Italians call it, Redipuglia also stands as a national military cemetery for Italy. Redipuglia and the many other nearby cemeteries and monuments make tangible the Julian March's historic position as a contested border zone and as Italy's eastern front in the Great War. In nationalist narratives, the Julian March occupies a symbolic space for Italy similar to that of Normandy and Brittany for France. The scene of Italy's principal Great War battles, this territory witnessed both the Italian military's disastrous rout at Caporetto in 1917 and its triumph at Vittorio Veneto that year against the armies of the Austro-Hungarian Empire. This victory ultimately led to Italy's acquisition of various "unredeemed" lands at war's end.

It is either fitting or ironic, depending on one's viewpoint, that the monument at Redipuglia embodies the fascist glorification of warfare and sacrifice which led Italy into a disastrous second world conflict in which a portion of the reclaimed territories of the Julian March were apparently lost forever. The original monument at Redipuglia emphasized the site's role as an actual and bloody battlefield between the Italians and Austrians. The initial cemetery created immediately after the Armistice contained individual graves interspersed with the damaged and deteriorating instruments of warfare, on which were inscribed poetic epigraphs. Although bearing a futurist impulse—a tumultuous riot of weaponry and poeticization of the machinery of warfare—the cemetery apparently did not convey a sufficient celebration of violence to satisfy the new fascist regime that came to power in 1922. Indeed, the intention to allow the weapons of the conflict to slowly deteriorate, intermingling with the bones of those soldiers whose lives the war had forfeited, sent a potentially powerful antiwar message about the futility of such carnage.

Under Mussolini, then, the existent cemetery at Redipuglia was refashioned into a Park of Remembrance (Parco della Rimembranza) and a new "sanctuary" or "shrine" (sacrario) built in the monumental, neoclassical style characteristic of Italian fascism. The massive tomb containing the remains of 100,187 dead consists of an enormous staircase (reminiscent of the famous "typewriter" monument to Vittorio Emmanuele in Rome) with twenty-two large terraces adorned with the phrase "PRESENTE PRESENTE PRESENTE PRESENTE" in a kind of roll call of the dead. The names, ranks, and dates of forty thousand fallen are inscribed on individual plaques, and a chapel at the apex of the staircase contains the remains of sixty thousand unidentified soldiers. Despite the triumphalist intention of the shrine and its continuing role as the site of elaborate annual celebrations for the national Festival of Unity (held each November), the monument's simplicity and the overwhelming quantity of names also potentially lend themselves to antiwar readings. Nonetheless, the sanctity of Italy's sacrifice in the First World War remains unquestioned in the official tourist pamphlets that recall the "glorious fallen" (*gloriosi caduti*) who made a "divine sacrifice" and now "repose in the sanctuary" (Italian Ministry of Defence 1994).

For many in postfascist Italy, this religiously charged language of nationalism (*sacrifici e sacrari*) associated with the Great War and its memorialization (which merged with subsequent remembrances of fascist dead) now appear anachronistic. As Patrizia Dogliani notes,

> More research is needed into these aspects of the Fascist political religion and its legacy in memory, but what is clear is that this cult, at least as linked to the Great War, disappeared swiftly after the fall of Fascism, and does not seem to have left a trace in popular memory. . . . The suspicions engendered by Fascist excess are still obvious in the limited surviving celebration of the suffering in the Great War. Vittorio Veneto Day (4 November) remains a festival of the army; then, the dead of all wars are not mourned, nor is it a proper moment to talk about a full and mature concept of the *patria*. In quite a few towns, the existence of two separate monuments, one to the Great War, the other to the Resistance, has exacerbated this sense of detachment from national history and led to a greater enthusiasm for the *feste* of Anti-Fascism and the Republic (25 April, 1 May, 2 June). (Dogliani 1999, 19, 26)

Although correct in pointing out the overall oblivion into which such traditions have fallen in Italy, Dogliani overstates her point in denying any continued popular resonance or in arguing that Vittorio Veneto Day remains exclusively a festival of the army. Groups like the Istrian exiles attach considerable ritual importance to this day and to monuments like Redipuglia. For many esuli, the "glorious" memory of World War I remains vivid, a symbol of a healthy love of the patria that had answered the hopes of those Italians in the "unredeemed" lands. Redipuglia likewise remains an important place at which to continue to honor those who defended such aspirations. In keeping with this, the major exile associations in Trieste organize annual outings to the massive Great War monument at Redipuglia every November 3–4 for the Festival of National Unity, recalling Italy's participation in the First World War.

In 1995 I accompanied the Istrian exile groups on their annual day trip to Redipuglia and nearby Great War sites. The outing was jointly organized and attended by members of the three principal exile associations in Trieste: the

Figure 3. Istrian exiles at Redipuglia

a. Fascist-era military cemetery and monument at Redipuglia

b. Exile leaders at Oslavia, Festival of Unity, 1995

the Associazione Nazionale Venezia Giulia e Dalmazia, Comunità Istriane, and the Unione degli Istriani. As noted in the last chapter, these associations have been roughly divided along principal political party lines. The coordination of the 1995 activities by the three major exile associations led to the first shared outing, an attempt at some sort of greater unity (fittingly, given the moniker the Festival of Unity) among the divided exile community and leadership.

Physical journeys through a landscape marked by war cemeteries and ossuaries also map out in a quite literal sense the esuli's vision of a unified Italy. Chartering four Pullmans, our group left Trieste's Piazza Oberdan—a monument to the irredentist "martyr" Wilhelm Oberdan, who was executed by the Austrians in 1882—and headed first to the Church of San Carlo in Gorizia/Gorica for a morning Mass. Such exile events almost invariably feature a religious observance, pointing to the importance of the church in Istrian Italian life—or, perhaps more accurately, the importance of the church to postexile representations of Istrian Italian life (for an analogous case among Cuban exiles, consult Tweed 1997, 29–30)—and of a Catholic liturgical tradition to nationalist-irredentist narratives in the region. This Mass, for instance, included association banners placed on the altar and the military playing of taps.

Afterward, we proceeded to Oslavia, a massive World War I ossuary on the outskirts of Gorizia. Gorizia, like Trieste, proved contested at the end of the Second World War, and the eventual border left the old Austrian town center in Italian territory and its outskirts in Yugoslavia, giving rise to the town of Nova Gorica (New Gorizia) across what is today the Slovene border. From Oslavia, one sees Nova Gorica in the distance and on the hillside the enormous words "Nas Tito" (Our Tito), as one of my companions bitterly pointed out. This proximity only highlights the exiles' sense of loss.

At Oslavia, three leaders from the respective exile associations laid a wreath to the dead and said a few words. Denis Zigante, then president of the Unione degli Istriani, underlined the importance of the date as that of Italian unity for which many youth sacrificed their lives. Renzo Codarin, representing the ANVGD, lamented that such deaths were in some sense futile given that the "war to reunite Istria and Dalmatia to Italy" was ultimately betrayed by the subsequent loss of these territories. An outspoken exile from Dalmatia then unexpectedly and spontaneously reminded the crowd of the fate of Zara/Zadar, "liberated" by the Italian navy on November 4, 1919. When the Italians entered and hoisted the national flag, noted this man, the Zaratini went down on their knees ("tutti in ginocchio") in gratitude and homage. Yet Zara lost its special status as an Italian enclave in Dalmatia in 1943, when most of the city was destroyed by Allied bombardment and the majority of the residents fled to Istria or elsewhere in Italy. This improvised speech points to the way in which exiles from Dalmatia seek both to include and to differentiate their experience within a narrative about the Istrian exodus, with events in Dalmatia being seen to have anticipated Istria's fate.

After the Dalmatian exile said his piece, the chorus of the Comunità Istriane sang patriotic hymns, complements to the religious songs that had accompanied the Mass earlier. This ceremony at Oslavia proved much more elaborate than the subsequent one at Redipuglia, which consisted of a brief laying of wreaths and playing of taps. More central to the exiles' activities that day was the three-and-a-half-hour lunch in a trattoria, with much socializing and singing, which underscored not only the ways in which an Istrian community is reconstituted in exile but also the social role such associations play for the predominantly elderly exile population.

The events that day concluded with a visit to a community center in an "Istrian village" (part of the Italian state's relocation efforts in the 1950s and 1960s) where exiles mingled over refreshments and the chorus sang again. The pieces selected included "Terra rossa"—a reference to Istria's differentiation along the lines of *terra grigia* (gray rock), *terra bianca* (white earth, rock/marble), and *terra rossa* (fertile, red soil)—and "L'Inno Istriano" (Istrian hymn). The latter serves as an anthem for the exiles, who rise when the song is played and, on this occasion at least, loudly applauded the line "Istria, salva salva" (save Istria); Istrian choirs often sang this piece in refugee camps, like the one at the Caserma Ugo Botti in La Spezia (Vivoda 1998, 77). While implicitly calling to save Istria from its present-day bondage, in the context of the celebrations of November 3–4 the appeal to save Istria more explicitly recalls the ways in which the demand to "redeem" the *irredenta* of Trieste, Trent, Istria, and Dalmatia rhetorically informed Italian participation in World War I.

After the 1918 Armistice and Italy's "redemption" of Trieste and Istria (the latter was redeemed in 1920), the Triestine literary critic Silvio Benco wrote of Italian patriots, "They live in a sort of stupor, since there is no more need to be irredentist. . . . They peer about them. Are there truly no more Austrians to despise?" (in Cary 1993, 43). Benco need not have worried, for the nationalists soon found a new enemy. With the disappearance of the Austrians and Italy's acquisition of Trieste and Istria, the threat posed by the new Yugoslav state easily assumed the structural position that "Austria" previously occupied within the irredentist framework. Well before the war, in fact, Adriatic irredentists had increasingly linked the threat posed by Slav aspirations to Austrian policies of divide and conquer. As the author of an irredentist tract declared, "A tremendous instrument in the war waged in the past against the Italians subject to Austria has been the Croatian. Hatred against Italians has for many decades been artfully stimulated in the Croatians, and the latter have waged a fierce war of suppression and violence against the Italians of the Julian Veneto, of Fiume and of Dalmatia, revealing themselves, as ever, faithful servants of the House of Habsburgs" (Alberti et al. 1917, 42). With the Austrians removed from the scene after 1918, then, Croats and other (Yugo)Slavs were seen no longer as "instruments" but rather as the principal enemies.

Drawing on biblical schemata of martyrdom and redemption, such transformed irredentist narratives offered a ready-made conceptual framework for understanding exodus, highlighting the fundamentally religious aspects of much of nationalism and the close relationship between Italian irredentism and a liturgical language derived from Catholicism; the popular cults of heroes developed during the French Revolution (Soboul 1983) may represent a direct link between Catholic and national traditions of hagiography. In addition, the experience of Julian internees and so-called political exiles (*fuoriusciti*) in the Great War, followed by the "first exodus" by Italians from Dalmatia after it passed under Austrian and, later, Yugoslav control, provided more specific traditions of exodus through which to interpret and fashion the events in postwar Istria.

Julian "Traditions" of Exile: Irredentist Martyrology

> Thus, through these glorious martyrs each unredeemed region is consecrated anew to the Italianism of its destiny. The blood of Battisti, of Chiesa, of Filzi, sanctifies the lands of the Trentino and of the Adige; the blood of Oberdan and of Sauro the Adriatic regions as far as the Quarnaro; the blood and the ashes of Francesco Rismondo, Dalmatia, which suffers and waits. In the name of these heroic dead, of these glorious sons, Italy now demands the security of her confines, the safety of her race and of her civilization. Together with them, and echoing their last shout before the executioner, all Italians cry in concord, "Death to Austria! Long live Italy!"
>
> . . . Surely Trieste and the Julian Region, after the long and glorious martyrdom for which they have suffered for the sake of Italy from 1799 to 1917, after having given so many heroes to the war, after the last three years of atrocious suffering and terrible persecutions, may believe that they have offered to the cause of national liberty more martyrs and champions of their rights than any other region of Italy.
> —Mario Alberti et al., *Italy's Great War and Her National Aspirations*

After World War II, some Istrians sought to understand their experience in terms of earlier population transfers (temporary and permanent) of Italians from Dalmatia and Istria, as well as a tradition of specific Italian patriots exiled or killed for their nationalist convictions. In doing so, these Istrians inserted events after the Second World War into a much more extensive narrative of Austrian and Slavic persecution. This narrative had, in turn, been forged by irredentists who during the Great War emplotted their accounts of persecution by Slavs into broader histories of the Italian Risorgimento (the struggle for a unitary state).

As a typical example, a 1915 book entitled *Il diritto d'Italia su Trieste e l'Istria* (The right of Italy to Trieste and Istria) reprinted documents and statements by figures such as the poet Ugo Foscolo and the Risorgimental hero Giuseppe Garibaldi praising the struggle of Italians in the unredeemed lands against "Austrian despotism." The invocation of Garibaldi located the irredentist struggle in a more extensive historical trajectory of Italian patriotism, thereby legitimizing actions considered "terrorist activities" by Austrian authorities. As Silvio Benco puts it, for Italian irredentists World War I "was a page from the history of the Risorgimento, and we can say, the last page . . . in the lands subject to Austria, the Julian and Trentine lands, the Great War spiritually raised everyone to the [task left by the] uncompleted Risorgimento" (Benco in Baroni 1939, iii).

Benco's description of the War of Redemption as the fulfillment of the Risorgimento appears in the preface to a memoir of Francesco Baroni, an Italian patriot from Trieste arrested and interned by the Austrians during World War I. Italians who could not countenance serving in the Austro-Hungarian armies against their Italian brothers and who managed to elude Austrian police forces slipped into Italy, often joining the military there as volunteers. Other *fuorusciti,* or "political exiles"—the term indicating "a person who has 'exited outside' or occupied the space beyond the territory or the walls of his home country or city" (Starn 1982, 2)—also made their way to Italy at this time, some of them coming as refugees *(profughi)* whose homes had become part of the front line. The majority of these refugees came from the irredentist lands of Venezia Giulia, particularly lower Friuli and the area around the Isonzo River (Coceani 1938). Baroni's work represents just one example of a literary tradition glorifying such Italian patriots and exiles from the *irredenta.*

Those Adriatic Italians who, in contrast to Baroni and his counterparts, did not "opt" for Italy were nonetheless seen as suspect by the Austro-Hungarian authorities, who interned entire families in Bavaria or Austria for the duration of the war. Internment constituted, at least in some accounts, another exile, albeit one that proved temporary. One author, for instance, denounced "the enormous tragedy of the deportation of Italian irredentists in Lower Austria" (Chersi 1938, 3), claiming that Italians were called "traitorous dogs" and interned in crowded camps where many died of illness and privation. In his memoir, Istrian socialist Andrea Benussi (1951) similarly decried Austrian brutality; at the front Italian soldiers were treated as traitors, and at home their women and children were loaded into wagons and sent off to unknown destinations.

A fascist-era publication notes that only after the war did the bodies of those Italians who died during this internment finally "return from their exile." In 1926, the remains of Triestines who had lost their lives in these camps were honored in a public funeral procession and placed in a common grave donated by the Commune of Trieste "in perpetual remembrance of the greatness of their sacrifice, their heroic faith" (Chersi 1938, 14). Such public funerals proved important to orchestrating Italian nationalist and irredentist sentiment (for the case of Fiume in 1919, see Ledeen 1977). After 1922, these irredentist traditions increasingly merged with those of mystic fascism and its cult of the "beautiful death." At the same time, the notion of these dead as redeemed from their exile also points to widespread understandings of exile and return in the former irredentist lands of Venezia Giulia.

Many of my informants in both Trieste and Rovigno recalled the stories told by their parents or grandparents of this period of "exile" in Austrian internment camps. Ita Cherin, an eighty-six-year-old retired schoolteacher and author of several articles on the Istrian experience in such camps recounted her family's experience in the camp of Pottendorf (near Vienna) between 1915 and 1917 (see also Cherin 1971, 1977–78; Fabi 1991; Malni 1998). In contrast to those who portray conditions in these camps as inhumane, as part of a long-standing Austrian campaign against Italians (Chersi 1938), in our conversation Cherin contended:

> The camp was a newly built camp, and thus from the point of view of public hygiene it was well done. Only that—let's say that the (social) assistance was good, too—only that the life of the refugee was always a difficult one, and those who most suffered the effects of this were children and the elderly. And, in fact, in two years over six hundred persons died, in *two years*. . . . The children, from childhood diseases and lack of medical treatment. The elderly for reasons of age, since they didn't have much physical resistance. . . . Only Italians from Istria had to go as refugees because when the war between Italy and Austria began, we were Italians and thus the Austrians didn't trust us much.

While Cherin and her mother remained in the camp, her father was conscripted to fight in the Austrian army. When Cherin's father finally returned home to Rovigno at war's end, he found his wife and daughter sick with Spanish influenza. Cherin's mother died a week later. Though Cherin refutes depictions of the camps as inhumane, she nonetheless contends that her story effectively "illustrates the tragedy of the refugees of another time" and underlines the privations and dislocations wrought by this temporary exodus. Another rovignese woman who detailed her grandparents' internment in such Austrian camps concluded, "My family's history is one of continual exoduses! But at least after World War I, Istrians were allowed to return to their homes [in contrast to the period after World War II]." This return home after World War I coincided with Italy's acquisition of Istria; exile is understood as a temporary trial preceding the glorious moment of "redemption." Many informants in Istria maintain that Istrians who left the peninsula after World War II believed they would ultimately return to a "redeemed" homeland, just as their parents and grandparents had after the First World War.

At the end of the Great War, many Istrians thus shared the sentiments of Francesco Baroni, who exclaimed that the conflict's end in 1918 meant that "[m]y exile was finished, my imprisonment ended" (1939, 293). Subtitled *Storia di martiri e d'ignorati eroi nella Grande Guerra, 1915–1918* (Story of martyrs and of ignored heroes in the Great War), Baroni's memoir builds on an established literary genre glorifying irredentist martyrdom (and ultimate redemption), a genre reinvigorated by the Great War and still important for exile understandings today. During the Great War, this Julian tradition of martyrs was readily taken up by the Italian state, which emphasized both the heroism and sacrifice made by these patriots. The Italian government, for example, consciously revived and propagated the "cult" of Wilhelm Oberdank, or Guglielmo Oberdan, a traitor for some and an irredentist martyr for others, on the eve of Italy's entry into the war. The fascist state would continue this hero worship, adding Great War martyrs to the irredentist pantheon and reinforcing the gendered aspects of this tradition (Alexander 1977, 205–8).[2] The sacrifice and suffering embodied by these patriots appeared, in turn, to offer further "proof" of the italianità of Venezia Giulia and Dalmatia, whose soil was sanctified by the blood of these martyrs. This blood was said to "cry out" for Italy to redeem these lands.

A 1914 pamphlet celebrating the life of Oberdan offers a typical example of the explicit linkage of this martyr's cult, together with its religious language of sacrifice, to the promotion of war and violence. Moving from the heroic example set by Oberdan, the author cites the declaration of the Comitato Pro Italia Irredenta (Italian Irredentist Committee), "Onward, brothers of Italy, to the war; awake, rise up united in the sacred fury and in the sacred cry! Onward! The Garibaldian epic needs new resplendent pages, the idea [needs] new martyrs, the country a new reparation. . . . Italy, understand that it is now or never!" in (Baldi 1914, 15). The 1918 work *Oberdan nella olimpiade storica dell'irredentismo italiano* (Oberdan in the historic olympiad of Italian irredentism) similarly links Oberdan to Garibaldi, specifically to Garibaldi's unrealized plans in 1878 to "invade Trentino and Istria" (Mirabelli 1918). This reiterates a common view of the "War of Redemption" as completing what the Risorgimento had left unfinished.

Genealogically linked with Garibaldi in this manner, Oberdan thus comes to embody the Garibaldian tradition of employing "direct action" in defense of a spiritual vision of the nation (one derived from the thought of Giuseppe Mazzini). A Great War account of Oberdan's life, for example, celebrated the Mazzinian "figure of the blond martyr who offered up his neck to the noose for the beauty of an idea" (BAR 1915, 6) and who justified his desertion from the Austro-Hungarian army thus: "I will never go . . . to fight against a people who struggles for its liberty; I could never be an accomplice of such murder" (ibid., 17). Throughout World War I, biographies of Oberdan continued to appear, treating Oberdan's life in the language of mystic nationalism characteristic of both Mazzinian nationalism and irredentism. According to the author of *Guglielmo Oberdan nelle note biografiche di un amico* (Guglielmo Oberdan in the biographical note of a friend), Oberdan's sacrifice transfigured him. "Who was Oberdan? Not a man, but the incarnation of an idea: *liberty;* the first step in the *liberation of the irredentist territories.* And he only breathed and lived for that ideal for which he made the sacrifice [*olocausto*] of himself" (Miceli 1917, 12).

Accounts of Oberdan's sacrifice strikingly evidence the nationalist hagiographic tradition within which the life of the hero/saint is narrated and celebrated.[3] One author characterizes Oberdan's life in terms modeled directly on a Christian saint: youth; flight to Rome; "the eve of the solemn sacrifice"; "the trip and the capture at Ronchi" [near Trieste]; "the accuser"; "the request for mercy"; "the week of the passion"; "death"; and, finally, the aftermath or "apotheosis" (Calcaprina 1935). In spite of the frequent anticlericalism associated with that tradition, Italian nationalists and irredentists clearly constructed martyrdom in fundamentally Christian terms. Anticlericalism, of course, does not prove synonymous with an antireligious stance per se; many Christian saints' *vitae* contrast the wandering holy man with the corrupt urban cleric (Kitchen 1998, 87).

Coon's description of hagiography as consisting of sacred fictions—whose motifs draw on "biblical *topoi*, literary invention, and moral imperative" (1997, xv)—thus proves apt for biographies of religious and nationalist (as well as communist) saints alike. In all cases, the story of the martyr tells of his or her achievement of spiritual and bodily purity (ibid., 3). One of the dominant themes in the lives of Christian saints is the battle against a hostile force (Kitchen 1998, 34), a motif readily taken over in the descriptions of nationalist martyrs like Oberdan. The biographies of Christian martyrs often feature imprisonment in subterranean spaces, compared to tombs. "A release from such a place is called a 'salvation,' a deliverance from darkness into light" (ibid., 40). This language resonates with the illuminist rhetoric of the esuli and informs irredentist descriptions of heroes' imprisonment in Austrian jails. Not surprisingly, Silvio Pellico's (1850) *Le mie prigioni* (All my prisons) remains one of the best-known documents of the Risorgimental patriotic/irredentist experience.

Within such a hagiographic tradition, not only does Oberdan's life offer inspiration but his physical remains or relics also acquire a powerful sanctity. The martyr's grave, for example, becomes the site of a figurative miracle: the rebirth of Italy sparked by "the flame that emerges from his tomb" (Miceli 1917, 29). This reflects the prominence of Christian martyrs' tombs as places for veneration (Kitchen 1998, 50). Another author, writing of "the relics of the martyr," laments that Oberdan's cranium remains preserved in a Viennese museum. With Italy's acquisition of Trieste, however, an "expiatory" statue had been placed in the city, prompting the author to hope that "perhaps the Italian government will also vindicate that relic [the skull] of our national rebirth for the veneration of the Italians" (Cuttin n.d., 6). Taking up the same theme, one author declares, "Oh, Guglielmo Oberdan, you are ashes: your decapitated head is relegated to the anthropological museum of Vienna, as if it were the cranium of a criminal" (Mirabelli 1918, 63–64). Yet, "under the unknown turf of the cemetery of Saint Anna [in Trieste] that covered your dissolved bones, the molecules that were part of you are transformed and are transported by the winds that flutter on the mountains and on the waters of our Patria . . . [they are] dispersed throughout our Patria—the country that Battisti, Sauro [other irredentist "martyrs"] made—that the soldier of Italy made" (ibid).

Here, Oberdan (himself genealogically linked with Garibaldi) stands as the direct precursor of Cesare Battisti and Nazario Sauro—two of the most celebrated irredentist "martyrs" produced by the Great War and accorded a status similar to Oberdan's—who partake of the "host" (Oberdan's scattered ashes) through their literal communion with the soil of the patria. Battisti, a socialist from Trento and an Italian volunteer in the Great War, was hanged for treason after being wounded and captured in battle against the Austrians (see Barbiera 1918; Ferrari 1935). Sauro's decision to serve Italy's navy similarly cost him his life when he fell into Austrian hands. A native of the Istrian town of Capodistria, Sauro was executed for serving on the side of the enemy. The Austrians ordered these executions in order to demonstrate to the Italian populations of its imperial lands that treason in wartime would not be tolerated.

Just as Oberdan symbolized the struggle for Trieste and Battisti the one for Trento, Sauro came to represent the sacrifice made for Istria. Biographies of Sauro echoed those of Oberdan, with his trial and execution treated as moments in the martyr's "apotheosis."[4] As in the case of Oberdan, much attention was paid to Sauro's mother, both her futile appeals for clemency and the son's determination (despite his mother's plea for mercy) to sacrifice himself as a martyr to the cause (see Rivalta 1934). Sauro's mother and sister were glorified as possessing the "soul of the Hero" and "for having followed the passion, the faith of their Nazario for Italy" (Cobòl 1924, 193). Verses dedicated to Sauro's mother in the 1921 work *Martiri e glorie* (Martyrs and glories) console her by reminding her "that the land that maternally receives you is today liberated, and liberated is the soil for which Nazario yearned. . . . Oh mother, mother, the people of Italy today pray and murmur to you:—Peace!" (Oliveri 1921, 54–55).

In other poems, such as *Canzone a Nazario Sauro,* the martyr is depicted as choosing his *madrepatria* over his biological mother. As the hero returns from the sea and kneels to kiss the earth, he vows, "Mother, I want to do the worst to your enemy" (Salvatori 1938, 5). In the decades following the Great War, fascist rhetoric reinforced this particular gendering and biologizing of nationalist appeals, with women cast as reproducers of heroic warriors like Sauro, whose sacrifice would regenerate the nation (Spackman 1983, 1990). In Istria, the fascist regime singled out the virile example of Sauro, "the great mariner of the people . . . immortal sentinel of Istria" (Del Vecchio et al. 1928, 10) and in 1935 erected a massive monument honoring him in his native Capodistria. (The Germans dismantled it in 1944 and used the memorial's materials in the war effort.) In his role as man of the people, Sauro was said "to remember all the martyrs, those known and unknown" (Rapetti n.d., 23).

Though Sauro's canonization had begun during the Great War, prior to the fascist regime's efforts, the conscious manipulation of these nationalist traditions in the service of militarism led to the twining of the memory of such "heroes" with those of fascism (for further examples, see Comune di Trieste 1932; Seri 1982). Writing in 1983 on the centenary of Oberdan's death, one author noted that the tragedy of fascism and its alliance with Nazism led many wrongly to conflate the Risorgimental and republican traditions of irredentist martyrs with those of a sterile and "indiscriminate patriotism" (Spadolini 1983, 29).

> The tragedy of Trieste in the post–World War II period is reflected in the tragedy of Oberdan. . . . The great hesitation to speak of "patria" ended up in distancing the hero from the admiration of young people, from the reflection of historians, from the "pietas" of the succeeding generations. The profound laceration that accompanied the fate of the city seemed to almost completely alienate the laic and democratic "reconsecration" of the patriot that had inspired so many circles. (Ibid., 29–30)

Patriots like Oberdan, continued Spadolini, suffered the unfortunate (and undeserved) fate of being seen as the precursors of fascism. The taint of fascism similarly led to an indiscriminate condemnation of all exiles from Istria as "fascists" who had been forced out with that regime's demise. When, after World War II, Istrian exiles called on the Italian state and Great Powers to "redeem" Istria from its brutal sacrifice, the rhetorical framework of redemption they employed had been largely delegitimized through its exploitation under fascism.

Just as authors such as Spadolini urged a reevaluation of the nationalist tradition embodied by Oberdan, some exiles have attempted to resuscitate the public memory of Nazario Sauro. The monument to the hero on Trieste's waterfront serves as a reference point for exiles from Sauro's native town of Capodistria. Beginning in the 1980s, Italo Gabrielli, the former president of the Unione degli Istriani, proposed to reconstruct the former monument to Sauro in Capodistria (at that time in Yugoslavia and today in Slovenia), or alternatively, to place a plaque on the house where Sauro was born (Sabatti 1996). Despite his lack of success, Gabrielli relaunched his plan in 1996, provoking controversy and discussion in the local Triestine newspaper. One reader wrote that such a monument would meet with opposition in Capodistria from both the Italian and the Slovene community there, given Sauro's documented antipathy to Slavs (Kocjan 1996).

Whereas for some esuli, then, Sauro and his heroic counterparts continue to symbolize the unselfish patriotic sacrifice made to redeem Istria and Trieste, for others this pantheon of martyrs embodies the chauvinism and imperialism associated with fascist nationalism. More so than Oberdan or other pre–Great War martyrs, Sauro symbolizes for many the expansionist path Italy embarked on with its entrance into World War I on the promise of the territories of Trentino, Istria, and Dalmatia. The fascist regime subsequently took up wellrehearsed arguments about "redemption" in order to make claims on Dalmatia, awarded to Yugoslavia after World War I in spite of Italy's protests.

The elaboration of a heroic pantheon embracing figures from the Istrian martyrs Nazario Sauro and Fabio Filzi (from Pisino/Pazin) to the Dalmatians

Francesco Rismondo and Tommaso Gulli (both from Spalato/Split) created a shared topography of martyrdom suited to the fascist regime's stated desire of reclaiming Dalmatia and joining it with the already redeemed Istria. The 1935 commemoration of the Istrian monument to Sauro thus prompted nationalistic declarations about Dalmatia, with one publication taking the occasion as appropriate for composing a "Dalmatian Hymn" (*L'Inno Dalmazia*). This song urged Italians forward: "We have sworn: death or liberty! Dalmatia, Dalmatia; what does it matter if one dies; when the cry of ardor is like an eternal footsoldier!" (Sartorio 1935, 23).

As evidenced by such bellicose pronouncements, claims to the Dalmatian coastline (as well as to North Africa) occupied a prominent place in fascist discourse about *Mare Nostrum* (Our Sea). These territorial claims in turn built on older, prefascist narratives about Italy's "right" to Dalmatia. The Latinate presence in Dalmatia had gradually diminished as a result of Venice's formal ousting in 1797 by the Hapsburgs and later with Dalmatia's passage from the Austro-Hungarian Empire to Yugoslavia after World War I. These events prompted the creation of a corpus of texts simultaneously lamenting the destruction of italianità in Dalmatia and calling for the mother country to heed the cries of its abandoned children there.[5] Literature produced around the time of the Great War, as well as subsequent works from the period of fascist imperialism, reiterates historical-cultural arguments about Italy's right to Dalmatia (see Combi 1878), to which are then added those of strategic position and geography. Dalmatia's essential Italian character is said to be demonstrated by the Roman and Venetian architectural patrimony, the presence of the Venetian dialect, and the love of Dalmatians (even those of apparently Slavic provenance) for Italy and its highly developed civilization, or civiltà. Nationalist writers, most notably D'Annunzio, recalled the scenes of Dalmatian loyalty, reportedly displayed in 1797 when the flag of San Marco was lowered for the last time and the Venetian Empire was extinguished; in Zara/Zadar, the flag was said to have been wet with the tears of *Dalmati fedeli* (Wolff 2001, 353). Wolff notes that the invocation of such historical episodes "suggests the intensity with which modern nationalism manipulated the imagined persistence of early modern imperial sentiment" (ibid., 355).

The various claims made to Dalmatia ostensibly express a sense of cultural nationalism much than an explicitly biological or racial one, reflecting one common view of Italian nationalism as generally free of racism. Some scholars have even found the nationalist invocation of civiltà italiana an odd one, instead seeing in it "[a] culture of inclusion, cosmopolitanism, and incorporation" (Gabaccia 2000, 33). As we have found with ideological expressions of Hapsburg cosmopolitanism in Trieste, however, cultures of inclusion may contain their own exclusions. Indeed, the language of cosmopolitanism may make exclusion and chauvinism that much harder to detect or combat.

Many propagandists for the Italian cause in Dalmatia, for instance, explicitly claimed to espouse a voluntarist notion of national identity. "The nationality of a people is like an individual's; it is determined not by the language that one speaks but rather by one's will [that is, self-identification]," declares one tract (De Santi 1919, 4). Similarly, an esule memoir of life in Zara maintains that the Italians of Dalmatia subscribed not to a racial concept of nationality but rather to a cultural one (Anzellotti 1990, 28–29). The authors of irredentist tracts often referred to *stirpe*—meaning "stock" (in the sense of a family lineage or genealogy) or "ancestry"—but almost never to *razza* ("race," in the English sense of the word). Harking back to ancient distinctions between Roman citizens and barbarians, references to the Latin stirpe or *popolo* (people) carried with them assumptions about a superior civiltà or "genius" into which other (barbaric) peoples could presumably be assimilated. Along the Adriatic coast, civiltà or civility, was particularly associated with urban living and urbane values.

Understandings of "race" as stirpe nonetheless coexisted with those of scientific racism (razza), which would become more prominent under the fascist regime and its imperialist "civilizing mission." The imprecise boundaries of the two concepts means that in practice they at times blurred (Sluga 2001, 60), permitting the proponents of a certain kind of chauvinist racism (against, say, Slavs or Africans or even southern Italians) to nonetheless deny any charges of racism. (For similar dilemmas with antiracist and "new racist" positions in contemporary Europe, see Gilroy 1987 and Stolcke 1995. On the Risorgimental elision of the biological and cultural understandings of "corrupt" Meapolitans, see Moe 2001, 125–26.) Appeals to the *madrepatria* by its children further underscore hidden histories of race. Danforth notes for the Macedonian context, "Metaphors identifying the personified national homeland as parent also support this biologized conception of national identity" (Danforth 1995, 224; also Loizos 1981, 146).

In the Adriatic zone, statements regarding the cultural superiority of Italian civiltà thus contain within themselves a chauvinism that easily elides with racism. "It remains to be noted that the Slavs who immigrated into Julian Venetia," contends one Italian supporter, "have not succeeded in forming even an elementary civilization of their own; they have contributed nothing to science or to art; for the most part they live in the country, under the most primitive conditions; they have no civilization as they have no history" (Alberti et al. 1917, 109). Among Italian nationalists, the terms *Slav* and *socialist* became synonymous (Pirjevec n.d., 25). The term *slavo-comunista,* still heard today in Trieste, suggests the ways in which Bolshevism was seen to follow from the Slav's innately "totalitarian" national character (for similar attributions of a "communistic character" to Slavs in the Greek context, see Herzfeld 1992, 58, 60, 137, 141).

Writing in 1920 about Dalmatia's fate, for example, one author denounced the Versailles Treaty as a "mutilation of the victory" and declared Slavic bolshevism the real enemy. Although the contrast with Italian antibolshevism or anticommunism is amplified in subsequent narratives about post-1945 Istria, basic collective narrative forms do not significantly alter. In discussing the way in which the Slavs assumed administrative control in Dalmatia in the second half of the nineteenth century, for example, pro-Italian authors recount violence, electoral fraud, and intimidation. They describe the "dead cities" of martyred Dalmatia, emptied of their Italian residents (Dompieri 1941, 9–11; Dudan 1915, 98–99; Federzoni 1941). Such descriptions resonate with subsequent accounts of the Istrian exodus.

Describing the first exodus from Dalmatia, the words of Ubaldo Scarpelli, for example, could just as easily describe events in Istria after 1945. After 1920, contends Scarpelli, in Dalmatia "[t]he 'hunt for Italians' was organized with subtle police tactics and lasted for a good while. They boycotted trade with the old Italian provinces, blocked maritime and industrial relations, imprisoned Italians, confiscating both their fixed and movable goods, and fixed matters by means of absurd trials. This is the history of yesterday, just like today" (Scarpelli 1933, 35). Another author, comparing Austro-Hungarian and Yugoslav policies toward Italians, declares, "More bitter, methodical, and disgraceful was the denationalization policy conducted by the government of Belgrade. It progressively attempted to suppress the typical character of italianità" (Missoni 1942, 35). This violence is seen to go hand in hand with the rewriting of history in the attempt to deny Dalmatia's Italian character and falsely assert a Slavic character. "The Dalmatians were thus obliged to abandon their hereditary homes, to detach themselves from their dead, but the past of their Land can be neither changed nor canceled: a past resplendent with romanità and italianità" (Teja 1949, 8).

From such narratives Istrians found a number of compelling accounts of irredentist martyrdom, exile, and redemption to draw on in making sense of events after 1943. The Dalmatian experience that became the subject of much fascist propaganda proves particularly important in offering a prototypical narrative of Italian exodus, the subject to which I now turn. The "denationalization" of Italians from Dalmatia is seen to have been initiated by the Austrian administration and the Slavic populations it favored, continued by the Slavs under royal Yugoslavia after 1919, and completed in 1943 by the Titoists who occupied Zara, the last Italian stronghold in Dalmatia. Whether these conceptual frameworks making sense of events in Dalmatia predisposed the population in Istria to opt for Italy can only remain a question of speculation. Most probably, however, they made many Italians in Istria receptive to Italian state-sponsored propaganda urging a "human plebiscite." Exiles would instead argue that the Dalmatian experience itself made it clear to Istrians what future lay in store for them in Yugoslavia.

The "First Exodus" from Dalmatia

In Dalmatia, as in Istria, Venetianized, Catholic populations had existed for centuries alongside and intermixed with "Slavs," both Catholic and Orthodox; these Venetian populations greatly enlarged the Latin presence dating from Roman times. In both Dalmatia and Istria, Latinate speakers clustered along the coast and islands, bequeathing a rich architectural heritage in the distinctive Venetian style. The period of Venetian rule reproduced the urban settlement preference typical to the Italian (and Istrian) peninsula, as well as a Venetianized ruling class complete with noble families. With the rise of nationalisms in the nineteenth century and Istria and Dalmatia's passage to Austrian control, social, class, and linguistic differentiations were increasingly mapped onto contentious-ethno-national identifications. For proponents of Italian Dalmatia, the period of Austrian control marked "the beginning of the tragedy of italianità in Dalmatia" (Bencovich 1935, 147). This tragedy resulted from Austria's "perfidy and political oppression" (Scarpelli 1933, 20), which the Yugoslavs are seen to have continued after the First World War.

Narratives of the Italian experience in Austrian Dalmatia depict the Hapsburg administration as pursuing a systematic and "implacable" suppression of the Italian population. The methods of this persecution sound exactly like those which Istrians accuse Yugoslavs of employing after 1943. As one Italianized Serb writes, "It is a proven historical fact that Austria tried, in all manners, to free itself from the Italians they found in their territories, including the other [eastern] coast of the Adriatic. Austria tried to depopulate Dalmatia; expatriating indigenous Italians, their agents guided them to our frontier, and the Austrians then populated Dalmatia with Croats, to whom they gave every type of benefit" (Alexich 1919, 20).

According to such accounts, this persecution of Italians occurred in spite of the good relations that existed between Italians and Slavs, the latter feeling themselves culturally Italian (or Venetian). One writer claims, "All the usages, customs, games, artistic, literary, and musical tastes of these Slavs of Dalmatia are Italian . . . all except for the language" (Dudan 1915, 71–72). He adds, "If at times there was hatred between the peasant and the owner, it was not racial hatred but rather class hatred provoked by the stinginess or the usury of some single founding squire" (ibid., 71). Others interpret these class relations as reflecting the superiority of Italian civilization, or civiltà, and proudly exclaim, "The wealth and the supremacy in public administration was Italian; and the peasant Slavs were willingly used to respecting the Italians of Istria and Dalmatia as masters [padroni]" (Federzoni 1941, 40).

Italian propagandists maintain that the Hapsburgs initially respected this Italian cultural and political predominance in Dalmatia, a situation that changed when the struggles for a unitary Italian state began (Dudan and Teja 1991, 82). Various publications thus describe the period 1848–60 as one in which political reforms within the Hapsburg Empire slowly stripped self-identified Italian speakers in Dalmatia of their political predominance. One by one, city administrations came under the control of the local ethnic majority, the Croats, encouraged by their political sponsors, the Austrians (Bencovich 1935; Sillani n.d.). "Autonomist" parties dominated by Italian influences emerged to oppose Croatian nationalist groups (Violich 1998, 106).

In many accounts, the year 1866—in which the Italo-Austrian War gave Italy the Veneto but simultaneously dashed Italian hopes of acquiring the Dalmatian coastline—represents a fateful turning point, after which Italians were increasingly constrained to take the path of exile (Federzoni 1941; Michelozzi 1919; Tamaro 1915). In addition to the more gradual process of diminution of Italian political control that began in 1848 (in the wake of Hapsburg reaction to nationalist revolutions) came new requirements for civil servants to know Croatian, as well as restrictions on Italian-language schools. To replace those Italian-language schools forced to close, private schools were funded by the Lega Nazionale, a nationalist association formed to defend italianità in the "unredeemed" lands. Despite such efforts, however, many Italian speakers began to either assimilate to a new Slavic reality or leave Dalmatia in a "voluntary exodus" (Dompieri 1941, 7–11). One author laments that with the favoritism for Slavs expressed by Austria in various areas of competition (jobs, scholarships, elections), many Italians became Slavicized. "Unfortunately, how many souls were sold for a single scholarship! I could document it with names" (Dudan 1915, 87).

In the decades that followed, the last strongholds of Italian municipal control— Sebenico/Sibenik, Spalato/Split, Trau/Trogir, Cattaro/Kotor, and Ragusa/Dubrovnik—fell under Croat administration. Individuals such as Antonio Baiamonti, Spalato's last Italian mayor, and his follower Ercolano Salvi figure in nationalist narratives as "martyrs" to the irredentist cause in Dalmatia (see Foscari 1921; Salvi 1919; Scarpelli 1933). After the capitulation of the Dalmatian cities in spite of the efforts of men like Baiamonti and Salvi, Zara remained the penultimate Italian foothold in Dalmatia (ibid.; Dudan and Teja 1991; Federzoni 1941).

In 1919, Zara officially came under Italian sovereignty while the rest of the Dalmatian coastline went to Yugoslavia, notwithstanding intense lobbying by Italians both during and after the Great War. One prominent argument voiced by the pro-Italian camp held that for reasons of strategic security for Europe in general and Italy in particular, Italy should control all of the Dalmatian coastline (Adriacus 1919; Foscari 1915; Michelozzi 1919). This would prevent Italy from nurturing any potentially destabilizing resentment. "Italy, once the complete redemption of all her people has been made sure, will always remain a Light of civilization and a Guarantor of peace and of justice for all mankind" (Adriacus 1919; see also Sillani n.d.). By giving Dalmatia to Italy, potential Croatian and Serbian rivalries over Dalmatia would also be resolved, thereby fulfilling the role of Italy as the guarantor of peace (Foscari 1915, 201–2).

While the strategic argument carried a certain weight, it was always underwritten by the notion of Italy's historical and "ethnic" or cultural right to Dalmatia. As Wolff comments, "More than a century of Habsburg rule seemed suddenly irrelevant as the discussion reverted to the Italian legacy of Venetian rule" (2001, 352). Immediately after World War I, Italian Dalmatia's supporters feared that Italy's leaders had forfeited their sovereign rights to the region in exchange for Trieste and Istria. Having been satisfied elsewhere, Italy would apparently leave Dalmatia to a Yugoslav fate; the Istrian exiles express a similar belief that Italy sacrificed Istria for Trieste after World War II. "All the world knows that in that part of Dalmatia abandoned to the Yugoslavs, persecution against Italians will continue implacable and constant! What will be the fate of Italians abandoned to Yugoslavia? It's easily said: destruction!" (De Santi 1919, 24). One typical tract lamented the "sacrifice" made by Dalmatia and its people and asked whether Italy would now abandon or sacrifice Dalmatia to the Kingdom of the Serbs, Croats, and Slovenes (Rambaldi 1919, 30). Such a sacrifice would entail a "mutilation of the victory" (Giglioli 1920). This theme, common in the period after World War I, echoed the popular notion of the Risorgimento as a betrayed revolution, or *rivoluzione mancata*. The poet Gabriele D'Annunzio would embellish this idea in his claim to "redeem" the mutilated victory by seizing Fiume, awarded after World War I to Yugoslavia in spite of Italian counterclaims, and urging the "return" of Dalmatia to the motherland.

With Italy turning a deaf ear to the cries of its "Dalmatian children," many self-identified Italians in Dalmatia (particularly in the islands such as Veglia/Krk and Arbe/Rab) chose either to relocate to the Italian enclave at Zara or to legally opt for Italian citizenship in a move similar to that which occurred in Istria after World War II. Some of these transplants to Zara hoped that Italy would eventually reconquer these lost homes. "We are exiles, we want to return to the houses that were ours, on whose thresholds await our brothers," exclaimed Tomaso Sillani in his fascist-era book *Mare Nostrum* (Sillani n.d., 26). These hopes for ultimate redemption from the condition of exile also echo in contemporary Istrian accounts, which figure the hope for "return" in various ways.

The narrative structuring of accounts of the "first" exodus (under Austria and Yugoslavia) and the "final" exodus (from Zara in 1943) from Dalmatia appears almost seamless at the same time that the Dalmatian experience is linked with subsequent events in Istria. Accounts of Zara's 1944 occupation by partisan troops temporally join the "final" exodus from Dalmatia with contemporaneous population movements from the Julian March, thereby emplotting events in Dalmatia and Istria into a larger narrative about Slavic persecution of Italians. Such a narrative reads the aims of "Slavs" under Austria as synonymous with those of the Yugoslavs (both royalist and socialist). By locating the roots of this extended anti-Italian campaign in an inherent Slavic nature, such a narrative deemphasizes the importance of fascism or communism in explaining or "justifying" events in Zara and Istria after 1943.

The fusing of the Dalmatian and Istrian experiences, however, reflects not only narrative continuities but also the fact that some individuals experienced both the Dalmatian and the Istrian exodus. Those Dalmatian Italians who abandoned their hereditary homes after World War I and moved to Istria, for example, would subsequently experience a second exodus at the conclusion of World War II. This double displacement was shared by those Italians who had relocated to Zara after 1919; the majority of these transplants within Dalmatia would later abandon Zara following the city's near-destruction by Allied bombings in 1943 and 1944. Italian hopes were raised briefly by the period of Italian rule over all of Dalmatia after 1941 as a result of the Axis occupation and partition of Yugoslavia. Such aspirations died quickly, however, as the 1943 capitulation of the Italian army left Italians in Zara (and elsewhere in Dalmatia and Istria) exposed and defenseless. "We had the impression of living on an island lost in the middle of the ocean" (cited in Calestani 1978, 73), comments one former resident of Zara, repeating and refiguring the familiar trope of Italian islands in a Slavic sea. Another exile reports the remark made by a former professor in Zara regarding the precipitous flight of many fascists from Dalmatia as early as July 1943, when the Grand Fascist Council overthrew Mussolini, but prior to the army's capitulation. "The fascists left. They left us, and we were destined to pay for their crimes" (Anzellotti 1990, 93).

In September 1943, the Italian military dissolved and its soldiers set out for home, some joining up with partisan units like those of the famous Garibaldi brigades (see Cuccu 1991 and Pacor 1968). Soldiers' accounts describe the desperate attempts by Zaratini to flee for Fiume or Istria (de Zambotti 1980, 91–92). The Germans occupied Zara for some months but began to pull out as repeated Allied bombings destroyed most of the city and Yugoslav forces drew threateningly near. As one author puts it, using the religiously charged language typical of irredentist narratives: "Who could describe the *calvary* of that ultra-Italian people, caught in a trap, on the enemy shore, without communications, resources, menaced from the hinterland by groups of assassins and implacably hammered from the sky?" (Calestani 1978, 74; my italics). Dalmatian Italians' accounts describe this situation of utter isolation, privation, and violence at the hands of Yugoslavs as prompting the "final" Italian exodus from Dalmatia, thereby violently completing the Slavicization process begun over a century earlier under Austria.

At war's end in 1945, then, Italians in Istria already had a powerful and specific framework in place through which to interpret and articulate their own experience as one of nationally motivated expulsion. The key themes heard in older narratives about exile from Dalmatia—the violent and treacherous methods of the Slavs, civiltà and Christian piety menaced by modern-day barbarism, Italian sacrifice and martyrdom—resonate powerfully in stories told today about events in Istria. These common themes inform even those accounts by exiles who disagree with the political orientation of the exile associations, the official mouthpieces for the Istrian and Dalmatian esuli. This suggests that these originally "irredentist" discourses serve as powerful master narratives or meta-narratives that continue to structure ostensibly disparate individual accounts in similar ways.

Trips through Memory: Narrative Continuities, Divided Politics

Participating in both the general exile associations and their own specific organizations, Dalmatian exiles want their fate to be remembered as part of the broader processes of population transfer that altered the Julian March's demographic composition after 1943. Simultaneously, however, Dalmatians seek to differentiate their experience from that of Istrians. Recall the Dalmatian exile's interjection at the annual Great War commemorations: "Remember Zara!" Although Istrian and Dalmatian exiles alike share a view of their experience as one of "denationalization" (or, in contemporary language, "ethnic cleansing"), these groups are divided among themselves in terms of political orientations and interpretations. The fissions within the Dalmatian community mirror those of the Istrian esuli, divisions that group commemorations like the Festival of Unity are meant to overcome.

These divisions emerged as I traveled with various esuli from both Dalmatia and Istria on an April 1996 boat trip down the Dalmatian coast. This trip, organized by a travel agency in Trieste owned by an Istrian exile, advertised itself as a "trip through memory" (viaggio di memoria) and represented the first large-scale tour of Dalmatian cities such as Ragusa/Dubrovnik since the Serb-Croat war of 1991–92. This occasion, entailing a physical confrontation with the actual traces of the exiles' lost world, rendered many of the returning esuli emotional and thus heightened certain tensions within those communities.

These tensions became evident as I spoke with individuals whose political loyalties ranged from the far right to the far left. The ship itself seemed to symbolize the fractious exile community. All literally "in the same boat," some exiles nonetheless returned to their lost homeland with trepidation or tears or anger, and others with pleasure and familiarity (having visited many times previously). The confined space of the boat intensified my usual awkwardness at being expected to take the side of members belonging to different political camps. On the first day, I sat looking out at some islands in the Coronati/Koronati archipelago near Zara when a woman approached me and began angrily denouncing the Slavs for having stolen this beautiful sea (and the region) from noi Italiani (we Italians). "This was the result of the nationalism of Yugoslavs, who haven't changed a bit!" continued the woman heatedly. She ranted on, making it sound as if this nationalism were an essential and inescapable part of the Slavic character. She then began pressing Italian claims to the area.

I could not but notice the irony of a critique of nationalism which was itself nationalist. Nor could an Istrian *esule* I knew well, who watched this scene with bemusement. A historian associated with the political Left, this man winked at me during the woman's diatribe, as if to signal that he and I (the broad-minded academics) knew better. When the woman concluded, she wanted me to concur with her. "Non è vero, signorina? Hai capito?" (Isn't it true, signorina? Did you understand?) Not only did I not agree with the woman's analysis, I also felt as if the scholar (with whom I had considerable dealings) expected me to agree with him by brushing off the woman. In the end, I offered a noncommittal response, shrugging my shoulders and muttering, "Mah," as if to say, "Who knows? Could be." The woman stomped away, probably convinced that I was either thick (*tonta*) or misinformed. The scholar merely laughed, adding, "Now you see the nationalism of the esuli. Here you have a fine example for your ethnographic work." He was right, of course, though I doubt he considered himself part of the ethnographic tableau!

Although individuals like the leftist scholar and nationalist exile on the boat tend to agree that they suffered a persecution that targeted Italians, they nonetheless diverge in their interpretations of Slavs, Italian fascism, and their assignation of blame for their postexodus sufferings in Italy. Gino Bambara, an outspoken man I met during this trip, endorses the "ethnic cleansing" thesis generally advanced by the Dalmatian and Istrian exile associations despite his adherence to the Italian far Left (the communist Rifondazione party). In his memoir, *Zara: Uno zaratino racconta la sua città* (Zara: A Zaratino recalls his city), Bambara describes Zara's occupation by the Yugoslavs on October 31, 1944. He claims that the new masters carried out some 150 executions. "In substance, the massacres—this is the exact term for describing those atrocities—are for the most part due to the atavistic rancor that the Croats had for the Italians and their culture: in this way was the *ethnic cleansing* continued that had been partly achieved with the Anglo-American aerial bombardments requested by the General Staff of the Croat partisan army" (1994, 111–12; my italics).

This account of massacres in Dalmatia echoes esuli descriptions of executions carried out by Yugoslavs in the karstic pits known as the *foibe* (see chapter 5). Interestingly, Bambara reiterates the ethnic cleansing thesis despite his disagreement with the exile associations' center-right political orientation. Bambara complains that the agenda of the associations has been set by fascist supporters. Carlo, an old school chum of Bambara's, does not share Bambara's communist loyalties (instead he is associated with the former Christian Democrats) but does agree that the tone of the exile associations has been dominated by those with fascist sympathies. Like Bambara, Carlo admits that much enthusiasm existed in Zara for fascism, since at the time support for Italy appeared synonymous with that for the fascist regime. "We were all fascists, *like in the rest of Italy.*" Carlo nonetheless disagrees with the postwar representation of Zara and its residents as die-hard fascists rather than patriots. According to Carlo, this representation has been perpetuated by both Italian communists—"When we came to Italy, Italian communists didn't welcome us as brothers but as 'fascists'"—and those right-wing refugees from Zara who attempt to "manipulate, instrumentalize our sentiments of pure italianità." This differentiation between patriotism and fascism underlines the ways in which fascism co-opted a distinct and separate irredentist tradition. Whereas some exiles complain that outsiders (like the communists) have wrongly conflated this earlier patriotic tradition with fascism and thereby falsely labeled esuli as fascists, Carlo suggests that some exiles themselves rendered Istrian patriotism synonymous with support for fascism and its neofascist legacy.

Carlo further maintains that exiles from noble and upper-class families have attempted to construct a patrician history of Zara that neglects the experience of Zaratini of a "democratic, popular extraction." This is reflected in the prominent role that descendants of such families—including Ottavio Missoni (the fashion designer), lawyer Renzo de' Vidovich, and Franco Luxardo (heir to the renowned Maraschino liqueur industry)—play in Dalmatian exile associations and the public events sponsored by these associations. Similarly, many of the volumes dedicated to the experiences of Zaratini highlight the fate of the Luxardos and other prominent families and neglect the more humble Zaratini.[6]

Through his activities in the Comitato Nazionale, or National Committee, of the Associazione Nazionale Venezia Giulia e Dalmazia, Carlo has sought to counter the political predominance of such Zaratini. As a member of the Comitato, for example, Carlo, since Yugoslavia's breakup, has labored to establish a branch of the Dante Alighieri Society in Zara. The Dante Alighieri, today an ostensibly apolitical organization, organizes cultural events for the small Italian communities that remain in Dalmatia; I attended one such initiative, a lecture given in Ragusa on the architecture of the Cathedral of Sebenico. Carlo complained that a certain faction among the Dalmatian exiles, dissatisfied with such purely cultural and scientific events, has attempted to imbue the Associazione Dante Aligheri with a political agenda set by the Italian Right.

During the course of our four-day trip to Dalmatia, a shouting match erupted between Carlo and a female representative of this opposing group over the role, cultural or political, that the Dante Alighieri should play. The name-calling degenerated into personal attacks, with the label of "fascist," which the esuli object to when applied by outsiders, used to defame political rivals. Carlo warned me not to let a man whom I'd interviewed earlier during the cruise know what he'd said, given that this fellow was a known "fascist." This not only underscores the challenges of talking to people with very different political agendas but also reveals the continued salience of such labels (at least as derogatory epithets) within the exile community. At a 1996 conference in Trieste announcing the formation of a group, the Amici e discendenti degli esuli (Friends and Descendants of the Exiles), Carlo jumped up and cautioned that such a group should not merely reproduce the "fascist" and irredentist tendencies of the associations. This prompted some members of the audience to hiss and silence Carlo.

Such incidents reveal the deep fissures within an "exile community" that seems united only to those looking in from the outside and further suggests why the exiles make so much of celebrations like the annual Festival of Unity (see also Thomassen 2001 for his analysis of differences and similarities in Istrian life histories and self-conceptions). At the heart of the political division among exile associations is a difference of opinion over the past and specifically over the role of fascism (and neofascism) as either historic defender or betrayer of the interests of the Italians of Istria and Dalmatia. As Carlo and those associated with the Left-Center see it, "Thanks to fascism, we lost these lands." Others contend that the Left-Center abandoned the exiles by acquiescing to Istria's partition; in their estimation, the only party that fought for the Italians from Istria, Fiume, and Dalmatia was the neofascist Movimento Sociale Italiano (rechristened the Alleanza Nazionale), which reiterated the fascist emphasis on national unity.

Exile debates thus refract broader currents of historical revisionism about the Second World War that emerged in both Italy and Yugoslavia during the 1980s. Long discredited for their association with both fascism and an older irredentist tradition (which fascism co-opted and transformed), exile accounts suddenly found a new hearing as the previously dominant readings of both the Italian and Yugoslav Resistance came under scrutiny. The very fact of this exile "memory trip" to Dalmatia reflects the profound reconfiguration of both political geographies and landscapes of memory in Italy and former Yugoslavia since the late 1980s and 1990s. Accounts of the denationalization of Istria and Dalmatia had found only a selective audience during the immediate postwar period and the intervening decades, confirming exiles' view of their history as submerged or forgotten.

CHAPTER THREE

Constructing the "Trieste Question,"
Silencing the Exodus

> Tracking power requires a richer view of historical production than
> most theorists acknowledge. We cannot exclude in advance any of the
> actors who participate in the production of history or any of the sites
> where that production may occur. Next to professional historians we
> discover artisans of different kinds, unpaid or unrecognized field
> laborers who augment, deflect, or reorganize the work of the
> professionals as politicians, students, fiction writers, filmmakers, and
> participating members of the public. In so doing, we gain a more
> complex view of academic history itself, since we do not consider
> professional historians the sole participants in its production.
> —Michel-Rolph Trouillot, *"Anthropology and the Savage Slot"*

HEEDING Trouillot's admonition to look beyond the academic
guild as the site for the production of both historical traces and silences, I explore the ways in which the Istrian exodus was variously constructed and silenced as a narrative event by different actors, including the Western Allies, the
Italian and Yugoslav states, and Istrian exile groups. Whereas in the previous
chapter I evidenced the manner in which Italian nationalists (both within and
beyond the territory) have understood post-1943 events in the Julian March
through narrative frameworks derived from older irredentist accounts, in this
chapter I consider how the population transfer from Istria unfolded within the
jockeying of state and superpower interests discursively coded as the Trieste
Question at the end of the Second World War. Between 1945 and 1954, the
Italo-Yugoslav territorial dispute known variously as the Trieste Crisis or the Trieste Question played out in British and American newspapers and strategy
rooms as one battle in the broader conflict between democracy and communism, West and East. This discursive framework shifted (even as it incorporated
certain aspects of) the terms of the symbolic opposition between fascism and
communism; within the Julian March, the fascism-communism dichotomy in

turn recoded distinctions between irredentism and cosmopolitanism, as well as those between Italians and Slavs.

The Trieste Question that refigured these older antinomies centered on long-standing territorial claims by both Italy and Yugoslavia to the region of the Julian March. Though Italy had acquired most of this area after World War I, during World War II the defeat of the Italian fascist regime and the establishment of a socialist state in Yugoslavia re-opened the issue. Originally a regional question, the conflict's dimensions expanded when the United States and Great Britain occupied Trieste at war's end to push back the Yugoslavs. Alfred Bowman, head of the Allied Military Government in Venezia Giulia from mid-1945 to mid-1947, claims that the Cold War began in northern Italy and "that its focal point . . . was the political and doctrinal confrontation at Trieste" (Bowman 1982, 7). This confrontation set the stage for the first Trieste Crisis, the Yugoslavs' withdrawal from the city and the provisional partition of the wider territory into Zone A (administered by the Anglo-Americans) and Zone B (run by the Yugoslav military). Zone B included the Istrian Peninsula. Their fate tied to the Trieste Question, the majority of Zone B's Italians wished to remain part of the Italian state and feared the installation of a socialist, Yugoslav regime in Istria. Between 1943 and 1954, the majority of these Italians left the peninsula in what became known as the Istrian *esodo,* or exodus.

Although the term *exodus* suggests a unitary event (and, indeed, Istrian exiles have presented it as such), the departure occurred for a variety of reasons (including outright persecution by Titoists, fear, the Italian state's promise of a better life in Italy) and at different moments over a twelve-year period. The periodization of population movements from Istria mirrored shifts in the complex political wrangling over the region. The first wave abandoned Istria in 1943, when the collapse of the Italian regime and army left vulnerable those individuals most compromised with the fascist state (including officials sent from other parts of Italy, especially the south); a second wave followed at war's end, as the Yugoslavs used force and intimidation to install de facto control (which led to the territory's temporary division into Zone A and Zone B); and a significant number of Istrians legally "opted" for Italian citizenship as a result of the 1947 Italo-Yugoslav Peace Treaty, which awarded two-thirds of Istria to Yugoslavia (leaving in dispute the remaining territory, subsequently redivided into a new Zone A and Zone B). The question's final settlement in 1954 recognized the territory's partition (with Trieste going to Italy and all of Istria to Yugoslavia) and prompted the last Big Exodus of those in Zone B who had held out hope of remaining in Italy. What the Great Powers understood as the Trieste Question's resolution, then, Istrian Italians viewed as partition and population transfer.

After its formal resolution in 1954, the Trieste Crisis was held up as a model of conflict solving and border delineation (Sluga 1994b, 285). Though the negotiations were largely dictated and imposed by the Great Powers, who saw an Italo-Yugoslav rapprochement as being in their interest, the Trieste talks "are still studied by scholars of international relations as a classic triumph of the art of diplomatic negotiation" (Rabel 1988, 159). A 1976 volume entitled *Successful Negotiation: Trieste 1954,* for example, features diverse perspectives by participants to the talks, which are presented as a successful model for dispute resolution. Similarly, a publication in the SAIS (School of Advanced International Studies) series uses the Trieste case as a teaching tool for students of international relations. The authors conclude,

> In the end, the Memorandum of Understanding produced by the secret Trieste negotiations of 1954 "settled" the Trieste impasse and has served as a binding agreement for more than thirty years. To be sure, the memorandum did leave open the possibility for future governments again to take up their territorial claims. But this has not occurred, and there is little on the political scene today—or anticipated—that suggests that this question will ever again arise to plague relations between Yugoslavia and Italy, as it did for so many years following World War II. (Unger and Šegulja 1990, 38)

Such optimistic conclusions were drawn in 1990, on the eve of the Yugoslav breakup that would resuscitate demands for compensation made by Italian "exiles" forced decades earlier to abandon their homeland as a result of the territorial dispute's "successful" conclusion. This mistaken assessment reflects the top-down, state-centric perspective common to traditional security and diplomatic history analyses. Although at different moments the exiles found allies among Italian and U.S. state actors, after 1954 the esuli's most vocal advocates (like the neofascist Movimento Sociale Italiano) occupied an oppositional position (at least until 1994). Mainstream histories of events in the Julian March failed to take account of the continued resentments of Italians whose exodus from the nearby Istrian Peninsula played out within the Great Power struggle known as the Trieste Crisis.

The very notion of the Trieste Crisis entailed the refraction of older narratives about competing Slavic and Italian nationalisms through the lens of an emerging Cold War discourse. The Cold War battle enacted on the terrain of Trieste remained largely one of propaganda, with furious attempts by pro-Italian and pro-Yugoslav groups to address Allied (Anglo-American) opinion. In all their troublesome materiality, however, bodies (live and dead) became crucial to these propaganda efforts, which in turn resulted in too-real physical consequences for those in Istria who abandoned their homes. In my analysis of competing narrative constructions and their very real effects, I aim to address the "central unresolved question about who invests a form of discourse or of practical activity with authority" (Feierman 1990, 31). The "who" is uncovered here only through a detailed discussion of the multivalent process of producing both dominant and alternative readings of the Italo-Yugoslav dispute. As Trouillot reminds us, "A warning from Foucault is helpful: 'I don't believe that the question of "who exercises power?" can be resolved unless that other question "*how does it happen?*" is resolved at the same time'" (1995, 28).

In this chapter, I answer these questions by means of a detailed reading of the Trieste Crisis, a story of ethnic and ideological conflict, Cold War partition, exile communities, and bitterly contested memories. This example has many obvious parallels to other divided territories and populations where displacement nurtures a nexus of deeply felt (and often explosive) claims about land, identity, and history; one need only look to Bosnia-Herzegovina, Cyprus, Ireland, Kashmir, Korea, or Palestine for other sites of contested partition and memory. Closer to home, the Cold War divisions separating Cuban exiles in Miami from their island homeland come to mind. Novelist Cristina Garcia has written of Miami's maddening proximity to Cuba and its almost unbridgeable distance: "Cuba is a peculiar exile, I think, an island-colony. We can reach it by a thirty-minute charter flight from Miami, yet never reach it at all" (1992, 219). Thus Miami, like Trieste, emerges as "a place in which world politics and local power groups prey on people's most intimate desires and identities. . . . It is a city held in the clutches of international national security interests" (de los Angeles Torres 1995, 39). Whereas the political environments of both Miami and Trieste have been shaped, in part, by the jockeying of international security interests, vocal exile communities in each city help sustain antagonisms by nurturing divisive histories that refuse to disappear. Typically overlooked by state-centric analyses, such groups may nonetheless revive issues—long presumed resolved or dead, as in the Trieste case—that complicate the international scene and confound confident predictions about conflict resolution.

Constructing and Contesting the Trieste Crisis

The 1954 Memorandum of London ostensibly resolved the territorial dispute, but in subsequent decades many Italian-speaking refugees from Istria scoffed at Italo-Yugoslav state propaganda celebrating "the world's most open border" and angrily denounced the sacrifice of their land and their culture in the name of international power politics and Cold War security. For many Istrians, the border represented an absolute division, both in symbolic and in political terms, between two worlds. The experience of border crossing recounted by Leonardo, whose family left Capodistria in 1954 after the memorandum, typifies the exiles' alternative understanding of the boundary that separated them from their former homes.

During the so-called years of tension, Leonardo's parents moved (albeit uneasily) back and forth across a still somewhat porous boundary. His mother went to Trieste whenever possible (though the Yugoslav authorities did periodically close the border) in order to make small purchases. When the family emigrated definitively in 1954, however, that boundary became a rigid demarcation between past and present, persecution and freedom. As Leonardo and his family waited to cross the border to Italy, brusque and threatening Yugoslav authorities rifled through their possessions, ignoring the tears and supplications of Leonardo's parents. After they crossed into Italy, an Italian functionary took the refugees to a bar and offered little Leonardo a hot chocolate. The sweetness of the Italian official (and of the chocolate treat) highlighted the contrast between the Yugoslav and Italian regimes, putting truth to the lie of a friendly, open border that sought to erase the symbolic boundary between esuli and "other" Italians. Though the exiles' fate had proved an emotional rallying cry for nationalists and anticommunists in the years before 1954, after the territorial settlement the refugees were expected to become mere Italians.

Glenn Bowman (1995) has argued that in situations of war the refugee becomes central to the imagining of the national space, serving as the symbol par excellence for the threat posed by the enemy to the national way of life (see also Volk 1999). The Istrian exiles certainly occupied this symbolic slot for Italian nationalists during the immediate postwar territorial dispute. In a sense they became the professional victims described by Bowman and thus felt even more embittered when the nation had no further need of their symbolic capital and dropped their cause after 1954. Long after Trieste had been declared a "noncrisis" at the international level, then, some local actors nurtured the galvanizing spirit of combat and profound insecurity that initially informed the postwar atmosphere in the city.

Through an analysis of the standard constructions of security and insecurity against which esuli write their own personal and group histories of betrayal, I follow Trouillot's suggestion (1995, 26) to examine processes of historical production at key moments; this requires considering in tandem the making, between 1945 and 1954, of sources, archives, and narratives about the Trieste Question. Attention is paid to the way that the situation of Italians in Istria either entered into or failed to figure in the story told by powerful actors, notably the Italian and Yugoslav states and the Western Allies, revealing the "strategic silences" engendered by traditional security readings.

After 1954 exile concerns and voices rarely, if ever, featured in either Italian (national) historiography or Anglo-American accounts of postwar events. Just as the dispute's genesis and conclusion were fitted at the time into a statecentric framework privileging security, as an object of scholarship the Trieste Question has been treated largely in terms of diplomatic history, with little attention given to the Italian exodus or to the aspirations and disappointments of the esuli.[1] The literature on this conflict draws heavily on Great Power pronouncements on the situation in Venezia Giulia, to which I turn first in my analysis of the making and assembly of historical sources, as well as narratives.

The very labeling of events as the Trieste Crisis or Trieste Question shows the manner in which power enters immediately into the apprehension and construction of events at the war's close. Let us first problematize the Trieste aspect of the formulation. For many exiles, the more appropriate descriptive term would be the Question of Venezia Giulia or the Istrian Crisis, rather than one that privileges the fate of the city to the exclusion of its surrounding territory. Although one might argue for the Trieste Crisis as a convenient heuristic or shorthand for the broader Julian Question, the identification of the problem as centering on Trieste *does* matter. It not only reflects the Italian state's strategic emphasis (dating from before World War I) on the port of Trieste rather than on its hinterland, but more importantly it signals the Anglo-American focus on the city as the "line in the sand" against the USSR and Yugoslavia.

The Anglo-American reaction to events in Trieste in 1945 rendered the situation an apparently unproblematic "crisis" (the second key term in our phrase), an evaluation that most exiles would not question or dispute. Yet, as Jutta Weldes (1999) demonstrates for Soviet missiles in Cuba, the naturalized appearance of crises works to efface the intense processes by which both security and danger, or insecurity, are continually produced. It is not only the Great Power reading of the Trieste Crisis that exiles find so questionable but also the eventual Anglo-American definition of events as having been successfully resolved and thereby rendered a noncrisis.

Events in Venezia Giulia first earned the designation "crisis" at the war's close in 1945 when the Western Allies adopted an increasingly hard-line stance toward the Yugoslav military. At the end of April 1945, the Yugoslavs were racing to "liberate" Trieste and Istria in advance of their allies, with the aim of installing administrative control there and thereby preempting Italian claims. Trieste thus constituted an important border both physically and metaphorically, becoming an early and key point at which an emerging Cold War discourse began to be articulated. The initial Anglo-American interpretation of the Italo-Yugoslav border dispute as a thinly veiled act of communist expansionism prevailed over (even as it interpellated certain aspects of) competing interpretations emphasizing a complex history of nationalist contestation. Before expanding on the Cold War readings of events as a crisis, it is important to note regionally specific interpretations and claims put forward by supporters of both the Yugoslav and the Italian position. This will help us better elucidate the manner in which Cold War narratives drew on selected elements of nationalist readings.

Alternative interpretations emphasized that Trieste and Istria, previously incorporated into the Austro-Hungarian Empire and part of the Italian state since 1918 and 1920, respectively, had long been objects of Italian and Slavic irredentism. Secretly concluded with the Italian government to ensure Italy's entrance into the war on the Allied side, the 1915 Treaty of London promised Italy Trieste, Istria, and Dalmatia (as well as Trento). Wilson's subsequent insistence at Versailles that secret treaties not be honored opened a phase of intensive propaganda and dispute between Italy and the nascent Kingdom of the South Slavs that foreshadowed many of the arguments heard at the end of the Second World War (see chapter 2).

With the Italian state's subsequent "redemption" of Trieste and Istria and the installation of a fascist dictatorship after 1922, Slovenes and Croats living in these territories experienced a denationalization campaign aimed at eradicating Slavic institutions in Venezia Giulia. These policies only nurtured many South Slavs' hope that Istria and Trieste—now the objects of Slavic irredentist passion—would eventually be joined with the Yugoslav state, a goal to which Josip Broz (Tito) accorded much importance in his refashioning of the "second," socialist Yugoslavia on the ruins of the former Kingdom of the South Slavs. In an address on May 26, 1945, in the newly liberated city of Ljubljana, Tito expressed the common view (see also Krleža 1944) that the Yugoslavs should finally be masters of their own house in recognition of their sacrifice during the war (Biber 1985, 44).

The arguments justifying Yugoslav claims to the Julian March were varied, Tito having picked up on a sentiment widespread among South Slavs of various political persuasions. Slavic populations who had suffered twenty years of fascist rule proved particularly vocal in demanding that Trieste (or, rather, Trst) become part of Yugoslavia. Pamphlets published in English and appealing to the Allies argued that the Julian March belonged to Yugoslavia by both history and geography, as well as on economic grounds. Some of these pamphlets were penned by prominent intellectuals (such as the Croatian writer Miroslav Krleža), others were by Yugoslav scholars capable of writing in English, and still others were anonymously authored and published by government presses and distributed through Yugoslav embassies and pro-Slavic committees abroad.

Yugoslav geographers such as Anton Melik proffered a number of arguments "evidencing" the Julian March's natural provenance within Yugoslavia. Melik argued, for example, that Trieste's historic development as an imperial port with a hinterland comprising the Balkans and Central Europe necessitated the city's return to Yugoslavia. "Only with its being united to Jugoslavia Trieste will be able to return to its primary function in which it arose when it represented the principal outlet of the whole Middle Danube territory" (Melik 1946b, 21). He further declared the region to be "but the continuation and the closing part of the Dinaric Alps" (1946a, 3). Although acknowledging the presence of mixed Slavic-Italian populations in the large cities and along the western Istrian coast, Melik concluded that the Italians in Istria have "no territorial connections with the compact Italian-Friulian national territory of the peninsula of Italy" (ibid., 13). The Slovene contributors to the volume entitled *The Julian March: Studies on Its History and Civilization* (Kos et al. 1946) similarly refuted arguments about an extensive and deeply rooted Venetian-Italic culture in the region and instead contended that the achievements of Slavic culture (art, architecture, poetry and prose, folklore and music) strikingly evidence that "[t]he Slavs arriving since the close of the sixth century, on the territory of present-day Slovene Littoral and Istria[,] were not short of civilization" (Kos 1946, 16).

The pro-Yugoslav pamphlet *Trieste and the Julian March* (Yugoslav Government), published in 1946, recapitulates these cultural and ethnic arguments. "The hinterland of Trieste, or the Julian March, is ethnically a compact Yugoslav block in which are to be found only a few small islets of mixed population. These are almost entirely limited to towns, and have resulted from foreign infiltration into Yugoslav-populated territory or denationalisation of such territory" (1946, 5). The struggle of the Slavic peoples against Italian conquest was here cast in broader historical terms, World War II being depicted as the culmination of Italian expansionism.

Other pamphleteers stressed the great sufferings of Yugoslavs under Italian rule and the particular sacrifices made by the Slavic peoples of the Julian region in the antifascist fight. The 1946 publication *Documents Concerning the Denationalization of Yugoslavs in the Julian March* (Yugoslav Institute of International Studies), for instance, offered 139 pages of photocopied documents demonstrating the systematic persecution of Slovenes and Croats under Italian rule. A volume by Francis Gabrovšek (1946) similarly narrated the Italian attempts to exterminate the native populations of the Province of Ljubljana, occupied by Italian forces after the Axis attack on and partition of Yugoslavia in 1941. Hostages were taken and killed in reprisal for acts of sabotage, villages were burned and bombed, and mass persecutions were undertaken.

Such tales of fascist brutality contrast with the glorious example of the Yugoslav antifascist movement. Discussing those inhabitants of the Julian March welcoming their Yugoslav "liberators," France Skerl's *Struggle of the Slovenes in the Littoral for the People's Authority* places the Slovenes "in the vanguard not only of all Slovenes but also of all Jugoslavs" (1945, 19) and stresses the fraternity between Slovenes and "democratic" Italians. Skerl linked the partisans' struggle with the Allies' fight for democracy.

Edvard Kardelj made a similar statement in the immediate months after the war. Summarizing the Yugoslav government's demands for Trieste, he floated the proposal to make Trieste the capital of a seventh Yugoslav republic.

> In spite of the persecution and killings they were subjected to at the hands of the Italian fascist authorities, the people of the Julian March resisted these attempts [at conquest]. Accordingly, they exerted superhuman efforts for their liberation and union with Yugoslavia. . . . The Italian minority of the Julian March participated in the struggle. The fighters from the Italian minority fought in the ranks of the Yugoslav Army. And in what other army could they have fought? Honest Italians know very well that this is a Yugoslav land, since the majority of the population is Yugoslav and since the province both geographically and economically is part of Yugoslavia . . . our government intend [sic] to give Triest under Yugoslav sovereignty the status of <u>separate state in the Yugoslav federation</u>.
>
> What does this mean? It means that the population, in addition to enjoying all democratic rights regardless of sex, race or religion, would elect its own assembly, the body, that is, which would pass laws on the basis of the federal Constitution of Yugoslavia and its own constitution; it means that the assembly would appoint its government responsible to it which, within the limits of both federal and state laws,

would govern the state independently. Since there would be no national discrimination and the Italians form the majority in Triest, both the parliament and the government would consist mostly of Italians. . . . The port of Trieste, like many other free ports in the world, would become a free port open to all the countries outside Yugoslavia's customs boundary. (In Yugoslav Government 1945, 2–3)

The battery of arguments employed by Yugoslav supporters and summarized in Kardelj's proposal was typically matched, point for point, by pro-Italian pamphlets that contended the diametrical opposite. Pro-Italian tracts used and inverted the same principal arguments—economics, historical culture, and ethnic composition—to refute Yugoslav claims. Maps showing population density, railroad networks, and "natural boundaries" (Bandiera and Bonetti 1946), for instance, depicted Venezia Giulia as dependent on an Italian hinterland. Other proposals instead recognized Central Europe as Trieste's traditional economic hinterland and thus called for an internationalized port (Ministero degli Affari Esteri 1946), echoing Yugoslav pronouncements like Kardelj's. As in the case of the pro-Yugoslav arguments, these Italian claims were well rehearsed, largely repeating arguments made at the end of World War I over the disposition of territory (on this, consult Sluga 2001, 32, 41).

Carlo Schiffrer, one of Trieste's most prominent historians and a member of the pro-Italian Comitato di Liberazione Nazionale, criticized in his pamphlet *Historic Glance at the Relations between Italians and Slavs in Venezia Giulia* both pro-Slavic and pro-Italian advocates who "project their own modern ideologies in the past" (1946, 10). In refuting claims that the region belonged to Yugoslavia on the basis of geography, economics, and history, Schiffrer nonetheless repeated the familiar argument about the split of Italian and Slavic groups in the Julian March along the lines of urban and rural values. Interestingly, Schiffrer agrees with those who view events in Istria as resulting from both class and ethnic divisions. Hatred of the tax collector became hatred of the Italian, notes Schiffrer, thus prompting the jacqueries of the foibe in 1943. Yet Schiffrer inverts this argument (one heard in Marxist and pro-Slav analyses).

> If the Istrian Italianity (as the Slav propagandists sustain) would have been represented only by exiguous privileged and exploiting classes, it would have been destroyed in that social crisis, as has occurred elsewhere in similar circumstances. But authentic Italians, who as a rule quite ignore the Croat language, are also the numerous cultivators of the coastal strip and the agricultural townsfolk of the interior, as well as the lower people of artisans, labourers, fishermen, mariners, etc. All these live chiefly by alternating the various local activities with long periods of navigation aboard the Triestine merchant fleet. From the economical and national point of view they belong closely to the shipowners and commercial centre of Trieste, which could not live without them, whilst they themselves would not live without the resources and the work which Trieste offers. (Ibid., 24)

Schiffrer thus maintains that Trieste and its Istrian hinterland cannot be separated and that both are fundamentally Italian in culture. (Even where mixed marriages occur, he adds, Italian language and culture predominate.) Furthermore, Italians numbered prominently in the antifascist struggle. Schiffrer concludes his tract by examining the much disputed figures for the censuses of 1910 (under Austria) and 1921 (under Italy),[2] arguing that even if bias is taken into account, the Italian element in the Julian March nonetheless predominates numerically. An articulate Italian intellectual and respected antifascist, Schiffrer's voice carried considerable authority with the Anglo-Americans.

Schiffrer's colleagues in the CLN of Trieste and Istria also solicited and collected hundreds of political declarations (dichiarazioni politiche) by residents of and refugees from what became known as Zone B, denouncing the abuses of Yugoslav "occupation." The nine hundred such documents preserved at the Istituto Regionale per la Cultura Istriana offer an interesting picture of events in Istria (extending through 1954), as well as the pro-Italian presentation of those events to an Allied audience. Most of the statements are written in Italian, but some translated copies in English and French survive, underscoring the way in which this new kind of cold warfare in Trieste was fought, in part, by propaganda. The documents suggest a climate of violence in Istria and, more importantly perhaps, a generalized sense of uncertainty and fear continually reinforced by relatively minor incidents.

In spite of the Italian examples cited here, the quantity and presentation of pro-Yugoslav propaganda produced in English in the early period of the Trieste dispute suggests that the Yugoslavs outdid their Italian counterparts in pitching their appeal to an "Allied" audience. Anglo-American documents repeatedly refer to the "poor organization" initially demonstrated by pro-Italian proponents in their propaganda efforts. One Allied account of political demonstrations in the city suggested that

[p]erhaps all that had happened in the years past . . . all combined to make the Italians timid about putting themselves forward. Second, the aggressive Yugoslavs and Communists had been well organized for years. They had been watchful. They had been ruthlessly willing to employ any force available to accomplish their ends. Hence, they had, with ease, been able to prevent or break up any pro-Italian attempts at a demonstration. (Allied Military Government 1947b: 5–6)

Many in the Allied camp thus appear to have remained unpersuaded by the more elaborate and abundant pro-Yugoslav propaganda produced in English, attributing this advantage to communist organization and careful, long-term preparation. The frequency of peasants and women among the pro-Yugoslav demonstrators was taken as a further sign of the orchestration of such events; using a language akin to that of contemporary exiles, Allied Information Services even argued that advocates of Italo-Slovene brotherhood desired to "submerge" the national question (Sluga 2001, 124, 126–27). An internal report entitled *A Political History of Zone A of Venezia Giulia under Allied Military Government (12 June 1945 to 10 February 1947)* (Allied Military Government 1947c), for example, describes the communists as using intimidation to create a false image of mass support. Furthermore, Italian violence is here posited as essentially reactive, merely responding to the one initiated by Slav-communists. As these comments suggest, the Anglo-American interpretation of events in Trieste as following communist manipulation and aggression helped transform the interstate dispute into a larger contest, the first "crisis" of what became known as the Cold War.

The initial Anglo-American reading of the Trieste Crisis as a clash between communism and democracy thus recast and simplified a complex political and ethno-national conflict with deep historical roots. The extremely contentious nature of the territorial question, however one interpreted it, ultimately necessitated nine years of Allied Military Government (AMG) within the disputed territory, divided into an AMG-administered Zone A (which included Trieste) and a Yugoslav-controlled Zone B (see figure 4). This Cold War partition had parallels, of course, in Berlin and Vienna, as well as in the broader demarcation of Western and Eastern "spheres of influence."[3]

Even before Allied troops arrived in the Julian March in May 1945, the region's difference from the rest of mainland Italy and its strategic importance had been recognized. The so-called race for Trieste in May 1945 between Allied and Yugoslav forces set the stage for what would become known in English as the Trieste Crisis. The memoir of intelligence officer Geoffrey Cox (1977) offers a Western account of this scramble, with the first Allied troops (New Zealanders) to arrive in the Julian March finding that Yugoslav partisans had already installed a civil administration in many areas. German forces in Trieste still offered resistance to the Yugoslavs, however, thereby enabling the New Zealand forces to assist in the final liberation of Trieste and stake a claim for a temporary Allied military government in the region. In order to preempt partisan claims to the liberation of Trieste, the Italian Comitato di Liberazione Nazionale had also staged an uprising in Trieste on the night of April 30, mistakenly assuming that the Allied forces were on the verge of entering Trieste. This confused situation, with various actors claiming to have "liberated" the city, set the scene for what would become almost a decade of Anglo-American mediation in the contested zone, the Trieste Crisis in fact representing a series of separate but related crises.

For participant-observers like Cox, the first and principal Trieste Crisis consisted solely of the showdown in May 1945 between the Allies and the Yugoslavs for control of the city and of regional administration. For Cox, the Yugoslav withdrawal from the city the following month and the establishment of the Allied Military Government in Venezia Giulia represented a Western triumph.

Figure 4. Map of the Julian March (Zones A and B) under the Allied Military Government, 1945–47. This map reflects the partition of the Julian March in May 1945.

"Trieste was the first major confrontation of the Cold War" writes Cox (1977, 7). He further contends that the example of Trieste may have provided a reference point for Truman in the subsequent crises of the Berlin blockade and the Korean War. Others have similarly identified this as the point at which the U.S. administration began to articulate a policy of containment (Rabel 1988; see Dinardo 1997 for a dissenting view).

Although initially hesitant to engage American troops in any military action against the Yugoslavs (who were, after all, still officially allies), by mid-May

1945 Truman had indicated his willingness to employ American military power if necessary. Truman and Churchill, as well as Cox, constructed the crisis within the terms of an Anglo-American struggle against the "Moscow tentacle of which Tito is the crook" (Churchill in Cox 1977, 225). Despite the fact that in foreign policy Tito acted independently of (and even in opposition to) Moscow, by reading the Trieste Crisis in Cold War terms Cox (like some Allied leaders) flattened the social and political complexities of the situation in Trieste.

As historian Glenda Sluga (1994b) has noted, many of the Anglo-Americans present in Trieste accepted long-standing Italian nationalist constructs—Latin-Italians versus Slavs, civilized versus barbarian, West versus East, and so on—and grafted onto them the bipolar identifications characteristic of the Cold War. These Cold War bipolarities proved essential to the production of symbolic boundaries through identity/difference (see Campbell 1992). For the British-American representatives, as for Italian nationalists, "Slavs were a political communist threat from the East. The two connotations of the term [*Slav*] overlapped politically and emotionally, enabling a rapport to be formed between the Allies and pro-Italian Triestines" (Sluga 1994b, 286). The *slavo-comunista* theme became particularly prominent from mid-1946 on (Giampaolo Valdevit, personal communication).

Geoffrey Cox's memoir illustrates this sense of identification with the Italians. He contrasts the friendly Italian men (and women [Sluga 1994a]) with the taciturn and rigid Yugoslav partisans, who tended toward a polite nonfraternization with the Allies. Cox and many others thus accepted at face value (or found politically convenient) the thesis of the CLN of Trieste and Istria that the Slavs represented an unpopular occupying force imposed on the predominantly pro-Italian Triestines (see Sluga 1994b, 287).

In critically analyzing the ways in which in fitting the Trieste Crisis into a Cold War mold the Allied administration built on the understandings of pro-Italian groups in Trieste, Sluga's work challenges many of the facile assumptions of subsequent Anglo-American political analyses of the situation. Her thesis seems most appropriate, however, for the years 1945–49, prior to the Yugoslav-Soviet split. After 1949, American attitudes and policies in Trieste altered significantly, provoking another "crisis" in 1953 when pro-Italian groups perceived the AMG to be hostile to the city's italianità. Prior to this, the Anglo-Americans had tended to favor Italian claims, although positions shifted according to the exigencies of the Cold War.

Admittedly, within the Allied Military Government a wide range of opinions existed, as evidenced by the AMG documentation on deposit at the U.S. National Archives. Nonetheless, at least until the period 1948–49, the AMG *generally* pursued pro-Italian policies in spite of its mandated neutrality. The preference at times shown toward Italian parties did not, however, translate into intense Anglo-American action regarding the fate of Italians in Istria. Although AMG documents reveal considerable awareness of the "refugee" problem from

Istria, the Istrian question does not feature prominently in either contemporary administration considerations or postwar assessments of the AMG.

The internally produced *Political History,* for instance, notes the migration of Italians from Istria while downplaying its dimensions. Writing of the year 1947, in which an Italo-Yugoslav Peace Treaty awarded a considerable part of Istria to Yugoslavia and led to an establishment of the Free Territory of Trieste (FTT),[4] *A Political History* concludes, "The year end [sic] greatly quiet and the only outstanding feature being the exodus of Italian residents of Pola" (Allied Military Government 1947c, 53).

The "only outstanding feature" cursorily mentioned here, the highly dramatic exodus from the naval port of Pola (situated at the base of Istria), occurred as a result of the city's passage from AMG control to Yugoslav sovereignty by the terms of the 1947 peace treaty. Within a few months, the city almost completely emptied as its residents exercised their "option" for Italian citizenship. While making its own preparations for withdrawal from Pola, the AMG was deluged with appeals from pro-Italian groups like the Lega Nazionale, a nationalist group dating from the irredentist struggle with Austria that was reconstituted in 1946. The Lega Nazionale office drafted a letter in July 1946 to the AMG stating that in Pola twenty-five thousand persons had applied to leave and urging the employment of departing workers in Trieste, as well as the adjacent towns of Monfalcone and Muggia. Revealing that the Italians of Pola realized they were leaving their homeland permanently, the letter added, "The population which has already seen the tombstones of the Italian martyrs lifted did not wish to leave even their dead to Jugoslavia. Several people are already taking steps to have their dead exhumed. Would you therefore approach the Trieste authorities to find a way of transferring bodies to Trieste."

AMG memos from the period of this appeal by the Lega Nazionale treat this "flood of people from Pola." One AMG document dated July 22, 1946, notes the numerous requests about arrangements for the anticipated exodus from Pola and Zone B after the peace treaty's signature and states the necessity that the AMG "have a plan ready for after the decision of the Peace Conference." By August 1946, AMG major J. A. Kellett, chief public welfare officer, had prepared a report on expected evacuations from those parts of Venezia Giulia to pass under Yugoslav control.

Though acknowledging the popular conviction that Pola's entire Italian population, estimated at 32,000 persons, would leave en masse, Kellett expressed skepticism at these dire predictions. He noted that only 150 persons had taken advantage of "free travel to Italy via Displaced Persons channels." Should such numbers increase, contended the memo, "it is the responsibility of the Italian Government to take care of their own nationals." This AMG disavowal of responsibility reflected agreements then being finalized between the Italian government and the International Refugee Organization (IRO).[5]

AMG memos from this period appear concerned for the most part not with refugees from Pola but rather with the evacuation of Allied personnel and their families from that city and the provision of accommodation for them.[6] A confidential paper dated August 27, 1946, and distributed to various AMG officials assessed the problem of Pola. The author noted the arrangements made by the Italian government to assist the city's evacuation and considered what role the AMG should play in the actual carrying out of the evacuation, the protection of abandoned property from potential looters, and the peaceful settlement of the refugees in Zone A. The author forcefully argued, "[W]e cannot morally take any measures which would delay evacuation and so risk the Italian population being left in any measure to the mercy of the incoming Jugoslavs." Other AMG documents, however, suggest that many within the administration viewed the Italian government as playing an instrumental role in orchestrating the speed and extent of the exodus (a view reiterated by Volk 1999, 271). One 1947 briefing noted of events in Pola, "As the Italian Government plan for evacuation was working reasonably well there was a tendency for a number of people to attempt to delay their departure until the last possible minute. The announcement however by the Italian Authorities that the evacuation ship 'Toscana' would not be available after the first week of March had the desired effect and nearly all intended to leave left before the middle of March" (Allied Military Government 1947d, 1).

AMG documents thus depict the exodus from Pola as a problem intensified and accelerated by an Italian government that bore ultimate responsibility for its consequences. A pamphlet prepared by Public Relations BETFOR (British Element Trieste Force) entitled *Birth of a Free Territory* and describing the six months immediately following the peace treaty and the establishment of the FTT barely mentions the exodus from Pola. Instead, attention is given to various demonstrations and manifestations within Trieste, the Yugoslavs being seen as "highly organised and their policy and publicity centrally directed," in contrast to the Italians, who "as usual . . . were behind-hand in their organization" (Allied Military Government 1947a, 4).

Even prior to the Western reappraisal of Yugoslavia's potential as a wedge in the socialist bloc as a result of the Tito-Stalin rift, internal documentation within the AMG suggests growing irritation with the Italians. As civil disturbances increased with the creation of the FTT, the BETFOR publication did not hesitate to condemn the strong current of anti-Allied sentiment prevailing among various Italian nationalist groups (ibid., 13). Increasingly, AMG officials appeared to view both Italian and Yugoslav groups as engaging in heavy-handed manipulation, suggesting a shift (locally, at least) from the earlier Cold War paradigm through which the Trieste situation was viewed. Even as the AMG increasingly came to view Italians, along with the Yugoslavs, as part of the problem in Trieste, electoral exigencies nonetheless led the Anglo-Americans to make concessions to the Italians in Zone A.[7]

Yugoslavia's definitive expulsion from the Cominform (as well as the electoral defeat of the PCI in Italy) in 1948, however, eventually prompted British and American leaders to redefine Western security interests. Whereas in 1945 Trieste had constituted the "last bulwark" against Soviet territorial advances, after 1948 the Anglo-Americans redefined Yugoslavia as the strategic buffer zone "between East and West." The AMG accordingly changed its role from protector of democratic Italians to neutral mediator.

Although some Anglo-Americans agonized over whether supporting *any* communists, even anti-Soviet communists, violated their basic principles, the Western powers soon decided to exploit the Soviet-Yugoslav breach. Brands argues that "[i]ndeed, when they considered ideology at all, American policymakers hoped Tito would remain a reliably orthodox disciple of Marx and Lenin, so he could become a guiding light to other would-be national communists in the Soviet sphere. Needless to say, those formulating policy did not trumpet this heretical view in public" (1989, 141–42). The redefinition of Western security needs thus induced British and American leaders to accept Tito's stubborn independence (especially in foreign affairs) and Yugoslavia's ambiguous position between the two blocs (see the discussions in Lane 1996; Lees 1997). Though scholars such as Brands and Heuser disagree slightly in their periodizations regarding the culmination of the West's opening toward Yugoslavia (and vice versa)—Brands sees 1948–50 as the formative years, and Heuser (1989) singles out the years 1952–53, the period immediately preceding what became termed the Final Trieste Crisis—they generally agree on the sharp shift signaled by the Cominform split.

As a result of these broader changes, in Zone A the Anglo-Americans increasingly adopted a more neutral position (Rabel 1988, 131–36). This perceived "betrayal" by their former defenders prompted various protests from pro-Italian groups, particularly those concerned with the fate of the Italian population in Istria. AMG suggestions for direct Italo-Yugoslav negotiations to resolve the impasse only deepened Italian nationalist anger (Novak 1970, 358). A national and international press campaign mirrored the agitation within Zone A, where the Anglo-Americans were now condemned for "selling out" Italy to Yugoslavia. Nationalists also instrumentalized the plight of Italians in Istria in order to contest the legitimacy of the Yugoslav regime in Zone B. In Trieste, irredentist protest against the AMG led to a series of riots in 1952. These disturbances were harbingers of the Italian nationalist anger toward the AMG that subsequently erupted in the course of the following year and helped the Anglo-Americans redefine their mandate.

Tired of a long and expensive military administration and now viewing themselves as allies of both Italy and Yugoslavia, the United States and Great Britain announced on October 8, 1953, that they would terminate the AMG and cede control of Zone A to the Italian state and Zone B to Yugoslavia. Both Yugoslav and Italian proponents responded angrily to the loss of half the desired territory. Tito rejected what he perceived as a humiliating and unilateral "*fait ac-*

compli" (ibid., 431), and a "'thoroughly organized'" crowd attacked the United States Information Office in Zagreb (Brands 1989, 193). In Trieste, rumors of an irredentist coup d'état spread. This atmosphere of panic and confused rumor in the city set the stage for the riots of November 1953, sparked when Italian protesters provoked the fire of AMG police who entered a church where the demonstrators had sought refuge. Six people were killed when AMG police fired on protesters throwing stones.

The interpretation various parties offered for the Trieste riots ranged dramatically (see Dunham 1954). Whereas Western and pro-Yugoslav papers tended to agree in their depictions of the Italian "agitators" as irredentist and neofascist elements, Italian nationalists interpreted these events as spontaneous demonstrations of patriotism by a long-suffering population. According to proponents of italianità, events became violent as a result of the AMG's false portrayal of all Italian patriots as neofascists. A publication of the Committee for the Defense of the Italian Character of Trieste and Istria (1953) charged the AMG with brutal tactics and linked the Trieste Question directly with the fate of Italians in Zone B, sacrificed for the larger security interests of the Western Powers. Written before the resolution of the Trieste situation, this document provides one example of the construction of an Italian discourse of betrayal at the time of the events.

Yugoslav pronouncements from the period 1953–54 also express a sense of betrayal. Reading Italian policy toward Trieste as a continuation of fascist imperialism, for example, Yugoslav leader Edvard Kardelj (1953) saw Western support of Italian aims as threatening to undo previous attempts at reconciliation with Yugoslavia. One tract entitled *Trieste: The Problem That Agitates the World* assigned blame for the failure of the Free Territory solution in practice to Italy, as well as its Anglo-American sympathizers. The authors conclude, "Once again the Roman Government has shown its reluctance to renounce its imperialist policy toward Yugoslavia or the time-honored methods of blackmail, provocations, threats and the taking of most drastic measures where the relations with Yugoslavia are concerned" (Sedmak and Mejak 1953, 79).

Confronted by both pro-Italian and pro-Yugoslav discourses constructing them as betrayers, the Anglo-Americans renewed their efforts to extricate themselves from Trieste, eventually serving as intermediaries in the secret Italo-Yugoslav negotiations that settled the territorial dispute. The 1954 Memorandum of London recognized the Italian acquisition of Zone A and the Yugoslav administration of Zone B while assuring respective protection of the minorities in both territories. As noted earlier, the 1954 talks are still studied by scholars of international relations as a classic triumph of the art of diplomatic negotiation. Only in 1975, however, did the Italian and Yugoslav states succeed in finalizing these Great Power arrangements by means of the Treaty of Osimo.

Though my own research focused on more recent efforts to revive the Istrian Question, exiles have never ceased to protest what they view as an unjust settlement. One of the most public and vocal moments of protest occurred in 1975 at the time of Osimo's ratification. This protest galvanized the city, reminding some of the people I spoke with of the charged atmosphere of the immediate postwar period. The protest against Osimo, in turn, constitutes an important memory of "resistance" within the exiles' collective narratives of their experience.

Protesting the Resolution of the Trieste Crisis

The Treaty of Osimo sparked an enormous popular protest in Trieste. Not only did Osimo recognize the long-standing partition of the region, it also proposed a transfrontier industrial zone (a free trade area) and economic cooperation between Italy and Yugoslavia in that zone, including shared or "mixed" infrastructure. In addition, the treaty contained clauses regarding indemnities for Istrian exiles' lost properties and for protection of the national minorities (Italians in Yugoslavia, Slovenes in Italy). Though the Italian and Yugoslav ministers of foreign affairs signed the treaty on November 10, 1975, protests had already begun in Trieste a month earlier. Large crowds continued to demonstrate in the city, and the following year a petition drive for signatures against the treaty's final ratification began. Approximately sixty-five thousand signatures were collected, the daily newspaper Il Piccolo playing an important role in this mobilization (Giuricin 1988, 97). Large "popular assemblies" became a common feature of city life, bringing together supporters of various parties ranged along the political spectrum and involving civic groups such as the Rotary Club. Prominent among such actors were the exile associations, as well as environmental groups fearing the effects of industrial development of the Karst above Trieste.

Out of these extended protests and lists of signatures denouncing Osimo was born the political party the Lista per Trieste (LpT), which had its origins in a political group (the Melone) formed in 1975 in Trieste's Communal Council. At its inception, this movement drew supporters from across the political spectrum, breaking down some of the usual barriers between Left and Right in Trieste. The original name, Melone, gave expression to this political hybridism. Christian Democrat and esule Giacomo Bologna notes, "I would like to observe, a little bit joking and a little bit seriously, that the 'Melon' belongs to the vegetable kingdom; and in the vegetable kingdom, exists the phenomenon of 'hybrids growing luxuriantly'" (in Giuricin 1988, 11).

As the Melone's successor, the LpT officially came into existence in June 1977 and the following year won the communal elections in Trieste. The party became associated with the esuli and the political Right, working closely with the Unione degli Istriani in promoting exile interests. The Unione and the LpT have also shared some leadership. One of the founders of the Melone's original Committee of Ten was Gianni Giuricin, a prominent exile from Rovigno associated with the political Left-Center (an adherent at that time of the Italian Socialist Party) and formerly a member of the Julian Delegation to the 1946 Paris Peace Conference.

Giuricin found support for his political activities among fellow exiles, such as Giacomo Bologna, who had built their careers in the ruling Christian Democratic (DC) Party that now sought to ratify Osimo. Even DC stalwarts like Bologna could not accept the state's "treachery" in agreeing to the 1975 treaty. Bologna proudly told me that in 1945 he had been the only person in his town (Isola/Izola) with the courage to openly enroll in the DC. Later transferring to Trieste, he began a long political career as a Christian Democrat. In his later role as parliamentary deputy, Bologna angrily voted against Osimo, which he denounced as an "imbecilic treaty." Bologna contended that the DC had promoted the fable about the "most open border in the world" in order to ram Osimo through parliament.

Other informants claimed that some Italian parliamentary representatives had been slipped envelopes of money by the DC in order to ratify Osimo. Whether true or not, these apocryphal stories reveal the treaty's illegitimacy in the exiles' eyes. Many in Trieste interpret the fact that treaty details had been kept secret until late in the negotiation process as further proof of the agreement's treachery and fraudulence. In this view, Trieste and the exiles had once again been "sold out" by Rome in the name of good relations with Yugoslavia. For the exiles, Osimo appeared to menace their refuge in Trieste at the same time that it revealed the continued lack of disregard for those Italians who had paid the ultimate price for Italy's lost war. In the exiles' estimation, Italy appeared unwilling even to defend Trieste, the last Latin stronghold against Slavic encroachment (Giuricin 1988, 195–96). Other publications on Osimo charge the DC with doing the bidding of the Vatican, here viewed as a longtime ally of Catholic Slovenes and an enemy of Trieste with its anticlerical nationalist tradition (Melonucci 1980, 5).

My fieldwork period coincided with the twentieth anniversary of Osimo, an event that prompted a spate of newspaper articles and public meetings in Trieste (see Spirito 1995). One such program, entitled "The Treaty of Osimo Yesterday and Today," took place at the Unione degli Istriani on November 4, 1995, also the traditional anniversary of Italy's victory in World War I, or the "War of Redemption." Unione president Denis Zigante commented that this meeting reflected the need to "always remember and denounce" Osimo, a treaty that legitimized the region's shameful partition. The organizers chose November 4, the Festival of National Unity, to remember the infamous day in 1975 when national unity was shattered. Zigante also stressed the secrecy with which the treaty was carried out and the means—"the dictatorship of the assembly"—by which its ratification had occurred in Italy.

At this meeting, Zigante introduced two journalists, Mario Oriani and Fausto

Biloslavo, who took up the theme of a "shame that endures." Oriani, formerly a journalist for the *Corriere della Sera,* noted that November 4 remained a day not only of sorrow (because of Osimo) but also of joy, given that it recalled Trieste's passage to Italy in 1918. Oriani remembered that his own father had been an Italian volunteer in the Great War and that on November 4 his father and his friends would gather together for a private commemoration of the War of Redemption. Oriani contrasted the honesty and goodness embodied by the Italian sacrifice in World War I with the squalid and secretive atmosphere within which Osimo took place.

Whereas Oriani used the Osimo anniversary to reflect on the more distant past, Biloslavo moved from the Osimo question to present-day debates. He placed the "ignoble treaty" in direct continuity with Italy's current relationship with the former Yugoslavia. He noted that the Italian government continues to pay out pensions to its former citizens in nearby Istria who had done military service or worked for the state sector under Italy. According to Biloslavo, the Slovene and Croat recipients of those payments include some ex–criminals of war responsible after World War II for the deportation, torture, summary execution, and *infoibamento* (death in karstic foibe, or pits) of the Italian population of Venezia Giulia. Though sharing parallels with wider concerns about what rights newly arrived emigrants to Italy should have (or be limited to), here the controversial and emotional issue of Italian pensions follows out of the specific context of the Julian March and debates over Osimo. Biloslavo's words also referred to the question of whether the Treaty of Osimo still remained legally valid, given that one of its signatories (Yugoslavia) no longer exists. In tandem with broad shifts in the global political economy, the legal ambiguities created by Yugoslavia's dissolution offered concrete hope to the exiles that the time had come to reverse the agreement ratified at Osimo.

Such meetings to "remember Osimo" represent one aspect of the multilayered struggle to reject the official narratives and constructions—and their very real consequences, that is, the partition of Istria and Osimo—of the Trieste Crisis which this chapter has outlined. Here I have focused on the perception and constitution of the crisis by the Great Powers, both at the time of events and in subsequent analyses by scholars of diplomatic history and security studies; the discourses of Italian and Yugoslav state actors have also received brief attention. As is clear from this discussion of the narrative constructions of the Trieste Crisis, the problem of the exiles from Istria entered consideration only as a tangential concern, if a concern at all. This neglect continues to anger many exiles, who view themselves as victimized pawns in the struggle over the Trieste Question.

Whereas for Italian national leaders Osimo merely ratified a two-decades-long reality, for some exiles and Italian nationalists in Trieste the conflict was far from over. They refused to accept the Great Powers' definition of Trieste as a noncrisis after 1954 (and, to some extent, after 1949). In the autumn of 1995, prompted by the extensive commemoration of Osimo, local historian Giampaolo Valdevit declared, "[T]he Cold War never ended in this city" (Valdevit 1995). At the same time, as suggested by the location of Osimo in a narrative extending from the War of Redemption to the contemporary Festival of Unity commemorating it, in Trieste a locally specific Cold War narrative appears to temporally join up with those about World War I. Perhaps, then, Valdevit would have been more accurate had he said, "The irredentist struggle never ended in Trieste."

As this ongoing contestation over the Istrian exodus makes clear, the centrality of history and culture to conceptualizations of identity proves crucial to understanding the production of insecurity for many of those, such as the esuli, whose voices were long drowned out by the official histories of the state. Issues of memory and identity not only matter for the security studies by which cases like the Trieste Crisis have been traditionally viewed but also force us to rethink power (its sites and operation) as we bring "culture" into such analyses. Understanding the politics of memory which have asserted themselves so forcefully in many contemporary cases means taking seriously Trouillot's comment that "[p]ower does not enter the story once and for all, but at different times and from different angles" (1995, 28–29); furthermore, the power relationships between the center and the margins do not prove stable. As the discussion here of the Trieste Crisis demonstrates, "Power is constitutive of the story. Tracking power through various 'moments' simply helps emphasize the fundamentally processual character of historical production, to insist that what history is matters less than how history works" (ibid., 28). The next chapter further takes up Trouillot's challenge to explore how "history works" by looking at broad currents of historical revisionism that intersect in powerful ways in contemporary debates over postwar events in Trieste and Istria.

CHAPTER FOUR

Revisiting the History of World War II

ALTHOUGH the "dual traumas" of fascism and communism have been hotly debated for decades in the Julian March, only recently have alternative histories of World War II and its aftermath come to the fore in Europe, East and West. In various ways, West European and East European societies today confront the question of extensive complicity and collaboration with authoritarian regimes (Borneman 1997; Rosenberg 1995). European debates about whether to seek out and retroactively punish such collaborators or, alternatively, seek reconciliation through "truth telling" and forgiveness parallel those heard in other former authoritarian societies grappling with past violence, among them South Africa, Chile, Guatemala, and Argentina. Revisionist debates among historians thus manifest the broad shifts and dislocations attendant to the end of the Cold War at the same time that they partake of more specific debates in which both the victors and the vanquished reevaluate the Second World War, processes intensified by attempts to commemorate major anniversaries of various events.

Contested Anniversaries, Battles for History

The period of my fieldwork in Trieste and Istria coincided with a spate of fiftieth-anniversary celebrations in Europe and the United States recalling the end of the Second World War. Italy saw its share of such ceremonies, centered around the Day of the Republic (April 25), the traditional holiday celebrating the end of the war. Such holidays have little resonance for many residents in Trieste, whose historical trajectory and "liberation" differ significantly from the rest of the country. As one would expect, then, in Trieste the fiftieth anniversary of the war's end did not meet with great enthusiasm.

In Trieste, for example, there is no consensus as to when the war actually ended in the city or whether the city experienced two "liberations"—one by Yugoslav partisans in the first days of May 1945 and another by Anglo-American troops the following month—or only one "true" liberation. The organizers of an exhibition sponsored by the Istituto Regionale per la Storia del Movimento di Liberazione nel Friuli–Venezia Giulia and held in Trieste to mark the fiftieth anniversary of the war's conclusion thus found themselves confronted with a sticky dilemma: given the highly divergent memories of the Yugoslav period in

Trieste, how could they represent this experience for a fractured general public? In Trieste, for example, pro-Italians recall the brief period of Yugoslav occupation as the infamous Forty Days, a time of summary arrests and executions, with many Italians (as well as Slovenes) meeting their end in the karstic grottoes known as the foibe. In contrast, many members of the city's Slovene minority (as well as Italian communists) viewed the arrival of Tito's partisans as liberation from two decades of oppression at the hands of a fascist state bent on denationalizing Venezia Giulia's autochthonous Slavs. Together with members of the Italian Communist Party, members of the Slovene minority had offered the first and principal armed antifascist resistance in the region. Organized belatedly, the Comitato di Liberazione Nazionale of Trieste and Istria represented the only significant alternative resistance force and proved explicitly nationalist and anticommunist in its orientation. After the war's conclusion, the local CLN dedicated itself to the fight to return Trieste and Istria to Italy and to provide assistance to refugees from those areas of Istria occupied by Yugoslav forces.[1]

Given this complex situation in the immediate postwar period, any attempts to offer an exhibition for the general public in Trieste commemorating the city's "liberation(s)" prove fraught with tension. In the end, the organizers played down the role of the Slovene resistance, angering many members of the Slovene community and prompting intense discussions within the scientific committee that organized the exhibition. Nonetheless, this slighting of the Slovene contribution did not protect the organizers from charges of being philo-Slavic (given the mere mention of the Slovene contribution), reflecting the persistence of anti-Slavic sentiment in Trieste.

In addition to this show, the Istituto Regionale per la Storia del Movimento di Liberazione nel Friuli–Venezia Giulia organized a variety of conferences and seminars, including a series of public encounters with the protagonists of what organizers billed as the "Difficult Years: Trieste, 1940–1954," which at times met with angry denunciations. Ceremonies at the Risiera di San Sabba, the former Nazi extermination camp in Trieste, reaffirmed a traditional narrative of the Resistance, one typically associated with the Slovene minority and the Left in Trieste. Italian "patriots" and exiles instead organized counterceremonies that remembered the fiftieth anniversaries of the foibe, the withdrawal of the Yugoslav troops from the city in June 1945, and the Italo-Yugoslav Peace Treaty, which awarded much of Istria to Yugoslavia. Such events made for a "ritual calendar" quite different from that sponsored by the Italian state and its custodians (like the Istituto Regionale per la Storia del Movimento di Liberazione)—as well as by the PCI's heirs (Kertzer 1996, 1, 25)—of the antifascist struggle's memory.

Furthermore, these alternative ceremonies told a story at odds with those heard in neighboring Slovenia and Croatia. The city of Capodistria/Koper, in Slovenian Istria, held a celebration in September 1997, in its main square, Piazza/Trg Tito. The program featured folkloric performances, a partisan choir, salutes from Istrian veteran groups, and films glorifying the Slovene struggle to "return to the madrepatria." Like a much more elaborate ceremony that took place the following week in Nova Gorica at which Slovene president Milan Kucan spoke, the event at Koper had state backing. In Croatia, as well, the state sponsored a gathering of ex-partisans and antifascists in the Arena of Pola.

In contrast, the elaborate ceremonies in Trieste to recall (and mourn) the 1947 Peace Treaty were organized primarily by the exile associations. Billed as part of a worldwide gathering of the exiles, events included round tables and seminars at which the exiles' bitterness toward both the Italian state and the Italian minority in Istria emerged, as well as cultural happenings such as musical concerts and photographic exhibits. The series of initiatives culminated in a public ceremony in Trieste's principal square, Piazza Unità d'Italia, the site of many meetings and protests during the protracted Trieste Crisis and still the focal point of the city's pro-Italian topography.

The turnout in Piazza Unità did not prove nearly as large as expected, perhaps the result of declining interest or merely a reflection of bad weather. Despite the September day for this ceremony, the weather proved cold, windy, and wet, with ample doses of the region's famous wind, the *bora.* Participants who braved the gusts of wind were bundled in winter clothes. Some participants wore pins showing the Istrian *capra,* or goat (symbol of the peninsula), superimposed on the Italian tricolor flag; one woman wore a small Italian flag in her hair. Another group carried an enormous flag bearing the message, "We want to return" (*Volemo tornar,* istro-veneto dialect for *vogliamo tornare*). In various ways, that day, esuli made a claim for the italianità of the lost territory.

After a series of speeches by different exile leaders, a representative of the Italian state—Antonio Maccanico, the minister of the post—began to speak, stressing the need to protect the Italian minority in Istria, as well as preserve neighborly relations with Slovenia. At this, the crowd erupted into whistles and catcalls. A group of young people (part of the "Children of the Exiles" group) with whom I was standing began to chant "Venduti! Venduti!" ("Sold out, sold out!"), giving vent to the sentiment of betrayal pervading the exile community. The minister's speech was abruptly terminated when three local politicians—Marucci Vascon, exile and former parliamentary deputy for Berlusconi's Forza Italia; Giulio Camber (a Forza Italia representative); and Roberto Menia (a parliamentarian for the Alleanza Nazionale, the neofascist party)—stepped to the front of the stage and sang a patriotic hymn (Verdi's "Va' Pensiero"), drowning out the minister's words.

Risorgimento nationalists had made "Va' Pensiero" their "chorus of liberation" (Robinson 1997, 165) when Verdi's opera *Nabucco* debuted in the 1840s. In *Nabucco,* "the political repression of Italy by the Austrians is metaphorically represented by the subjugation of the ancient Hebrews under the Babylonians" (ibid). The analogy drawn between the ancient Hebrews and the Italian nation in exile continues to hold significance for groups like the esuli today. More recently, Verdi's hymn has been adopted as the anthem of Padania, the separatist

Figure 5. World Congress of Exiles, Trieste, 1997

a. Italian exiles protesting in Piazza Unità d'Italia, Trieste, 1997; the sign reads "Volemo tornar" (Istrian dialect for "We want to return")

b. Embodying identity: esuli and supporters commemorating/mourning the Italo-Yugoslav Peace Treaty of 1947, Trieste, 1997

state proclaimed by the Lega Nord, or Northern League. Although the exiles claimed that "Va' Pensiero" has long proven meaningful for the Istrian esuli and that its spontaneous performance in Piazza Unità did not reference the Northern League in any way, it nonetheless sent a doubly ominous message to Rome.

Though some exiles I spoke with believed that these actions were "over the top" and showed a lack of respect toward the government's representatives, many others justified it, telling me that this incident represented a spontaneous outburst by the exiles to fifty years of lies, deceit, and hypocrisy. Exiles were incensed not only by Maccanico's speech, which revealed a lack of sensitivity to the esuli's feelings, but also by the fact that the Italian state had sent only an "unimportant" minister to the ceremony. In contrast, a few days earlier then Italian president Oscar Luigi Scalfaro had attended a ceremony held at Gorizia honoring the city's return to Italy in 1947. Many exiles interpreted Scalfaro's absence in Trieste as a snub and symptomatic of the exiles' continued neglect by the Italian state. The protest in Piazza Unità, however, got the attention of the government, and an exile delegation immediately went to Rome to meet with leaders there.

Prime Minister Prodi's government declared itself cooperative to dealing with esuli concerns. Maccanico recognized the "patrimony" constituted by the exiles' faith in the nation at the same time that he denounced the long historical "repression" (rimozione) of the Istrian experience (Il Piccolo 1997). The fact that representatives of a Left-Center coalition—including former communists in the Partito Democratico della Sinistra (PDS)—made these conciliatory statements, endorsed the values of patriotism, and acknowledged the esuli's suffering highlights the ongoing reevaluation in Italy of such alternative histories. These transformations reverberate throughout Europe as historians, politicians, and others engage in various "battles for history," particularly histories of World War II.

The former "truisms" about that war—their authority previously underwritten by both the official historiographies of postwar regimes and the testimonies of witnesses and survivors—have come under scrutiny from a variety of directions. At the same time, elderly individuals whose experience had previously been written out of official historiographies are still alive to bear witness to their experience. A generational aspect thus works in tandem with broad shifts in the political economy of historiographical representation. John Keegan's slim volume The Battle for History: Re-fighting World War II summarizes many of the debates that presently occupy historians of the conflict, historiographical disputes that do not remain isolated within the academy but instead entail broader political struggles over the meaning of the past. Keegan insists that "the Second World War must engage our moral sense" (1996, 52). Yet it is precisely those moral narratives about the war—in tandem with the former exigencies of Cold War politics and the post–Cold War reevaluation of those politics—that have rendered so contentious the dual memories of Nazi occupation and antifascist resistance within countries such as France, Italy, and Yugoslavia.

These countries experienced German occupation as a civil conflict that divided loyalties and left a fractured collective memory of the war. For many years, however, official narratives glorifying the Resistance worked to silence or paper over disturbing issues of widespread complicity, collaboration, and internecine strife between competing factions of the Resistance. For France, Henry Rousso posits a case of unfinished mourning that subsequently prompted a bitterly contested examination of that past. "An objective (and optimistic) view of the postwar period customarily sees it as divided into two successive phases: Liberation and Reconstruction. First night, then light" (1991, 15), writes Rousso; Rousso's characterization reveals the pervasive use of illuminist imagery to discuss memories of World War II generally.

Rousso dates the shattering of the French myth of "resistancialism" to May 1968. Originally a pejorative epithet used by the victims of the postliberation epurations, resistancialism signifies,

> first, a process that sought to minimize the importance of the Vichy regime and its impact on French society, *including its most negative aspects;* second, the construction of an object of memory, the "Resistance," whose significance transcended by far the sum of its active parts (the small groups of guerrilla partisans who did the actual fighting) and whose existence was embodied chiefly in certain sites and groups, such as the Gaullists and Communists, associated with fully elaborated ideologies; and, third, the identification of this "Resistance" with the nation as a whole, a characteristic feature of the Gaullist version of the myth. (Ibid., 10).

This process of elaborating a myth of the Resistance—a myth central to many postwar regimes' legitimacy in Europe—holds in different ways for both Italy and Yugoslavia, where revisionist debates emerged much later than in France. (Peitsch [1999] has suggested, however, that debates in Germany in the mid-1990s highlighted issues common to the French and Italian cases.) The Italian and Yugoslav cases resemble in a very general way the French experience for the actual period of the war: rapid collapse upon Axis invasion, followed by partition and the establishment of quisling republics, as well as the development of competing partisan groups. For the postwar period, however, the Italian case more closely resembles the French situation, with political grappling between communists and Gaullists, or in the Italian case, between communists and Christian Democrats over ownership of the memory of the Resistance. These struggles over memory mirrored struggles for power, with heated electoral campaigns and defamatory portrayals of communists as a Soviet "fifth column" (see Bocca 1996b).

In Yugoslav public and political discourse, this contest did not exist, and the other "resistance" movement—of the Četniks under the leadership of the Serbian nationalist and royalist Draža Mihailović—instead became a wholly discredited and shameful memory. In Titoist narratives, Četniks figured as Serbian "fascists" on a par with the Croatian Ustaša and the German and Italian occupiers they at times collaborated with. Alternative histories of "resistance" were instead nurtured outside Yugoslavia, largely by embittered émigré communities. In Trieste, the Istrian exile community similarly ruminated obsessively on its experience and on an alternative, nationalist-anticommunist tradition little acknowledged in Italy or instead conflated in the public imagination with that of Mussolini's final republic at Salò.

In both Italy and Yugoslavia, major shifts in the balance of power (post-1945, as well as post-1990) were accompanied by reconfigurations of "history," with some aspects emphasized and others submerged. For the case of Istria, both domestic political exigencies and external strategic interests resulted in the Italian and Yugoslav states' "silencing" the story of violence and refugee flows from Istria during and after the Second World War. In Titoist Yugoslavia, for example, the fact that Istria was largely emptied of its population put into doubt its claims to being a socialist paradise. If the socialist experiment in Yugoslavia was so wonderful, why would so many people abandon their homes and properties for an uncertain future in Italy? The claim (later seconded by Tito's former collaborator and subsequent critic, Milovan Djilas) that the regime had purposefully targeted ethnic Italians in Istria further exposed the Yugoslav leadership to the charges of nationalist imperialism, used by Stalin to justify the Yugoslav Communist Party's expulsion from the Cominform in 1948. The divisions and conflict in Istria also provided yet another example—like the wartime massacres perpetrated by Croat Ustaša and Serbian Četniks against their enemies—of civil strife in Yugoslavia during the war, an inconvenient history that the Titoist slogan "Brotherhood and Unity" papered over.

How did the Yugoslav leadership counter these charges and explain—or explain away—the exodus? The answer given was that those who had fled were fascists, whereas a minority of uncompromised Italians remained. In 1953 Edvard Kardelj argued that Italians who had settled in Istria during the fascist period had naturally returned to Italy after the end of Italian rule there with no pressure from the Yugoslav regime but rather as a natural process of "decolonization." Thus denying the existence of a sizable autochthonous Italian-speaking population dating from the Roman and Venetian periods, Kardelj noted that there remained "only approximately 20,000 Italians in the Yugoslav portion of Venezia Giulia. Those are mostly decent citizens and working people whom nobody in Yugoslavia wishes to drive away from their homes nor deprive of their national rights or complete equality with all other citizens of Yugoslavia" (Kardelj 1953, 14).

Yugoslav literature glorifying the partisan struggle during the Second World War detailed the actions of those Italians from Istria who had participated in the Resistance (Benussi 1951; Ehrenburg 1944; Kumar n.d.; Unione degli Italiani 1945), thereby implicitly linking all other Italians who left Istria with the tainted fascist regime. Within this logic, the exiles' flight implicitly evidenced their illegitimacy in both ethnic (that is, not autochthonous to Istria) and political-ideological terms. After the settlement of the Italo-Yugoslav dispute in 1954, the story of the exodus remained a tabooed topic in Yugoslav public discourse. Only in 1972 did Tito even acknowledge, in a speech given in Montenegro, that some three hundred thousand Istrians had left the peninsula after the war. Like other troubling tales of ethnic and ideological conflict, these alternative histories of exodus were transmitted through family memories, oral accounts, and contact with historiographical circuits outside Yugoslavia.

The possibilities in Italy for public discourse about the exodus thus differed sharply from those available in Istria. In Italy one could talk about the exodus as much as one liked, but outside Trieste one found little audience for such a discussion. In contrast to Yugoslavia, then, the problem was more of the *reception* than the production of histories, although historical production admittedly remained confined to a local-regional circuit and a broader but suspect right-wing historiographical tradition that spoke of the civil war that had divided northern Italy between 1943 and 1945. Just as the Istrian question did not dovetail with Yugoslav accounts glorifying World War II as a war of resistance against foreign occupiers, it also did not fit with a popular narrative about Italy's "self-redemption" from fascism by means of the Resistance or with the Left's glorification of the antifascist struggle fought by communists. A series of political shifts in the 1980s and 1990s, however, provided the opportunity to reconsider the Istrian experience.

Reopening the Istrian Case

From 1954 until the end of the Cold War, the exodus and its victims remained largely forgotten outside the region of Venezia Giulia; if acknowledged at all, the esuli were remembered merely as "fascists" forced to flee Istria once it passed to Yugoslavia. This blanket labeling of Istrians as fascists reflects the fact that even today Italians on the whole have not fully come to terms with fascism as a system within which most people proved (to varying degrees) complicit (see Passerini 1979). It proved much easier to treat fascism as an anomalous parenthesis in the narrative of post-Risorgimental history—as did the idealist philosopher Benedetto Croce (1963)—and thereby attribute the guilt for that aberration to others, singling out political leaders or groups such as the Istrians. Istrian Italian exiles repeatedly complain, "Italy lost the war but *we* paid the price," a price understood as both material and spiritual. Forgotten by the madrepatria toward which they had looked for protection, exile groups thus saw in the recent regime changes in Italy and former Yugoslavia the opportunity to reposition their histories of the exodus.

From 1992 onward, the collapse of the postwar Christian Democrat political machine in the wake of the political corruption scandals known as *Tangentopoli*—part of what some analysts have deemed a "political earthquake" (Gundle and Parker 1996, 1)—provided one such opportunity. In broad terms, "the end of the Cold War in Europe undermined the anti-communist cleavage around which much of the political system had been organised, and caused various irregularities and forms of gross maladministration to be exposed to empirical scrutiny and political sanction on the part of an electorate that had long seemed impervious to them" (ibid., 2). Specifically, political changes in Italy reflected the redefinition of U.S. and NATO interests in Italy, whereas for the previous forty-five years the Christian Democrats had been perceived as the bulwark against victory by the Italian Communist Party.[2] With the fear of the communist threat removed, many in the Italian electorate apparently no longer felt obliged "to hold [their] noses and vote for the DC," as the journalist Indro Montanelli had famously quipped (in Gundle and Parker 1996, 7).

The expected victory of the Left did not occur, however, in part because its internal scission (the PCI bifurcating into the more moderate Partito Democratico Sociale [PDS] and the hardline Rifondazione) absorbed its political energies. In contrast to the new Right composed of Berlusconi's Forza Italia party, Umberto Bossi's Lega Nord (separatist Northern League) and Gianfranco Fini's Alleanza Nazionale (AN, formerly the Movimento Sociale Italiano), "the Left seemed old, static, defensive and short of ideas" (Ginsborg 1996, 35). The 1994 electoral victory by this right-wing coalition brought to national power for the first time the formerly neofascist party AN-MSI. Fini had transformed the neofascist party, to some extent distancing it from its Mussolinian heritage and positioning the AN as a respectable "reformed, post-fascist, European movement" (Fini in Ruzza and Schmidtke 1996, 152) at the same time that he "subtly questioned the suitability of old Resistance values from the 1940s for the Italy of the 1990s" (ibid., 152). In addition, Fini sought to demarcate the fascism of Mussolini's regime from a more generalized fascist movement. This signaled, then, a discourse shift within Italian politics and society; the former taboo against praising *any* aspects fascism removed, President of the Parliament Irene Pivetti declared that fascism had brought positive changes to Italy, old-guard fascist Mirka Tremaglia became president of the Foreign Commission, and AN supporters began to take up the exiles' cause in demanding compensation for the Istrians' lost properties.

The dismemberment of the Yugoslav state in 1991 also provided a legal and political pretext for the Italian exile associations and their political allies to present claims to their lost lands, given that the Titoist state whose representatives signed the 1975 Treaty of Osimo had ceased to exist. Exile associations currently seek to reposition their histories, as well as claims to property restitution and/or compensation, for a transnational audience. The principal exile associations in Trieste have all worked to make this "forgotten history" known.

The Death of Tito and the Crisis of the Yugoslav Past

The Resistance served as a powerful source of postwar legitimacy and papered over the reality of fratricidal warfare in Yugoslavia, as well as Italy. In contrast to Yugoslavia, however, the antifascist struggle did not become widely recognized as the Italian First Republic's foundation myth until the 1960s and 1970s (Crainz 1999; Giampaolo Valdevit, personal communication). The ideological divisions of the Yugoslav civil war during World War II were further complicated and intensified by ethnic and religious differences generally absent in the Italian case. In Tito's Yugoslavia, the process of mourning the losses of the Second World War proved highly selective and orchestrated by the regime. In spite of the image of an open or tolerant socialism, the limits for criticism and historical debate in Yugoslavia proved much more restrictive than in the neighboring democratic state of Italy. "It was obvious that, in the years immediately following the end of the war and the advent of Communism, historiography in Yugoslavia would be made to serve the revolution and the construction of socialism. History was then made to begin when the Communist Party went over to the resistance in 1941" (Pavlowitch 1988, 129).

The effects of Marxist orthodoxy (specifically *Yugoslav* Marxism, after the 1948 split with Stalin) on historiography proved uneven, however, as scholars of the Byzantine, medieval, and Ottoman periods did not feel constrained in their studies to make major concessions to Marxist schemes of history. Such areas of history proved relatively uncontroversial, in contrast to the vexed interwar period (the "First Yugoslavia") and the Second World War. Predictably, in the 1950s historians from different republics collaborated on a massive two-volume history of the Yugoslav peoples; due to disagreements over how to understand and represent the rise of various national movements, the history concluded at the early modern period (Vodopivec 1996a, 131).

The 1960s and 1970s saw the first glimpses of a more critical historiography exploring the modern period, with an intensification of historical production about the "People's Liberation War" in tandem with a critique of the "'sclerosis' of the official historiography of the Second World War" (Pavlowitch 1988, 132). The ultimately "nervous and inconclusive nature of historical polemics in the early 1970s," however, reflected an unsettling political tug-of-war between centrists and decentralizing reformers (Banac 1992, 1087). After the open expression of nationalist sentiments (especially in Croatia) during the years 1968–71, the party sought to reassert control over the teaching of history in schools and to recentralize key political decision-making processes (Vodopivec 1996a, 131).

In his useful analysis of historical revisionism in post-Tito Yugoslavia, Ivo Banac identifies a milestone in the 1979 congress of historians of Yugoslav unification at which Momčilo Zečević and others delivered a radical challenge to a dominant institutional Yugoslav historiography "still bound by the ideology of the Titoist party-state" (Banac 1992, 1085). The official historiographical line that Zečević took exception to had been laid down in Tito's 1948 address to the Fifth Congress of the Communist Party of Yugoslavia. Tito depicted the First Yugoslavia as a product of bourgeois, Great Serbian hegemony and the royal dictatorship of King Alexander after 1929 as a "monarcho-fascist dictatorship" (in ibid.). Within this narrative, the Četnik leader Mihailović figured (in Tito's words) as "the last remnant of armed power of the old, rotten, bourgeois order, [which] in no case wanted to struggle against the occupiers but, at all costs, wanted to safeguard the old bourgeois social order under the occupation" (ibid., 1085–86). Tito's condemnation of the Četniks was matched by an excoriation of the Croatian Ustaša. The notorious concentration camp of Jasenovac run by the Ustaša became a national monument—indeed, "a metonym for the entire Ustaša campaign to eliminate the Serbs from Croatia" (Hayden 1994, 177)—and the figure of six hundred thousand Serbs killed there was enshrined in official statements.

The assault launched by Zečević on these sacred narratives of Titoism was neither novel nor isolated, as Tito's death a year later demonstrated. This prompted what Banac describes as an "outpouring" of revisionist histories, most of them originating in Serbia. (For the different trajectory of Slovene historiography, consult Verginella 1999 and Vodopivec 1996a, 1996b.) This revisionist flood reflected Serbian insecurity in the face of growing demands for autonomy by ethnic Albanians in Kosovo (the "Albanian specter," one that historians helped construct [Marjanović 1996, 291]), as well as the broader uncertainties created by Tito's death and the winding down of the Cold War, which stripped Yugoslavia of its privileged position between East and West (see Woodward 1995). At the same time, however, this revisionism also gave expression to an interest in the Second World War, interest that had increased during Tito's final years. Quite simply, "People wanted to find out what had been kept hidden. They wanted to grasp the extraordinary complexity of a complex period. They wanted to know what had happened in those years that had given birth to the Communist regime. They wanted to learn about themselves" (Pavlowitch 1988, 132).

The 1981 publication of *New Contributions to the Biography of Josip Broz Tito* responded to this curiosity and signaled the definitive close of the era of Titoist historiography. Written by Vladimir Dedijer, the Yugoslav leader's former wartime comrade and official biographer, this volume painted a highly unflattering portrait of Tito. A hodgepodge of testimonies, rumors, and archival work, the book described the traditional history of the liberation struggle as largely mythic and deliberately falsified or "doctored." Banac credits this controversial and widely read account as having "legitimated sensationalist debunking and diminished genuine scholarship" (1992, 1094). In its wake, came Branko Petranović's 1983 *Revolution and Counterrevolution in Yugoslavia, 1941–1945,* a reappraisal of the Četniks as both committed antifascists and anticommunists; formerly the official historian of the Tito regime, Petranović possessed a reputation as one of the best scholars of contemporary Yugoslavia. His ideological volte-face played a major role in the "decapitation" of Titoist historiography (Marjanović 1996, 287). The following year, Veselin Djuretić's *The Allies and the Yugoslav Wartime Drama* reevaluated both the Četnik and partisan movements, part of the process of rendering the once-vilified Četniks nationalist heroes and martyrs. This period also witnessed the publication in the United States of Kosta Čavoskí and Vojislav Koštunića's *Social Movements and Political Systems in Yugoslavia, 1944–1949*, banned in Yugoslavia for its account of the Communist Party's ruthless elimination of any political opposition at war's end.

This story of the war's forgotten "losers" and the communist regime's brutality in liquidating its rivals quickly became a topic of newspaper and magazine articles, books, novels, and plays. In the memoir *Wartime* (published outside Yugoslavia in 1977), Milovan Djilas had already described the massive executions that accompanied partisan victory. "These killings were sheer frenzy. How many victims were there? I believe that no one knows exactly, or will ever know" (1977, 447). Those executed included Croatian, Slovene, and Serbian soldiers who, fleeing the partisan advance, had sought protection from the British in Austria. In his 1986 study of these massacres, historian Nikolai Tolstoy charged Sir Harold Macmillan with having knowingly turned these military personnel (as well as the civilians encamped with them) over to Tito's partisans. Placed on trains the British claimed were destined for Italy, these "refugees" found themselves returned to Yugoslavia and as many as thirty thousand of them executed in mass liquidations like that at Kocevje and Bleiburg. Although Slovene historians—widely accused of having been the handmaidens of the communist regime (Verginella 1999; Vodopivec 1996b)—were relatively slow to take up this topic of the collaborationist *Domobranci* (home guard), articles in popular journals and newspapers praised as "national heroes" those collaborators executed by Tito (ibid., 268).[3]

In addition to the deaths of domobranci, the "cleanup" of Četnik units resulted in perhaps as many as one hundred thousand further deaths in 1945–46 and led to the capture, show trial, and execution of their leader Draža Mihailović (Lampe 1996, 224; on postwar retributions, also see Tomasevich 1969, 111–14). Not all enemies of the partisans and Yugoslav socialism were physically liquidated, however; rather they found themselves imprisoned or interned in concentration camps. The 1948 split with the Soviet Union led to the further arrest of thousands of *ibeovci*, or "Cominformists," that is, those siding (or accused of doing so) with Stalin against Tito. Banac estimates that up to one-fifth of the Yugoslav party membership supported Stalin over Tito (Banac 1988, x). Many of these ibeovci, secretly arrested and tried, ended up at Goli Otok, the "Marble" or "Naked" Isle in the Adriatic. Here, prisoners underwent a horrific political "reeducation" process, with release conditional on complete silence about this experience. Goli Otok thus remained an open and shameful secret during much of the Yugoslav period, a strategic silence that underlined the regime's power. "Their citizens must know there are secrets so terrible they must be kept secret, even while these states make it publicly known that secrets exist—a situation that the states hope will create precisely the climate of fear and paralysis in the citizenry they desire" (Schirmer 1994, 191).

After Tito's death, a body of "camp literature" sought to break the regime's hold by baring the secrets of Goli Otok and demystifying the Stalinist punishments meted out there. Branko Hoffman's novel *Night Till Dawn* came out in 1981, and testimonies like that of the well-known Macedonian poet Venko Markovski detailed the treatment of prisoners on Goli Otok and the attempts to physically and mentally demoralize them. Survivors described the moment of arrival, for instance, at which naked prisoners had to "run the gauntlet" through a human tunnel formed by the other inmates, who beat and cursed the newcomers. This was intended to break any potential solidarity that might form among the prisoners, isolating them psychologically. Subjected to extreme heat in the summer and terrible cold brought by the wind known as the *bura* in the winter, prisoners also had to undertake senseless tasks such as threading sand through a needle. As Markovski writes, such jobs were expressly devised to wear the inmates down, "[t]o fracture the granite of our convictions. To take from us the principal thing that differentiates a man from a beast" (1984, 62).

The testimony Giacomo Scotti offered in his 1991 *Goli Otok* confirms the picture already well established by Markovski and others imprisoned on the Marble Isle while illuminating the still little-known drama of Yugoslavia's Italians after the Cominform expulsion. Scotti, like many of the Italians who finished at Goli Otok, had come in a "counterexodus" to Fiume from the Italian peninsula, motivated by a belief in the socialist utopia heralded by Tito's regime. Typically loyal to the internationalist line of the Italian Communist Party, these Italian communists soon came under the scrutiny of the Yugoslav secret police (OZNA and later UDBA) as the dispute between Tito and Stalin emerged.

Scotti contends that the Cominform split provided the Yugoslavs with a handy pretext for "cleansing" the leadership of the Italian minority of any suspect elements while it encouraged even more autochthonous Italians to emigrate from Yugoslavia. Interviews I conducted with descendants of such Italians who ended up on Goli Otok describe both the climate of fear these events created (especially for the years 1948–52) and the shamed silence that even family members of victims maintained. Relatives of the accused typically lost good housing privileges and jobs. One woman from Rovigno whose mother had been stigmatized and forced to clean the streets as a result of her husband's imprisonment stated her regret that she had never asked her father and brother (both sent to Goli Otok) about their experiences. After their release, such a topic remained taboo within the family, mirroring the overall silence surrounding this phenomenon. Emir Kusturica's film *When Father Was Away on Business* captures the ways in which such silences operated within families. The story of a high-ranking party official imprisoned during the Cominformist period, the events are seen through the eyes of his children, who are merely told that "Father is away on business." Like the exodus of Italians from Istria—as well as the flight at war's end of other minorities, notably ethnic Germans (Schechtman 1962, 271–74) and Hungarians—the fate of Cominformists remained a public secret on which few dared to remark until Tito's death.

Ironically, in a 1987 review of the Yugoslav camp literature shattering the long silence about Goli Otok, Oskar Gruenwald interpreted the historical revisionist trend toward "de-Titoization" as a positive sign lending support to the thesis that "[j]ust as Yugoslavia was the first Communist party state to break away from the Soviet Empire, it may also be the first totalitarian dictatorship to metamorphose into a pluralistic, democratic, multiparty socialist system" (1987, 528). Tragically, the result has been the opposite. Written four years before the onset of the wars in Slovenia and Croatia, Gruenwald's piece nevertheless underscores the manner in which during the early post-Tito era Yugoslavia's internationally recognized "dissidents" played important roles in propagating divisive nationalisms. Gruenwald mentions the novelist (and well-known Serbian nationalist) Dobrica Ćosić as voicing the "first public demand for civil disobedience" (ibid., 527) and mentions that one of the chairmen of the Democracy International Committee to Aid Democratic Dissidents in Yugoslavia (CADDY) was Franjo Tudjman, the first president of independent Croatia.

Tudjman, a former partisan general and a historian, became one of Yugoslavia's more prominent dissidents for his controversial revisionist studies of Serbian victims at the Ustaša concentration camp of Jasenovac. In the 1960s, Tudjman claimed that the official figure of 600,000 victims represented a gross exaggeration, given that he had arrived at a total net direct loss of 750,000 Serbs for the entire war. Tudjman argued that approximately 60,000 Serbs had perished at Jasenovac. "Like many Croats, Tudjman believed that these large figures of *Ustashi* war victims were part of a so-called 'black legend' invented to bring the whole Croat nation into disrepute. . . . Tudjman was one of the first to be imprisoned in 1971 when the Croat 'Spring movement' was crushed by President Tito" (Pasic 1989, 70). Arrested again in 1981, Tudjman was accused of releasing "state secrets" through the public disclosure of a 1964 census that he had copied at the Zagreb Statistics Office.

At the same time that Tudjman's cause was being taken up outside Yugoslavia, Yugoslav newspapers such as *Politika* and *NIN* disclosed former state secrets about the location of mass graves in Gradina, Bosnia. Sealed over by the Titoist government and their existence denied for decades, these ossuaries contained the bodies of Serbs massacred by Ustaša during World War II. Such disclosures prompted, on the one hand, further debate over the numbers of victims on all sides,[4] and on the other, exhumations and ritual displays of the bones of massacre victims. In Serbia and Bosnia, the disinterred bodies of victims of Ustaša massacres received elaborate reburials in televised ceremonies; this stirred memories of Ustaša genocide against Serbs at the same time that Tudjman and other Croatian nationalists revived state symbols of the Pavelić regime, including the flag and currency (Denich 1994, 382). In Croatia and Slovenia, similar "un-burials" and ceremonies recalled victims of massacres, like those at Kocevje Rog, carried out at war's end by the victorious partisans. "The result of this new accounting of death and transfiguration of the dead has been to produce a propaganda war of competing nationalist histories of violence and injustice," suggests Robert Hayden (1994, 173). Hayden thus sees a "verbal" civil war as having preceded the actual conflict that broke out in former Yugoslavia. Denich (1994) similarly posits a "symbolic revival of genocide" prior to the actual instances of genocidal policy in the wars in Croatia and Bosnia.

In the Yugoslav case, revisionist historiography thus sanctioned "new totalizing histories" (Hayden 1994, 181) that became a powerful tool in the hands of politicians seeking to sharpen ethno-national differences and to ultimately legitimate civil war. The debate over formerly repressed histories of the Second World War increasingly came to center on the deadly Ustaša-Četnik rivalry and the revival of those movements' symbols by contemporary Croatian and Serbian nationalists. Although the story of the Istrian exodus no longer proved taboo, in the increasingly polarized atmosphere of Yugoslav politics it nonetheless remained overshadowed by these more gruesome accounts.

The "revival" of the past in Istria and the opening of formerly tabooed topics there has differed from the general tenor of revisionist history elsewhere in former Yugoslavia. The tale of the exodus has instead informed the attempts of the Istrian regionalist movement to *reinforce,* rather than destroy, multiethnic cohabitation in Istria. Where nationalists in former Yugoslavia readily instrumentalized massacre accounts in service to martyrological complexes justifying "self-defense," Istrian regionalists (comprising both reformed communists and political newcomers) instead saw voicing the traumatic memory of the exodus as an exercise that would *strengthen* the delicate multiethnic, cultural, and linguistic fabric of Istria. The regionalists thus positioned themselves as offering an alternative political model, drawing different lessons from the past than elsewhere in former Yugoslavia. The regionalists also offered alternative historical interpretations to those put forth by most of the exile associations in nearby Trieste.

For the most part, the regionalists' initial attempts to reach out to the "Istrian diaspora" in Italy and beyond met with suspicion, particularly in Trieste, where demands to remember the foibe, the pits in which Yugoslav partisans executed locals in 1943 and 1945, resembled nationalist rhetoric about massacre sites in Yugoslavia more than they did the Istrian call for ethnic cohabitation and tolerance. The stridency of nationalists in Trieste, reinforced by the 1994 election of the Forza Italiana-Alleanza Nazionale (neofascist) coalition, led some alarmed observers in the early 1990s to view Italy as succumbing to neofascism (Bocca 1995, 5; Magri 1995). Others feared that the rise of the separatist movement known as the Lega Nord (Northern League) would fracture Italy into a wealthy north and an undeveloped south, as had happened in neighboring Yugoslavia.

At the time of writing, such dire predictions have not come to pass. Instead, in the spring of 1996 a Left-Center government under Romano Prodi (and in its 1998 and 2000 incarnations) replaced the Center-Right Berlusconi government (the Berlusconi coalition, in turn, again came to power in April 2001). An important shift accompanied this transition in government, as the Italian Left began to own up to its errors and to acknowledge the "victims of communism," including the Istrian exiles. Central to contemporary and ongoing debates in Italy about the Second World War is a reconsideration of the "excesses" or "crimes" (depending on one's viewpoint) of communist partisans hand in hand with a reappraisal of fascism and, in particular, the Republic of Salò established by Mussolini and the Germans in 1943.

Italian Fascism and World War II Reconsidered

A critical historiographical reappraisal of fascism and the Second World War received considerable impetus in the 1970s from the monumental work of historian Renzo De Felice (Cotta 1977, 11), author of a multivolume biography of Mussolini and numerous books on fascism and accused by some of being an apologist for the regime. A more widespread public reexamination of Italy's fascist past, however, began only in the late 1980s (although the intervening years had witnessed a lively debate over the fascist legacy). The seemingly endless series of corruption scandals and the brutal murders of two leading anti-Mafia judges (Giovanni Falcone and his colleague Paolo Borselino) led some Italians to nostalgically recall fascism as a time of relative order and stability. (The old line "Under Mussolini, the trains ran on time" was once again trotted out, and only half in jest.) The open greed that had ruled politics in the 1980s and the absence of a civic sense appeared symptomatic of a spiritual malaise. Clientelism and loyalty to restricted social networks were widely seen as prevailing over any sense of duty and obligation to the Italian nation-state. Some observers explicitly linked the defects of contemporary Italian political culture to the absence of a healthy patriotism, the catastrophe of the Second World War having led to the discrediting of all forms of nationalism (see Guarino 1989, 10; Galli della Loggia 1996).

Although much of the recent public discussion in Italy about the Second World War has focused, as it did in Yugoslavia, on those whose experience had previously been excluded from official histories, the overall result has tended toward creating more-inclusive narratives embracing the diverse experiences of Italians in the war. Once the Left came to power in 1996, figures such as Massimo D'Alema of the Partito Democratico della Sinistra (heir to the former Communist Party) publicly urged a reconsideration of the errors made by the communist leadership and its supporters. D'Alema and others were responding to a common (if not wholly accurate) criticism that the communists had exerted a quasi monopoly on the memory of the Resistance (Bocca 1996b). Cynics read these reconciliatory moves as motivated by the desire of leftist politicians to break the Right's traditional "monopoly" on nationalist mobilization and thereby shore up a national unity threatened by the secessionist designs of the Northern League. Regardless of the motivations, these moves to overcome the "divided memory" (Rusconi 1995) of the war implicitly linked the political Left and Right in the late 1990s, uniting them against the threat of the Northern League.

For much of the postwar period, however, the memory of the war divided the Left from the Right at the same time that it created competition for its usage between the Christian Democrats and the Italian Communist Party. The Resistance provided the Left specifically and the democratic Italian Republic more generally with key (if competing) legitimating myths (Cotta 1977; Gobbi 1992). As Kertzer notes,

> In the universe of PCI symbolism, the Resistance stood above all else as the source of legitimation of both the party's past and its present. . . . From the perspective of the PCI, this Resistance-focused history not only had the virtue of assigning the party a heroic role but, perhaps as important, established its patriotic credentials. Indeed, in the years following the war no symbol of nationalism was more powerful than the Resistance, and no patriotic credential was more valuable than having been a partisan. (1996, 49, 114)

The Resistance also inspired an enormous historiography, disproportionate to its actual military weight though not its symbolic impact, and led to the establishment of a network of regional institutes for the history of the Italian liberation. As in the First World War, the Resistance (as well as the earlier struggle of antifascists exiled or interned under the fascist regime) spawned a pantheon of martyrs.[5] Sites where partisans had died became hallowed ground, memorialized by both PCI and DC supporters (ibid., 25). The deaths of these heroes confirmed their courageous lives, as one ex-partisan recognized when he suggested that the account of one comrade's end seemed the stuff of legend.

> After three hours [sic] interrogation, during which the Fascists had yanked at his wounds to torture him, Giancarlo was carried outside, and leaned against the wall in front of the barracks. While the black-uniformed brigade pointed their guns, Giancarlo shouted 'Long live the partisans! Comrades, move forward!' These seem like sentences reconstructed from legend. But this was how Giancarlo had actually died. (Pesce 1972, 268)

The Resistance thus became a story of the nation's redemption, of the people (il popolo) finding the soul they appeared to have lost during the long, dark night of fascism (Ben-Ghiat 1999, 87). The defeat of the Nazi occupier in the North became a tale of the defeat of the masses' passivity and indifference to the policies of a corrupt fascist leadership. One author concludes,

The Italian resistance in World War II was a people's war. It began as a spontaneous rebellion against Nazi oppression in the days following Italy's unconditional surrender to the Allies on September 8, 1943. There was no great leader in the beginning, no organization to weld individuals into a fighting force. Yet people fought with unexpected fury. . . . It was a desperate, uneven attack on the German invader, but it was also a civil war, a final recognition that the real enemy, fascism, was within. (Wilhelm 1988, 1)

These fratricidal aspects of the "War of Liberation" became the subject of a wider discussion in the 1980s, as Italian politicians and mainstream historians began to question the standard received wisdom about the Resistance. Regarding the Julian March, antifascist historians such as Elio Apih had already begun to sharpen their analyses in the 1970s with a discussion of a "frontier fascism" whose particular violence provoked an extreme reaction in the postwar period; this nonetheless left in place an image of partisan violence as a "score settling," a kind of appendix to fascism (Valdevit 1997, 19). Only in the following decade would a more widespread critical reappraisal come about. Some scholars have rightly noted that the degree to which one standard line or myth of the Resistance operated, as well as the predominance of leftist historians in fashioning this myth, has been overstated in these recent debates. The tempering of the claims of the "Anti-Anti Fascist historians" (Bosworth 1999) and the recognition of a varied historiographical debate since 1945, however, does not contradict the fact that certain key myths or narratives about the Resistance did prevail at the more general level of public consciousness and ritual commemoration.

The prevalence of the term *Resistance* rather than *civil war*, for example, reflected one of the long-held truths that came into question in the 1980s.[6] The authors of *L'Italia della guerra civile* (Italy of the civil war [1983]), for example, attached a "warning" to their text, justifying their choice of the term *civil war* over the usual *Italy of the Resistance*. This civil war had several faces, according to Montanelli and Cervi: the conflict between the Allies and the Germans (both of them occupiers), that of the Kingdom of the South versus the Italian Social Republic (RSI), that of antifascists against fascists, and finally that waged by communist partisans against their democratic opposition (1983, 6). Despite a common antifascist front in the umbrella organization known as the Comitato di Liberazione Nazionale, a split had rapidly developed between the Communists and the Action Party (a democratic coalition); this mirrored the divided positions within the Allied camp on the support to be given these groups (see Lamb 1993, 202–54).

In regions such as the Julian March, where ideological loyalties at times mapped onto and at other times conflicted with ethno-national identifications, the picture of the Resistance became increasingly fractured. Some Italian communists supported their Slovene and Croat comrades and agreed that at war's end the region should become part of Yugoslavia, and some Italian antifascists associated with the CLN instead fought for a vision of an anticommunist patria. Slovene historian Nevenka Troha (1997) has described the Slovene resistance (OF) and the CLN di Trieste e dell'Istria as rivals for the annexation of the Julian March rather than partners in the antifascist fight. Simultaneously, collaborators with the fascists and Nazis after 1943 included not only Italians but also Serbs, Slovenes, and Croats, the Slavs' anti-Italianism at times encouraged by the German institution of a divide-and-conquer policy in the reconstituted Adriatic Littoral, or *Küstenland*. The territorial dispute between Italy and Yugoslavia at war's end would both intensify and further complicate these divisions, particularly those between CLN and communist supporters in the Julian March.

The myth of the Resistance as a popular rebellion uneasily and inadequately accommodated these divergences within the antifascist camp, even as it later gave rise to a leftist notion of the Resistance as a revolution "betrayed" by the postwar republic. Where Mussolini's propagandists had proclaimed fascism the "culmination" or fulfillment of the Risorgimento, the partisans condemned it as the "anti-Risorgimento" and instead heralded the Resistance movement as a second Risorgimento in the Garibaldian tradition of direct, popular action (Pintor 1970, 426). On April 25, a series of insurrections against the Germans began in the major cities of the North, enabling Italians to claim they had liberated themselves.

These insurrections were accompanied by executions of "fascist" traitors, including Mussolini and his mistress, Claretta Petacci. Richard Lamb notes, "The partisans set up *ad hoc* tribunals to try Fascists, and great numbers were summarily executed; some estimates are as high as 30,000, and may be correct" (1993, 236). This settling of scores extended to nonfascists and in some cases included members of rival resistance groups, particularly those associated with the Christian Democrats and the church. The PCI's official line on the Resistance omitted any mention of this internecine strife, instead stressing the cooperation of communist partisans with other resistance forces and the predominance and decisive role of the communists (Kertzer 1996, 49; also Bosworth 1999, 196).

As the next chapter will take up at length for the foibe, violent score-settling at war's end helped make for a problematic and shameful memory whose selective and fragmented nature was mirrored by the shifting and subterranean locales that were the physical sites of many of these liquidations. As Triestine writer Paolo Rumiz notes, the symbolic borders between Left and Right and their divided memories of the war created "an infernal topography of incommunicability" (Rumiz 1998c), one that found literal expression in the grisly cartography of death at the conclusion of the war. Some accounts recalled sites where, "in April–May of '45, the cadavers of 'fascists' slaughtered in the valleys and thrown in the rivers ran aground, forming a type of bank or floating island that gave off a nauseating stench for hundreds of meters" (Mazzantini 1995, 170).

These grisly accounts of clogged rivers of corpses find parallels across the border in Yugoslavia, where postwar massacres in Slovenia led peasants to complain, "[U]nderground rivers were casting up bodies . . . and piles of corpses were heaving up as they rotted in shallow mass graves, so that the very earth seemed to breathe" (Djilas in Hayden 1994, 174). Though such testimonies— what Hayden deems "almost the stuff of epic poetry" (1994, 174)—were not officially tabooed in Italy, in contrast to Yugoslavia, they became the subject of national attention in Italy only in the late 1980s and early 1990s. A 1990 article in the magazine *Famiglia Cristiana* (Christian family) (Pagnotti 1990), for example, detailed crimes committed by Italian partisans and claimed that between 1,200 and 1,500 persons disappeared and/or were killed in mass graves in Reggiano alone, part of an area that includes the cities of Bologna, Modena, and Reggio Emiliana and that has come to be known in the last decade as the "triangle of death" (Pagnotti 1990; Pisanò and Pisanò 1998).

Ironically, the existence of this grisly cartography received publicity in part due to the efforts of Otello Montanari, a local PCI leader and former partisan who organized a meeting examining such relatively little known events of the immediate postwar experience. Kertzer (1996, 134–36) has vividly described the confrontation between PCI and MSI (neofascist) supporters provoked by this conference. Members of the partisans' association maintained a vigil at the monument to the Resistance in the central square while *missini* sang fascist songs and gave the Roman salute. In that year, neofascist deputies protested the existence of a similar "triangle of death" around Gorizia (contested by Yugoslavia and Italy after World War II), blaming members of the Italian Communist Party for having carried out much of this postwar violence. Both the demonstrations in Reggio Emilia and the political spat in Gorizia underline the way in which these ritual confrontations with the "subterranean" past initially unfolded largely within the terms associated with the political divisions and narratives (red versus black, PCI versus MSI) that had dominated Italy for forty-five years. Within a few years, however, the Italian Communist and Neo-Fascist Parties (like the Yugoslav state) had ceased to formally exist. Their political heirs today inhabit a reconfigured landscape of politics and memory.

With the Italian state's growing crisis of legitimation in the early 1990s, for instance, the voicing of such resentment against partisan tactics and of the historiographical tradition glorifying them began to emerge in the popular press, as well as among historians. In June 1994 I attended a conference held in the Italian town of Arezzo and entitled "In Memory: Revisiting Nazi Atrocities in Post–Cold War Europe," which reflected the growing dissension over the memory of the occupation. As the conference co-organizer Leonardo Paggi noted, "Many things have happened in Italy and Europe since we started work on this conference. . . . The task which we took as our starting point—to establish a shared memory of Nazism in the completely new cultural and political conditions created by the fall of the Berlin Wall—seems all the more important today, but at the same time considerably more arduous" (Paggi 1994, 1; see also Paggi 1997).

Though the conference featured academic specialists discussing the war's memory in diverse European contexts, it also gave space to area locals offering testimonies about a brutal Nazi massacre that took place in the nearby village of Civitella della Chiana. The final night of the conference concluded with a ceremony in Civitella and a dinner offered by the commune. In the course of the conference, an elderly woman from Civitella recounted the events of June 1944, when Nazis came and killed the entire adult male population (about 150 people) and burned the village in reprisal for a partisan action that had left two German soldiers dead. The woman recounting these tragic events expressed her bitterness toward not only the Nazis but also the partisans, who thoughtlessly engaged (as she saw it) in imprudent acts that placed local communities at risk. Caught between the Nazis and their partisan opponents, many such locals felt trapped between the proverbial rock and a hard place.

Given this, Paggi noted the divergence in Italy between the broader national "collective memory" about the Resistance and the "social memory" of events like those at Civitella. After the elderly survivor's emotional and angry account of the massacre at Civitella, a former partisan approached the microphone with tears in his eyes and insisted that he and his comrades had done what they thought was right in order to save the patria. He thus reaffirmed a standard narrative of the Resistance. Another affirmation occurred later that evening after dinner, when many of the scholars in attendance nostalgically sang partisan songs—from "Bella ciao" to the "Internazionale"—in various languages. This standard narrative continues to be heard and cherished in places such as the village of Stia-Valluccioles, which, like nearby Civitella, also suffered a vicious Nazi reprisal but where this instead "provoked a whole-hearted adhesion to the anti-Fascist values that were to be the cornerstones of the Italian Republic" (Paggi 1994, 5).

In contrast to Yugoslavia, then, the questioning or tempering of the myths of the Resistance in Italy has not led to a wholesale reaffirmation of fascism but rather has encouraged a more diversified and less romanticized view of the Resistance. It has simultaneously, however, prompted a renewed interest in the Republic of Salò (Repubblica Sociale Italiano), the fascist government in Northern Italy over which the Duce—rescued from his Italian prison in the Gran Sasso by German paratroopers—presided as little more than a figurehead.

Salò represented the last stand made by fascism in Italy after the regime's collapse and the army's capitulation in September 1943. Largely stripped of his power by the Germans and no longer needing to consolidate support, Mussolini appeared at Salò to seek a return to his radical anticlerical and antibourgeois roots, with the ideal of the warriors' brotherhood that had dominated the early fascist movement reappearing. The intransigents who surrounded Mussolini in his final days at Salò have typically been viewed as giving expression to the "radical" fascism of the early movement, as violent fanatics willing to engage in a fratricidal war. As Giordano Bruno Guerri contends in his preface to the diary (1982) of diplomat and RSI supporter Luigi Bolla, Italians' inability or unwillingness in the postwar period to confront the past led to this facile equation of Salò with cruel and fanatic fascists. Films in the 1960s and 1970s—perhaps most notoriously Pier Paolo Pasolini's *Salò*, which updated Sade's *Les 120 journées de Sodome*—frequently represented this political deviance in terms of a sexual perversion (Forgacs 1999; see also Ben-Ghiat 1999; Bosworth 1999).

Guerri urged Bolla to publish his diary in order to offer average Italians a glimpse of a personage utterly at odds with the stereotypical image of the violent and pathological "fascists" at Salò. More influential in sparking interest in Salò and empathy for its defenders, however, was the 1986 memoir of Carlo Mazzantini, an ordinary volunteer. Seeking to humanize the vilified *ragazzi di Salò* (boys of Salò), Mazzantini's *A cercar la bella morte* (In search of a glorious death) helped prompt a more widespread reappraisal of those adolescents who turned out to fight what was clearly a lost cause. Mazzantini's account shifts back and forth between his own narrative of the war—a bloody civil conflict in which volunteers were expected to kill other Italians and in which the local populations proved increasingly hostile and dangerous to the volunteers—and recollections of that period by his wartime companions and their relatives.

These recollections are marked by shame and silence, by alienation from one's family and from one's cocitizens. Upon his return home after the war, for example, the author's mother urges him, "Be silent, my son! For pity's sake, be silent!" and his schooltime chum advises him, "You've got to forget about it" (1992, 250, 252). Mazzantini notes the profound gulf separating him from that majority of Italians who welcomed the war's conclusion as a liberation. In spite of this onerous burden of memory, Mazzantini continues to defend his decision to answer the RSI's call for volunteers as born out of a desire to save the patria's honor. For "patriots" like Mazzantini, the armistice with the Anglo-Americans, the spectacle of the army's instantaneous collapse, and the ignominious flight of the king and the Badoglio government from Rome betrayed the Italian nation (see also Bolla 1982, 38; Guarino 1989).

As one of Mazzantini's brothers-in-arms declares, these young recruits consciously sacrificed themselves and thus made themselves victims: "For a lost cause—a cause we knew was lost from day one! . . . Why? Because accepting that defeat meant accepting everything which had led up to it: the hypocrisy, the lies, the cowardice! What did we have to do with all their shit? We weren't the least bit responsible for it" (1992, 164). In *I ballilla andarono a Salò: L'armata degli adolescenti che pagò il conto della storia* (The Balilla went to Salò: The army of adolescents who paid the bill of history), his exposition on the "dual" myths of Salò and of the Resistance, Mazzantini elaborates his view that most of these young boys were motivated by larger, more diffused notions of honor and patria than fanatical devotion to fascism.

Mazzantini argues that under the guise of carrying out justice in order to establish a new civil state after the war, thousands of people were arrested and killed under the pretext of having been fascists. Placing fascists like Mussolini on trial would have exposed the ambiguities of Italy's "cobelligerent" status, continues Mazzantini, thereby forcing the Italian people to examine their own culpabilities rather than merely displacing their guilt onto those select few punished as fascists.

Despite this critique of the Italian disavowal of responsibility for fascism's crimes, Mazzantini himself employs a similar logic by positing the absolute innocence of the lads, like himself, who fought at Salò. Mazzantini contends that the civil war in Northern Italy really began only when the partisans embarked on a campaign of sabotage and assassination. Whereas partisan attacks created a deep-rooted hatred among the volunteers and motivated their ferocity in carrying out reprisals, Mazzantini maintains that the communists viewed fascists as nonhuman and hence deserving of "ethnic cleansing" (1995, 174–75). It is interesting to note the use of the term "ethnic cleansing," drawn from the context of the contemporary conflict in former Yugoslavia, to explain "atrocities" committed by members of the same ethno-national group divided along political lines. Such a rhetorical strategy clearly works to portray the victimizer as victimized. In current debates over wartime events in Venezia Giulia, this theme of ethnic cleansing features prominently and operates to portray the exiles—like the "boys of Salò," widely condemned as fascists and their experience dismissed—as victims. Rather than recognize the complexities of complicity, both esuli accounts and Mazzantini's narrative emphasize ingenuity and idealism.

The reaction to Mazzantini's sympathetic portrayal of the adolescents who fought at Salò and his thoughts on their postwar demonization has proven varied. One response has been to endorse a traditional narrative of the Resistance. In the preface to an illustrated album celebrating the Italian Resistance, for instance, the editor scoffs, "Today, however, there are people who speak of the German 'presence' in Italy rather than occupation; and others, who say that the Resistance was a myth. Yes, a myth. With almost half a million victims. We aren't joking!" (Luraghi 1995, 27). The well-known journalist Giorgio Bocca has sarcastically written of the Resistance that, sooner or later, "[w]e'll say that it never was or that the communists invented it" (1996a, 9). Elsewhere, Bocca denounces the revisionism of both the Right and the Left, particularly the latter's desire to create consensus (1995; 1996b). In general, however, there has been renewed curiosity about (if not complete approbation of) Salò. Luciano Violante, formerly a member of the PCI and president of the Camera under the Prodi government, for example, urged the need to reconsider the "vanquished" of Salò. In March 1998 he also participated in a public forum with Gianfranco Fini, leader of the Alleanza Nazionale, on the question of the foibe (discussed in the next chapter).

A spate of publications further evidences renewed interest in the RSI.[7] Some earlier works on Salò have seen republication, including the 1969 *L'esercito di Salò nei rapporti riservati della Guardia nazionale repubblicana, 1943–1944,* by Giampaolo Pansa. In his preface to the expanded and retitled 1991 edition, Pansa notes that had he been old enough in 1943 to make such a choice, he would have become either a partisan or a *repubblicano.* Though finding it more probable that he would have joined the partisans, Pansa nonetheless admits that such a decision could have easily been swayed in another direction by the simple example of a friend or a relative. The only certain thing, argues Pansa, is that he would have chosen to take up arms rather than remain passive or hidden away *(imboscato),* as many young men did. Pansa thus implies that at the time the two paths leading, respectively, to Salò and the partisan cell did not necessarily appear so divergent and that many of those who chose to fight fascism's final battle did so, like the partisans, for "noble" (if ruined) principles.

The more sympathetic treatment now accorded the volunteers at Salò also offers an antidote to the image of Italians as passive and apathetic about both the regime and the war, as well as lacking in martial spirit. Interestingly, this view of the shallow support for fascism has underwritten a pervasive self-image: that of the "good Italian" *(il bravo italiano).* The "good Italian" contrasts with the "bad German" (or in Venezia Giulia, the "barbaric Slav"). Italians appear as good because, unlike the Germans, they never "really" supported the regime, and they subsequently freed themselves from fascism. Even as interest in Salò grows, this image of the bravo italiano remains deeply rooted in Italian popular culture.

Although some analysts trace this "myth of the good Italian" back to the nineteenth century (Bidussa 1994), the image comes to the fore in postwar evaluations of fascism. Not surprisingly, exile self-representations draw on this archetype, thereby constructing Italians in Istria as good and humane and rejecting the thesis that fascist brutality precipitated (and perhaps "justified") the events of the foibe and the exodus. Such a depiction inverts the description of Italians as fascists and, hence, "perpetrators." Hand in hand with the increasing interest in accountability for crimes during the Second World War, then, goes a tendency to depict oneself as among the victimized.

The distinction, forcefully articulated by the historian Renzo De Felice, between an essentially humane Italian fascism and anti-Semitic German national socialism is the pivot on which the myth of the bravo italiano resides. In De Felice's influential formulation, Italian fascism lacked a "racist tradition," and anti-Semitic policies came about belatedly and only as a result of the unequal alliance between Mussolini and Hitler. De Felice contends that (1) racism was "unknown" in Italy and an anti-Semitic tradition was lacking; (2) Italian Jews were well assimilated and numerically small; (3) with the exception of some individuals, Italian fascism was not anti-Semitic, and indeed the fascist ranks included Jews; (4) Mussolini's anti-Semitic turn in 1938 occurred for pragmatic political reasons, as well as colonial concerns in connection with Italy's new

African "empire"; (5) the racial legislation of 1938–39 had a different, more "civil" character than in Germany; (6) the majority of the Italian people disagreed with the racial laws; (7) until the Republic of Salò, the racial laws were interpreted liberally and enforced unevenly; and, finally, (8) the concerted enactment in Italy of anti-Semitic policies occurred only during the period of Salò and as a result of German domination (De Felice in Caracciolo 1986, 7–15).

That significant numbers of Italians defied the 1938 racial laws by sheltering and helping Jews confirms De Felice's description of the very different receptions in Germany and Italy of anti-Semitic measures. An estimated 85 percent of Italy's Jewish population survived the Holocaust, placing Italy, alongside Denmark, "at the top of the list of occupied nations for its percentage of Jewish survivors" (Zuccotti 1987, 272). Italian efforts to rescue Jews—efforts that extended beyond national borders—have rightly been recognized and lauded at the same time that they have reinforced a view of Italians as a humane and essentially *brava gente,* good people (Bosworth 1998, 3–5; Walston 1997, 182).[8]

The rescue of Yugoslav Jews by Italian soldiers has received particular attention as "something unique in the annals of the Holocaust," given the moral resolve displayed by numerous Italian high officials and officers in disobeying official orders (Shelah 1989, 205). Steinberg describes this as a "silent mutiny of the mighty and the well-connected" (1990, 58), a mutiny not to change leadership but to do what was morally correct. While emphasizing that the Italian fascist and German Nazi regimes had much in common, Steinberg nonetheless concludes: "On one point there can no longer be any doubt: in their attitudes to Jews the two Axis allies inhabited different moral universes" (ibid., 219). Similarly, a Zaratino exile whom I met on the "memory trip" to Dalmatia stressed that although Italians treated Slavs badly both before and during the war, the rescue of Jews in Dalmatia "told an important story about disobedience to orders" and thus revealed the different response of Italians and Germans to the ethical dilemma posed by the Final Solution.

Though attention to the historical particularities of Italian fascism brings out important differences with Nazism effaced by broad categorizations such as totalitarianism, the almost exclusive focus on Italians' lack of anti-Semitism glosses over the Italian interest in questions of race well before the axis pact with Germany. Admittedly, the Italian demographic campaigns launched with Benito Mussolini's 1927 Ascension Day Speech and elaborated over the course of the 1930s reflected a positive eugenics of pronatalism rather than the negative one of the Nazis, based on euthanasia and ultimately genocide. Nonetheless, a discourse of hygiene linked what Ferdinando Loffredo, a Catholic fundamentalist and prominent proponent of a racist totalitarianism, deemed "a politics of family and a politics of race" (1939, 29). Far from being a slavish imitation of German ideas and policies, this demographic discourse had deep roots in Roman Catholicism and the Italian social sciences. The Italian conquest of Ethiopia in 1935 also raised concerns over miscegenation and prompted laws forbidding intercourse (social and otherwise) between Italians and Africans; these racist policies coincided with the first official articulations of fascist anti-Semitism (Michaelis 1978, 114–15).

The emphasis on benign, tolerant Italians thus not only glosses over such homegrown discourses about race and population but also effaces the reality of fascist violence toward subject peoples in Africa and the Balkans (see Schieder 1995, 82–83; Walston 1997). The Italian military did not hesitate, for example, to use poison gas in an effort to quell resistance in Abyssinia (Del Boca 1969). Many of the brutal tactics employed in Ethiopia—including deportation and internment—had been tested in the 1920s and early 1930s in the campaign to subdue Cyrenaica, Libya; a few Italian scholars have gone so far as to label these policies "genocidal," though this judgment finds little trace in popular consciousness (Walston 1997, 173–74).

Fascist-era presentations of Africans, as well as Slavs, suggest that national and racial chauvinisms were not unique to the Nazis (see Carter 1997 and Pinkus 1995 on fascist images of "black bodies"). The renewal of debates about the exodus and the foibe have led some politicians and historians in Slovenia and Croatia to demand that Italians own up to the atrocities and brutalities committed during the fascist occupation of Yugoslavia. The attention paid to the "good deeds" of Italians in Yugoslavia—from the officers and soldiers who regarded the Ustaša with horror and tried to protect Jews and Serbs to fighters who, after the 1943 capitulation, joined the partisan Garibaldi Battalions—has served to reinforce the image of the good Italian. Yet some of the Italian officers singled out for praise in the rescue of Jews in Yugoslavia, notably Generals Mario Roatta and Mario Robotti (mentioned, for instance, by Steinberg [1990, 50–84, 122]), are remembered by Yugoslavs as having perpetrated genocidal acts toward Slovene and Croatian populations. As will be discussed in greater detail in the following chapter, those who suffered the negative effects of the Italian occupation and what some consider its "genocidal" policies demand that these episodes be accorded space in the Italian collective memory.

In response, exile figures such as Renzo de' Vidovich reject these claims about Italian war crimes in Yugoslavia, deeming them

> [a]bsolutely unfounded theses, given that [Yugoslav] terrorism, actuated systematically with infoibamenti, drownings and mass firing squads, was finalized with the denationalization of Istria, Fiume and Dalmatia. . . . It does not follow, instead, that the Italian forces ever determined, either by force or by pacific means, to transfer populations to the interior of Yugoslavia, and *it is universally recognized that Italian nationalism cannot be confused with the racism that is at the base of the ethnic cleansing of the time,* as well as what is today in course in the Balkans. (*Il Piccolo* 1996; my italics)

De' Vidovich's explicit invocation of the "universally recognized" notion of Italian nationalism as lacking a racial (and racist) base reminds us of the need to critically interrogate claims about an Italian tradition of tolerant, "cultural" nationalism (for additional details, refer to chapter 2). Although such distinctions usefully bring out differences between Italian nationalism(s), fascism, and Nazism, this portrayal of a benign Italian patriotism is itself a powerful ideological statement that has often been widely accepted at face value both in Italy and abroad. In the Istrian context, the image of the "good Italian" works to paper over a history of violence and chauvinism toward Slavs. The irredentist narratives previously examined, for example, reveal one way in which Italian accountability for such chauvinism is erased through the construction of Italians in Dalmatia and Istria as victims.

Even the popular and humorous image of Italian military incompetence and cowardice has worked to obfuscate the more brutal aspects of fascism and the Italian experience in the war. Enjoying popular success in Italy and abroad, the 1991 film *Mediterraneo* reflects a fairly widespread take on Italian "bellicosity." The motley crew of bumbling but ultimately lovable (and utterly harmless) Italians sent to subdue a small Greek island prove absolutely indifferent to warfare and instead concentrate on women, food, soccer, friendship, and poetry. Portrayed as victims of the fascist war machine, the Italians come to know and admire their Greek "subjects" (who, in fact, hold the Italians' fate in their hands). Within such a narrative, then, the Italian people appear equally exploited by the fascist regime as do those populations Italian soldiers must ostensibly fight against and conquer. That Italians in the North also endured Nazi German occupation after 1943, the occupier becoming the occupied, further underwrites a memory of victimhood that works in tandem with the myths of the Resistance. Although writing from a Dutch perspective, Ian Buruma's words could apply to the Italian experience. "It was comforting to know that a border divided us from a nation that personified evil. They were bad, so we must be good. To grow up after the war in a country that had suffered German occupation was to know that one was on the side of the angels" (1995, 4–5).

The status of "cobelligerent" awarded by the Allies in 1943 to the Italian state under General Badoglio captured Italy's ambiguous space between aggressor and ally, perpetrator and victim. Whereas the historiography of the postwar First Republic emphasized Italy's status in the war as simultaneous victim and ally, the recent revisitation of the Second World War in Italy suggests that some greater accommodation is being made for the ambiguity and ambivalence implied by the notion of cobelligerent.

Revisionism Refracted

Italians in Istria and Dalmatia ultimately paid a heavy price for the ambiguity implied by Italy's cobelligerency and the postwar emphasis on Italy's Allied role. A prominent response of the exile community in Trieste has been

to counter official historiographies with equally totalizing histories about genocidal victimization by Slavs. This move seems more akin to a nationalist revisionism across the borders in former Yugoslavia than to the tentative and open-
ended historical reevaluation characteristic of Italian politics in the 1990s. Exile
discourse intersects at various points with these broader currents of historical
evaluation while nonetheless remaining something apart, as the next chapter
demonstrates.

Although in some ways resembling revisionist trends in former Yugoslavia,
exile efforts to reposition their group histories also parallel the German debates
launched with the *Historikerstreit* (see Eley 1988). This label actually encompasses myriad positions, but one prominent tactic in the German debate has
been to relativize Nazism in light of other totalitarian (and genocidal) regimes
and, in particular, in light of the "red threat" posed by the Soviet Union. Communism, not Nazism, becomes the real enemy and villain. Some Istrian exile
groups' accounts similarly downplay fascist violence in contrast to that wrought
by Slavic nationalism and communism.

The handwritten manuscript *Il fascismo a Rovigno: Un giudizio a quasi mezzo
secolo dalla fine* (Fascism in Rovigno: A judgment almost half a century after its
end), penned by exile Mario Rossi in 1994 and on deposit at the Centro di
Ricerche Storiche di Rovigno, offers just one example of this exile "relativizing"
strategy. In my interviews with esuli, I often heard views similar to Rossi's. Fascism is seen to have contributed considerable material and social "progress."
Rossi, for instance, details the construction and amenities that fascism brought
to the Istrian town of Rovigno: street paving; electricity; a *dopolavoro* (afterwork
center) including a cinema, theater, and lecture room; a system of social security; public health campaigns against TB and malaria; and summer camps for
young people.

Recalling the beginning of the war and the obligatory premilitary service,
Rossi notes that the regime became the object of many jokes. In the bathroom
of the Casa del fascio, for example, graffiti mocked the Duce.[9] Yet this humorous "resistance" to fascism implicitly suggests that the regime proved relatively
benign, a bit of a nuisance and something to scribble about on the toilet stall,
perhaps, but not the ruthlessly efficient regime of terror constructed by the
Titoists. Rossi maintains that in spite of the excesses committed by some fascist
fanatics, these did not prove comparable to those of the Yugoslavs, particularly
the foibe.[10]

Such a judgment contradicts the early postwar account of Andrea Benussi, a
fellow Italian from Rovigno who, unlike Rossi, remained in Istria after the Second World War. Benussi's *Ricordi di un combattente istriano* (Memories of an Istrian combatant) reflects an alternative Italian socialist tradition in Istria and
focuses on the violent suppression of this tradition by Italian fascism. Benussi
begins his memoir by narrating his childhood in the last two decades of Austrian rule in Istria. Denouncing Austrian authoritarianism and militarism,

Benussi nonetheless contends that irredentist groups found few supporters in Istria. Italian sovereignty over Istria rendered the Istrians a "colonial population"—"Istria seemed at that time a colony of Africa" (1951, 67)—and encouraged the growth of underground workers' movements in Pola. Fascist squads wreaked terror, burning and looting villages and arresting striking workers. Benussi, like many other socialists, was arrested and forced to drink castor oil in order to purge him "of the obscure ideas of Lenin" (ibid., 85). In celebrating the socialist triumph of Yugoslavia in World War II, Benussi rejects the notion that Italy brought liberation to an oppressed people. "They brought terror, hunger, and imprisonment. This was the liberation that Italy brought to our suffering Istrian people" (ibid., 50).

While many Croats, Slovenes, and Italians living in contemporary Istria desire acknowledgment of the suffering wrought by Yugoslav socialism, narratives of the Istrian antifascist movement like Benussi's retain considerable meaning for many of my informants, in spite of broader revisionist trends in Italy and former Yugoslavia. In Istria, then, the response to the renewed debate over the foibe and other wartime atrocities, as well as to exile demands for compensation, proved relatively cautious and circumspect throughout the Tudjman era. Whereas in other parts of former Yugoslavia, street names and monuments honoring Tito and Titoist-era figures were rapidly changed or effaced, Istrian towns continue to bear the names of antifascist martyrs such as the Italians Pino Budicin and Giuseppina Martinuzzi. On building facades in small towns in the Istrian interior, one can still discern traces of painted slogans proclaiming, "Long Live the Popular Power!" or "Evviva Tito!" Such images, viewed in the context of decaying structures often abandoned since the period of the exodus, constitute ghostly reminders of both the antifascist front and the protracted postwar struggle over Istria. And like Trieste's topography, which reveals the continued power of irredentist narratives and heroes—Piazza Oberdan, Via Felice Venezian, and so on—these material traces in Istria point to the deep structures that delimit historical discourse, as well as to the complexities of repositioning alternative local and regional histories vis-à-vis larger national and statist narratives.

Throughout part 1, my aim has been to situate debates in contemporary Trieste and Istria within broader geographies of history and memory, geographies that have been dramatically reconfigured in the last decade, as well as over the course of the last century. Looking at the Italian and Yugoslav cases in tandem highlights issues common to much of the ongoing debate about the European experience during the Second World War, as well as other current attempts to deal with authoritarianism's legacies: questions of memory and silencing, of guilt and innocence, victimizer and victim. In Italy and Yugoslavia, these questions have been asked primarily in the context of liberation movements that pitted not only fascist against communist but also antifascist against antifascist. (On debates about the massacre at Porzûs of Catholic Italian antifascists by their

Italian communist "brothers-in-arms," see Kersevan 1995.) The discussions in the 1980s and 1990s about the resultant "divided memory" varied widely in Italy and Yugoslavia, as my analysis has suggested. The general tendency in Italy has been toward creating more inclusive narratives, and in Yugoslavia toward exclusive ones; at the local and regional level, however, the picture proves much more complicated, as the following chapter on the foibe demonstrates. In Trieste, as well as in much of former Yugoslavia, narratives about civil strife are increasingly read in terms of ethno-national divisions rather than political ones, part of a broader tendency in the post–Cold War world.

Part II

MAKING MEMORY

CHAPTER FIVE

The Politics of Submersion: The Foibe

IN PART I, I explored how various moments of war and state-sponsored violence—the Great War, World War II, and Yugoslavia's breakup—provided key opportunities for actors within and without the Julian March to articulate and reconfigure their historical narratives. In part 2, I look closely at the contemporary production of group histories in order to reveal how actors forge memories about such historical episodes through practices, discursive and otherwise. In particular, I focus on the creation of narratives of suffering and victimization, which have been, and continue to be, couched in claims about purity and hybridity, discourses whose terms were largely set by earlier processes of state formation. In the Julian March, this long-standing vocabulary has increasingly been merged with the legal one of the "victims" and "perpetrators" of "ethnic cleansing." This language emerges most powerfully in debates about the foibe, those karstic pits in which Yugoslav partisans executed civilians and military personnel in 1943 in Istria and again in 1945 in Trieste during the "Forty Days."

In their role as what Pierre Nora (1989) calls *lieux de mémoire*, mnemonic sites around which discourses of memory are constructed and contested, the foibe serve as a focal point for intertwined debates in Trieste: on the one hand, those defining the relationship between the Italian majority (including the esuli) and the autochthonous Slovene minority and, on the other, those understandings of the Istrian exodus as an act of ethnic cleansing prompted by such violence. Within "Italian" accounts, Italy's present-day Slovene minority frequently becomes equated with Slavs who carried out Istria's "ethnic cleansing" and subjected Trieste to the "Forty Days." Slovenes, in turn, stress their own suffering under fascism and seek to ally themselves symbolically with the memory of the Holocaust. Slovenes and Italians/esuli alike therefore aim to make marginal histories more visible by linking them (often through analogy) with other, better-known histories and by claiming exclusive "ownership" of victimhood.

The end of the Cold War has revitalized and transformed the language of victimhood and "genocide" which gives the foibe debate its emotional resonance. At the same time that we appear to be witnessing an increase in practices labeled genocidal (with observers struggling to label and prosecute for atrocities and massacres in Bosnia, Kosovo, Rwanda, and elsewhere), esuli and many other groups have found a new hearing for *retroactive* claims regarding injus-

tices and atrocities committed by communist groups and/or regimes. Because
the 1948 Genocide Convention omitted "political groups" as targets of genocidal persecution,[1] crimes such as the Stalinist purges of the 1930s or Khmer
Rouge massacres in Cambodia have hitherto remained outside the legal definition of genocide (Chalk 1994). The powerful moral capital attached to the
charge of genocide has nonetheless paradoxically made for the term's increasingly broad application by groups—like the esuli and the rimasti—claiming
past persecution.

   This persecution remains understood primarily in the racial and ethnic terms
of genocide's legal definition, however, and many victim groups now depict
their "political persecution" by communist regimes as bound up with ethno-
national antagonism. As a result, we may be witnessing the increasing ethni-
cization of claims about past violence, particularly "genocidal" violence, together with a more receptive response to such claims. Since the phenomenology of genocide entails particular kinds of attacks on the body (Adelman 1998),
practices concerned with recuperating the body and restoring its dignity become central to the construction of these memories of genocide. Linke notes of
the German case, "[T]he fundamental tension is between corporeality and liq-
uidation. The potential site of confrontation is the body. Its solidity, its physical boundaries, and its internal integrity are always deemed threatened by dangerous internal or external flows" (1999, xiii). In the Julian March, similar fears
about submersion on various levels (metaphorical and physical) are expressed
through debates about the disinterment of bodies, as well as the exhumation of
"submerged" histories of victimization.

The Politics of Submersion: Raising up the Dead

   The rocky plateau of the Carso, which extends for a large area in [the
   region of] Venezia Giulia, can be compared to an immense piece of
   Gruyère. The soil, often shot through with water, is marked by numerous chasms—people have counted 1,700—which descend for hundreds of meters into the bowels of the earth. These are the mysterious,
   frightening, impenetrable foibe. Near them there exist cavities of every
   kind, underground passages, grottoes, and underground rivers . . . the
   foibe have become an instrument of martyrdom and a horrid tomb for
   thousands of victims. . . .

   The elimination technique in the foibe [in Trieste] had already been
   used and tested by Tito's partisan groups when Istria was first invaded,
   on 8 September, 1943. . . . The corpses [found in the foibe] are shocking evidence for the cruelty and ferocity of the "infoibatori": naked and
   mutilated bodies, their hands bound with wires that cut to the bone,

people bludgeoned, horrendous tortures of all kinds. . . . The lorries of death arrived filled with victims who, often chained to one another and with hands cut up by wire, were pushed in groups from the edge of the chasm. The first ones in line who were machine-gunned fell and dragged the others into the abyss. Whoever survived after a fall of 200 meters lay in agony from the lacerations caused by the spiky rocks that broke the fall. . . . When the tombs were covered, the tragedy of the foibe was also covered by the conjuration of silence. No government, no judge—no one—pushed for an investigation of the massacres.
—Marcello Lorenzini, *Le stragi delle foibe*

The politics surrounding the foibe, as well as the broader nexus of claims about genocide in Trieste, operate as what I have called a politics of submersion. The notion of submersion here works at various levels. Metaphorically, the trope of submersion refers to silenced histories. Advocates for foibe victims, for example, claim that the memory of these crimes has long been "buried" by the Italian state, part of a general tendency toward the "clandestinization" and nontransparency of Italian politics or what Curi (1989) deems a submerged politics (*la politica sommersa*). Literally, the notion of submersion refers to subterranean spaces and an "exhumatory politics" (Verdery 1999). The metaphorical and the literal intersect powerfully in cases like the foibe, just one example in a broad field of contemporary political claims about ancestors, where dead bodies come to evidence not only "genocidal" victimization but also the nation's right to the territory sanctified by the remains of its martyred subjects.

As noted in the previous chapter, debates in Trieste about the foibe echo similar polemics heard in post-Tito Yugoslavia about World War II atrocities and mass executions, as well as in other countries that experienced World War II as a civil war and in post-1989 Eastern Europe more generally. Hand in hand with the tearing down of the symbols of the post-1945 regimes has been the simultaneous raising up (often literally) of those regimes' victims. In the case of faceless massacre victims, the movement is upward from the very soil, the roots, of the nation. These mass graves often become sites of religious veneration.

In his work on nationalist cosmologies, Kapferer (1988) compares Sinhalese identity in Sri Lanka, explicitly informed by Buddhism, to the ostensibly secular sense of national identity in Australia, built around the cult of the Anzac soldiers; he demonstrates that in both cases, the conjunction of religious *forms* of nationalism contributes to the making of nationalist *passions*. As we have seen, the Christian notion of passion acquires particular importance within an Italian irredentist discourse privileging themes of sacrifice, martyrdom, and eventual resurrection or rebirth. Given that "[d]eath in war . . . is the quintessential gift of the people to the state" (Kapferer 1988, 167), the sacrifice of individuals, particularly patriots and soldiers, thus becomes a prime object for memorialization.

The sacralization of the nation expressed in war monuments and tombs to Unknown Soldiers (Anderson 1995, 9) has its counterpart in the cenotaphs to massacre victims. Whereas both Unknown Soldiers and atrocity victims are figured as anonymous, the soldier is represented as an individual who *willingly* sacrificed his life in service to the nation. In contrast, the atrocity victims venerated as national martyrs have been brutally sacrificed in "illegitimate" acts of warfare or violence. Bringing to light the remains of these victims evidences sacrifices made for the nation, its ground sanctified by the blood and bones of its martyrs. When such territory is contested, histories (like Istria's and Dalmatia's) may invoke such notions of passion and sacrifice to assert the nation's right (or duty) to redeem that land and avenge its martyrs.

Veneration at mass grave sites may prove religious not only in the figurative sense of nationalist passions but also in the more literal sense. Priests often perform services at these locations in order to bless those denied peace for so long and, as has occurred in Eastern Europe, to confirm the ultimate triumph of the church over communist regimes. Objects associated with these sites and their victims can come to function as relics possessing a sanctity transferable through contact. The bones exhumed from caves in the Krajina, for example, were displayed publicly as (neo)relics, and those who gazed upon them or touched them could thus be considered to have received a holy "charge." Taussig (1997) has deemed such processes part of the "magic of the state," and the worship of the nation's humble martyrs is often paralleled by the attempts to restore or return the bodies of its "spiritual fathers." The exhibited bones of ordinary Serbian victims of the Ustaša, for instance, had a counterpart in the publicly displayed remains of Prince Lazar, the Serbian ruler killed by the Turks at Kosovo in 1389. In a revival of "the old Orthodox custom by which the mortal remains of a ruler were carried through all the monasteries of the country before burial" (Salecl 1993, 105), Lazar's bones made a tour of Serbia's old monasteries six centuries after the Serbs' mythic defeat.

Susan Gal (1991) examines a relevant case in Hungary: the dramatic return of the body of classical composer Béla Bartók. Bartók's funeral in the Hungarian "homeland" forty years after his death abroad was celebrated by both the waning socialist state and its democratic opponents. Such a lavish reburial, however, could not silence the demand for the body of Imre Nagy, the hero of the 1956 revolution who had never been officially buried after his execution and whose "ceremonial burial and political resurrection" (Ash 1990, 49) provided the opposition with important symbolic capital in the days leading up to the communist regime's collapse (for a review of such cases, see Verdery 1999). Similarly, in Croatia the tomb of Archbishop Alojz Stepinac, accused of collaboration with the Nazis and Ustaša and imprisoned under Tito, became a site of pilgrimage, and in Trieste efforts have been undertaken to restore the lavish monument in Capodistria to irredentist hero Nazario Sauro. In the Julian

March, such efforts draw on the long and specific tradition of irredentist hagiography detailed in chapter 2.

At the same time, however, imaginings of the foibe or similar sites elsewhere in ex-Yugoslavia and Eastern Europe build on a much broader and longer tradition of imagery about such subterranean spaces. Although "[s]tories of strange disappearances and labyrinthine underground chambers dedicated to human sacrifice" (Taussig 1997, 22) recur cross-culturally, the cave—one of the most powerful and primal symbols in European literature—possesses particular resonance within various Mediterranean traditions. The cave variously suggests refuge or entrapment (Odysseus's visits to the pleasure cave of Calypso and to the lair of Polyphemous), sources of potentially dangerous knowledge and power (the oracular tradition of Delphi), sites of dimly perceived truths (Plato's "shadows on the wall"), or death (the cavelike imagery of the underworlds depicted by Homer, Virgil, and Dante [Lesser 1987; Macdonald 1987; Weinberg 1986]). Not coincidentally, the *topoi* of both the cave and exile often figure in epic tales from the Mediterranean. As Starn observes, "The theme of return from exile in the earliest Greek epics has been shown to chart an archetypal passage from lands of darkness to lands of light or, ultimately, from the world of the dead to the world of the living. To return home to Ithaca, Odysseus traversed the islands, caves, and underworlds which gave geographical expression to darkened understanding and death" (1982, 8).

In a specifically Christian tradition, the association of death and darkness or exile (for those who fled in time) with the infernolike foibe lends victims' accounts particular emotional power and reinforces the theme of Catholic piety confronted with barbarism. Specific folk traditions, such as the *cane nero*, or black dog, placed in the foibe in order to watch over the victims' spirits and prevent them from escaping to torment their killers (Spazzali 1990a, 66–67), probably intensified the fear and mystery surrounding the foibe. Various legends spoke of the foibe as the homes of witches and spirits who left treasure in the grottoes and punished intruders with death (Oretti 1994, 190–91; Predonzani 1950, 339). Local authors of literary works have played upon the foibe in their role as "outlets, pitfalls, 'trous,' black holes" (Pizzi 1999, 92), rendering them fitting metaphors of "border anxiety."

In the Julian March, then, different groups struggle to define histories bound up with the traumatic events of fascism, World War II, and Yugoslav communism through the metaphors of submersion, hiddenness, and mystery evoked by caves and pits. Demanding official recognition of the hidden and "uncomfortable truths" (Bevilacqua 1991) that they claim lie buried in the foibe, Italian nationalist groups and exiles have long recognized that these caves represent powerful sites of potential knowledge and of ritual return. Publishing maps that mark the location of such foibe around Trieste and Istria (see De Simone, 1992), these exile associations reinforce their sense of a historical and territor-

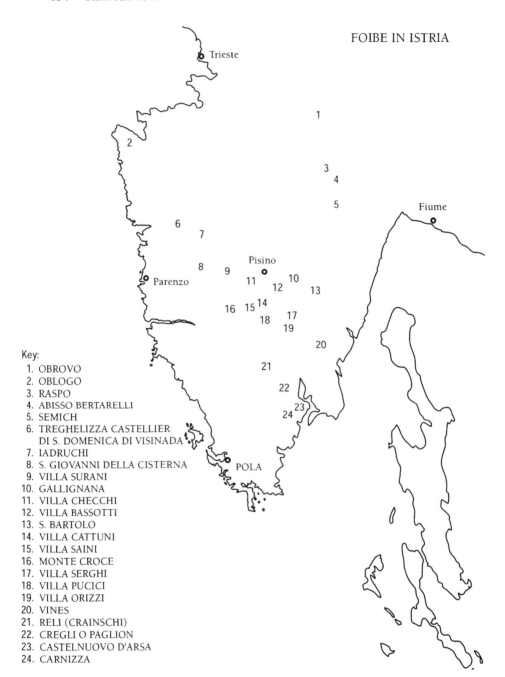

FOIBE IN ISTRIA

Key:
1. OBROVO
2. OBLOGO
3. RASPO
4. ABISSO BERTARELLI
5. SEMICH
6. TREGHELIZZA CASTELLIER
   DI S. DOMENICA DI VISINADA
7. IADRUCHI
8. S. GIOVANNI DELLA CISTERNA
9. VILLA SURANI
10. GALLIGNANA
11. VILLA CHECCHI
12. VILLA BASSOTTI
13. S. BARTOLO
14. VILLA CATTUNI
15. VILLA SAINI
16. MONTE CROCE
17. VILLA SERGHI
18. VILLA PUCICI
19. VILLA ORIZZI
20. VINES
21. RELI (CRAINSCHI)
22. CREGLI O PAGLION
23. CASTELNUOVO D'ARSA
24. CARNIZZA

Figure 6. Map of foibe in Istria. Taken from *Le Foibe, Il Diktat, L'Esodo* (Associazione Nazionale Venezia Giulia e Dalmazia). Courtesy of Unione degli Istriani

ial identity that confounds current border arrangements. The call by some exile associations that "the young who don't know [of the foibe and exodus], must know" (De Simone et al. 1991, 3) uses the device of the caves to temporally link generations. In their capacity as chronotopes—offering a "primary means for materializing time in space" (Bakhtin 1981, 250)—the foibe thus offer a means for better narrowing in on the organization and production of various contemporary group histories of "submersion" in the Julian March.

Like the esuli, some local Slovene authors similarly describe themselves as members of a "submerged community" (Stranj 1992), as victims of "silent assimilation" or a "canceled identity." "We're like your American Indians," suggested one Slovene man I interviewed. An Italian cab driver in Trieste volunteered his view that the Slovenes proved analogous to "my" Mexican Americans. In positioning themselves as an autochthonous population subject to genocidal policies, Slovenes thus liken themselves to First Americans, whereas their Italian opponents see them as troublesome "newcomers" from across the border who threaten to supplant and submerge the real "natives." This theme of autochthony runs through the discourses of various competing groups in the region and underwrites their accounts of "authentic" and exclusive victimhood.

This exclusivity constructs the other side's victims as compromised or guilty (hence meriting their fates and not genuine victims). As a Yugoslav diplomatic note put it in 1945, the foibe's victims were "guilty" individuals, "fascists who fell or disappeared alongside the Germans in the course of fighting the partisans or in Yugoslav army operations, or criminals of war whom the people themselves disposed of in the act of liberation" (in Pupo 1997, 37). From the other direction, in the 1975 trials of individuals charged as war criminals responsible for the Risiera di San Sabba, Justice Sergio Serbo applied the category of noninnocent victims to members of the Yugoslav resistance who met their end in the concentration camp. "By emphasizing a Yugoslav threat and by questioning the ethical role of local Anti-Fascism, Serbo distinguished between 'innocent' and 'non-innocent' victims of the Risiera. This latter comprised all those engaged in anti-Nazi and Anti-Fascist activities" (Sluga 1999, 183). On this slippery slope of criteria for victimhood have group identities such as "Slovenes" and "esuli" been reconfigured through storytelling and memorialization practices. In the remainder of this chapter, I analyze Italian efforts to "raise the dead" in Trieste and Istria and to submerge the memory of other victims, notably the Slovenes.

"Bitburg History": Redefining Victims and Aggressors

In Trieste, both Slovenes and Istrian Italians put forward collective histories centered around claims of genocidal persecution. Positing its members as victims of ethno-national hatred on the part of the other, each group tends to reject the other group's calls for protection or recognition. The battle cry "Remember the foibe!" has been repeatedly raised in conjunction, for example, with the question of bilingualism for the Slovene minority resident in Italy, a right guaranteed by the Treaty of Osimo. For some Triestines, the "crime" of the foibe and the presumed collaboration with Tito's forces leave the Slovenes no moral high ground on which to demand that Italy honor its international treaty agreements. In response, some members of the Slovene minority in Trieste—such as the small Slovene movement known as Edinost—have pursued two different but interconnected strategies: (1) to minimize the foibe by questioning the numbers and identities of the victims and, more commonly, (2) to contextualize and relativize the episode by directing attention to the injustices suffered by Slovenes at the hands of fascists and, in the postwar period, neofascists (see Tonel 1991).

As suggested by its centrality to arguments about the rights of the Slovene minority, the foibe debate has great importance at the level of local and regional politics at the same time that it involves questions of international significance between Italy and its neighbors. Although in theory Slovenes have prevailed at the national-international level, with their rights guaranteed by Italian-Yugoslav treaties, in local practice bilingualism has never been fully instituted. Despite the political predominance of Italians/esuli in Trieste, however, after 1954 their own demands were rarely promoted by politicians at the national level in Italy. With Yugoslavia's breakup and the 1994 Italian elections that brought to power a Forza Italia—Alleanza Nazionale—Lega Nord coalition, though, the foibe and the exodus became tied up with demands that Slovenia be denied admission into the European Union until the esuli received compensation for their lost properties (beni abbandonati). In response to these demands, Slovenes in both Italy and Slovenia countered that they themselves were the victims of ethnic cleansing and that the properties of those forced to flee fascist Italy had never been returned.

Three days after my arrival in Trieste to conduct fieldwork, I found myself thrust into the emotional maelstrom surrounding the foibe when I attended a public meeting on the Istrian *beni abbandonati* issue. Moderated by a journalist for the Triestine paper *Il Piccolo,* speakers included both exile association leaders and Slovene officials. Although this meeting ostensibly had nothing to do with the foibe, being organized around the legal question of restitution for the Istrians' lost properties, the arguments made by both Slovene and esuli representatives—as well as angry interjections by audience members—reveal how such issues are politically bound with memories of the foibe and heated debates over collective victimization (who suffered first and/or the most). In his remarks at the meeting, for example, the Slovene consul in Trieste complained that Italians do not know all the wrongs done to Slovenes under fascism. Not only did the Italian state forbid Slovene-language schools, it also initiated an "ideological and social ethnic cleansing in Istria," he claimed. At this, a man in the audience rose to his feet. Gesticulating, he shouted about the "savagery" of the foibe. (The consul had already been interrupted earlier when he began his remarks in Slovene and members of the public yelled, "Speak in Italian!" "You know he knows how to speak Italian," and so on.) This prompted a Slovene woman in the crowd to chastise the Italians present, "*Basta!* You are making a bad impression for your country. We had fifty thousand dead, and I myself have twice been made an exile."

As some audience members left in disgust after these exchanges and others began rustling papers and talking among themselves, exile representatives took the microphone and presented their demands for restitution. Lucio Toth, an Italian senator and president of the ANVGD, admitted that Slovenes had suffered from "nonliberal policies" under fascist Italy. Nonetheless, contended Toth, Slovenes had been compensated generously for their losses financially and in terms of historical atonement by an Italian state that had "paid its bills" for fascism. In contrast, continued Toth, the exiles had received neither real restitution nor acknowledgment for the traumas of the foibe and the exodus. In their comments, both Toth and the Slovene consul each represented his own group's sufferings as greater than that of the other. In the past, Slovenes have been losers in these debates at the local level but successful at a broader level, winning national recognition for Risiera di San Sabba, as well as Italian state support for its minority associations and newspapers. This situation shifted in the 1990s, as the Slovene minority underwent a financial crisis and exile claims about having suffered ethnic cleansing gained new credibility in Italy.[2] Tales of victimization have real and significant political stakes both within and without the region, the local contexts in which such stories are told becoming important sites at which memory is made.

In refuting the image of Slovenes as victimizers, many Slovenes in Trieste appear to agree with one of my informants that "it's time to forget the foibe and move on." Others, notably Samo Pahor and the supporters of his movement, Edinost,[3] believe that Slovenes have mistakenly felt ashamed about the foibe, a shame that has promoted their community's political and cultural submersion by "keeping them quiet and making them submit." Pahor maintains that the number of nonfascist Italian victims in the foibe has been greatly exaggerated;[4] instead he emphasizes the Slovene minority's persecution under fascism (personal communication).

This interpretation reflects the long-standing tendency of Slovene scholars to analyze the foibe solely in the context of the "War of Liberation" (Valdevit 1997, 11), a position articulated forcefully in Triestine journalist Claudia Cernigoi's 1997 book *Operazione foibe a Trieste*. This work consists largely of a critical (and polemical) reexamination of various published lists of presumed *infoibati*. Cernigoi concurs with Pahor that the numbers of the foibe's victims have been grossly exaggerated, with victims of deportation and other violence falsely lumped together with those of the foibe. In addition, victims of Nazi-fascist violence and dead German soldiers have been counted among those "thousands of Italians" presumed dead in the foibe. Cernigoi considers the case of the various foibe on the Karst around Trieste in which executions are thought to have occurred, noting inconsistencies or gaps in the data. In her estimation, the so-called foibe (actually a mining shaft) at Basovizza, a national monument since 1992, epitomizes the construction of "false histories." This site stands as a metonym for all the foibe in which Italians met their end in a manner similar to the pit of Jadovno in Yugoslavia; Živković notes, "One of the most notorious pits was called 'Jadovno' and, just as Auschwitz came to stand for all concentration camps and the Holocaust in general, so Jadovno came to stand for all the pits and for the genocide [of Serbs by Croatian Ustaša] itself" (2000, 71).

In the summer of 1992, in the company of Dušan, Pahor's colleague, I visited both the memorial at the foibe of Basovizza (above Trieste) and a nearby monument honoring four Slovenes executed by a fascist firing squad in 1929. After the war, the pit at Basovizza was sealed on the grounds that explosives and wartime weaponry had been dumped into it, making exhumation impossible. As a result, a rough calculation of victims was made based on an estimated number of bodies per cubic foot; Dušan pointed out that the commemorative plaque includes a hypothetical cross-sectional diagram of the foibe which presents these controversial body count estimates as straightforward. Dušan thus employs a strategy designed to minimize the foibe by questioning the very facts; Pahor and his supporters have long called for the reopening of this "common grave" in order to know the truth, a demand echoed by scholars such as Cernigoi and Sandi Volk. At the same time, by taking me to the nearby memorial to the four Slovene antifascist martyrs executed in 1929, Dušan implicitly told a story about Slovene persecution. Not only did this persecution precede (and thereby explain?) the episode of the foibe, but it also remained underacknowledged, grumbled Dušan, pointing out the lack of care given to the Slovene memorial. This story of the Slovenes' persecution under fascism is told by the minority community in myriad ways, with annual commemorations ranging from large ceremonies at the Risiera and at Trieste's Slovene Theater to small village programs with neatly dressed schoolchildren giving recitations about the heroic antifascist struggle. Through such practices, Slovenes reproduce a sense of collective identity tied to victimization, positing themselves as victims of genocide and ethnic cleansing. After our visit to Basovizza, for example, Dušan lent me a book (published in English and thereby suggesting its potential audience) that he felt illustrated the reality of the fascist period. Entitled *Twenty-nine Months of Italian Occupation of the "Province of Ljubljana"* and written by an Italian socialist from Gorizia, this 1946 work details the tactics of the Italian military in Yugoslavia. The most damning proof of Italian cruelty is provided by the words of the Italian officials themselves. Commander Mario Robotti, one of the officials lauded elsewhere for his efforts to rescue Dalmation Jews (Steinberg 1990), complained in one memorandum, "One kills too few!" Robotti's successor Gastone Gambara, in response to the reports brought back about terrible conditions, similarly stated that "concentration camps are not camps in which people are fattened . . . a sick person is a person who keeps quiet" (Piemontese 1946, 5).

Such attitudes informed the 1942 Spring Offensive, designed not only to wipe out the partisan menace but to replace the local population with an Italian one. Italian General Roatta suggested "that the houses and fields of the rebells [sic] should be assigned to the families of our soldiers killed or wounded in action throughout Slovenia" (ibid., 17). The minutes of a command meeting reiterated this desire to make the "national frontier coincide with the political one" and "to intern all Slovenes and to replace them with Italians" (ibid., 32). In accordance with this, a number of internment camps for Slav civilians were created in places like the islands of Molat and Arbe/Rab, as well as at Gonars (between the cities of Trieste and Gorizia). Yugoslav diplomats protested that the treatment of prisoners at these camps amounted to genocide (Walston 1997, 174–78). In response to such complaints, by 1945 Italian military leaders were protesting their innocence. In a statement made by Robotti and today on deposit at the archive of the Ministero degli Affari Esteri in Rome, the former commander noted that the Slovenes in those territories occupied by the Italians expressed "satisfaction" at being under the rule of the Italians rather than of the dreaded Germans (Robotti 1945, 2). He went on to detail the crimes of Yugoslav partisans, concluding (in capital letters meant to express his apparent indignation): "INSTEAD OF TALKING ABOUT ITALIAN CRIMINALITY AND ITALIAN CRIMINALS [OF WAR] IN YUGOSLAVIA, IT IS NECESSARY ONLY TO SPEAK ABOUT YUGOSLAV CRIMINALITY AND YUGOSLAV CRIMINALS AND, ABOVE ALL, ABOUT THE FEROCIOUS YUGOSLAV HATRED AND THEIR ARROGANT CONTEMPT TOWARD OUR COUNTRY AND ITS MILITARY FORCES" (ibid., 26). Other statements made in the same period and collected under the title "Presumed Italian Criminals of War According to the Yugoslavs" similarly exonerate the behavior of Italian officials by referring to atrocities committed by Yugoslav partisans and "bandits."

Written at the same moment as such Italian self-exonerations, a work like *Twenty-nine Months* fuels contemporary Slovene-Italian contests—given vocal expression at the *beni abbandonati* meeting described earlier—over which side originated ethnic cleansing in the area; priority becomes crucial to the arguments here, since the response of the wronged side then appears more justifiable. Piemontese's book positions Slovenes as the first victims of an Italian "genocide," thereby rejecting the widespread image of "good" Italians. In renewed debates over the foibe, a few Italian intellectuals have invoked this work in order to temper self-laudatory accounts of Italian humanity during the war and to emphasize the broader context of Nazi-fascist violence that preceded the foibe and exodus (Sala 1996), a rhetorical move akin to that made by many Slovenes in Trieste (again, see Cernigoi 1997 for an example of this strategy).

Slovenes in Trieste thus see themselves as victims of "genocidal" policies before and during the war, a tragedy embodied by the concentration camp at Risiera di San Sabba, where the majority of the three thousand antifascists killed were ethnic Slovenes (Bon Gherardi 1972). Locating narratives of group identity within broader discursive configurations constructing the Resistance and the Holocaust, members of the Slovene minority have sought, with much success, to associate the memory of Risiera with that of Slovene victims. Slovene associations played an important (but by no means singular) role, for example, in the establishment in 1965 of a national monument commemorating the Risiera. In March 1970, the Italian government further responded to Slovene demands and initiated an inquest into crimes committed at the Risiera, prompting a series of trials of "war criminals" in 1975–76.[5]

In response, pro-Italian associations in Trieste demanded a similar investigation of the foibe's perpetrators, as well as national recognition for the monument at Basovizza (Spazzali 1990a, 259–60). Employing a dual strategy, this lobby sought to minimize Slovene martyrdom by highlighting the Italians included among Risiera's victims and elevating the foibe to a status equal to or greater than Risiera's. In the years immediately following World War II, some politicians in Trieste and the local Italian press focused on the location of foibe and the recovery of remains in an attempt to deemphasize (or at least deprivilege) the horror of Risiera; pro-Italian parties (including the DC), for example, used the foibe to create anti-Slavic feeling in the local elections of 1949 (Sluga 2001, 149). In the 1950s the focus shifted to the symbolic struggle for ritual remembrance and official recognition of the *infoibati* as victims of a "holocaust" against the Italian people equivalent to that of Risiera (Spazzali 1990a, 262–63).

Though the term *holocaust* in this context undoubtedly refers to the Jewish *shoah*—and, indeed, authorizes claims about the foibe by association with the Jewish Holocaust[6]—it also reflects the older irredentist framework of martyrdom and redemption/rebirth. When the nationalist poet Gabriele D'Annunzio seized the port of Fiume Rijeka in 1919, for example, he declared it *la città olocausta*, "the city of the holocaust," from which would be resurrected phoenix-like a new, "model" community embodying the Italian national spirit (see Ballinger 1994). While referencing the Holocaust of Jews, then, the holocaust of Italians is figured in specifically Christian terms,[7] and its commemoration typically involves Catholic prayers to honor the dead.

For the sealing of the foibe of Basovizza and Monrupino in 1959 the Associazione Nazionale Venezia Giulia e Dalmazia organized a commemorative ceremony and Catholic Mass that attracted two thousand people. Giulio Andreotti, then minister of defense, represented the Italian government in dedicating the rock slab that covered the pits. The slab featured an inscription from Antonio Santin, the bishop of Trieste, that read, "Honor and Christian mercy to those who are fallen here. May their sacrifice remind men of the road of Justice and Love, on which flourishes true Peace" (Secco 1991, 90). Flaminio Rocchi, an

Istrian exile and a priest, then dedicated a memorial stone (the one that Dušan pointed out to me) showing the internal cross-sections of the foibe at Basovizza (Rocchi n.d.; 1990, 23).

Bishop Santin, himself an exile from Capodistria, said a prayer at the ceremony and in subsequent years participated in the annual commemorative Masses organized at the foibe by the Lega Nazionale (Lega n.d., 12–17). For the fortieth anniversary of the tragedy, the Lega published cards bearing the image of wrists bound with metal wire, in reference to the manner in which victims were found in the foibe, as well as to Christ's "crown of thorns" (Secco 1991, 89). The explicitly religious frameworks by which the violence of the foibe has been interpreted and remembered reflect not only the antagonism between the church and socialism but also, as discussed previously, the sacralization of the nation and its martyrs. For the case of Italian irredentism, this sacralization draws heavily on Catholic liturgical language and rites, as well as actual religious personnel such as esuli priests Santin and Flaminio Rocchi.

Rocchi, head of an exile foundation in Rome and author of the comprehensive volume *L'esodo dei 350 mila Giuliani Fiumani e Dalmati,* writes of the "Calvary of the Infoibati" and uses photographs to illustrate the victims' *Via Crucis.* He outlines the steps along this painful journey; capture, condemnation, the path toward the sacrifice *(il cammino verso il sacrificio),* the tomb, the *infoibamento,* exhumation, the identification of the remains, and the burial. Rocchi depicts these victims in Christ-like terms, as having been sacrificed for the sins of others. Their surviving relatives and friends endured another *Via Crucis,* however, that of the exodus, one of whose first causes Rocchi locates in the "anti-Italian vendetta" given its most violent expression in the foibe. (Esule Gigi Vidris' cartoon in figure 7 depicts this calvary of the Istrians.)

The beleaguered exiles who fled this violence in Istria found that their trials did not end upon arrival in Italy. There, they often found themselves placed in crowded refugee camps with only the barest amenities. Father Rocchi notes that in Trieste some exiles were housed in the Risiera di San Sabba, the former concentration camp. "Entire families, including, in 1959, my sister's (comprising five persons), women, the elderly, children, were amassed in the same cells, dirty, moldy, without light. . . . The walls and the beams still bore scratched names, dates, Stars of David, crosses, invocations" (1990, 82). Such a statement reclaims the memory of the concentration camp from the Slovene minority (as well as the Jews). The Christian framework of martyrdom and exodus that provides an overarching metanarrative for a variety of exile accounts also makes an implicit claim about moral Italians and "godless" slavo-communists while rhetorically figuring an eventual return to the Promised Land.

Hand in hand with this ritual remembrance of the Italian holocaust of the foibe and the exodus has been vocal protest against what esuli see as the exclusive linking of Slovene victims with the Risiera. The Lega Nazionale and some exile associations, for example, objected to the use of the Slovene lan-

Figure 7. *L'Esodo* (The exodus), by Gigi Vidris. Courtesy of Istituto Regionale per la Cultura Istriana.

guage at the inauguration ceremony of the Risiera museum. Many viewed the opening of the "case" of San Sabba as a move engineered by the Slovenes to create a kind of moral imperative for the ratification of what would become the Treaty of Osimo, finalizing the de facto territorial agreement outlined in the 1954 Memorandum of London (Spazzali 1990a, 266).

The agitation surrounding Osimo, combined with the fear that the tragedy of Trieste's concentration camp would overshadow that of the foibe, led to a loud reaffirmation in the 1970s of the resistance displayed by Italian Triestines against Tito, deemed an "infoibatore [acting] on the orders of Stalin" (Ugo Fabbri in Spazzali 1990a, 273). This represents a kind of tit-for-tat strategy—or what Charles Maier calls "Bitburg history" (Maier 1988, 14)[8]—in which the violence of the foibe, some of whose victims were undoubtedly collaborators and fascists, becomes posited as symbolically and morally equivalent to that of San Sabba. As we shall see, these debates, culminating at the local level in the mid-1970s, were replayed at the national level almost twenty years later.

The national recognition awarded to the Risiera in 1975 and the presence of Italian President Giovanni Leone at that ceremony only intensified the campaign to nationalize the monument to the foibe at Basovizza. In 1992 the Lista per Trieste, formed in reaction to the ratification of the Treaty of Osimo, finally succeeded in its decade-long campaign to have the foibe declared a national monument. This belated acknowledgment has merely highlighted the foibe's importance as a site of ritual return.

One of the more elaborate of such rituals marked the fiftieth anniversary of the tragedy of the foibe. Held in June 1995, the ceremony also recalled the city's "liberation" after the withdrawal of Tito's troops on June 12, 1945. The commemoration featured a Mass by Monsignor Bellomi, Bishop Santin's successor. Bellomi remembered the infoibati and the scomparsi (disappeared), together with the victims of the Risiera and all extermination camps. His voice cracking with emotion, the priest urged the need for peace together with the recognition that the sacrifice of the foibe's victims be recorded in the "moral conscience of humanity." Despite the call for reconciliation and their participation in the group prayer following the priest's sermon, some esuli present at the ceremony expressed to me on other occasions that they could neither trust nor forgive the "Slavs" who had carried out such executions.

One such woman, an Istrian exile and daughter of an Italian civil servant killed in the foibe, read Santin's "Prayer for the Infoibati" at this 1995 commemoration, thereby referencing the elaborate memorializations of 1959. Chosen to represent the family members of those killed in the foibe, this woman had tears in her eyes and recited the piece with a quavering voice, perhaps as much in continued anger as in sorrow. The objects of her anger may have included Monsignor Bellomi, viewed by some as too "open" to the city's Slovene minority, in contrast to his predecessor Santin. For the surviving relatives of the foibe victims, such ceremonies and monuments offer a site of mourning, given that many of the "disappeared" were never recovered and families have no gravesite at which to honor their loved ones. Indeed, at this ceremony the vice president of the Commemorative Committee demanded, "Where are the remains of our various disappeared? Where are our dead?" The question was really an accusation, one directed as much at the representatives of the Italian state present—including Trieste's mayor (at that time Riccardo Illy), whose conciliatory words recognizing the dual tragedies of the Risiera and the foibe struck some esuli there as "false and hypocritical"—as against Slavic "perpetrators."

Although on the surface this elaborate and well-attended ceremonial appeared to have satisfied esuli and others seeking recognition of their tragedy, the equation of the Risiera with the foibe still left many disappointed and revealed some victims' continued resentment toward the Italian state. Some of these "victims," including those who were not directly affected by the tragedy but who have nonetheless come to identify with a collective "we," want recognition of the foibe in and of itself, or as a tragedy greater than that of Risiera in terms of numbers and historic silencing.

The vice president of the Commemorative Committee, which organized this ceremony, noted that this fiftieth-anniversary gathering at the tomb of Basovizza initiated a "pilgrimage" that would continue into the following autumn, with various components. Such events included modest commemorations organized by various exile groups in September and November 1995. The first such homage at Basovizza was one of many events in the program for the thirty-third National Meeting of Fiumans, held in Trieste. This low-key commemoration proved quite similar to the one held in November 1995 by a delegation of representatives from the three principal exile associations. In this case, the honoring of the dead consisted of a few words of remembrance and the laying of a large wreath; this brief ceremony formed part of the exiles' traditional activities for November 3–4 (recalling the First World War), discussed in chapter 2. In neither instance was any mention made of the region's "other" wartime tragedies, such as the Risiera di San Sabba. Rather, these ceremonies emplotted the tragedy of the foibe in an unbroken narrative of Slav aggression toward Italians and posited them as the ultimate "sacrificial" victims. That a stop at the Basovizza monument proves de rigeur for exile programs (particularly those stressing unity within the exile community) reveals the foibe's centrality as a site of remembrance at which a collective identity as victims is reproduced; even if the ceremony lasts only five minutes, one must nevertheless acknowledge Basovizza.

The importance now accorded to the foibe as a "national shrine" reinforces, in turn, the Slovene minority's sense of victimhood, given that the countermonument remembering four Slovene antifascists executed at Basovizza/Basovica in 1930 has been largely overshadowed by the foibe memorial. For Trieste's Slovenes, Basovica (along with the Risiera) has served as the site for various commemorations of their "martyrdom" (*Bolletino,* September 1–30, 1980). These memorializations have in turn prompted countercelebrations, for instance, the neofascist MSI's honoring of the fascist who organized the 1921 burning of the Slovene Narodni Dom, or National House (*Bolletino,* April 1–30, 1983). In addition, the Slovene monument at Basovizza has been repeatedly defaced, and an additional marker memorializes these desecrations, noting the dates of such vandalism (see Sluga 1999, 188); as Taussig observes, "[t]hrough desecration and sacrilege, defacement creates value" (1997, 142). When such defacement and sacrilege involve the body (Adelman 1998), as occurs with atrocities like those perpetrated by both Nazis/fascists and Yugoslav partisans, the corresponding stock of moral capital or value also rises, giving claims of genocide their enormous power.

In Trieste, then, both Slovenes and Italians, feeling "submerged" and marginalized, fight over the "ownership" of victimhood and "genocide" as if they must be exclusive. This reflects the increasing tendency of a politics of identity and memory to understand genocide not in its more circumscribed, international legal definitions but rather in vaguer, morally charged terms, precisely what imbues the term with such symbolic import and makes it the object of such contestation. At the same time, in popular usage genocide remains understood primarily in ethno-national terms. To acquire legitimacy, group claims about genocidal persecution must increasingly be cast in terms of ethnic or racial conflict. An older view of the foibe as the product of a conflict of political ideologies has steadily yielded to such an ethno-national reading, one nurtured over the last fifty years by exile groups.

The Foibe as 'Ethnic Cleansing'

From roughly the mid-1980s until 1991, an initial effort was made to incorporate the memory of the foibe—long contested at the regional level in the Julian March—into a broader Italian collective memory recuperating "victims of communism." Although reflecting the beginnings of an Italian reevaluation of fascism, these efforts more explicitly assumed their direction from similar debates in former Yugoslavia and Eastern Europe. A March 1986 article in Trieste's newspaper Il Piccolo, for example, noted that Gorbachev's policy of "transparency" had borne fruit in Yugoslavia. Similar articles lauding the "air of glasnost" in Yugoslavia appeared in other Italian newspapers (Paladini 1988). These articles initially read events in Yugoslavia as a variation on Soviet state socialism's confrontation with the past and its acknowledgment of anti-communist victims.

In the same period, new scholarly work on both the foibe and deportations from the Julian March began to appear. Within Trieste, an important advance in the restoration of the city's dead came about with the publication of Roberto Spazzali's monumental tome Foibe: Un dibattito ancora aperto (Foibe: A debate that remains open). Like Triestine historians Giampaolo Valdevit (1997) and Raoul Pupo (1997),[9] Spazzali views the foibe as part of a precise plan to cancel the Italian presence in Venezia Giulia, motivated not by some primordial ethnic hatred but rather by the desire to sever the territory's ties with the Italian state and install a communist Yugoslav regime there. Spazzali sees this plan as proceeding alongside, or perhaps utilizing and working under the guise of, more popular discontent. For Spazzali, this explains the targeting of Italian antifascists in the CLN, as well as the nonpersecution of some prominent fascists. The persecution of noncommunist antifascists by communist partisans echoes other cases in Italy.

In the late 1980s, then, journalistic and scholarly revelations about events in Trieste paralleled those coming to light at the national level in Italy, as well as in Yugoslavia, about the communist settling of scores after the war. Within the last six years or so, however, the Italian discourse concerning the foibe has increasingly been dominated by an account of these events as an ethno-nationally motivated violence directed specifically against "innocent" Italians, killed for the "sole crime of being Italian."[10] In asserting their claims about ethnic cleansing, Italian exiles from Istria employ both implicit and explicit analogies to victims of other genocidal campaigns, thereby deriving powerful moral capital in their struggle to reshape national narratives about the exodus and the foibe. The most obvious references are to the Jewish Holocaust and to the Yugoslav wars of the 1990s. The latter furnished the exiles with apparently powerful "proof" of the Slavs' genocidal character even as dominant metaphors employed to understand the conflict in former Yugoslavia drew heavily on the Holocaust narrative, thereby underlining the role of the Holocaust as the West's "central morality story" (Živković 2000, 82). Almost every exile I have spoken with has told me, "What the Slavs are now doing to one another they did to us fifty years ago." Seen to confirm widely held stereotypes about Balkan butchery and fanaticism, the specific events of the foibe have thus been attached to broader discourses about the exodus as an act of ethnic cleansing. At the same time, the problematic of fascism and possible complicity lurks at the margins of these accounts. By positing absolute Italian innocence, these stories labor to counter an alternative narrative to those depicting such events as retribution for fascist sins.

One elderly exile couple from Orsera/Vrsar voiced the pervasive view that the foibe gave expression to both an inherent Balkan cruelty and a hatred of (essentially good) Italians. This couple came from a modest background in Istria; the husband, Beppe, did not follow in his father's footsteps as a fisherman but rather had been a small landholder. His partner, Lina, proudly told me that she stayed at home, made clothes, and never worked the land or in a factory (a common occupation for women in the nearby town of Rovigno). Neither had much education and spoke standard Italian with some difficulty, frequently slipping into istro-veneto dialect. Having met them while attending an event at the Unione degli Istriani, I subsequently visited them in their modest and tidy home, where Lina showed me her needlework and photos of her son and grandchildren. Their son and his family had moved away from Trieste, and Beppe and Lina's loneliness, far from their beloved Istria and from their son, became painfully obvious. Eager for company, they treated me as they might a grandchild and expressed curiosity that someone so young would undertake this program of research.

After providing what they saw as the necessary contextualization for their personal stories, the two focused on the topic of the foibe and the tragic end met by Beppe's brother and Lina's cousin, both found guilty by the partisans of the "sole crime of being Italian."

> *Lina:* Those who didn't go away [from Istria], they threw all in the foibe, and they hadn't done anything; his brother was twenty-two years old, my cousin was twenty.
> *Beppe:* That was the time of terror.

Both victims had served as soldiers under Italy. According to Lina, they "went to do military service in Italy because they [the partisans] wanted them to do military service under Yugoslavia, and they preferred to go to Italy." Confused, I asked if this had occurred in 1943 with Italian capitulation, at which time soldiers would have had a "choice" as to whether to fight for Italy or for Yugoslavia. Beppe replied that these events took place before the war had ended. Before I could inquire if, in choosing Italy, these soldiers had joined the fascist forces at Salò or those fighting with the Allies, Lina insisted that they had done no harm, contrasting these "innocent" soldiers with the partisans who attempted to force Istrians into joining them in their "murderous" activities. This glossing over of the (possible) taint of fascism and the violence associated with it recalls Passerini's (1987) findings about the frequent ellipses and silencings in the memories of fascism. The following interview excerpt reveals this hedging around of the question of individual complicity with the fascist regime. At the same time, the couple's statements place the foibe and the exodus in a direct and continuous narrative. Note Lina's habit of ending her statements with a question ("no?"), which points to my ambiguous position as simultaneously the ignorant novice ("Do you understand? *Capisci?*") and the *dottoressa* whose agreement and approval Lina seeks.

This rhetorical strategy also renders the ethnographer complicit by forcing her to agree with the informants' interpretation of the events. The use of reported speech further distributes (or dissipates) responsibility, by creating the "effect of multiple participation in a speech event" (Hill and Zepeda 1993, 197). Similar strategies figure in memoirs of former fascists, such as that of the journalist Curzio Malaparte, in which "memory becomes a means of assuming a series of identities which absolve the writer from any responsibility" (Burdett 1999, 113).

> Lina: And signorina, they didn't do anything, these soldiers, and when they returned home, there was still Yugoslavia, no? They had finished military service, and they hadn't even hurt a flea. Signorina, they returned. . . . They are Italians, we were born Italians, and just as you are born in your land, that's where you're born. We were never Slavs, and they came home, signorina, and they [the Slavs] asked after my brother-in-law—that would be his brother, no [indicates husband]? And he had just arrived, and [my husband] didn't know right away that he'd arrived. . . . And a quarter of an hour after he'd [the brother] left to go for a swim, our devils of communists come along, the *druzi* [Croation for "comrade"]; this signaled that they were Slavs, no? And they asked his mother, and his mother said, "He went. . . . My son went to have a swim." And they said, "When he comes back, send him to the military barracks [*caserma*]."
>
> And his mother said, "But why must he go to the caserma?"
>
> "No, no, it's nothing, signora. Only for an interrogation. We just want to ask him something."

The husband and wife continued their story, contrasting the brother's trusting nature with Slavic treachery, seen here as an innate characteristic. At every step in the process of the brother's arrest, detention, and execution, the Slavs revealed their false and deceptive nature.

> *Lina:* Assassins . . . And my brother-in-law when he came, he was tranquil, for he hadn't done any harm to anyone, he went. We never saw him again. They took him to the prison of Parenzo, which is a nearby town, no?
>
> And there they have a prison. We didn't have a prison here [in Orsera]. And every morning his mother brought him something. She sent sausages, eggs, bread, a bottle of wine, some little thing. She sent it to the prison, and they never let her see him. These druzi said, "Give it to me and I'll take it to him," but then they ate it, wretched ones, they didn't give him anything to eat, and this went on for a couple of days. I don't know how many—five or six, no? . . . But this lasted during the time he was at Parenzo. It was five, six days. And one day his sister went, always with this purse full of things to eat, no? And they told her that he wasn't there, that he'd gone.
>
> And she asked, "Where?"
>
> And one of them, he was a little more humane, told her, "He's there, in that truck."
>
> There were big trucks covered with a tarp, no?
>
> And my sister-in-law, his sister [indicates her husband], went there and didn't even get to see him because they had left, and we never saw him again. Because, instead of taking them—I don't know where they intended—they threw them alive in the foibe.
>
> How could we stay with those people? We were terrified of those people because they, these youth, they hadn't done anything, they hadn't even hurt a lamb, and they killed them because they were Italian. Because the soldiers didn't go in the woods with them [the partisans] to kill people, because they [partisans] killed every day. They were cursed and they still are, you know.

In telling the story of Beppe's brother, the couple described an incident that they indicate as having taken place at the end of the war in 1945, although the pressure applied to the young soldiers by the partisans to join them "in the woods" suggests that the episode might have taken place in 1943. This may represent a temporal collapsing of the war's two "conclusions" (in 1943 and 1945) and the two episodes of violence involving the foibe. The subsequent discussion of the foibe, clearly identified with the events of 1943 in Istria, suggests such a possibility. At the same time, the couple linked the events of 1943 to those of the exodus, inserting all these happenings into a unified narrative about a deliberate and systematic campaign to Slavicize Istria. For this couple, this ethnic cleansing followed out of a deeply rooted hatred on the part of the Slavs ("them") against Italians ("us," "our people"), as well as long-standing territorial ambitions.

Beppe: Because they took them [the Italians] at night, took them away, one didn't know where they went. Soon after when the Germans were here and raised them out of the foibe, one knew that they were inside the foibe and after, in '45, when the war finished, they [the Yugoslavs] commanded, because the Allies gave Istria to Yugoslavia, and after a short time they began to Slavicize Istria. Then all the Italians had to go away, leave all their things, all this or if not, eh, eh, eh.

Lina: Finish in the foibe . . . all of them thrown in because we were Italian.

Beppe: Thus they emptied the land, everyone gone. . . .

Lina: And our people were very good, they worked . . . they didn't hurt anyone, and they hated us because we weren't Slavs.

Beppe: They always hated the Italians. The hatred of the Slavs for Italians, always hatred.

Lina: . . . Because they weren't workers. . . . The majority [in the interior] were Slavs, signorina. And in the houses [abandoned by the Italians], they were afraid when they came in [and saw the accoutrements of "civilization"].

These comments about the Slavic hatred of the Italian work ethic echo long-standing distinctions between civilization and barbarism, urbanism and rurality; Venetian reports on the Dalmatian Morlacchi, for example, stressed the laziness, economic irrationality, and indiscipline of those populations inhabiting the interior (Wolff 2001, 132). At the same time, the couple's judgment deflates the pomposities of socialist rhetoric about the "workers' struggle." For this couple, the "barbarism" displayed in the recent Yugoslav wars proves identical with that of the Slavs who threw Italians to their death in the foibe. The couple dwelled on the horrific method employed in these executions, the kind of defacement of the body and its dignity that makes such stories powerful and persuasive today to a larger Italian audience.

Lina: We always have in our hearts these people whom they killed, signorina, [because they] are still assassins today.

Beppe: Do you know how they did it? With iron wire they tied two—one to another, thus—and they threw them in alive.

Lina: Do you know what kind of wire? Not straight but barbed.

Beppe: Not even a beast you'd treat the way they treated them.

Lina: How could they kill people in such a way?

Beppe: Worse than beasts because they bound one to another with the barbed wire and threw them in. The foibe had water inside—

Lina: Alive, signorina, still [alive] (tears).

Having recounted their tale, Lina asked me, "How could we live with such people?" When the husband chided his partner for still being fearful of the Slavs, she exclaimed, "They're beasts! They were, are, and always will be. Always will be because one who is born a beast doesn't ever become Christian." This language of beasts and Christians echoes narratives dating as far back as

the time of the Turkish invasions, when the devastated landscape left by fleeing Christians (including Slavs) was often figured as the domain of wild boars
and other "demonic" animals (Blažević 2000), the triumph of savage nature
over cultivation/culture. In his memoir of Istria, an esule priest described in
these exact terms the desolation of the postexodus peninsula, now marked by
a "poverty of the people and of cultivation" (Parentin 1992, 45); empty houses,
fallen buildings, and the uncontrolled grazing of "pigs and black goats of *Balkan
origin*" (ibid., my italics) evidence this decay. Whereas older narrative conventions pitting Christians against Turkish infidels placed Slavic peoples on the just
side of the holy crusade, in contemporary accounts of the exodus and foibe they
occupy the structural slot of the godless invader (for a reading of contemporary
Turkish occupiers as barbarians, see Loizos 1981, 143–44). Exiles like Lina and
Beppe interpret contemporary events as proof of the fact that in their barbarism
"the Slavs have not changed" (and, indeed, cannot change), thereby situating
events in Istria (and those of Trieste in 1945) in a much more extensive and
well-known story about destruction and genocide.

In recalling the story of her father's death in the foibe in 1945, an exile from
Pirano made a similar argument, denouncing both the Slavs and the Italians
who stayed in Istria. I saw Liliana frequently at exile events, where she cut a
glamorous and stylish figure and sometimes made dramatic and emotional
statements. A published author, she was one of a small group of strong-minded
women who participated in the male-dominated leadership of the exile associations. At times, these men (whose wives usually stayed well in the background)
appeared merely to tolerate the presence of these women, who inserted their
"emotion" into the meetings at moments where "cool heads" were needed.
(These men nonetheless often rose to the occasion with emotion when denouncing the crimes of the foibe and exodus.)

Liliana's participation in the exile ambit proved a key means by which she remained part of the Istrian community, given that she had married a Triestine
who had little interest in Istria (and even preferred the mountains for vacations).
In contrast to Beppe and Lina, then, who married in Istria before the exodus
and had family roots in Istria, Liliana lived in two fairly separate spheres: her
home life and the exile associations. Perhaps because of this she never invited
me into her home but would instead meet me at the exile associations or restau-
rants. One day over lunch, Liliana recounted her family's experience during the
exodus. She spoke forcefully and steered the conversation in the direction she
wanted. Liliana returned several times to her father's story, sometimes upon my
insistence, which she narrated in bits and pieces. Whereas the couple from
Orsera seemed unable to talk about much else besides the foibe, Liliana's fragmented telling reflected another mechanism by which exiles narrate traumatic
and difficult firsthand memories.

An employee in the Commune of Pirano, Liliana's father had brought his family to Trieste once the partisans arrived in Istria, only to have the Yugoslavs take

control of Trieste as well. Early on in the interview Liliana described her father's arrest in May 1945, in Trieste, from where he was transported to Pirano and then to the prison at Capodistria. After recalling her mother's desperate search for her father, who apparently numbered among prisoners transferred from Capodistria to an unknown destination, Liliana quickly changed the subject and touched on a number of other issues. She later returned to the story of her father's arrest, embellishing it little by little. Her father, warned that he was in danger, had attempted to return to Pirano on the regular boat service from Trieste but was unable to obtain the necessary permission, since the office was closed for a holiday. The following morning, he was arrested.

I asked Liliana why the Yugoslavs targeted her father. "Was he known as an Italian patriot?" I asked delicately, trying to tease out whether her father might have been compromised with the fascist regime. Liliana's usually sure manner of speaking suddenly gave way to long pauses and silences.

> He was known as an Italian patriot, and [pause] it seems that my father hadn't denounced Mussolini, he hadn't denounced fascism after the capitulation [in 1943] because it seemed to him that [long pause] . . . He was ingenuous; to him it seemed a betrayal of one's ideals because he was really an idealist. It seemed a dishonorable and villainous act [to betray one's ideals] in the moment of danger of dissolution. So he hadn't denounced fascism, and therefore he was called a fascist, right-wing.
>
> PB: An idealist?
>
> Liliana: Yes, right. And thus he didn't . . . Everyone today, if you meet people from Pirano, they say, "Ah, a fine man that." He was at the Commune because he hadn't done harm to anyone. Just think, one day, around '43, my sister . . . [returned] to the house, and she said to my father, "Do you know what Radio London says? It says that the Germans have concentration camps in which they imprison and kill all the Jews." My father said, "Extreme propaganda, subversive." He didn't believe it, and he absolutely didn't know anything about this.

Note once again the silences and rationalizations typical of many memories of fascism in particular and difficult experiences more generally. "In accounts of personal experience speakers attempt to construct a favorable presentation of self, and to mitigate representations of experiences that might tend to damage this construction" (Hill and Zepeda 1993, 197). Having asserted her own father's innocence and ingenuousness (particularly as a "good Italian" unaware of the Holocaust), Liliana goes on to refute the more general claim that fascist brutality in Venezia Giulia "precipitated" the foibe. Though the fascist regime made mistakes, such as forcing Slavs to Italianize their names and forbidding them to speak their language in public, such actions cannot compare with Yugoslav crimes, according to Liliana. In particular, the Yugoslavs' gruesome attacks on the body came to symbolize their barbarism and the difference between fascist and communist tactics.

The communists there say that in Istria the fascists made the streets run with blood. Don't believe these things, you know. They're absolutely not true. . . . And then they say that in the schools they had prohibited Slovene and Croat, one had to teach Italian, and this was a big mistake, according to me, because one must learn one's own language. . . . However, all the women of the countryside who came to bring fruit, vegetables, or milk to sell in the piazza spoke their dialect, and no one ever said anything. I, with these ears of mine, I was in the tram many times, and I heard it [Slavic dialect] spoken, and I never heard anyone say to them, "Don't speak in this language or else [you'll go to] prison." I also asked my woman [her domestic], who used to come to bring milk to Pirano, if she remembered being looked at or prohibited from speaking by anyone. But not even in one's dreams, because they spoke in their mixed dialect, which was a Slav dialect with curses in Italian [laughs].

Liliana does provide a brief opening for examining the wrongdoings committed by fascists, pausing to say, "Certainly, during the war . . ." She quickly forecloses any further commentary, however, by contrasting the "errors" of Italian fascism to Yugoslav atrocities. "But the partisans, do you know what they did? What they did to the Italian soldiers they took as prisoners?" In answering her rhetorical question, Liliana moved from the third to the second person. "They took out their eyes, they pulled out *your* eyes." Such a shift renders more immediate and persuasive the repetition of atrocity accounts. Liliana concluded: "This is what they do today; they're always the same race. Then they got it in their heads that Istria, Trieste, and all the zone as far as the Tagliamento are theirs by a historic right. . . . They still expect to arrive, in peace, in war, as far as the mouth of the Tagliamento. Because this is the zone they've been expecting for centuries."

Liliana thus saw contemporary Slavs not only as equally "barbaric" as those of fifty years ago, then, but also as equally threatening to Italian Venezia Giulia; the Slavs had changed in neither their methods nor their aims. Later in the interview she noted that she "would be ready to prepare her suitcases for another exodus," given that Trieste had become a "degenerate" city where one hears empty rhetoric about reconciliation with Slovenia and Croatia.

Interestingly, Liliana rejected an identification with Jews and other genocidal victims when she noted:

I have dreamed, and I dream and I will continue to dream of belonging to a race that isn't a race like ours, renunciatory, that loses. . . . I would have wanted to be a Palestinian, because (in other circumstances, of course) they have lived in contact with their land. We instead are scattered throughout the world, we've lost contact, we are dismembered, we don't have much consciousness, and maybe our memories aren't so tangible.

This admiration for Palestinians points to the ambivalent attitude some exiles have toward the analogy drawn between esuli and Jews and other seem-

ingly "passive" victims of genocide. Liliana, for example, symbolically connected her dream of an eventual return to the Promised Land to the histories of
Palestinian refugees, rather than of the Jews. Liliana's comment also expressed
ambivalence toward the general lack of armed resistance against the Yugoslavs
in Istria. This absent resistance rhetorically reinforced a sense of victimhood and
"civility," given that Italians did not engage in counterviolence but merely fled
Istria. This image of civility, in turn, played into the view of Italians as a humane people, lacking a martial spirit. Yet, as suggested by the ongoing reevaluation of Salò's defenders and by Liliana's idealization of Palestinian fighters,
this stereotype about Italian pacifism and military incompetence is double-
edged. As Federico, a second-generation exile put it, "The Slavs are a combat-
ive people in respect to the Italian people as a rule. Italians are people with their
tail between their legs." This remark implies a certain (if grudging) respect for
the Slavs, or at least for their martial traditions.

The son of exiles from Buie/Buje, fifty-year-old Federico recounted a story
about the foibe that, initially, seemed quite at odds with those analyzed so far.
This appeared to accord with Federico's explicit disagreement with the right-
wing tendencies of exile politics. In contrast to exiles who, like Liliana, minimize or relativize fascist crimes, Federico stresses that "[w]hen one speaks of Istria one needs to always consider the things that happened [under fascism]."
Noting the injustice of the fascist Italianization campaign in the Julian March,
he added, "Then, unfortunately, the war brought hatred, and hatred brought
vendettas, and people who probably had nothing to do with it suffered from
vendettas. For what reason are many Istrians dead? Probably something happened before which brought about this type of death."

Federico made these comments as I stood talking to him at the Unione degli
Istriani, where he works as a volunteer. He frequents the Unione in spite of his
well-known disagreement with the political orientation of the association, in
part because it helps him maintain contact with the land his parents left. Born
in Trieste, Federico's childhood memories are not of Istria but of the period of
the Allied Military Government and the "heavy hand" of the English. As a child,
he and his friends would throw rocks at those Slovenes who presumably sought
the city's annexation to Yugoslavia. These actions reflected the family sentiments
Federico absorbed; during the time of Austria, his grandfather had helped
found the irredentist/nationalist Lega Nazionale di Grisignana, and Federico's
father later joined the forces at Salò after the Italian army's dissolution in 1943.
In 1945 Yugoslav partisans threw Federico's uncle in the foibe. Despite this nationalist genealogy, Federico loudly disagrees with the prevalent interpretation
of the foibe and the exodus and stresses that he and his wife (whose family had
left the island of Lussinpiccolo only in 1963) "talk about the past but always try
to find the reason [il perchè—in this case, fascism] for why things happened."

Lina, the housewife from Orsera who lost her cousin and brother-in-law in
the foibe, overheard Federico giving me his opinion on the foibe. She came over

to us, shaking her head with a look of concern that I might be "taken in" or mis-led by such information. Disagreeing violently with Federico's contextualizing interpretation, Lina stressed the absolute cruelty that Slavs displayed. Rejecting the popular image of *brava gente* which informs the contrast drawn by Lina and Liliana between fascists and communists in Istria, Federico countered that Ital-ians proved equally vicious.

> *Federico:* They [Italians] did such things in Africa, Signora, in a very heavy-handed manner. Marshal Graziani in Abyssinia and in Libya, he threw blacks out of air-planes in order to test parachutes.
>
> *Lina:* But the foibe . . .
>
> *Federico:* In Libya they did the same thing, in Abyssinia. Signora, unfortunately the Americans dropped a bomb on Hiroshima with I don't know how many thousand dead. The Russians had gulags. Unfortunately, war brings much loss, every type of loss.

Up to that point, then Federico's account sounded quite different from the stories told by other exiles who had lost close relatives to the violence of the foibe. And perhaps this is what one might expect, given Federico's avowed left-ist political orientation and his sense of generational difference, describing him-self as part of the postexodus *(dopo esodo)* generation raised in Italy. Yet when Federico returned to the subject of the foibe, he unhesitatingly described it as "genocide" and the Slavs as "wild animals."

> With the genocide, they killed innocent people. I don't want to debate whether they killed soldiers . . . people butchered, people, entire families. . . . I don't know, young people, wives who didn't have anything to do with it, were killed. It was in the logic of wild animals *(belve)* because they are wild animals, and they demonstrate today that they are wild animals because the genocide that they are carrying out there against the Muslims, or with the Serbs against the Croats and vice versa, demonstrates what they did fifty years ago in Istria. It's a mess. What they did also in 1912 in the Balkan Wars, all that stuff there.

Despite contextualizing the foibe in the events of fascism and the war, then, Federico ultimately validated the orientalizing rhetoric that other exiles articu-lated, including Lina. He telescoped multiple instances of violence in the Balkan into an extended narrative, one that ultimately depicted Balkan Slavs as bestial. This example underscores, once again, the power of the "ethnic cleansing" mas-ter narrative to ultimately unite even discordant exile accounts. This may ex-plain, as well, how Federico managed to reconcile his work at the Unione with his conflicting political loyalties.

It would be easy to assume that this current reading of the foibe and the ex-odus reflects a wholesale remaking of memory on the part of the esuli, who today radically reinterpret the events of more than fifty years ago in light of the recent Yugoslav wars. Yet, as the previous discussion suggested, since at least the 1950s memory practices centered around commemorations of foibe victims have taken place in Trieste. Though having deep roots in older irredentist practices, the precise template for these ceremonies to honor "innocent Italians" was forged in 1943–44. When the Germans pushed the partisans back from Istria in October 1943, they began, together with their Italian allies, to exhume many foibe. Featuring tearful relatives identifying mutilated bodies, Nazi-fascist newspapers, newsreels, and pamphlets lost no time in denouncing "slavo-communist perfidy." An anonymous pamphlet published in Italian describes the solemn rites held in churches in the Italian RSI (Salò) for these Istrian "martyrs" (Anonymous 1943, 19). While declaring that the massacres were carried out in perfect accordance with instructions from the Communist Party, the author further comments that the killings were undertaken in the "typical Slav" manner, with no discernment for persons, ideologies, age, or sex.

Many contemporary exile accounts of both the foibe and the exodus (including the three analyzed here) display considerable continuity in terms of form and content with those produced at the time of the events, although the current ones tend to use a contemporary language of genocide. Beppe, the man from Orsera whose brother was killed in the foibe, for example, continues to employ an older language of "denationalization" and "Slavicization" rather than of ethnic cleansing. Whether described as Slavicization or ethnic cleansing, however, the interpretation of events remains largely unchanged. One could even contend that the exiles view recent Yugoslav events through the prism of the foibe and the exodus as much as they read the *esodo* (exodus) in light of Yugoslavia's breakup.

A recent documentary on the foibe produced by Claudio Schwarzenburg, head of the Commune of Fiume in Exile, dramatically underscores the continuities between many contemporary exile accounts and state-sponsored propaganda from the time of the foibe executions. The film draws heavily on a 1943 Italian newsreel showing the recovery of badly decomposed remains and the emotional responses of friends and relatives called to identify the bodies. This wartime propaganda film features loud pealing, superimposing the "Bells of Death in Istria" on images of Istrian churches, symbols of the peninsula's Italian civilization, which was so brutally violated by the Slavs.

Although instances of sexual assault by Yugoslav partisans in Venezia Giulia appear to have been relatively infrequent, the foibe documentary links Istrian events in the 1940s to contemporary Serb campaigns of mass rape in Bosnia, asking "Are Karadžić's troops so different from those of Tito?" Schwarzenburg's film recalls the sad fate of Norma Cossetto, a student taken by the partisans from her home in S. Domenica di Visinada and repeatedly raped before being thrown in the foibe at Surani. Cossetto represents perhaps the quintessential victim of the foibe for the Istrian Italians. The Unione degli Istriani, for example, displays a large photograph in her memory and has a cultural circle bearing her name. In his volume on the exodus, Father Flaminio Rocchi notes that the Italians of

Istria considered Cossetto "a true martyr" to the cause of italianità (Rocchi 1990, 31). Describing Cossetto as a cultured and respected university student, Rocchi emphasizes her youth and gender; this not only underlines her vulnerability against the masculine aggression of the partisans but also figures her as "apolitical" and hence uncompromised by fascism (since she was young and female). Indeed, Rocchi notes the irony that Cossetto's thesis advisor at the University of Padua was Concetto Marchesi, a communist who in 1949 arranged for the murdered student to be awarded her degree posthumously (ibid., 33). Cossetto thus comes to stand in for the entire Istrian population, trusting and innocent, which due to its "civilized" and civil traditions chose to flee Istria rather than take up arms against Yugoslav violence. In pro-Italian literature from the period of the exodus, Istria is often represented as a violated woman. (See esule artist Gigi Vidris' use of such imagery on the next page.) This symbolism recalls the frequent representation of Christian female (but not male) martyrs as sexually violated or mutilated by the enemy (Abou-El-Haj 1994, 27); such images of a violated purity also prove a common feature of nationalist rhetoric.[11]

Having linked the violence against Cossetto with contemporary campaigns of rape, the Schwarzenburg video concludes with a discussion of the shocking and "shameful" discovery by historian Marco Pirina that some "criminals of war" responsible for such acts continue to receive pensions from the Italian state. That Italy pays out pensions to citizens of Slovenia and Croatia who were born and worked under Italian rule—including some of those individuals today charged as perpetrators of the foibe—infuriates many exiles. While an account such as Schwarzenburg's film reiterates arguments made at the time of events, then, it also inserts these arguments into new debates about both historic and legal justice; these debates reflect the broad and ongoing polemics about accountability opened up by the Cold War's end. In accusing the Yugoslavs of genocide, for example, esuli and their advocates not only demand that the Italian state end its policy of giving pensions to Istrians but also seek out and prosecute those responsible for the foibe who are still alive. Making the story of the foibe as ethnic cleansing known to a wider audience, then, has also raised thorny legal questions as esuli and their advocates seek redress on the basis of their once-marginal histories.

Owning up to the Foibe

In 1994 and 1995 newspaper articles began to appear at the national level as the foibe increasingly became bound with legal questions about "war criminals" responsible for genocide, Italian pensions abroad, and compensation. An article in the popular Italian weekly *Panorama,* for example, described the submission to the government in Rome of a ninety-page dossier on the foibe filled with names and photographs. Detailing crimes committed in Tri-

Figure 8. *La fine dell'Istria* (The end of Istria), by Gigi Vidris. Courtesy of Istituto Regionale per la Cultura Istriana.

este, Istria, and Dalmatia, the article's author employed the kind of language that for the past fifty years had dominated the local debate in Trieste (Tortorella 1995). Such reports, together with the publication of sensational accounts like those of Marco Pirina and Annamaria D'Antonio (1994), prompted a lawyer (Augusto Sinagra) and later a judge (Romano Pititto) to take up the foibe as a legal issue. Pititto heeded the "call for justice" demanded by Pirina and D'Antonio in a series of books. These volumes consist largely of the recovered voices of witnesses, survivors, and victims' families, interspersed with photographs and various documents. Playing on a language associated with such survivors, Pirina and D'Antonio see themselves as "bearing witness" to the *scomparsi,* or disappeared.

In pursuit of "justice and truth," Pirina and D'Antonio's volume *Scomparsi* (Disappeared) listed the names of more than four hundred presumed perpetrators of the foibe, some one hundred of whom were presumed living. Cernigoi, among others, has attacked the methods by which Pirina and D'Antonio arrived at their conclusions and their numbers of victims, commenting sarcastically that Pirina's research was so badly done "that if we had produced a similar research while in elementary school, the teacher not only would have given us a big fat F but also would have asked how we could have strung together such a series of errors" (1997, 62). Cernigoi even mentions that she was motivated to write her book *Operazione foibe a Trieste* out of a desire to correct such inaccuracies; exile Giorgio Rustia (2000) has, in turn, written *Contro operazione foibe a Trieste,* picking apart Cernigoi's methods of argumentation.

Despite possible inaccuracies in Pirina's work (or Cernigoi's, for that matter), his accounts provided Judge Pititto with a starting point for his investigations, leading him to press for the prosecution of infoibatori on the charge of "genocide" (*Il Piccolo* 1996c). (Ironically, in May 2000 Pititto was removed from the case of Oskar Piskulic, charged as an infoibatore, on the grounds that his involvement in a libel case against Cernigoi created a conflict of interest.) In November 1995, Pititto published an appeal for individuals to provide testimonies about their experiences in Venezia Giulia during the Yugoslav occupation. Pititto expressed his sense that gathering such testimonies was necessary to the task "of *translating a historical fact into a juridical fact*" (Bar. 1995; my italics).

Those providing testimony to Pititto included historians, together with survivors of partisan "terror" and relatives of those killed. The Triestine paper *Il Piccolo* published interviews with descendants and survivors at the same time that it tracked down several of the "most wanted" on the Roman magistrate's list (see Maranzana 1996; Maranzana and Coretti 1996; and Radossi 1996). Such pieces inevitably stress the fact that these presumed criminals enjoy good health in their advanced age and live comfortably, often on Italian pensions. Like accounts of former Nazis apparently living the good life in exile, these articles helped fuel a public outcry that those responsible for the foibe should be brought to trial.

At the same time, these debates renewed Slovene and Croatian fears about Italian exile demands for compensation in Istria. Slovene politicians countered that if the Italians wanted to open a "Pandora's box," they must also be willing to prosecute those Italians responsible for atrocities committed during the occupation of Yugoslavia between 1941 and 1943. As Pititto's inquest got under way in February and March 1996, the Slovene magazine *Mladina* published a full-page photo of Slovenes massacred by Italian troops during their occupation of the Province of Ljubljana. Under the title "883 Italian Criminals of War," the accompanying text stated that Slovenes had obtained from the UN Commission for War Crimes 883 names registered in category A (reserved for criminals); Foreign Minister Zoran Thaler warned that if Pititto continued his investigation, the Slovenes would push for prosecution of Italian war crimes (Manzin 1996).[12]

The Ljubljana paper *Delo* made a similar report and charged the Italians with using the question of the foibe in order to block Slovene entrance into the European Union (*Il Piccolo,* 1996). Other Slovenes, including members of the Association of the Slovene War Veterans, expressed outrage at what they saw as Italian efforts to transform aggressors into victims and thereby rehabilitate fascist collaborators. In Croatia the minister of foreign affairs similarly complained about Italy's one-sided rewriting of a history that forgets fascist criminals (Štorman 1996, 10–11).

While the legal issue of the foibe has yet to be resolved, in August 1996 this debate in national newspapers pushed the question of the foibe to national prominence in Italy. The catalyst for this discussion came when a member of the Italian Left urged his colleagues to finally "own up" to the tragedy of the foibe. The appeal made by Stelio Spadaro, local secretary of the Partito Democratico della Sinistra of Trieste, elicited a variety of responses. Though the "ethnic cleansing" thesis has by no means been universally accepted in Italy, the reaction to Spadaro's declaration, like that of Pititto's inquest, reveals the increasing tendency to read the foibe as part of a genocidal design.

Urging the Left to assume responsibility for its part in the crime of the foibe, Spadaro stressed the need to move beyond the old, ritual schemata (that is, those of fascism versus communism) employed in such discussions. Spadaro noted that in contrast to the rest of Italy, the history of the foibe had never been silenced in Trieste. Instead, the obsessive and ongoing polemic there had psychologically isolated the city from national politics, rendering the region a "remote appendix to this country" (Spadaro 1996). In Spadaro's vision, reintegrating Trieste into the nation, at the level of both politics and historical memory, will not only reinvigorate the declining city but also heal the wounds that have divided the country since the civil war. Roberto Cuilli, coordinator for international activity in the Quercia, picked up on Spadaro's comments and added that the future of Trieste and the entire Italian Northeast lay in a politics of integration, integration here being identified not just at the national level but also with Italy's Slavic neighbors (Spirito 1996a).

Trieste's potential as both the symbol and the economic center of the new Europe is a theme heard of late in the city, in spite of the fact that the national elections of 1996 and 1998 which brought a Left-Center coalition to power only reinforced Trieste's political isolation (a situation reversed by the elections of 2001). In contrast to national trends, the Left fared poorly in Trieste in 1996 and 1998. Spadaro's appeal may thus be viewed in more cynical terms, as it has by many, as an attempt by the PDS to appropriate the political and symbolic capital associated with the foibe that has traditionally been the property of the political Right (see Galli della Loggia 1996b). The PDS's appeal to national unity also came at a critical moment of increasing radicalization by Umberto Bossi's Northern League. One could more charitably suggest that having finally assumed power, the Left could at long last abandon its defensive guarding of the patrimony of the Resistance and begin, from a position of strength, to critically interrogate the myths of the partisan movement.

Not surprisingly, Spadaro's statements met with both approbation and criticism in Trieste. Exile leaders such as Renzo Codarin, the vice president of the Associazione Nazionale Venezia Giulia e Dalmazia and a parliamentary deputy representing Alleanza Nazionale, noted that Spadaro's mea culpa was a necessary first step in rewriting the history of the foibe but that much more remained to be done. Many others in Trieste shared the suspicion that the PDS cynically mouthed empty rhetoric. Attacked from one side for not doing enough, Spadaro came under heavy criticism from the other direction for having gone too far. In his radio show, for example, Edinost leader Samo Pahor blasted Spadaro for pandering to Italian nationalism.

Though the local debate prompted by Spadaro's pronouncement built on long-standing polemics within the city, it also resonated beyond the region, as evidenced by the spate of articles and editorials dedicated to the foibe that appeared in national newspapers and magazines. The titles of such articles clearly indicate the manner in which the tragedy has been reread in terms of a "forgotten history" of ethno-national "genocide": "Hypocrites: It Was Genocide" (Aquaro 1996b), "The Historic Taboo of the Left" (Galli della Loggia 1996a), "Another Canceled Memory" (Galli della Loggia 1996b), "The Gulags without Trial" (Strada 1996), "Prisoners of Tito. And of Silence" (Pansa 1996).

Many of these accounts highlighted the horrific aspects of the foibe. The national newspaper *La Repubblica,* for instance, ran an article that included testimony by a survivor. Decrying the fact that "[t]he executioners are still alive," the journalist noted that Titoist atrocities did not stop with the executions in the foibe but extended to cutting off testicles and placing them in the victim's mouth, using decapitated victims' heads as soccer balls, and placing "crowns of thorns" on the heads of priests thrown into the foibe (Sergi 1996). Such descriptions echo those of atrocities committed during the recent Balkan Wars.

The timing of this renewed interest in the foibe reflected not only happenings in former Yugoslavia and shifts in Italian politics but also the trial of Erich Priebke, the SS officer responsible for the massacre of 335 Italian civilians in the Ardeatine Caves near Rome in 1944. Extradited from his Argentinian refuge, in 1996 Priebke stood trial and was acquitted in Rome (though a later reversal led to his house arrest). The Priebke trial prompted an extended polemic over the commensurability of Nazi crimes and those of the foibe; this debate took up on a larger scale themes long familiar in Trieste, where local contests about the foibe and Risiera di San Sabba have centered around these issues. Not surprisingly, as in Trieste, much of the emotion of the national debate concerned the issue of how to construct (and thereby interpret) monuments to such atrocities and then locate these commemorative sites within larger historical narratives and topographies of memory.

A proposal to establish a museum of exterminations in Rome, for instance, provoked intense comment and, at times, angry debate. Victor Magiar, a founder of the Jewish Pacifist Group in Italy and one of the museum's advocates, stated that his group's aim was to create a museum detailing the great tragedies of the past: the Inquisition, the destruction of Native Americans, the Jewish Holocaust, and so on. In an interview published in the national paper *Corriere della Sera,* Magiar noted that although he understood the emotion surrounding the Priebke case, the example of the Fosse Ardeatine (the Ardeatine Caves) proved too "provincial" for such a museum. When questioned on the foibe, Magiar reiterated that the intention was not to create a museum to *all* the massacres of the Second World War. Here the issue of scale of such specific histories emerges as a key issue. When repeatedly pressed about the foibe, Magiar stated that he wished to talk about something more "serious" (and presumably of more universal significance), like Hiroshima (Aquaro 1996a).

Although such comments expectedly provoked outrage in Trieste (see Spirito 1996b), at the national level the debate about situating the foibe vis-à-vis Nazi reprisals and the Holocaust proved more varied. Some public figures (notably those with a Marxist bent) continued to endorse an older fascism-versus-communism thesis and deny that the foibe followed out of ethnic hatred. Marxist historian Luciano Canfora, for instance, stressed the uniqueness of the Holocaust and dismissed any comparisons of the Ardeatine to the foibe, given that the latter did not originate from "racial prejudice" (*pregiudizio razziale* [Cavadini 1996]). With the revision of narratives about the Resistance, however, other members of the Left (such as Stelio Spadaro) have begun to rethink the categories through which this history has been read.

Other writers and politicians, particularly those associated with the political Center and the Catholic press, instead took up the theme of the foibe as a long-forgotten act of ethnic cleansing. Some denounced the silence that fell "like a tombstone on this anti-Italian ethnic cleansing" (Ruggiero 1996). The historian Gabriele De Rosa, interviewed in *Avvenire,* cautioned that one must remember the larger context in which the violence of the foibe occurred, notably fascism and Yalta, at which Italy's fate as a defeated nation was decided by others. De Rosa concluded, however, "Within the war of liberation there was another war, which had this ideological and ethnic character, that was brought by Tito, and that has nothing in common with other wars of liberation. The foibe are the first episode of ethnic cleansing" (ibid.). On one hand, De Rosa's statements reveal the range of possible interpretations of the foibe and the potential for individual positions to encapsulate a variety of arguments. On the other hand, these comments reveal the increasing prominence of the ethnic cleansing thesis, indicating the shift that has taken place outside Trieste in the last decade.

The flurry of articles at the national level dedicated to the foibe tapered off by early September 1996, to be replaced by other items of concern, notably Umberto Bossi's rally of "green shirts" on the Po River to proclaim the secession of the northern republic of Padania from the Italian state. The emotion that this national debate aroused in Trieste, however, did not subside and furthered agitation not only to finally bring infoibatori to justice but also to end Italian pensions abroad (that is, in former Yugoslavia) for those who worked for the Italian state or served in the Italian military. After opening his inquest on "war criminals" responsible for the foibe, for example, Judge Pititto took up the pension question. This aroused anxiety among Italian emigrants abroad, who feared that the unfortunate fact that a few infoibatori received retirement monies from the Italian state may lead to the denial of pensions to tens of thousands of Italians outside the former Yugoslavia (Spirito 1996c).[13]

This also, expectedly, caused great concern among members of the Italian minority in Istria, many of whom scrape by in the ruins of the Croatian economy thanks only to their Italian pensions (see La Voce del Popolo 1996b). In general the response of the Italian communities in Slovenia and Croatia to the foibe question proved more circumspect than among the exiles in Trieste, at least in the Tudjman era (1991–2000). This reflects, in part, the precarious economic and political position that the Italian minority occupied until very recently in the successor states of former Yugoslavia and the need to distance itself from politically explosive contentions about Croat and Slovene "guilt" for the foibe. At the same time, the suspicion with which many exiles view those who remain—as having collaborated with slavo-comunisti—renders the Italian minority in Istria somewhat analogous to the Slovene minority in Trieste. Viewed by some esuli as perpetrators, the rimasti nonetheless insist that they were equally victimized by Istria's ethnic cleansing.

Today in Istria one hears among Slavs and Italians alike both an older narrative about "fascists" having been thrown in the foibe and, alternatively (especially among Italians), a view of these events as part of a campaign of ethnic cleansing. Although Italians have begun to make the latter claim in both print and political meetings, until Franjo Tudjman's death and the electoral defeat of his Croatian Democratic Union in January and February 2000, respectively, there remained considerable fear in Croatia that the regime would persecute rimasti who spoke of this "ethnic cleansing," and thus the public response proved more muted than in Italy. Alessandro Damiani, a noted figure in the Italian minority in Istria, offered one of the relatively few voices in Istria on the 1996 Italian debates. Writing in the popular Istrian magazine Panorama, Damiani lamented that contemporary Italian accounts of the violence contain much misinformation. Though he agrees that the silencing of the foibe proved a grievous error, he contends that the current revisitation of the past displays disrespect to the dead buried in the foibe and symbolically repeats the desecration suffered by its victims fifty years ago. "From the dispute centering around the foibe one can construct nothing . . . do we want to also negate the future?" (Damiani 1996, 19).

The contrast established here between backward-gazing versus forward-looking perspectives—akin to the alternative laid out by Spadaro and Cuilli, among others, of Trieste as a "dead" city obsessed with its past and of Trieste as the focus of a new Central European region—also figures in the Italian minority's imaginings of the exile community and itself. Depicting the rimasti as the real victims, left alone and defenseless in Istria when the mass of Italians abandoned the peninsula, this judgment subverts the terms of the debate, largely set by the exiles, within which the foibe and esodo have been reconsidered. According to Damiani, it is the Italian minority in Istria that has suffered a true infoibamento, or submersion. Damiani thus posits the Italians in Istria as "would-be victims of the first ethnic cleansing" (ibid.). I heard the "ethnic cleansing" thesis repeated by members of the Italian minority in Istria, as well as by some ethnic Croats there. This signals a significant discourse shift in Istria, where in the past those who chose to remain often defensively labeled those who left victims of Italian state propaganda.

In an editorial in *Il Piccolo*, the Triestine historian Giampaolo Valdevit made an argument similar to Damiani's when he maintained that it would be a grievous error if the suffering of the foibe's victims and their descendants "become a type of hunting ground for a category of hunters that still has some adherents: those dedicated to chasing after ghosts" (Valdevit 1996). Contending that fifty years after the fact *historical* truth proves more important than *juridical* truth, Valdevit stresses the need to reconcile with the past and look toward the future. He appeals to "his fellow citizens, in the conviction that a serene relationship with our past is the prologue for a serene vision of our present and our future . . . we all need this" (ibid.). Such comments echo the (West) German discourse of *Vergangenheitsbewältigung*, of "mastering" or coming to terms with the (specifically Nazi) past, a language often phrased in terms of success or failure (Rosenfeld 2000, 2).

Not surprisingly, Valdevit proved an enthusiastic supporter of the "historic" meeting held on March 14, 1998, at the University of Trieste between Gianfranco Fini, head of the Alleanza Nazionale (heir to the neofascist MSI), and Luciano Violante, then-president of the House and member of the PDS (successor to the communist PCI). This encounter, structured as a question-and-answer session with faculty and students enrolled in a political science seminar devoted to the "political uses of memory," returned the issue of the commensurability of the foibe and Risiera to the national stage, which it had occupied in August 1996. The announcement of the meeting sparked a lively discussion in Trieste and beyond. Although a poll of six hundred individuals in Trieste suggested a general approval of the initiative (Garau 1998), predictably a wide range of opinion prevailed. In the days preceding the conference, for example, many letters were sent to the editor of *Il Piccolo*. Some letter writers defended the initiative as an important step forward, others complained about the need to recognize the memory of Trieste's Slovenes as part of that "unitary national memory" that both Fini and Violante sought to construct, and still others saw the lumping together of the crimes of the Risiera (associated with the German Nazis) and the foibe (considered a crime of Titoists) as yet another inscription of the *brava gente* myth.

As with Spadaro's pronouncements on the foibe two years earlier, many observers suspected that the basest political ambitions motivated what Giorgio Marchesich, secretary of the Movimento Indipendentista Nord Libero, deemed the "incestuous embrace" of Fini and Violante (Marchesich 1998). Protesters from the extreme Right (members of the old MSI who do not approve of the Alleanza Nazionale's more centrist and reconciliatory approach) and the extreme Left (Rifondazione Communista) rejected what they saw as an opportunistic move by the "postfascists" and "postcommunists." Casting themselves as defenders of the pure faith (*veraci*, or true ones) and embracing the older narrative terms about the war, those few dissidents who turned out to protest bore the old symbols (the tricolor with the black flame for the MSI, the Yugoslav flag with the red star for Rifondazione), which the parties represented by Fini and Violante had discarded.

Fini's and Violante's comments during the course of the meeting reveal the increasing convergence of discourse from the Left and Right about the foibe and a newfound interest in Trieste on the part of national politicians who now see it as a bridge to the East, a vital link between the Mediterranean and Eastern Worlds. According to Violante, "The pain of this part of Italy separated it from the rest of Italy. But now Trieste has much to teach Italy about living together [*convivenza*]" (Zeriali 1998). Violante also lamented the amnesia or "dismemory" (*dismemoria*) that had long rendered Trieste a marginal and lacerated place, a city whose residents had paid for Italy's defeat in World War II. Both Fini and Violante agreed on the need to "resew a torn memory" (*ricucire una memoria strappata*) by recognizing the dual tragedies of the Risiera and the foibe. As they saw it, this would constitute a common denominator of values for a nation that had been stillborn. On one point Fini and Violante did, however, clearly disagree: protection of the Slovene minority. Fini countered Violante's expression of support for further guarantees with the argument that the Slovenes enjoyed more than enough rights (Manzin 1998b).

In the days following the much-discussed encounter, a group of seventy-five scholars published a protest in the leftist newspaper *Il Manifesto*. The scholars charged that by failing to place the events of the foibe in their proper context (two decades of fascist violence toward Slavic populations), Violante had "offended" the memories of those who had died in the Resistance (Palieri 1998).

According to these intellectuals, political initiatives like the ones organized by Fini and Violante proved incompatible with "historic truth" and obscured the real difference between those who created gas chambers (the Nazis and fascists) and those who fought for a better world. As two commentators for *Il Manifesto* concluded, inverting the celebratory rhetoric of Fini and Violante regarding the city's newfound role as a "national resource," Trieste itself had become the true foiba of history (Chiarusi and Moder 1998). Such responses indicate that although increasingly overshadowed by a revisionist reading of Italy's civil war, the interpretations that predominated in the immediate postwar period continue to hold significance for some individuals.

The arguments waged in national newspapers about how to understand the events of the war and immediate postwar era paralleled those heard in the city itself. Rows broke out among the historians at the traditionally left-oriented Istituto Regionale per la Storia del Movimento di Liberazione nel Friuli–Venezia Giulia over how to judge the Fini-Violante meeting. Giampaolo Valdevit, at that time scientific director of the institute, had publicly thanked Fini and Violante for what he saw as an important gesture. He argued that in postwar Trieste, the divided memory of the war had hardened into exclusive memories (as we have seen in this chapter). This had resulted in "memories surrounded by barbed wire" *(memorie circondate da filo spinato),* an image invoking the deportation camps of both the Nazis-fascists and the Yugoslav partisans. For their effort to break the tight nexus of memory and politics in Trieste, Valdevit concluded, Fini and Violante deserved gratitude, regardless of whether they were also motivated by self-serving political ambitions (Valdevit 1998). For his stance, Valdevit received considerable criticism at the institute and eventually resigned his position after a fiery meeting of the executive committee.

Like the city's professional historians, representatives of the esuli and rimasti did not agree on the event. One group of Istrians wrote an open letter to the two political leaders in which they expressed the sense of betrayal that pervades esuli understandings. They viewed this political reconciliation as reflecting the desire to bury the problems of the border in the "archive of history." Just as exiles rejected the notion of "the world's most open border," these Istrians mocked the idea that the boundary confirmed by Osimo could become the "frontier of expiation" *(frontiera dell'espiazione).* In their estimation, Trieste and its Istrian population would again be instrumentalized for their symbolic value to the national center (Gruppo Memorandum 88 1998). Other esuli saw the gesture as a crucial first step that nevertheless demanded concrete political action.

A number of other important symbolic gestures have followed, including the participation in February 2000 of Head of State Carlo Ciampi in a commemoration at the monument of Basovizza. The following month, a general monument to the "martyrs of the foibe" was dedicated in Trieste's Park of Remembrance, originally created under Mussolini to remember the heroes of Italy's War of Redemption. This location proves fitting, underscoring the emplottment of the foibe and exodus in broad irredentist narratives and demonstrating the reclamation of a national(ist?) history separate from that of fascism. Whereas some esuli hailed this symbolic recognition, others complained about the haste with which officials conducted the ceremonies and the absence of the expected solemnity and religiosity. One esule remarked, "It is up to us now to make sure that this memory is not canceled" (*Derin*, 2000). This statement renders the exiles the true and exclusive custodians of the foibe's memory, challenging the political appropriations of this memory by leaders such as Fini and Violante (as well as the Slovene minority's contestation of this memory). Ironically, then, both this exile and the observer for the communist paper *Il Manifesto* fear (though for different reasons) that the true history of these events will remain tragically *infoibato*, buried, canceled in the name of a new national "pacification" and "reconciliation."

Moving beyond the specificity of the foibe case, the comments made by Valdevit and others about establishing a "serene relationship with the past" raise difficult questions for victims of such violence, as well as for scholars of atrocities. In the post–Cold War world, victims whose claims were previously ignored or looked at with suspicion because of the exigencies of Realpolitik have demanded acknowledgment and atonement from their victimizers. Long-silenced groups now may merely invert the equation and present themselves as unambiguous victims ("Istrian Italians = fascists" becomes "Istrian Italians = genocidal victims," "Slovenes = antifascists" transmogrifies into "Slovenes/Slavs = ethnic cleansers"). How to allow for shades of gray—particularly in the case of the population of a territory traumatized by rapid regime changes (Italian fascism, German Nazi occupation, and Yugoslav communism) and various degrees and types of complicity—in order to really reconcile with the past and look toward the future, as Valdevit and others propose? How to recognize victimization without creating a pervasive and exclusive sense of victimhood that, as this chapter has shown, can provide a powerful basis for group identity and action? Answering these questions acquires urgency, since some "victim" groups employ claims of past genocide in order to justify new genocides, as has been seen in Bosnia and Rwanda. As Borneman has suggested, in places such as ex-Yugoslavia, where the successor states to the authoritarian socialist regime have failed to take demands for retributive justice seriously enough, retributive violence may take its place (1997, 155). Yet in Trieste, the slide from demanding the legal prosecution of guilty individuals to broader calls for "symbolic and historical justice" also easily elides into theses of collective guilt, complicating Borneman's contrast between postauthoritarian societies that establish the "rule of law" and those which do not.

Alarmed by the proliferation of groups claiming to be victims of genocide and thereby justifying intolerance, some analysts lament that the concept of genocide itself has been so trivialized and "debased by semantic stretch that its use stirs suspicion" (Fein 1994, 95). With the Cold War's eclipse, many groups have pressed forward retroactive claims of injustices and atrocities committed in the name of socialist-communist ideologies. Although changed political realities often lend these stories a new hearing, the very definition of *genocide* nonetheless offers powerful incentives for groups to increasingly cast their persecution in specifically ethno-national terms rather than in those of other political ideologies. For the case of the esuli, during the Cold War a collective identity centered around victimization was forged through semantic and nonsemantic practices of memory. These practices included exhumations and commemorative rituals that by emphasizing the bones of ancestors linked questions of rootedness and genealogy to group claims about genocide. Such processes have worked in tandem with a powerful interpretation of the contemporary Yugoslav crisis as an inherently ethnic conflict, rendering the "ethnic cleansing" thesis all the more plausible for Istria and Trieste.

As the Istrian case reveals, attempts to determine which "genocidal" policy has priority and which is more or "truly" genocidal—that of the fascists against the Slavs, of the Germans against antifascists, or of Titoists against Italians—perpetuate a potentially dangerous logic of recrimination. At the same time the persistence of claims about the foibe and exodus—nurtured and voiced for the past half century in Trieste—reveals that whether labeled genocide (or "ethnocide" or "linguicide") or not, the victims of such violence neither forget nor renounce claims to territory and properties. Such claims receive powerful support when embedded in a narrative framework casting events in fundamentally moral terms.

CHAPTER SIX

Narrating Exodus: The Shapes of Memory

My land is very far
As if it didn't exist outside of my mind.

—Anonimo Giuliano, *"La Terra"*

CLAIMS to genocide and ethnic cleansing construct Italian exiles from Istria as the only genuine Istrians and hence as survivors. Yet what does it mean to be an esule istriano? What multiplicity of experiences does the narrative of exodus efface and/or embrace? How is an identity as an esule (re)produced? What shapes does memory take in the construction of this exile identity?

At the technical or legal level, individuals who left Istria between 1945 and 1955 were recognized by the Italian state as *profughi,* or refugees, and became eligible for aid administered by the Opera per l'Assistenza ai Profughi Giuliani e Dalmati (OAPGD). As one scholar has put it, "Although at the moment of departure the refugees were active subjects . . . after the departure they could no longer decide whether to be a refugee—*they were*" (Volk 1999, 270; my italics). Many individuals initially left Istria believing (or hoping) that their displacement would be temporary, as had occurred during World War I (see chapter 2; for a similar sentiment among Greek refugees from Asia Minor, consult Hirschon 1998, 9). One man, an adolescent when his family left the Istrian port of Pola, noted Istrians' common practice of taking the keys to their houses with them when they departed from Istria.[1] "I remember, too, the day we left. He [his father] went to close the door of the house with the key, and he put the key in his pocket as a token. He went like this [gestures], 'Let's go, let's go.'" Indicating that many refugees hoped for an eventual return to their homes, such practices also embody a view of Italians as the rightful owners of the land and property. After 1954, however, Istrians such as this man's father realized that their loss had become permanent (although many still dreamed of a distant "redemption"), rendering them esuli.

In her memoir, *Vento di terra perduta* (Wind from a lost land), esule Giuliana Zelco describes the moment in which this transformation (semantic and conceptual) took place. Having left Istria in 1943, Zelco's family resettled (temporarily, they thought) in the Veneto region. The locals there considered the family members refugees (profughi). Only after the war did they learn a new word: *esilio* (exile). This word captures the pain of exile and yet cannot express it: "There are no words to describe an exodus of biblical proportions" (1993,

92). Zelco's characterization of her displacement highlights the the initial flows of refugees from Istria became emplotted in a bro nationalist narrative about exodus, "temporary" refugees coming the fact that their condition was one of permanent banishment from their land. When, in 1947, Zelco's family members learned that their house in Istria had been sacked and her father and brother condemned *in absentia* as enemies of the people, "At that moment I ceased to be a refugee and became an exile" (ibid., 93). The physical degradation of the family's house thus rendered "homeland" something to be preserved only in memory, positioning the esuli as the true custodians of *istrianità* (for similar tensions in the semantic status of the displaced, consult Bisharat 1997; Loizos 1981; Peteet 1998).

By attending to the various "shapes of memory" (Hartman 1994)—written accounts (memoirs, fiction, and poetry), oral and life histories, funerary traditions, and other rituals—in this chapter I examine how exiles such as Zelco construct memories that map out their "lost world." Although I focus on those who self-consciously describe themselves as esuli, not all individuals who left Istria agree with Zelco's vision of the exodus as an event of epic (and biblical) proportions or even accept the designation *esuli*. This self-selection draws even tighter boundaries of purity around the esule identity. Needless to say, Slovenes and Croats from Istria who resettled in Italy usually do not call themselves esuli; nor are they considered by "Italians" from Istria as esuli.

Some Istrian Italians prove reticent to identify themselves as such, as well. I had known Giovanna, for example, for almost two years before she ever revealed that she too had come from the Istrian town of Isola at the age of ten. She and I first met at the Istituto Regionale per la Storia del Movimento di Liberazione nel Friuli–Venezia Giulia, where Giovanna collaborates on the photographic collections. She has never felt like an esule, she told me, and with her participation in the city's leftist intellectual and artistic circles (including those of the Slovene minority) has always sought to distance herself from what she sees as a politicized rhetoric promoted by the exile associations. Nonetheless, Giovanna does find that being Istrian sometimes produces unexpected reactions, as when she made her first solo visit to her hometown twenty-five years ago. The visit induced a strange reverie, almost a trance. Given that Giovanna's childhood in Istria had always seemed like a dream to her, she indeed felt as if she was dreaming. She could hear the sound of childhood friends laughing and playing. Reality intruded, however, when she heard Slovene being spoken. At this, Giovanna began to cry—an irrational reaction, she said—because her dream had been spoiled; here, the "shapes of memory" included sight and sound. Returning to Istria induces a malaise that is hard to explain, admits Giovanna, who does not view herself as a typical esule, or even one at all.

Two cousins expressed a similar discomfort with the esule label, an unease shared by many of the younger generation of Istrians who either came to Trieste at a very young age or were born there. Annamaria, born in Capodistria in

1939, stated emphatically that because her family had left during the war (her father transferring to Padua with the Italian military), "We were profughi, not esuli." Although she remembers Istria, she feels rootless (senza radici) and goes to Istria only infrequently. Her cousin Elisabetta, born in Capodistria at war's end in 1945, similarly feels disconnected from the exile identity that other family members embraced; instead she considers herself a Triestine, much to her mother's dismay.

Like Federico, the son of exiles whose vision of the foibe complicated the thesis of "killed for the sole crime of being Italian," Betta grew up as part of the dopo esodo (postexodus) generation who nonetheless shared what she calls a "patriotic education." Her family despised Slovenes and "Titoists," an aversion she does not feel. Betta's parents often sent her on exile-sponsored trips and activities designed to instill a sense of italianità in the younger generation. The family would also visit her maternal grandparents, who remained in Capodistria until 1954, and Betta still recalls her fear while crossing the border (especially when her parents hid money and gifts on her person).

Whereas Betta grew up fully integrated in the Triestine context and has dedicated herself to researching the fate of the city's Jewish population and the crime of the Risiera di San Sabba (she and Giovanna are colleagues), her mother reconstructed an Istrian world for herself in her adoptive city. Most of her mother's closest friends in Trieste hail from Capodistria. The mother maintains these friendships through her participation in the Unione degli Istriani, over which she and Betta have had tense exchanges, and through her residence in a refugee quarter; in the 1960s Betta's parents obtained an apartment, fittingly enough on Via Capodistria, built for refugees. Betta's mother has frequently returned to Capodistria and with pleasure. In the past, she often drove for forty-five minutes to buy vegetables and other foods there, insisting that the food in Istria was healthier and tasted better.

I focus here on the ways in which self-conscious esuli, such as Betta's mother, remember and idealize a lost world (as symbolized by her faith in Istria's purer and more wholesome foods). The children of the dopo esodo often inhabit the interstices and margins of this re-created community, sometimes rejecting it altogether, sometimes (re)discovering contemporary Istria for themselves, and sometimes sharing in their elders' understandings more than they like to admit (as with Giovanna's "outburst" upon hearing Slovene or Federico's depiction of the Slavs as "wild animals").

Architectonics of Memory

Remembering the house in which an uprooted culture originated and developed involves reversing history and sinking symbolic roots into a vanished human and geographical world. The remembered house is a small-scale cosmology symbolically restoring the integrity of a shattered geography. (Bahloul 1996, 28)

Place-names, churches enshrining icons, even stones transported from the homeland: all were elements aiding in reconstructing a meaningful environment. (Hirschon 1998, 25)

For exiles and their children, Istria's nearby presence (what I earlier called its maddening proximity) serves as the ultimate mnemonic, daily reminding them of a world that is so near and yet so far, physically just over the horizon but whose social and cultural fabric has been rent forever. In reconstructing their communities in memory as well as in dreams (for many esuli note that at night they still dream about their homes after all these years), displaced peoples typically refer to the actual landscape and to individual houses (Bahloul 1996; Hirschon 1998; Nemec 1998). In mapping out the physical landscape of their natal land in their mind's eye, poetry and prose, and artwork, the exiles' abode thus serves as a metonym for the homeland. The story of Vittorio's house illustrates the ways in which dwellings often become the locus of the intense and frequently contradictory emotions—nostalgia, anger, and sorrow—experienced by the displaced, for whom *casa mia* (my house) stands in for *casa nostra* (our house, our land).

Vittorio inherited the apartment of a great-aunt who remained in Rovigno under Yugoslavia. Visiting the house and his hometown after many years in exile brought to the surface long-buried memories of childhood. The trauma of his mother's imprisonment in 1948 for the "crime" of possessing sugar and eggs and her subsequent heart attack had proved so painful that for many years Vittorio neither wanted to nor could remember many incidents from that period. Only by rewalking the streets of Rovigno and encountering former classmates who had remained there did Vittorio begin to recuperate his past, little by little recalling events he had believed were long forgotten. These encounters often proved ambivalent, as when he found he had a "nondialogue" with old childhood mates who had become party faithfuls under Yugoslavia: "It's only a monologue with them; their minds have been formed in a completely different way from ours." Nevertheless, Vittorio and his wife (not an esule) decided to spend a good portion of their summers in Rovigno.

When I met them, Vittorio and Elisa were embroiled in a nasty dispute over the house Vittorio had inherited. The apartment was in an old palazzo on the waterfront. Below the apartment, an enterprising family (of "Albanian Mafiosi," according to Vittorio) had built a large restaurant catering to tourists. They had done much of this work *abusivo*, that is, illegally, without all the necessary permits. Vittorio also charged that the restaurateurs had taken out supporting walls in a neighboring apartment (which had belonged to a well-known Istrian partisan hero), rendering Vittorio's own home precariously unstable. Vittorio filed various complaints with the authorities and hounded the town's architectural code officer but with little success. His failure in the Croatian legal and political system (which Vittorio, rightly or wrongly, chalked up to corruption and clientelism) embittered Vittorio so much that he eventually shuttered up his house and sold it. His apartment's shaky existence symbolized his own unsuccessful attempt to "reintegrate" into an Istria whose social maps and relations had irrevocably changed. The removal of his home's proper supports by illegal means and without any hope of recourse proved an all-too-apt metaphor for the common fate of Italians in Istria. Vittorio realized that as an exile he could go home again only in his memories. "After all these years, I still feel like an exile. . . . I began to realize that the real Italians are no longer here [in Istria]."

Other exiles often agree with Vittorio, finding that a visit to contemporary Istria merely reinforces their memories, to which they cling as an act of faith when confronted with the peninsula's contemporary face. Writing in a volume of works by second-generation esuli, Gianni Sirotti notes that he has returned many times to visit his native town of Pisino. "Even the people who live there are so different from us that I found myself out of my element [spaesato, literally out of one's paese, or country]. Certainly it is not anymore those Istrian people that I was used to" (in Famiglia Pisinota 1967, 37). Unlike Sirotti, several other contributors to the volume on Pisino had never visited their parents' former homes in Istria; nonetheless, these exile descendants feel that they can mentally re-create that lost world about which they have heard so much. One woman admits, "I never went to Pisino, but in my imagination I already have an idea of this town located in a hilly zone" (ibid., 23). Similarly, another son of esuli paints a vivid picture of Pisino's cemetery, where he envisions his grandfather resting among the dead. "I've never seen that cemetery, which has perhaps only a few flowers, but I want to visit it just as I wish to visit that town [recreated] in my parents' stories and my imagination" (ibid., 46). These secondhand images of Istria appear to be built largely out of stories told by parents, a world of abandoned houses and cemeteries reconstructed from words and whose "truth" proves greater than that offered by the actual landscape.

Many exiles attempt to relocate and re-create Istria not just mentally, however, but also in their new dwellings. Photographs and paintings (oil and watercolor) of their birthplace frequently adorn their homes. Some keep more tangible bits of Istria in the form of stones, fragments of their family home's foundation, or vials of seawater. (Tweed [1997] discusses similar practices whereby Cuban exiles in Miami re-create their home with soil and seawater, particularly by incorporating them into diasporic shrines, such as the one for Ermita de la Caridad.) Telling me that she feels as if "she is still living with her people," freelance journalist Liana showed me her "piece of Istria," an Istrian stone that she preserves in her home in Trieste. Stella, Liana's childhood friend, similarly attempts to re-create Istria in her house, where she has placed photographs of her parents, the family coat of arms, and a piece of the wall of her former home in Capodistria. When Stella enters her home in Trieste, she can imagine the house she *should* have had.

Stella's fashioning of her home as a literal mnemonic, Vittorio's recall of memories upon revisiting Istria, and the second-generation esuli's mental mappings of Pisino all remind us of the well-remarked connections between memory maps and actual maps. As we have seen, cartographic maps feature prominently at some exile (as well as rimasti) associations and institutes, highlighting these groups' claims to alternative boundaries and maps. Whether spoken (as in the case of Vittorio) or written, many such accounts present the story of the exodus as trips through memory *(viaggi di memoria)*, triggered by physical traces of history that "testify" to the Istrian Italians' autochthony and purity as Italians.

Penned by a priest, *Incontri con Istria: La sua storia, la sua gente* (Encounters with Istria: Its history, its people) takes the form of a literal and a figurative journey. Luigi Parentin constructs his history as both a "trip through memory" and an actual visit to the small towns of Istria many years after the events of the exodus. Parentin thus organizes his history like a guidebook, with sections corresponding to places; each stop on his itinerary provides the occasion for him to revisit the history of the locale. Parentin focuses on small towns and villages such as Materada, "heavy with a melancholy silence" (Parentin 1992, 29), churches and monasteries abandoned to the "silence of the countryside" (ibid., 31), and dead cities such as Vergnacco, where the windows of ruined houses serve as "mute mirrors" (ibid., 54). Parentin also notes the cemeteries with their "old tombstones, all Italian, different from those recent ones, which are for the most part Slav" (ibid., 83). For Parentin, the tombs testify not only to the Italians' historic presence in the peninsula but also to the "Istrian" religious tradition and the barbarity of those who defaced cenotaphs and monuments, destroyed churches, and persecuted the clergy. "The foundation of Istria, the roots of our people," concludes Parentin, "is the land *[terra]* with traditions that have sunk in over the centuries" (ibid., 52). This emphasis on soil and materiality reminds us of the etymology of *exile,* defined in the seventh century by Isidore de Seville as meaning "outside the soil—*extra solum*" (in Starn 1982, 1).

The kinds of memory maps fashioned by esuli such as Parentin draw on a long history in Western thinking about not only exile but also the "art of memory," which in turn rests on a storage or archival model of memory as the retrieval of indelible traces. From the ancient rhetoricians of Greece and Rome, medieval scholars inherited a mnemonic art of memory privileging visual images or maps as aide-mémoire. During the Renaissance and under the influence of Neoplatonism (Yates 1978, 140; see also Carruthers 1990), such maps assumed more elaborate forms in the memory theaters of men like Matteo Ricci and Giulio Camillo. A later generation of rationalists including Descartes and Leibnitz would reject these detailed representations, seeking a simpler mnemonic method based on "not images, but causes" (Fentress and Wickham 1992, 13). As a textual model gradually supplanted a visual one, "the dominant mode of mnemonic connection became logical, a chain of connections and causes articulated in syntactic 'space,' rather than in a visual representation of space" (ibid.).

Despite this broad shift in scholarly perspectives on memory (from a visual to a semantic model), the older tradition of maps and visual images as aide-mémoire was by no means extinguished. It remains particularly pronounced for groups such as the esuli, who preserve a literal vision of their lost world as they focus on architectural monuments, cemeteries, houses, and family trees in legitimating their historical claims. Many commentators have remarked on this close association between memory and space, as well as on such symbols of rootedness (Schama 1995). Feeley-Harnik has even gone so far as to suggest that the prevalence of root metaphors derives, "like the spatial dimensions of memory, from more general human capacities of laterality, movement, or uprightness" (1991, 467).

In the esuli's case, "uprightness" also has a figurative sense, the Italians in Istria depicting themselves as morally just and pious (particularly through references to cemeteries and churches) in contrast to the "godless" Slavs who persecuted them. By linking semantic discourse to physical landscape, the exiles offer powerful "evidence" of Istria's destruction, evidence that resists various efforts to silence the story of exodus. Like Istria's ruined landscape, the exile's body itself (and those of the ancestors in Istria's soil) also bears testimony to the "truth" of the esuli's claims. In a variety of ways, then, exiles (re)construct memories of their lost world, which remains open only to those "authentic" Istrians with roots in the land of Istria. The ultimate sign of this rootedness is the presence of dead ancestors, who have become part of the soil.

Ghostly Landscapes: Istria as Tomb

These, Oh Italy, are your boundaries! but every day they are violated by the avarice of nations. Where are your sons? You lack nothing but the force of unity. . . . Even as we invoke the magnanimous shades [of our ancestors], our enemies trample their sepulchers underfoot. And the day will come when, losing our possessions and our dignity and even our voice to cry out in protest, we will be reduced to the condition of slaves, or bought and sold like Negroes, and we will see our masters open the tombs and empty them and scatter to the winds the ashes of those Heroes to annihilate their memory.
—Foscolo in Carolyn Springer, *The Marble Wilderness*

I looked at the tombs. What with all their weeds they looked like mounds of earth on the backs of enormous moles. And I thought of our deceased, their ears and nostrils filled with sweet basil; I thought of so many other people who'd been born and bred and then buried there with a rosary and a black book in their hands, and of whom nothing was left but bones and more bones, the ones on top of the others, and books and beads strewn through the soil. An acre of that rockless land had sufficed for them all; it could have sufficed for us and our children too.

"Farewell to our dead," said one woman aloud.

—Fulvio Tomizza, *Materada*

The dead figure prominently in exile understandings in a dual capacity: as ancestors who testify to the peninsula's italianità and as the bodies of those killed or desecrated by the partisans. This duality mirrors the ways in which architecture stands as both a sign of civilization, or civiltà (the Roman and Venetian heritage), and its destruction (a ruined landscape). Such a language has a long genealogy in the region; in the 1770s, for instance, the Venetian priest Alberto Fortis lamented the destruction of Dalmatia's archaeological splendors at the hands of the greedy and ignorant barbarians who resided on the ruins of a splendid past (Wolff 2001, 109–10). As one of Trieste's most popular mayors, a prominent exile, similarly put it in the decade following the exodus, "There in 'Istria nobilissima' remain falling walls and noble stones, but the irreplaceable leaven of civilization, which makes for life and progress, is extinguished" (Bartoli 1960, 7). Here older discourses about the Italian civiltà threatened or destroyed by occupiers begin to be articulated with the postdestruction imagery of genocide. For exiles such as Bartoli, Istria's crumbling architecture (its monuments to "civilization") and devastated landscape symbolize the way in which the peninsula has become a vast sepulchre, metaphorically but also literally: a dead land, despoiled by the Slavs, where the light of civilization has been snuffed out.

Photos of postexodus Istria included in exile publications or presented at slide shows and exhibitions perpetuate this view of Istria as a devastated and emptied land. A 1996 exhibition at the Istituto Regionale per la Cultura Istriana entitled "Forgotten Istria" featured photographs of present-day Istria's ruined and abandoned buildings. The organizers put this set of photographs together with portraits of Italian Istrians dating from the Austrian and Italian periods. This juxtaposing of portraits and ruined landscapes brings to mind Glenn Bowman's 1993 analysis of Palestinian "tales of a lost land." Bowman found that whereas in late-nineteenth-century Europe commercial photography developed largely as a medium of portraiture, contemporaneous pictures brought back by Western visitors to the Holy Land showed decaying monuments and empty territory. This Western vision of Palestine as a site of historic importance and contemporary desolation neglected and silenced the area's residents, just as Istrian exiles' use of photos of Istria does. In depicting Istria as a dead land, ravaged by barbaric Slavs, exiles thus ignore its present-day inhabitants and posit themselves as the territory's only indigenous and authentic peoples.

This funereal portrayal of the Istrian landscape further underwrites esuli claims to authenticity and autochthony by referencing those dead ancestors, buried in Istrian soil, who give silent testimony to Italians' historic presence in the peninsula. The image of cemeteries, the site of proper mourning, provides an antidote to the anonymous and sealed-over mass graves of the foibe, "which speak by virtue of their silence" (Pizzi 1999, 103) and signal the inversion of proper, moral relations. Envisioned as a spectral landscape, Istria paradoxically rings out with the sounds of silence: the silence of the deserted cities and countryside of Istria, the silence of the nation and the world that expressed no outrage at this event, the silence of the dead and of the grave.

Though these images of emptiness and funereal quiet prove common to understandings of displacement, as well as of genocide (Patterson 1992), in the Istrian case they also refer to a specific mode of meditating on ruins and tombs that Risorgimental poets like Ugo Foscolo made central to the practices of Italian nationalism (Springer 1987, 117). Foscolo's 1807 poem, "Dei Sepolcri," has particular resonance for many esuli (Spazzali, personal communication). "Dei Sepolcri" is a meditation on the tombs of Italy's great heroes and martyrs, the politicization and secularization of a Christian elegiac tradition of poetry in which the resurrection now imagined is political (ibid., 122). As with esuli's mental returns to Istria, Foscolo's poetic text of political exile consists of a literal voyage or journey through a territorially dismembered Italy, whose desecration is symbolized by laws forbidding the use of individual tombs and prescribing "the dispersion of bodies in unmarked communal graves" (ibid., 123). Mentally traversing the Florentine Church of Santa Croce, the poet finds himself before the cenotaphs of Italy's great men: Dante, Petrarch, Machiavelli, Galileo, and other national geniuses, whose tombs mark the "station of a civic via crucis" (Springer 1987, 119). Foscolo's call for Italians to "[p]lacate the souls of your great heroes" (Foscolo 1970, 38)—whose graves risk being vandalized at the hands of barbaric invaders—echoes generally in later irredentist reworkings and more precisely in esuli accounts. Just as Foscolo depicted Italy as a vast tomb, so too do exiles envision Istria.

As the Istrian esule Guido Posar-Giuliano wrote in 1955, "The interior of Istria is a sweet land of saints and cypresses, but it is also a land of the dead; it has the air of a sepulchre" (120). For this man, Istria's atmosphere of decay belies both the destruction wrought by the exodus and the Italians' historic (and civilizing) presence in the peninsula. The Italians' interred ancestors lie at the heart of a cult of remembrance stressing piety and respect for the dead. Remembering the dark and silent Istrian nights in which "the dead slept tranquilly" (119), Posar-Giuliano suggests that the silences of times past were signs of an ordered universe in which the living honored and respected the dead. This situation contrasts with the desolate silences of postexodus Istria. "[T]hat Istria of my youth," laments this exile, "no longer exists. It is only a ghost, the most luminous memory of my life, which I preserve in my memory and return to ever more frequently. . . . A land dear to me because there rest my people" (113).

Through manifold practices that recall ancestors, saints, and nationalist martyrs, Istrian Italians honor and reconstruct in exile their lost, dead world. These practices invoke those aspects of life in preexodus Istria now labeled traditional. Not coincidentally, the fascist era in which most exiles came of age witnessed an intense exploitation of "popular traditions" by the regime (De Grazia 1981; Horn 1991; Simeone 1978). In Istria such traditions were often recorded by local Italian scholars, who in the 1920s and 1930s increasingly used ethnography in the service of political aims, specifically those demonstrating the Julian March's italianità and thus silencing the presence of other ethnic groups (Oretti 1994, 19, 27–38). Among those Istrian Italian traditions often noted was the intensive care and attention given to tombs, particularly on the Day of the Dead (October 31).[2]

Visiting and honoring family tombs continue to hold great importance for Istrian Italians, both those exiles and those rimasti with whom I worked in Rovigno. In Istria I accompanied members of the Italian minority on different occasions to lay flowers and clean tombstones; this was done at least several times a year. Many exiles in Trieste similarly said that they returned only reluctantly to Istria yet would force themselves to go at least once a year to visit their families' tombs. Narratives of the exodus often described the first emotional return to Istria years later as prompted by the desire, as well as the duty, to visit family graves. Leonardo, who at the age of nine left the small interior town of Verteneglio/Brtonigla with his family, first "rediscovered" Istria when he accompanied a woman from Capodistria who occasionally returned to visit her former home. She took him to the cemetery, where he saw the tombs of Capodistria's illustrious and noble families. Like Giovanna (who began to cry upon hearing Slovene spoken in the town of Isola), Leonardo speaks of the "strange sensation" induced by such return visits to Istria. He nonetheless feels compelled to rediscover his identity. In seeking out "testimonies of italianità," Leonardo constructs a literal itinerary of cemeteries and churches.

During the 1996 cruise down the coast of Istria and Dalmatia, described in chapter 2, several of my companions also felt compelled to visit graveyards. Although our group had only a few brief hours in which to visit Zara, several of the Zaratini on the trip insisted on paying a visit to the old cemetery. When the ship arrived behind schedule, my companions and I hopped into the waiting car of an elderly Italian, one of the small number of Italians who had remained in Zara and who now participate in the newly constituted minority association there. As we arrived at the cemetery, the Zaratini quickly located their family graves and laid flowers. They detailed their family genealogies to me and also pointed out the headstones of members of notable families and renowned patriots, as well as the memorial stone to Zara's Great War dead. In a city in which

Figure 9. The Cult of Remembrance
a. Tomb for Girolamo Luxardo, prominent Zaratino, Old Cemetery, Zara
b. Zaratino esule placing flowers in Zara's cemetery

much of the rich architectural patrimony left by Venice was obliterated by aerial warfare, this cemetery remains a tangible trace of the "Italian" past.

Indeed, after the city's bombing, one exile proclaimed Zara *una città morta,* "a dead city" (Bambara 1994, 110). The cemetery offered refuge to the city's harassed Italians during these bombardments. Survivors of the bombings who had lost their homes or feared being trapped in them in case of further attacks took shelter in the graveyard. Reflecting a world turned upside down, the ancestors protected the living from the death that came from the skies. The place of the dead *(luogo dei morti)* thus nurtured the last signs of life of the dead city of Zara (on Zara's cemetery, consult Ivanov [1986] and Madrinato Dalmatico [1986]). One of my guides at the old cemetery, a fifty-nine-year-old retired army general who left Zara at the age of four, pointed to the Italian surnames on the tombs as irrefutable evidence of Italians' historic presence in the now "dead" city. Piero also recounted the city's "liberation" by the Italian navy in November 1918. Cemeteries themselves become powerful aide-mémoire for the esuli, paradoxically preserving life through memory. Paying their respects at the cemetery, my Zaratini companions simultaneously honored their personal dead, gave thanks to the ancestors who watched over them during the city's destruction, and mourned their lost city.

The preservation of these graves becomes a moral concern, as well as a legal one, given the taxes imposed on tombs. The burial plots of families who are unable to pay or who have no living representatives are often emptied of their contents, to the horror and anger of many exiles; such desecration echoes the profanation of Italy's dead lamented by the poet Foscolo. Stella, born to a noble family in Capodistria and resident for many decades in Trieste in the house modeled on that which "she should have had," first told me of this situation and of various exile efforts to both protest the practice and collect money to pay the taxes. Maintaining that "our history is in the cemetery," Stella is one of several exiles who argue that the Croatian and Slovene governments' actions represent an attempt to rewrite Istrian history, one that recalls the Yugoslav effort to "Slavicize" Italian tombstones immediately after World War II. Stella, together with exile association leaders, has called for a law to protect Istrian cemeteries and to recognize as "protected tombs" those of illustrious Istrians. "Our cemeteries represent a historic patrimony of great importance and an irrefutable testimony of the centuries-long italianità of the Istrian land," she argues. In line with this view, researchers from the Istituto Regionale per la Cultura Istriana and the Centro di Ricerche Storiche di Rovigno have visited 209 cemeteries and assembled a photographic record of more than 16,700 Italian tombs in Istria. Highlighting the urgent need to protect the graves of former generations, this photographic record is also intended to offer further testimony of Istria's italianità.

Desiring to protect their ancestors' resting places, some exiles hope ultimately to join them there upon their own deaths by having their ashes scattered in Istria. Others, aware that their exile would be without return, took the remains of their dead with them at the time of the exodus. The best-known case occurred in 1947, when departing Istrians disinterred the body of irredentist hero Nazario Sauro. In the months preceding the dramatic exodus of Italians from Pola in 1947, Italian propaganda frequently invoked Sauro's heroic figure. Proponents of the removal of Sauro urged that "[t]he remains of the pure Mazzinian martyr, symbol of the Istrian people's love of country, cannot and must not be desolately abandoned to the foreigner" (L'Emancipazione, January 27, 1947). Such arguments won out, and film footage and photos from that time show the transfer of these "sacred remains" to the ships that took the refugees to Italy. Priests on board blessed the remains of Sauro, as well as those of other Istrians removed from their graves, and newspaper headlines proclaimed "Sauro an Exile with His People" (ibid., March 10, 1947). Such a practice demonstrates the intense importance Istrians attach to their dead, as well as continued fears that those remains will be desecrated.

In addition, the removal of Sauro's body brings to mind the peregrinations of saints' bones common to Catholic hagiography, offering yet another example of the close links between a cult of national ancestors and those of religious martyrs. Although Sauro represents a nationalist martyr for esuli throughout Istria, his name specifically recalls San Nazario, patron saint of his native town of Capodistria. The relics of San Nazario, like those of his namesake fourteen centuries later, endured several moves; tales relating the desecration of San Nazario's remains may have underwritten the exiles' reluctance to leave Sauro's body to modern-day "barbarian" invaders. According to one legend, San Nazario was originally buried in an unmarked grave in order to shelter the saint's relics from the vandalism common in that era of "barbarian" invasion (Oretti 1994, 174). Over time, however, the secret location of this tomb was lost, only to be rediscovered sometime between the seventh and eighth centuries; the recovered relics were said to have cured the sick who touched them. From this point on, Capodistria recognized San Nazario as its patron saint.

The festivals surrounding these saints' days—traditionally featuring religious processions, Masses, and celebrations and still commemorated today in "exile" together with celebrations of nationalist martyrs such as Nazario Sauro—represent another important memory practice by which Istrians honor their dead and thereby reaffirm their attachment to the place where their dead rest. The celebrations honoring San Nazario, held annually in Capodistria on June 19, were traditionally among the most elaborate of such Istrian festivals (Radole 1976, 127–28). Today Capodistrians living in Trieste celebrate this day in exile by participating in the festival at Borgo San Nazario sul Carso, a village on the Karst above the city. Participants in the procession to the church there carry sheaves of lavender, re-creating a traditional aspect of the Capodistrian celebrations. Among the adherents I recognized and greeted when I attended the celebrations in 1995 were many esuli not from Capodistria. This suggests the manner in which San Nazario (like the nationalist Nazario Sauro) has become symbol of a pan-Istrian esule identity, an "ancestor" common to all Istrians (for a similar process whereby exile fosters a regional identity among refugees, consult Loizos 1981).

Another Capodistrian tradition faithfully preserved in exile—the celebration held the second Sunday after Easter—remains specifically local and offers an example of how more particularized identities are also maintained in exile. In Istria this traditional festival took place at the Church of Semedella, on the outskirts of Capodistria. Dedicated to the miracle of the Madonna (the so-called Madonna delle Grazie) that ended the pestilence of 1630–31, the chapel at Semedella sits in the cemetery where many of Capodistria's plague victims were interred (Pusterla 1996). Since fleeing their homes, Capodistrians in Italy have continued to celebrate the Madonna's divine intervention. Today the esuli hold their traditional Mass and lunch in Fiumicello, a burg west of Trieste. When I joined the Capodistrians at Fiumicello in 1996, they told me that they had chosen Fiumicello for their celebration because the church's positioning resembled that of Semedella, dated from the same period, and was similarly built to remember the plague. The church at Fiumicello thus stands as a mnemonic for the chapel at Semedella, reflecting the ways in which "[d]iasporic religion is translocative" (Tweed 1997, 95), and thereby symbolically mediates between the lost homeland and the new land of settlement.[3]

Fiumicello not only recalls the original church at Semedella, however, but also contrasts positively with the damaged and decaying original structure. In the Mass given at the Fiumicello celebrations in 1996, the priest closed with a sobering reminder that the chapel at Semedella lies in a state of degradation, and he urged the representatives of the exile associations to work to restore the church structure there. A few Capodistrian exiles did not hear the priest's exhortations, having opted instead to attend the newly revived celebration at Semedella. Under the Tito regime, such religious festivals, as well as those honoring patron saints, were frowned on (particularly before the 1966 protocol between the Yugoslav state and the Vatican), though Istrians told me that they had celebrated such days privately, in their homes.[4] Since Yugoslavia's breakup, public festivals for saints' days have been revived in Istria. In stressing their strict adherence to tradition, many exiles not surprisingly view the revived public saints' festivals in Istria as largely commercial events—with booths selling sweets and toys, games, and events designed to attract tourists—that miss the "real" religious and communal significance of such traditions.

When I asked some of those in attendance at Fiumicello whether they had considered going to the revived ceremony at Semedella in Capodistria, one person expressed fear, and another disinterest in the "squalor" that such a celebration in Slovenia would presumably entail. This squalor is seen as both physical (wrought by decay and neglect) and moral (arising from Slovene hypocrisy). For participants at Fiumicello, the world they have lost cannot be recaptured by revisiting Istria. "Istria" resides no longer in the physical territory bearing that name but rather in the moral community constituted through memory practices by the esuli who reproduce Istrian traditions. The caption for a 1948 drawing by exile Gigi Vidris reads, "Now Pola is but a dream [or a memory]"; this holds more generally, of course, for Istria.

In various ways, then, Istrians' devotion to their dead ancestors stakes a moral claim for the exiles' history and indigenousness, reinforcing their status as members of a lost world. The bodies of ancestors make manifest, for example, extensive Italian genealogies in the peninsula. Honoring the dead connects with deep-rooted traditions, which in turn reconstitute a community in exile. My emphasis here has been on practices and rituals, but I now turn to different types of texts, which, in telling the tale of exodus, similarly relate a story about Istria and its true inhabitants, its *gente verace,* through a focus on the material traces (especially cemeteries and churches) left by those who fled Istria.

Figure 10. *Ormai Pola è solo un sogno* (Now Pola is but a dream), by Gigi Vidris. Courtesy of Istituto Regionale per la Cultura Istriana.

Narratives of Displacement, Semantics of Exile

Exiles feel, therefore, an urgent need to reconstitute their broken lives, usually by choosing to see themselves as part of a triumphant ideology or a restored people. (Said 1994, 140–41)

As Bahloul suggests, remembering lost houses is a powerful way of "symbolically restoring the integrity of a shattered geography" (1996, 28). Another means by which groups such as the esuli reconstitute "broken lives" is inserting their specific histories into a larger framework—usually the prototypical biblical story of sacrifice, martyrdom, and redemption—that positions esuli as a "restored people." As Said points out, such a strategy proves common to (and, indeed, may be said to define) the state of exile, as opposed to that of refugeeism. Regardless of the specificity of the broader histories to which displacement accounts are connected, the "semantics of exile" (like the rites of passage) typically entail a tripartite structuring of accounts: the original state of innocence, the liminal moment of rupture and transformation, and the phase of (partial) integration. Written and spoken narratives of the Istrian experience, for example, usually describe an idyllic life in pre-*esodo* Istria, the exodus itself (figured as the encounter between Italians and "barbarian" Slavs), and the difficult conditions of the esuli's arrival in Italy and/or the destruction of Istria's cultural integrity.

The recollection of an idyllic lost age of innocence is underscored by the fact that many exiles also remember their own childhood, usually figured as a happy and carefree time. As one commentator puts it in a preface to a volume of poetry by an esule, *"There is a land that Antonio Angeli [the poet] was forced to abandon that once perhaps he was indifferent and ungrateful towards but that now, seen with regret, is transformed into a Lost Paradise. And, together with that place, there is an era that perhaps once seemed heavy and boring but that now, in retrospect, has become a golden age"* (Piero Bargellini in Angeli n.d., ii).

These Istrian tales of a lost paradise and expulsion from the Garden (presumably for the original sin of fascism) display structural affinities with "contact narratives" (see Harkin 1988), stories of encounters between Europeans and aboriginal populations. Such narratives of first meetings prove particularly revealing of group self-conceptions (Carrier 1987). In casting the exodus as a tale of the fateful encounter between the Italians of Istria with the "barbaric" Slavs, at different points the esuli assume the role of either Western civilizer or "native" (that is, genocidal victim, survivor). In all the accounts analyzed here, as in those of the foibe, the Slavs clearly occupy the "savage slot" (Trouillot 1991), inciting terror rather than pleasure. Esuli instead figure as representatives of a rich and ancient civilization that has brought to the peninsula spiritual and intellectual enlightenment, as well as technological progress. However, esuli simultaneously occupy the structural position of "natives" in a "last of the Mohicans" sense, as members of a lost world *(un mondo perso)*.

The image of exiles as the survivors of an autochthonous and now decimated culture, a culture rooted in the soil of Istria and today preserved in the hearts of the esuli, thus informs a strong sense of moral community (for a similar case, see Malkki 1996, 73), as well as concrete demands to return to that land. Here, a religiously charged vocabulary of exile conjoins with the diplomatic language of "governments in exile." Previous winners and current losers, the Istrian Italians hope for eventual redemption: redemption at the symbolic level (the recognition of the esuli's "forgotten history"), in memory (Istria living again in the hearts of these survivors), and in pragmatic terms (the actual return of properties in Istria). Demands for legal and historical justice rest on the moral quality of exile accounts as biblical epics, telling a tale about the betrayal and sacrifice of Istria's Italians, innocent victims who paid the price for fascist Italy's sins just as Christ paid for those of humankind. Writing of Greek refugees, Layoun's judgment proves equally apt for the esuli case: "The assertion (in the narrative present) of trust betrayed is the assertion, at least implicitly, of a claim for what *should have been* (in the past of the story), for the necessity of a critical community 'then'" (Layoun 1995, 80).

Memoirs such as Giuliana Zelco's *Vento di terra perduta* (1993), for instance, employ a variety of rhetorical strategies that make powerful claims about the authenticity of the Istrian Italians and the illegitimacy of those who supplanted them. Italians are seen not only as authentic but also as trusting and ingenuous, unaware of the fate that awaits them. Exhibiting the tripartite structure common to such narratives of displacement, these texts also evoke funerals, cemeteries, and other material traces. In her memoir, Zelco makes a specific funeral symbol of Istria's imminent fate, one of death and dispersion (see Giuricin 1993 for a similar strategy); the attendant emphasis on religiosity and propriety underlines the exodus's character as a biblical epic. Zelco recalls the idyllic Istria of her childhood, into which intruded the specter of death when her grandfather passed away in 1942. Zelco remembers with nostalgia the vigil and the funeral, seen in retrospect as the last moment in which the entire family would be gathered together. Although this funeral was a portent of the death yet to come, the collapse of the Italian state and army the following year nonetheless was "an unexpected storm" (24) for the Italians in Istria. Rumors of Tito's rebels reached their ears, but Istrians thought of Slavs as belonging to another world. "Croatia was beyond Fiume, beyond the Julian Alps, which signaled our frontier, thus far from Italian Istria and having nothing to do with it" (ibid., 26). Zelco does admit, however, that some Slavs lived near them in the Istrian countryside.

When telling their life stories, few Italians from Istria distinguish between the Slovene or Serbo-Croatian languages, referring to the languages and their speakers as "Slav." "For us, they were generic Slavs, without distinction between Slovenes and Croats," writes Zelco (ibid., 29). This reflects the general ignorance of Istrian Italians about the Other in their midst, in contrast to the Slovenes and Croats, who were compelled under fascism to speak Italian. That these local Slavs would "treacherously" join up with Slavic "invaders" and turn on their "innocent" and "trusting" Italian neighbors seems to have shocked many esuli I knew, a sense of betrayal that Zelco registers in her story. Zelco describes her fear and anguish as Tito's partisans occupied her town and arrested her father, uncle, and family friends. Left alone in their house, Zelco's mother and aunt returned to find that the steward had forced his entry and proceeded to eat the family's food. When her mother protested, the man exclaimed, "Enough with 'Signora' Maria and 'Signora' Alba. I will use *tu* [the informal 'you'] with you because we are all comrades now" (ibid., 48). Zelco writes that they had long considered this man affectionate and loyal, even obsequious, given that in the past he had seemed honored to sit at the table when invited for lunch by the "masters" *(padroni)*. Incidents of this nature prompted Zelco's family to abandon Istria in 1943 and resettle in the Veneto.

In the final section of her narrative Zelco discusses her subsequent life in Italy as one of the thousands of those exiles "dispersed throughout Italian territory . . . or placed in squalid and humiliating refugee camps: a final form of annihilation" (ibid., 92). Although enjoying a tranquil existence in the Veneto, Zelco can forget neither her land nor her feeling of being *sradicate,* "uprooted." Returning to Istria twenty years later, she finds a sad and melancholy landscape and her town half abandoned. Zelco visits her former house, where only a few traces of a lost time remain, significantly the brass lamps associated with the death vigil. Among Greek refugees from Asia Minor, the oil lamps that hang before Orthodox icons and at the graveside similarly serve as powerful symbols of human life and death (Hirschon 1998, 208–9).

The brass lamps in Zelco's former house stand as mute metonyms for the house itself (and, in turn, for Italian Istria), which remains like a dead person who has been neither buried nor properly mourned.

> In the dusk I hoped for the fascinating mystery of another era, but there remained only two brass lamps that one placed in the room for the dead [during the death vigil]: the only things not taken, perhaps because of superstition, during the sacking. I hoped with all my soul that the house would collapse, become dust, and be dispersed with the *bora* [strong wind]. I loved the house too much to see it so fallen and violated. (Zelco 1993, 101)

Zelco adds that her family has made its new home in Italy but that "her" house will always be the one at Visignano, whose memory she preserves. In the account's final line, Zelco writes of that lost land, "I neither know how to nor can I forget it" (ibid., 108).

The impossibility of forgetting and the moral duty to remember—a theme expressed in myriad ways through the exiles' cult of remembrance—frame Zelco's memoir, a tale of a people's tragedy and a family's dispersion. Through "truth" telling, esuli like Zelco attempt to preserve the memory and traditions of *una terra perduta,* a lost land, even as time erodes the population of aging Istrians. "We are irremediably in danger of extinction," writes Zelco, "and we don't have protectors" (ibid., 107). Zelco thus depicts the esuli as survivors of a culture (a *pure* Italian one) decimated through genocide, as well as a "novel" community forged in exile. Like the Greek refugees from Asia Minor, the exiles preserve "a sense of separate identity in the face of close similarity . . . [by working] continually at constructing a 'boundary'" (Hirschon 1998, 5).

In the Istrian case, an emphasis on genealogies and roots and hence authenticity and autochthony is among the primary means for constructing this symbolic boundary (in contrast to the "total cultural milieu" that religion provided in the Asia Minor case). Repeated references to these boundary markers characterize the approximately fifty formal oral histories and interviews I conducted with exiles, to which I now turn. In contrast to some recent books on exile (Malkki 1996), I do not claim that these oral narratives are "prototypical" tales, although the more time one spends listening to Istrian exiles the more one becomes aware of commonalities (as well as discordances) between individual stories.

Echoing written accounts, almost all individuals I spoke with had an idealized vision of preexodus life in Istria, particularly for the years before the war. Exiles often disagree considerably in their representation of the Italian, as well as German, regimes during the war. In her aptly titled book *Un paese perfetto* (A perfect town), based on interviews with thirty exiles from Grisignana, Nemec (1998) similarly notes this pervasive idealization of prewar life. Just as the exile writer Posar-Giuliano depicted Istria as a land characterized by proper relations between the dead and the living, esuli I spoke with frequently viewed preexodus life as marked by a proper ordering of relations between God and people, the dead and the living, the old and the young, men and women. Exile accounts, particularly men's, treat these relations as "traditional" and hence authentic, thereby obscuring the ways in which Italian Istria became the object of intervention by a fascist regime bent on inscribing hierarchical class, gender, and ethnic relationships as "traditional."

As a result, even when speakers describe life in fascist Istria as economically difficult, they see it as pervaded by a sense of collective solidarity, honest labor, and religiosity. Other books on displacement, both in Istria and elsewhere, report similar examples whereby informants acknowledge economic hardship but nonetheless remember life as better, more convivial, and intimate (Bahloul 1996, 36; Hirschon 1998; Nemec 1998, 45). The family, threatened or torn apart by the exodus in the most dramatic manner, symbolizes this unity; in turn, empty houses stand as a "spatial reminder of the absent family" (Hirschon 1998, 132). Seventy-five-year-old Renzo, born in Pirano to a family of sailors, noted the misery *(miseria)* under fascism that led Istrians to dream of America and some (including his uncle) to go abroad for work. In spite of this, Renzo remembered life in Istria with great nostalgia. In particular, he praised the virtues of the patriarchal family. By rendering many male family heads wards of the Italian state or forcing women to stay alone in Istria for long periods after men were forced to flee (because of the fear of the foibe or forced labor), the exodus inverted such key societal values and power structures.

Another Capodistrian described the Istrian people as "economic and good," as religious people who placed the family first. Giuseppe, a retired pharmacist and an authoritative voice within the exile community, asserted:

> [In Istria of old] mothers and fathers lived frugally. . . . All for the children, all for the family. . . . We, I can say this, had all good people, good people, thrifty people, people who knew how to act solely for the good of the children. . . . Yes, religion [was strong] back then, in a particular way. Now [it's] different, but once, for the love of God, there was your religion. . . . If a piece of bread fell, a child kissed it because bread was a grace from God, and it was necessary to kiss this bread that fell. All this marvelous religion, no? . . . Of this [came] the unity among Istrians.

Giuseppe's statement emphasized unity, virtue, and religiosity as central to the Istrian way of life, symbolized by the respect with which even apparently such humble objects as bread are treated. The reference to bread recalls its importance as primary food, given the economic difficulties of the fascist period. More important, however, Giuseppe invoked bread's symbolic connection to the Eucharist, as well as to a variety of popular beliefs about protection against the evil eye and illness. Radole reports the Istrian custom of never keeping bread in one's hand during a meal; if by chance a piece fell, one kissed it (1997, 55), as Giuseppe claimed. Hirschon mentions the similar importance attributed to bread in the Greek context (1998, 137). Bread thus figured as part of a cosmological ordering of relations between the human and the divine, as well as between men and women, the young and the old. When circumstances forced Giuseppe's father to buy the daily bread, for instance, everyone teased his father for doing "women's work."

Giuseppe fondly remembered the respect Istrians displayed toward both gender hierarchies and seniority. At meals, men typically sat and women stood; only the elderly spoke. Children often used the formal *you* (*Lei*, or as the fascist regime decreed, *Voi*) with their father, as did women with their husbands. Although an extreme hierarchy may have reigned in Giuseppe's family—not surprisingly, Giuseppe's wife always put off my requests for an interview by saying, "My husband has told you everything"—and as an ideal social model, the degree of formality varied considerably within families (see also Nemec 1998, 113). Similarly, the degree of formality in my relationship with Istrians older than myself as symbolized by the use of the polite address also ranged widely; some individuals, both men and women, insisted that I use the informal *tu* with them immediately, others used the *tu* with me (appropriate with a younger person or a social inferior) while I employed the formal *Lei,* and still others addressed me with *Lei.* Giuseppe, for example, unfailingly addressed me in formal and respectful terms as *dottoressa.*

Giuseppe concluded of life in Italian Istria, "It was good, the father was always right" (*Era bello, il papa ha sempre ragione*). To my ears, Giuseppe's statement uncannily recalled the fascist slogan "The Duce is always right" (*Il Duce ha sempre ragione*), highlighting the fact that most esuli alive today came of age in a fascist state marked by paternalist and pronatalist discourses. Giuseppe also maintained that under Italy, no real "class conflict" existed, thereby refuting the socialist view of fascist Istria as rent with division. On a piece of paper, the retired pharmacist mapped out for me (again, note the importance of such aide-mémoire) the social distinctions in his town, Capodistria.

In Capodistria, Istria's cultural and intellectual center, noble families (relatively rare elsewhere in Istria) owned extensive tracts of land, including the salt flats at nearby Sicciole/Sečovlje. These marshes were worked in the summer by fishermen and their families; land was cultivated by sharecropping peasants, who gave half their yield to the owners (the *mezzadria* system). Insisting that conflicts between the sharecroppers and landholders never occurred, Giuseppe noted that the padrone typically served as a *compare,* or godparent, to the peasants. Giuseppe added that around 1935, a Capodistrian who bought the salt flats tried to bring workers from the Veneto by offering them the terms of mezzadria. This man gained a false reputation as a hard-nosed master, contends Giuseppe. In fact, when after the war socialist committees interrogated this landlord's workers, they defended their former landlord, saying that they were the real padroni and that they could not have been treated better by a brother.

Giuseppe notes that whereas most of the peasants (*contadini*) who worked such land were Capodistrians, others were *cortevani,* those who came from outside the city walls. "These Slavic workers got along well with us," insisted Giuseppe. They often came to his mother, a seamstress, and Slavic women selling bread and milk were a common feature in the town. Accounts differ as to the degree of contact and number of intermarriages between Slovenes, Croats, and Italians. A small number of my informants reported close friendships with Slavs. When intermarriage did occur, it usually entailed the linguistic and cultural assimilation of a Slavic woman into an Italian family; such marriages appear to have been more common in small villages than in towns (Nemec 1998, 63). Furthermore, such intermixing proved more common in certain zones of Istria, such as the Buiese (central Istria, the territory surrounding the town of Buie). A semiautobiographical account of a small Istrian village during the exodus, Fulvio Tomizza's celebrated novel *Materada* captures the mixed (or hybrid) nature of this area, in contrast to southern Istria, where Italian coastal towns like Dignano, Valle, and Rovigno remained isolated within a Slavic-speaking rural hinterland. The Buiese's greater degree of cultural mingling is reflected in local dialects, which contain words of both Slavic and Italian origin, and in the fact that many ethnic "Italians" from this area spoke some Croatian dialect, a reality expressed in Tomizza's depiction of village life.

Sergio, who became an antifascist and CLN activist as a young man during the war, noted that historically his small village in the Buiese lay at the limits of that territory which the Venetians had controlled. A mere four kilometers away villagers spoke the Istrian Slovene dialect; they frequented the store in which Sergio's family sold goods like tobacco and wine. Despite these frequent contacts with both Slovenes and Croats, however, Sergio admitted that "like the in-habitants of coastal cities, we knew very little about what went on within the Slavic community. . . . But we lived in a condition of serenity. No one could have foreseen what happened." Sergio came from a long line of Italian patriots; his ancestors included irredentists, and he recalled a 1918 photograph, cherished by his aunt, of King Victor Emmanuel III descending from a navy ship in the "redeemed" city of Trieste. This patriotism for Italy did not, however, translate into support for fascism (although his father was a party member), and despite Sergio's claim that no one could have predicted what occurred after 1943, his father complained that the regime's mistreatment of its Slavic minorities was a sure way to alienate them. "He would often say, 'This is the way to lose Istria anew' because he understood that you can't govern with police. . . . He always said this, 'It will end badly.'"

Some exiles, like Sergio, attach considerable blame to fascism for the subse-quent violence toward Italians, which occurred during and after the war. Oth-ers, like Giuseppe, maintain that interethnic relations were fine until outside agitators came and "educated these people in hatred." (For similar views about the inculcation of hatred from the outside as expressed by exiles from Asia Minor and Algeria, see Hirschon [1998] and Bahloul [1996].) Like Giuseppe, Piranese exile Renzo contended that Italians and Slavs lived together well until the war. He recalled with nostalgia the milk woman (donna del latte) who came every day to their house "like an aunt." Similarly, a Slovene peasant who sold Renzo's family wood was "like a father for us." As such comments indicate, in Italian Istria inequalities of class and gender appear to have been encoded in traditional kinship idioms and reinforced by paternalistic state discourses. Those, like Giuseppe, who were part of the educated classes, thus remember Istria as one big happy family, just as Istrian Italians generally recall Slavs be-fore the war as the grateful recipients of Italian magnanimity.

These halcyon descriptions of life before the war set the scene for the dra-matic rupture that followed, an event usually presented as unforeseen by the trusting and unsuspecting Italians. Sergio cited an episode in 1942 as an early sign of the transformations under way. At that time, many Istrians (particularly those in small villages) had little awareness of the military disaster unfolding, and the war seemed distant (a sentiment reiterated by Nemec's informants [1998, 162]). Heavily censored news reports offered little warning of the com-plete collapse of the army the following year. On a summer's day in July 1942, an overheated stranger arrived in Sergio's family store, where his father was working on the bank books. "He [the stranger] came in and asked 'Could I have a little wine?' My father, while he was pouring the wine, said, 'It's hot, huh? This heat really makes you thirsty.' 'Yes, it makes you thirsty, but we are thirsty for blood'—remember, this is July '42—'we're thirsty for blood, not for water.' And this made both my father and me really think."

Despite this ominous warning, Sergio's family confidently invested a sizable amount of money in home improvements. "This meant that we thought that things would turn out well enough." The collapse of the Italian state and army in September 1943 came as a complete surprise, bringing with it a sense of "total defeat" and the terror of formerly subservient Slavs who had become partisans. In a story similar to Zelco's, where the once-servile steward now assumed the role of padrone, Sergio recounted the moment in which this shocking new reality arrived at their doorstep.

> Toward the middle of the month [of September 1943], we were having dinner at home. A knock at the door. There were two persons from that village I mentioned, on the border with Slovenia, a village in which they spoke Italian but also Slav. There was a carpenter and another person from the village with him. We didn't know why [they had come]. They knock on the door, it was already dark, and one of us went to open it. "Good evening." "Oh, Franjo"—the carpenter was named Franjo, this carpenter who until two months earlier had worked at my house doing the entryway and so on. He was always treated well, he had nothing to complain about, he was paid, and he ate lunch with us; it's not as if he was considered—I don't know—a Slav, a *schiavo*.
>
> They sit down, then have a glass of wine. At a certain point—I don't know, I don't remember well—there arises a discussion. This guy was armed with a hunting rifle, this Franjo; he stands up [and says to my father], "Ah, it's finished. It won't be you to command anymore, now we're in charge." And he takes the rifle and points it at my father, saying, "Now we're in charge, *basta* [enough], it's over for you," and so on. With threats. Threats of all sorts. The villager who was with him grabbed the rifle from his hands, my mother jumped on him, shouting and yelling, and he got out of there. Evidently this was the symptom of a general sickness. He expressed himself in this way, though to tell the truth his companion apologized.

The shock and bewilderment at the Slavs' apparent treachery, as registered in the accounts of Sergio and many others, suggest a self-deception implicit in the paternalistic ideologies that governed both ethnic and gender relations in Italian Istria. For an interesting comparison, see Genovese's 1975 discussion of the paternalism that undergirded the slave system in the American South. Paternalism created dependency in both directions, with the affection and loyalty of the slaves (particularly the house slaves who shared an intimate relationship with the masters) proving a vital component of the self-image of the masters. Whereas the slaves came to view the master's duties toward them as rights, the masters considered them as privileges and hence expected gratitude from the recipients. The slaveholders' self-deception led to profound trauma during the war and afterward when "treasonous" slaves abandoned the plantations. Genovese suggests that both masters and slaves accepted a paternalistic system but understood it differently, a contradiction giving rise to violence. Although obviously not as rigid or tyrannical as the slaveholding American South (though in Istro-Venetian dialect the derogatory term for Slav is *schiavo,* or "slave"), Italian Istria was characterized by a cultural, economic, and ethno-national hierarchy, one reinforced by the state paternalism of Italian fascism. Such paternalism appears to have blinded many Italians in Istria to the discontent brewing in their midst, one that became violent in the context of the war and the Italian state's collapse.

Narratives of the exodus, like the related ones of the foibe, thus cast Slavs as villains and Italians as innocent victims. Slavs are often referred to in exile literature, interviews, and iconography as "druzi." Although the term *druzi* merely signifies "comrades" in Serbo-Croatian, its usage by exiles carries extremely negative connotations. Exile artist Gigi Vidris, whose work appeared in clandestine Istrian Italian papers such as *Il Grido dell'Istria* and *El Spin* during the long contestation over the Julian March, depicts the druzi as not only deceptive but coarse and animalized, a cross between man and ape (see figure 11). Glenda Sluga has noted the particularly demonized representations of the female partisan, or *drugarizza,* described in *Il Grido dell'Istria* as

> an animal that belongs to the human species, of the female sex; as a result of special living conditions and of practices contrary to nature, it is facially, corporeally and spiritually transformed. In that transformation what was most delicately feminine becomes a monstrous being, huge and muscular, masculine. Its spirit harmonises with its body and accumulates all that is most vile and ferocious in human nature. (In Sluga 1994a, 192)

Characterized as monstrous human-animal, male-female hybrids, the partisans were associated with the woods *(il bosco).* As an archetypal space of liminality, danger, and transformation (Nemec 1998, 156), the woods also stood for the space outside of culture, thereby mapping neatly onto the long-standing association of Italians with an urban-based civiltà. The fact that during the war partisans typically came to towns at night—knocking on doors with a terrifying *buh-buh-buh* that reverberated throughout small towns—only heightened their fearful aspect as both human "bandits" and something more sinister and nonhuman (ibid., 177–78, 195).

In contrast, Italians appear as a refined and civilized people (again, see Vidris's representations) who suffer both physical and psychological violence at the hands of the druzi, a violence said to be rooted in an ethno-national hatred that inverts all that is sacred, good, and civilized. The emphasis on psychological intimidation and fear (one reiterated by Nemec's informants) connects the experience of Istrians who endured violent persecution firsthand with the experience of Italians who left the peninsula in a calm and peaceful manner, never having suffered actual violence. Although one might possibly read the latter as pointing to the varied motivations for and circumstances of leaving Istria—an interpretation that complicates a neat "ethnic cleansing" thesis—the linkage of physical violence with psychological terror constructs a unified narrative tying together the different migratory movements out of Istria over a period of more

Figure 11. *Druzi,* by Gigi Vidris. A 1946 cartoon printed in the journal *El Spin* showing druzi with a suitcase full of propaganda and illusions. Courtesy of Istituto Regionale per la Cultura Istriana.

than ten years. These different experiences come to be seen as part of a larger phenomenon, enabling esuli who did not experience such traumatic events to nonetheless identify with what others ("we") went through.

Although cast as the culmination of a long-standing campaign of aggression by the Slavs, the exodus itself is said to have begun in September 1943 with the capitulation of the Italian forces, at which time the Yugoslav partisans briefly gained control of various parts of the Istrian Peninsula before the Germans arrived; this is the period of the foibe, in which Istrians were executed by partisans. Even when interviewees were not directly affected by the tragedy of the foibe, it figured in many oral histories, revealing how intimidation (physical and psychological), combined with rumor, created a climate of pervasive fear and insecurity (again, see the similar conclusions drawn by Nemec [1998, 221–25]).

In some cases, the mere threat of the foibe encouraged Italians to leave. Born in Portole/Oprtalj, a tiny town in the Istrian interior, eighty-six-year-old Gianfranco (a retired factory worker) noted that when he returned from the war in 1945, he heard frightening rumors that the partisans intended to throw him in the foibe. He maintained that he was targeted because he refused to collaborate with the Titoists, begging off participation in various political activities on the grounds that he had to work and provide for his family. Here, then, the Yugoslavs are portrayed as disturbing those proper relations and duties that Giuseppe, Renzo, and others described.

> I came home from military service in '45, the 26th of October. I'd been with the Americans in France, and when I came home, Tito was in charge. Then, I didn't want to get mixed up in anything [intrigare]. People came to ask me to help with a festival, one thing or another, and I said: "I have to work my land and maintain my family. I can't afford to lose time." And then, for that, they thought about throwing me in the foibe in order to kill me. A cousin of mine told me, "Watch out, they're thinking of taking you off to the foibe."

In addition to the foibe, esuli recount other methods of intimidation employed by the Yugoslavs; they depict the Yugoslavs as foreign (and brutal) occupiers, as well as resolutely anti-Italian. Liana, a prominent political figure in Trieste's exile community who kept her bit of Istria (a stone) in her home, narrated the entry of the Yugoslav troops into Capodistria in 1945 in order to illustrate the partisans' "unmistakable antagonism" toward the Italian population of Istria. In telling her story, Liana employed considerable rhetorical skill and polish; this no doubt reflects her freelance work in journalism, as well as her forays into regional and national politics, in which she has had ample opportunity to present her story as representative of the esuli's tragedy. Throughout her account, Liana exploited the ironies and disjuncture between the partisans' self-presentation as liberators and their actual behavior (as padroni, or masters) when they arrived in Istria.

"All the population rushed outside the city walls," Liana began, suggesting the good faith and hope with which the Italians greeted war's end. Referring to the city walls also highlights the antiquity (and autochthony) of her city and its population. "You see, it was an ancient city, and we went to greet these, our liberators." The identity of these "liberators," dressed in German uniforms and bearing German weapons, proved unclear; Liana implies that these Yugoslavs, dressed in "stolen clothes" and arriving from afar, represented an illegitimate occupying force. As the soldiers approached, the crowd fell silent. People began to applaud, then stopped. Ordering the soldiers to face the crowd with their machine guns, the army's commander declared: "'You are expecting the Americans? We are not who you are waiting for. If in five minutes you're not all out of here, we'll start firing.' And this was the first 'buongiorno' that we had from the liberators who then became occupiers. This was the beginning."

To these tactics of intimidation, Liana added brainwashing. A loudspeaker in the city's main piazza broadcast propaganda, with names of the "enemies of the people" listed. Incongruously, advertisements followed these lists. "Then there were jingles, a little song, 'ding dong,' and the advertisements came on. . . . A so very sweet voice would say, 'If you want to live to be one hundred years old, drink Vato Vanni orange drink" (laughter).

Although such laughter constitutes a subversive act, puncturing the posturing of Yugoslavs as liberators, it also may help esuli voice difficult memories. At the same time, ridiculing the enemy helps mute questions of complicity with fascism, a strategy that the fascist journalist Curzio Malaparte employed in his wartime memoir *Kaputt* (Burdett 1999, 113). In my interview with her, Liana relied on another moment of comic relief as she told a particularly emotional story. She began by noting the panic created by the regime's sudden introduction of the "Yugolira" (a short-lived hybrid currency for the contested border area) in 1945–46. This event instantly reduced many families to poverty and led to one of the few real rebellions against the new regime. Consisting of a strike by Capodistrian shop owners, the protest ended tragically when the partisans gathered together a force of men from the city's suburbs. The soldiers, many of them drunk, broke the shop windows. Then,

> they took a shopkeeper. It was a food shop, and then they took my uncle, who had a trattoria—an uncle of my father . . . he was nicknamed 'fried fish' [*pescefritto*] [she laughs and stops before continuing].
>
> They took them and put them in the piazza, and they murdered them with their blows. I was with some other people near the fountain where one got water, and I saw these tremendous things. My uncle had his eyes gouged out, but they weren't dead yet. He was in agony and cried for help and called out. These people began to dance the *kolo*, a dance where everyone joins arms and forms a circle, around these persons, who were no longer alive. They were dead.

Such dramatic stories of "Slavic barbarity"—highlighting the perversion of *slavo-comunisti* who broke up families, destroyed property, and turned executions into bacchanalian celebrations (grisly twists on the ritual inversions of car-nival)—reinforce exile claims to having suffered ethnic cleansing. They also reflect the long-standing stereotypes of Slavs (or what Venetians labeled Mor-lacchi) as being prone to violence and moments of heightened excitement (as in the kolo dance), as well as "the blasphemous perversion of religious obser-vance" (Wolff 2001, 138). As did many others, Liana contended, "All the strate-gies known today as ethnic cleansing are perfectly identical [with those of the exodus]."

In response to this genocide, exiles claim to have staged a "human plebiscite" that demonstrated both the peninsula's true, Italian character and the illegiti-macy of Yugoslav rule. Due to its dramatic nature and scope, the massive 1947 population transfer from Pola has become emblematic of events of that period (with the conclusion of the Italo-Yugoslav Peace Treaty), as well as of the exo-dus more generally. Within two months the city emptied; Pola had passed from Yugoslav control at war's end to the Anglo-American Allied Military Govern-ment, which ceased in 1947 when the Peace Treaty awarded the city and the central and southern part of the peninsula to Yugoslavia. Dramatic photos de-picting the departure from Pola—with aged patriarchs, women, and children boarding the steamers furnished by the Italian state to transport the refugees to Venice, Ancona, and other Italian ports—have come to represent the "quintes-sence" of the exodus and feature prominently in recent newspaper articles and documentaries. Such images of "people voting with their feet" played an im-portant role in the emergent Cold War discourse, sending (as they were in-tended to) powerful messages to the Anglo-Americans, as well as Italians de-ciding between the Christian Democrats and the Italian Communist Party in the contested 1948 elections.

Departing from their city, the Polesi sang a hymn that expressed their "mys-tic communion" with the Istrian soil, a communion so strong that it prompted them to disinter their dead heroes, like Nazario Sauro.

> . . . I want to say goodbye to the little house
> where I passed my youth. . . .
> Two things I want to take in order to remember
> In a bag a little piece of the [Roman] Arena
> in a bottle a little of your beautiful sea. (Daici in Bogneri 1994, 196)

This song mentions the common practice of taking a material trace of Istria by which to remember it. Marcello Bogneri translated this song for me from istro-veneto into Italian. Shortly before I met him in 1993, he had performed the "last rites" at his brother's funeral by bathing a sack of Istrian soil in sea-water. Bogneri thus perpetuated in exile those religio-nationalistic practices en-acted during the moment of exodus itself. Despite Bogneri's personal political leanings (he had gone to Salò after 1943), he read the exodus not as primarily a conflict between fascism and communism but rather as one following out of the Yugoslavs' expressed anti-Italian antagonism. The residents of Pola responded by leaving en masse and taking cherished bits of Istria with them, he argued, evidencing their historic attachment to (and right to remain on) that land.

Bogneri's interpretation, as well as his mention of the physical attachment to the homeland, was echoed in the account of Fulvio, a retired veterinarian. Although Fulvio professed to be a life-long leftist, his explanation of events in Pola jibed with that of "unrepentant fascist" Bogneri, revealing the way the ethnic cleansing interpretation unites those exiles otherwise divided on political grounds. In contrast to Bogneri, Fulvio described his family as resolutely antifascist and claims Pola had a strong (albeit clandestine) tradition of socialism. At the same time, Fulvio proudly detailed his family's Italian patriotism, which he identified with the Garibaldian tradition, separate from fascism. The fact that even communists left with the exodus, he contended, evidences that nationalism—not the ideological conflict between fascism and communism—lay at the heart of the conflict.

> There is a question that I always ask myself: How is it possible that a city like Pola, a city dominated by the Left, was abandoned in 1947? The so-called Yugoslav socialists arrived, but the Italian communists and socialists all left. Why? Because the Italians had already understood that what predominated in Yugoslavia was not communism but nationalism and that they [Yugoslavs] had installed a regime of terror.

Returning to his city in May 1945 (his family had taken refuge during the war in the Istrian town of Orsera), the young Fulvio found the Roman Arena there covered with Yugoslav partisan flags bearing the communist red star. Vivoda (1998) has described this period preceding the arrival of the Anglo-Americans as a "red May," similar to that of the "Forty Days" in Trieste. Trucks traveled the streets, broadcasting partisan songs in Serbo-Croatian. Fulvio soon heard his father's name denounced as an *affamatore del popolo,* a "starver of the people," since he owned a delicatessen. Echoing Liana's ironic phrase about the Capodistrians' first "buongiorno" from their Yugoslav liberators, Fulvio recalled, "This is the first contact I had with the 'liberation' of Pola."

Fulvio's family left Pola in 1947, "like everyone else," without even considering the possibility of remaining. The family departed Istria on one of the many ships provided by the Italian state to facilitate the population transfer. Fulvio noted that his father retained the key to their abandoned house, paralleling other Istrians who took a piece of "home" with them as both token of their lost land and symbol of their "roots" there. Other Polesi took doors and windows (Vivoda 1998, 30), which often come to symbolize the family and enclosure (Bahloul 1996, 31); as we have seen, the bodies of ancestors (illustrious and humble) also joined the exodus from Pola. In addition, departing Italians dismantled many of Pola's factories, reflecting their desire to leave the Yugoslavs with as little gain as possible and physically to remove as much of their homeland as they could. Such efforts to reconstruct the homeland necessarily proved incomplete. As Fulvio noted, only with age did he fully understand the import of his father's gesture. "With age instead you search for conclusions and you realize that you are truly a plant without roots," he commented resignedly. As part of his own search for *radici*, Fulvio moved to Trieste upon his retirement in order to be closer to Istria and became an enthusiastic participant in the Circolo di Istria, which makes frequent forays to Istria.

Whereas Polesi like Fulvio abandoned their city in a dramatic collective protest against Yugoslav socialism, other Istrians describe uncoordinated, individual efforts to leave the peninsula in response to various acts carried out by the socialist regime. Italians resident in the newly drawn Zone B between 1948 and 1954 recounted heavy-handed measures: the creation of socialist cooperatives, the confiscation of private property, and the elections of 1950 in which armed soldiers forced many Italians to vote. Though such events would appear to be part of the installation of a communist regime, many of my informants expressed the belief that they were specifically designed to drive Italians away; socialist initiatives, particularly the confiscation of land and homes, appear to have targeted Italians disproportionately. Some esuli, like Leonardo (who first rediscovered Istria in the cemetery of Capodistria), noted the suppression of religious festivals (particularly those of Easter and Christmas) and the persecution of clerics. Many Istrians nonetheless described enduring these injustices and making tremendous sacrifices in the hope that Zone B would eventually return to Italy and Istria would be "redeemed" as it had been after the Great War.

The 1954 Memorandum of London dashed this hope and prompted the final *Esodo Grande,* or Big Exodus. At this time Italian speakers left Istria en masse, emptying the cities of Pirano, Capodistria, Isola, Buie, and many of the rural centers in the territory of Zone B. As a carpenter from Capodistria put it, "It wasn't a choice we made. Everyone did it." This man did not recall many dramatic instances of persons forced to flee from Istria—"Certainly, there were a few people in certain political positions who were persecuted"—but stated simply that they left for their children's future. This reason for leaving was expressed by several informants: To live under a communist regime and under "foreign" masters meant to live in a trap with few prospects. Though the final phase of the exodus appears to have been marked by less overt violence than in the immediate postwar period, the accumulation of threats, insults, and insecurity persuaded an overwhelming majority of Italians to leave Zone B forever.

The years 1955–56 marked the end of this massive exodus, although trickles of people continued into the 1960s. These latter arrivals were often viewed with suspicion in Trieste and were considered compromised with the socialist regime and/or impure Italians (if so, they would have left with the exodus, that plebiscite of italianità, the reasoning went). Nora, born in 1951 on the island of Lussinpiccolo/Losinj and the wife of Federico, came to Trieste only in 1963. When I asked why her family waited so long, she said that in Lussinpiccolo things had been relatively uneventful for her family during the difficult years immediately after the war and that all her relatives had remained there. Nora nevertheless recalled always feeling out of place because her family went to church (frowned upon by the communist authorities) and spoke Italian at home. Eventually, her father lost his job when he refused to join the party; his brother had his bread oven appropriated. As a result, the family left Lussinpiccolo on tourist visas and never returned. Nora commented on the irony that in Lussinpiccolo, she was seen negatively as the "daughter of Italians," and in Trieste, others eyed her suspiciously as the "daughter of Croats." Given that the story of exodus has been cast in terms of purity and authenticity, as the discussion here has shown, little room remains for those who appear to be "hybrids" or in some way liminal.

Despite this questioning of her family's pure Italian genealogy, Nora's family— like many others—found temporary housing in the refugee camp at Risiera di San Sabba, still operating in 1963. In contrast to those who fled Istria during or immediately after the war, many such later arrivals were housed in refugee camps located throughout Italy; laws seeking a definitive and organized solution to the refugee crisis were passed only in 1952 (Volk 1999, 273). Prior to this, refugees often sought accommodations with friends or relatives. Marcello Bogneri, who was working in a hospital in Udine (a city to the north of Trieste) at war's end, reported unfortunate Istrians "living in a stable together with animals . . . millions of flies . . . and these people were cooking there, in those conditions." The bitter irony that the esuli, having left often intolerable conditions upon the promise of aid in the Italian homeland, were reduced to this state of animality, herded together in former concentration camps and prisons, and were often resented by other Italians for stealing jobs or were even spat upon as "fascist pigs" still rankles in the hearts of many.

Although regional scholarship has focused more on the exodus itself than on the fate of esuli in their new homes, exile stories usually devote considerable space to discussing the exodus' aftermath: arrival and life in Italy. During my fieldwork I heard again and again the refrain that exiles feel "strangers in our own home" (stranieri a casa nostra). Istrians feel strangers in a double sense: on return visits to their natal land, Istria, which they no longer recognize, and in Italy, paradoxically both their adoptive and "home" country (country of "ethnic" origin). Labeled as fascists by their own countrymen and mistreated in a number of ways by their Italian "brothers" who questioned their authenticity as victims of genocide, the exiles reiterate the theme of purity in asserting that they are ultra-Italian (italianissima). This, in turn, questions the political legitimacy of the various parties seen to have "sold out" the esuli.

Some exiles who spent as many as twelve years in makeshift refugee camps blame the Italian state for failing to defend the esuli's interests. The refugee camp appears to have been an important site for reinforcing a pan-Istrian identity, as well as a specific exile identity. In her study of Hutu refugees, Malkki (1996) considers the refugee camp as both a technology of power and a site of identity formation. Comparing Hutus in camps with those dispersed in a large township, Malkki found that refugees living in camps nurtured visions of ethnonational purity, whereas those in townships expressed more cosmopolitan and multivalent understandings of identity. Some Istrian exiles I interviewed made similar distinctions between those who spent long periods in camps and those who succeeded right away in finding accommodation in Italy.

Alfonso, a retired engineer, noted that his family adapted to life in Italy easily. Leaving Rovigno in 1948 by means of the citizenship option, his family settled in Bari; a civil servant, his father automatically obtained a job. Fourteen years old in 1948, Alfonso entered the *liceo* (high school) in Bari and found a much more cultured atmosphere than in Rovigno. For Alfonso, then, coming to Italy meant a broadening of his horizons; he claimed that for 90 percent of the esuli, life in Italy similarly brought greater prosperity and opportunities. He recalled that in contrast to Rovigno, at Bari one slept easily (without fear), and food proved plentiful. Yet in the summer of 1954 Alfonso visited some refugee camps in Puglia (southern Italy), where he saw his old schoolmates. He recalled the squalor and crowding, "truly a dramatic situation." According to Alfonso, those who endured such conditions for long periods proved much more intransigent in their demands and sentiments. As Peter Loizos (1981) has said of Greek Cypriot refugees, in the camps one often found "the heart grown bitter."

Giuseppe, the retired pharmacist from Capodistria, expressed similar bitterness about the five years he spent in the San Sabba camp. He and his aged mother inhabited what the esuli called a "box," a cubicle separated by paper partitions. Giuseppe remembered having to help his infirm mother to the outdoor bathrooms late at night; some people grumbled about his presence in the women's bathroom. This lack of privacy and the mingling of men and women greatly offended the Istrians' "inherent" sense of dignity and propriety, which had already been insulted by the Yugoslavs' disruption of proper social relations. In a bitterly ironic twist, the boxes mimicked the socialist partitioning of houses into multiple-family dwellings.

Fellow Capodistrian Liana also spent time in the camps. Having fled to Trieste on foot, the rest of Liana's family joined her six months later, and together they shared the hard life of refugees. Her parents lived in one refugee camp, her grandparents in another. The latter had to traverse the city each day in order to eat at the soup kitchens organized for esuli. In spite of these conditions, for Liana even a former prison cell seemed like "the maximum" after a life of oppression in Istria. In contrast, Giuseppe and others complained about the esuli's inhumane treatment at the hands of the Italian government.

The difference of opinion precludes any facile assumptions about the camps as making for a particular understanding of identity among esuli. Many of the most "hard-line" exile leaders I spoke with, for example, did not spend much or any time in the camps. Instead, other esuli who express no bitterness did spend part of their youth in the camps. Marino Vocci, founder of the Circolo di Istria and a well-known proponent of collaboration with the Italian minority in Istria, told me of living in a camp at Opicina, on the Karst above Trieste; one of his overwhelming memories is the sanitized odor of the camp, so different from that of the countryside in which he spent his first years. This suggests that the camp experience was neither sufficient nor necessary for creating a particular view of Istrian Italian identity. Furthermore, my research suggests that views of the refugee camp experience tend to divide along generational and gender lines (on generational differences among refugees, see Daniel 1996, 154–93). This complicates Malkki's dichotomy between camp residents and townspeople; although Malkki's findings may reflect the specificity of her case, the fact that she relies on composite narratives rather than examining individual stories and their speakers makes it difficult to ascertain who claims to speak for the Hutu refugees and how issues like gender and generation figure in such accounts.

Several persons I interviewed contrasted their experience in the camps to that of their adult parents, who had much more difficulty adapting. Indeed, many informants spoke of a generational conflict, with younger persons wanting to leave Istria and older individuals desiring to remain on the land. Laura, a friend of Stella's and an adolescent when her family left Capodistria for Trieste, recalled living in several camps over the course of twelve years. The family first lived in Campo Marzio, a transit camp for newly arrived refugees. Upon seeing the crowded camp, Laura's mother began to pull her hair and cry that she wanted to go home. Laura also recalled a Christmas spent in another camp. She was standing in the cafeteria line, joking with young men and enjoying herself, but her mother simply could not take it. Her mother subsequently suffered a mental breakdown, was hospitalized, and recovered only after electroshock therapy.

Other informants told me of grandparents and parents who died soon after leaving Istria, their hearts broken by the experience. Sergio, who like Liana fled Istria for Trieste on foot and then by boat under the cover of night and was only later joined by family members, contrasted his mother's tough character with that of his father. His father died of a heart attack in 1951, broken by the war and the exodus, as well as his concern for Sergio's mother. After both Sergio and his father had transferred their residence to Trieste, Sergio's mother remained firm, saying, "No, we're not moving." Sergio's father, in contact with Allied officials who advised him to "remain strong" (in the hope of an eventual return), agreed with this strategy. Even after her husband's death and when members of local socialist committees interrogated and threatened her about her "reactionary relatives in Trieste," Sergio's mother held out on the land. The authorities finally expelled her in 1953, transporting her to the border with neither documents nor possessions.

In contrast to his mother's tenacity, Sergio's father was "completely undone after 1943." Sergio remembered his father's despondence at having to leave Istria and the painful nostalgia that tormented him. Not surprisingly, Sergio's father sought to "see" the land he'd lost. Trieste's proximity to Istria makes such actual seeing possible at the same time that it reinforces the "vision" maintained purely in memory.

> In Trieste he bought binoculars, and he would go to Gretta [an area above the city] or to the cemetery of Saint Anna from where he could see the tree—the big oak that was at the entrance of our town—and he went there to look. Ah, yes, he stayed there for hours just looking. In '48 my father was sixty-two years old, and thus it wasn't easy. Because I know that [also] my uncles, who were older, how much they suffered from being separated from their land and their way of life, because their way of life was an agricultural one and now these people lived in the town. These people were used to working in a certain way and living in a certain manner. Living in the city or in a refugee camp signified death.

The experience of exile in general, and the refugee camp in particular, thus appears to have proven more difficult for the older generation (as well as for rural dwellers); in some cases women are described as more resilient, in other cases as more fragile than their husbands.

In contrast, several women I spoke with recalled their adolescence in the camps with nostalgia. Just as Laura mentioned joking with young men her age, Anita—who spent several years in a camp in Florence—remembered the camp with affection as a place for flirtations and romantic intrigues (for fond memories of the camps expressed by exiles from Grisignana, see Nemec 1998, 332). While I was interviewing a ninety-year-old man who complained about his eight years in the large Triestine camp known as SILOS, his daughter-in-law broke in to remember her days in the camps with pleasure. Another woman said that coming to Italy meant an "opening up of one's world" and that in the camps one lived alongside not only Italians from other parts of Istria but also Italians from former colonies like Ethiopia, Libya, and the Dodecanese Islands. Such memories suggest that many young people, and women in particular, found in the camps a sense of freedom from the rigid gender and age hierarchies of Istrian life described by Giuseppe and others. Bahloul's (1996) book on the gendered memories of a Jewish family's displacement from Algeria reveals the similar ways in which women perceived in exodus certain opportunities and freedom from a rigid, patriarchal regime. Fiuman esule Marisa Madieri, who lived with her family in a "box" at SILOS, perhaps speaks for many young people who left Istria: "Even the tragedy of the war was for me a curious adventure: bombings, fires, alarms, and flights to the shelter seemed undecipherable episodes that didn't endanger me but rather made my life more interesting" (1987, 12).

Some exiles cheerfully accepted the camps as part of their youth, others continued to harbor resentment. Many embittered exiles did not necessarily blame the Italian state for their difficulties, however, but rather singled out Italians who greeted the Istrians with hostility, specifically the Italian communists who spat (in some cases literally) on the newly arrived refugees. Despite his leftist political orientation, Fulvio from Pola reiterated a common resentment toward those Italian communists who meted out abuse to esuli. Fulvio became a member of the Italian Socialist party only in 1956, when the socialists distanced themselves from the communists, "because I could never, for reasons of logic and dignity, become part of a party that supported that situation there [in Istria], because the Communist Party defined us all as 'fascists.'" In Fulvio's opinion, the PCI's hostility to the exiles enabled the Italian neofascist party to present itself as the Istrians' protector. "Those who pretended to be our defenders were those very fascists who started the war, lost it, and for which we paid [with our land]."

As a result, claimed Fulvio, many exiles have rewritten their own history, neglecting and silencing the traditions of socialism that existed in preexodus Italy. Fulvio offered one such story of erasure, locating the exiles' psychological and political divisions in their hostile reception in Italy. After settling in Italy, Fulvio's father, who had fought for Austria in World War I, applied to become a Knight of Vittorio Veneto, an honor reserved for those Italian citizens born in 1909 who had fought for Italy on the Isonzo front.

> My father made the request and became Knight of Vittorio Veneto, convinced that he merited this, *even if he was on the other side* [fighting for Austria]. But the most moving thing is that when he died, my mother gave me his certificate and medal as if it was an important thing, something I should keep as a sign of his suffering because this was part of his disturbance. This is the case of my father, but many other refugees also suffered this perturbation, this form of self-deception because, for example, many of them were Austrophiles, but when they came to Italy they became more Italian than the Italians just to show that they weren't pro-Austrian. This is why many became nationalists. . . . And when I say these things, everyone [in the exile associations] insults me.

Fulvio viewed his father's nationalism and rewriting of his personal history as a response to the exiles' treatment in postwar Italy, to the widespread questioning of the Istrians' legitimacy. According to Fulvio, this mistreatment of esuli by fellow Italians led them to reinforce their claims of purity, of being ultra-Italian.

> Let's try to understand my father, this pain of his. It's much more painful this fact of not being 100 percent Italian in a country that doesn't even welcome you anyway, that has yet to give the exiles restitution, a country that labeled you a fascist because you left [Istria] and not because you really were a fascist, a country that practically said to you "You lost the war" when you didn't lose it. Understand that this is a real psychological problem . . . this betrayal, by the communists but also by others. If the Slavs treated you this way, they were Slavs who were your enemies, but when your mother country treats you in this way. . . . Because of this fact of being unwelcome, many refugees left [Italy], the majority went to Australia, the United States, Canada, Sweden. They preferred to go there without even asking for Italian citizenship.

The greatest betrayer of the esuli, suggested Fulvio, was not Yugoslavia but Italy. Fulvio and many fellow exiles blamed not only the Italian Communist Party, however, but also several other groups for maltreating the esuli. Istrian refugees encountered hostility, for example, from those Italian citizens who viewed them as taking away already scarce food and jobs, since exiles and their children were given preferential treatment in job applications (see also Nemec 1998, 344–45). Resentment of exiles continues to this day, at least in Trieste, where I heard Italian Triestines and Slovenes alike grumble about the unfair privileges that *figli dei profughi* (children of refugees) enjoy in *concorsi*, or job competitions. Betta, who grew up in the exile milieu but identifies herself as a Triestine, recalls sports events that became violent confrontations between Istrians and Triestines. Faced with this situation, many Italian Istrians—together with Triestines, as well as Slovenes and Croats who had left Istria for various reasons, both political and economic—chose to emigrate. Some exiles (for example, Giuricin [1993] and Fulvio) interpret this as another phase in a process of cultural genocide begun by the Tito regime and its allies in the Italian Communist Party and subsequently abetted by the Italian state.

That the Italian minority in contemporary Istria and the Slovene minority in Italy enjoy(ed) certain rights guaranteed by international treaties further angers some esuli, who feel abandoned by their own country yet again; admittedly, the last few years (especially after I concluded my fieldwork) have seen a considerable opening toward the rimasti. Although some exiles complain about being viewed as "inauthentic" Italians in their own country, they at times depict those who remained in Istria as "inauthentic" Italians. This parallels the manner in which Italians construct themselves in the foibe debate as exclusive victims and fail to admit the possibility that Slovenes (or Italians in Istria), who are seen unambiguously as perpetrators, might also have been victimized during the same period.

Authenticity and Purity: Andati and Rimasti

Esuli emphasize their own rootedness while frequently questioning that of Istria's present-day Italians and their leaders. Though exiles often absolve younger Italians born in Istria in the 1960s and 1970s of the "sins of the father," they do not prove so forgiving of an older generation of leadership linked with the state-sponsored organizations of the Italian minority. For example, Liana claimed that many individuals charged with crimes committed during the partisan war in Italy fled to Yugoslavia. She mentioned an individual, tried and found guilty in Italy of assassinating an Italian partisan, who escaped to Yugoslavia. This individual "still lives in Capodistria, and he is the father of a current city official of Capodistria," contended Liana. Her charge of treachery and murder implicitly questioned the political legitimacy of this individual's two sons, both prominent members of the Italian minority in Istria. Not only did these individuals gain power in a dubious manner, suggested Liana, but they are obviously not autochthonous Istrian Italians, since they fled to Yugoslavia only after the war. Roots and ancestors have high stakes, then, in current political struggles, as well as more individual efforts at reconciliation.

Liana's fellow townsman Giuseppe similarly emphasized that most "Italians" today living in Capodistria do not have authentic Capodistrian names. When I mentioned that I would be going to Capodistria to speak with a young leader in the Unione Italiana, Giuseppe remarked of this man's name, "That is a Capodistrian [name], yes. That is a Capodistrian, true, genuine [*verace*], a Capodistrian name." Despite his admission about this man's authenticity, Giuseppe concluded that such instances prove rare. "Today one can't say that there is an Italian community in Istria because one finds only a handful of people who have typical Capodistrian [Italian] surnames."

Indeed, Giuseppe did not prove generous in his assessment of the Italian minority representative to the Slovene parliament.

> This [man] is the grandson of a Roman who was in Pola under Italy working in a big insurance office. The father followed in the footsteps of the grandfather . . . these are not true Istrians [*Istriani d.o.c.*]. . . . I ask you, is this a rightful Capodistrian in the true sense of the word? If his father, his grandfather, were not Capodistrians and one is not born in Capodistria?
>
> My daughter was born in Trieste, for example, but she doesn't say, "I am Professoressa V. of Trieste." [Instead she says,] "I am Capodistrian because my parents [were] Capodistrian, my grandparents [were] Capodistrians." . . . There was a time, once, when a young woman [came] who was from Yugoslavia; she said Pola. "I am Istrian." Istrian? Eh, it's like Sicilians who come to work in Trieste and say, "I am Triestine."
>
> She, by my account, [was] Croatian, born in Istria, in short. If she was born in the Croatian part of Istria, she should say so but she can't say, "I am Istrian." For me, Istrian signifies someone who lived there, the parents, the grandparents.

Giuseppe's statements brought together the criteria of authenticity that dominate these esuli accounts, all of which take a number of markers (names, genealogies, ancestors in cemeteries) as evidence of the exiles' historical presence in, as well as right to, Istria. For Giuseppe and others, very few genuine Istrians—or *Istriani d.o.c.*, the term here referring to the certification used in wine making (*di origine controllata*, of confirmed origin)—remain in contemporary Istria. Here, the metaphorical theme of roots is expressed through references to actual plants/vines (those of wine grapes); similarly, Annamaria claimed to feel "rootless," and Fulvio spoke of the exodus as rendering him a "plant without roots." Many other informants prefaced their life stories with detailed family genealogies that often went back to the fourteenth or fifteenth century, irrefutable proof of their authenticity and rootedness. Here vines and roots appear to stand in for the unspoken: "blood" or "birth." As Danforth notes of the distinctions self-identified Macedonians from Florina draw between themselves and Greeks, "Wheat is wheat, and corn is corn. You can't change one into the other. Even if you call it corn, it's still wheat. Its nature doesn't change" (1995, 224). Such horticultural imagery also proves common in contemporary Istria, though usually in service to the notion of an autochthonous hybrid.

Not surprisingly, the various exile associations have generally responded cautiously to initiatives stressing reconciliation and rapport with those Slavs and Italians who currently inhabit Istria. As my analysis of exile narratives of various sorts demonstrates, the sense of horror remains vivid for those who lived through such experiences. With the tragic end of Yugoslavia, some exiles feel vindicated, as they were never taken in by the reconciliatory post-1954 rhetoric of the Yugoslav and Italian states. In this view, the "mask" that accorded Tito's Yugoslavia international legitimacy has been pulled back to reveal that forty-five years of socialism did not significantly alter the bloodthirsty, bestial Slav (the monstrous druzi).

This view of the treacherous and dangerous Slav surfaced during the esuli boat cruise I took down the Istrian and Dalmatian coasts (discussed in chapter 2). When the boat's propeller broke, forcing our group to stay on the island of Curzola/Korčula longer than expected, rumors began to circulate within the group that the "Slavs" had caused the breakdown and were keeping our group hostage for some nefarious purpose. A woman in the group telephoned her husband in Trieste with this theory; he duly called the newspaper *Il Piccolo,* which reported this unsubstantiated opinion and thereby prompted various worried relatives in Italy to phone members of our group. Some of us on the trip laughed that we threatened to create a diplomatic incident!

For many, though not all, esuli (like those on the cruise ready to attribute the first glitch to sabotage), the Slavs have not changed in either their tactics or their aims and thus cannot be trusted, even when, as in Istria, they don the guise of European regionalists. The main exile associations in Trieste for the most part have not collaborated officially with the Istrian regionalist movement, founded in Croatia in 1990. The exile organizations do, however, have diverse contacts with the associations of the Italian minority in Istria. Individual initiatives in Istria have been undertaken by esuli groups from particular towns, at times in collaboration with the corresponding Italian minority association and sometimes unilaterally. Some Italian minority communities, like that of Rovigno, have succeeded in establishing a fairly good rapport with their diasporic counterparts, and others, like that of Pola, have more acrimonious relations. In the 1990s, for example, the division over how to respond to political shifts among the rimasti and the rise of the regionalists led to the fracturing of the community of Pola in exile; individuals such as Lino Vivoda, formerly associated with the journal *L'Arena di Pola,* created a new publication, *L'Istria Europa,* stressing cross-border cooperation. Political parties such as La Lista per Trieste have also made some initial and surprising moves toward an opening with the rimasti and their associations. The wars in Yugoslavia thus revived old issues but also offered the possibility for greater rapport between the exiles and the Italians who remained in Istria (the rimasti).

In spite of these tentative moves, exiles nonetheless may view the rimasti in general (and in particular, its leadership) as a dubious lot, yet another group that has betrayed them by collaborating with slavo-comunisti. The moves toward a greater esuli-rimasti rapport thus remain tempered by the continued suspicion with which some exiles view Italians in Istria, often believed to have stayed out of opportunism or fervent communism. As we have seen, the very autochthony and authenticity of these Italians also comes under question. In extreme cases, exiles deny that any real Italians are still to be found in Istria, as in the case of Maddalena's father (see the introduction), who exclaimed furiously, "If you haven't understood that there are no Italians left in Istria, you haven't understood *anything!*" Such suspicion of the rimasti as a group may persist in spite of the fact that exiles often have relatives and friends still living in Istria, whose memory practices often mirror those of the exiles.

In myriad ways, then, esuli practices of remembrance make powerful and frequently exclusive moral claims about legitimacy and autochthony which work in tandem with the narratives of the foibe explored in the previous chapter. Constructing themselves as victims, the esuli thus depict themselves as "pure" in two senses: as innocent victims and as "genuine" Italians persecuted by a Yugoslav regime bent on installing a communist regime in an ethnically cleansed Istria. Both senses of Italian purity emerge dramatically in exile tellings (written and oral). Like the shtetl Jews described by Barbara Myerhoff (1978) as "double survivors" who have reached old age and survived the destruction of their social-cultural worlds during the Holocaust, aging esuli in Trieste make a powerful claim for themselves as the last members of their generation and of a lost world, as survivors.

Those Italians left behind in Istria similarly see themselves as survivors of a nearly extinct culture. Whereas esuli tend to see themselves as the last bearers of a culture that exists today only in their hearts and in their "traditional" practices, Italians in contemporary Istria seek to reforge ties with their long-alienated kin through a recognition of their mutual suffering and their shared *istrianità*, or Istrianness.

CHAPTER SEVEN

Remaking Memory: The View from Istria

INVESTIGATING the long-term consequences of the Istrian exodus for those who lived through it on both sides of the border points to the paradoxical fragility and resilience of kin ties: the possibility for their fragmentation together with their endurance despite spatial and temporal separation. Tomizza nicely captures the sense of betrayal and fear that often divided families from within at the same time that kin loyalties determined the decisions of many others about whether to leave or stay.

> For them the ten years [that] just passed [1944–54] had meant a continuous waiting, it had meant talking under their breath about putting their kids to bed, fearing their wives or their brothers or their own shadows, because times had changed, and it seemed everyone had gone crazy: people had their own ideas and interests to defend, and you heard about brothers who'd stabbed each other, a wife who'd denounced her husband . . . old stories came to the surface, stories of jealousies and betrayals, ancient ties long since forgotten. One person wouldn't leave unless another person did, and that other was tied to a third. . . . The young people had taken over: the old mostly prayed, trembling at the thought of being left alone in the house they'd built for their children; they let themselves take advice and then be led by the hand. (1999, 33, 90–91)

Recognizing the ways in which state ideologies and violence fundamentally penetrated, fractured, and shaped families in Istria and beyond offers an important corrective to understandings of kinship that treat family structures as if existing outside of either history or larger political structures. Though anthropologists of the Mediterranean region have devoted disproportionate attention to family forms and kinship structures, as well as related gender relations and norms (notably the so-called and much debated honor and shame complex), only recently have they located such relationships within a wider web of social and political networks. (For key studies of European kinship systems as the objects of ideology, see Kligman 1988; Loizos 1975; McDonogh 1986; Todorova 1993.) Some scholars have tied the prevalence of notions of honor and shame to an underdeveloped sense of community or civic loyalty and an overdeveloped sense of selfishness, particularly in the Italian case, where the continued lack of national and civic identifications remains a puzzle to be explained (and solved). In some influential analyses, brittle kin structures and the reliance on nuclear families (whether seen to derive from tradition [Banfield 1958] or a cul-

tural ecology determined by scarce resources and inheritance patterns [Schnei-
der 1971]) in areas like the Italian South are posited as the *cause,* rather than
the result, of political fragmentation.

The Istrian case makes painfully clear, however, how the fragmentation of
families may reflect the all-too-modern dynamics of state building, warfare, and
displacement. Prior to the exodus, Istrian families had long been subject to the
pressures of separation and emigration for economic reasons. Though a large
literature, anthropological and otherwise, exists on migratory patterns (including those of "return") from Europe, refugees from violence have remained
largely outside the purview of this scholarship, which in anthropology centers
on questions of kinship and social networks (Brettell 2000, 106). Furthermore,
many of the family and gender norms eulogized as traditional by exiles and sus-
ceptible to analysis as "folkways" by anthropologists of a certain bent were, if
not altogether novel, reinforced and transformed by the modernizing fascist
project (which made the family and pronatalism central to its vision of a modern nation). The fraught relationship between esuli and rimasti (as well as
among themselves, particularly across gender and generational lines), then, is
best explained not in terms of ostensibly static family forms but in light of the
historical circumstances in which families were rent asunder by the political
and economic policies of states and the attendant ideological struggles fought
on the ground in Istria.

Although many exiles rejected and denounced their labeling as fascists in the
postwar period, instead depicting themselves as upstanding citizens of a democratic Italian state in which fascism proved a shameful memory, they nonetheless condemned as communists those fellow Italians who did not leave with the
exodus. By consorting with Slovene and Croat "comrades," these Italians were
also seen to have renounced, to some degree, their own Italian-ness or were
deemed as nonautochthonous Italians who had come to Istria to build socialism. In extreme cases, exiles disavow any kinship with Italians in Istria. Rimasti,
in turn, often portrayed the exiles as having been "politically compromised" or
manipulated by Italian right-wing propaganda. This mutual negative labeling
maintained the symbolic and literal borders between fascism and communism
forged in the Second World War and the Cold War. The end of the Cold War
and Yugoslavia's breakup removed the supports of both ideology and state
power for this fascism-communism dichotomy.

Whereas exile memory practices tend to reproduce a logic of recrimination
(victims/perpetrators), Italians in Istria in the 1990s remade memory in a somewhat different manner, attempting to express the complexities of their position as a minority in a non-Italian state and the difficult choices made at the
time of the exodus. In doing so, some Italians in Istria began to talk—still ten-
tatively in the mid-1990s, but today, in the post-Tudjman era, with greater
force and frequency—about an ethnic cleansing that exacted tremendous sacrifices from both those who left and those who stayed. Positing themselves as

victims together with the esuli, these Italians also seek greater rapport with their long-alienated kin and acquaintances. In this chapter I explore the ways in which Italians in Istria incorporate memory practices into a vision designed to strengthen and sustain the minority community at the same time that it challenges the narrative means by which the minority was incorporated into the (periphery of) Yugoslav socialist state during and after the war. Whereas during the Yugoslav period leaders of the Italian minority wanted to see themselves as central to the state established through the partisan struggle, in the post-Yugoslav period rimasti stress their marginality (and hence their lack of accountability for the errors of Yugoslav socialism and the wrongs done to their alienated kin).

Rimasto Identity

As among the andati in Trieste, not all Italians in Istria adhered to the rimasto identity as defined by the Italian minority associations. On the one hand, the choice for Italians who stayed behind proved much starker than for the Istrian Italians in Trieste: in contrast to the plurality of positions embodied by the diverse exile organizations, in Istria there existed only one, state-sanctioned vehicle of expression for the Italian "national group." On the other hand, many (though not all, since assimilation into the Slavic milieu did not prove uncommon) of those who generally opted out of active participation in the Unione degli Italiani dell'Istria e di Fiume e felt themselves to be Italian and thus frequently took advantage of resources associated with the Unione, such as the Italian-language schools. In addition, they had the option to move through various stages and types of engagement with the Unione. The story of Tina and her family illustrates these complexities.

Tina, a retired worker from Rovigno's tobacco factory, was a minor at the time of the exodus and stayed in Istria with her father. Under the Yugoslavian regime, she participated in the Unione but only in its cultural activities, specifically its folkloric groups. In the 1950s and 1960s, for example, Tina performed in many locales in Istria, as well as other parts of Yugoslavia. After she married, she and her husband, Antonio, became well known locally for their performances and even cut some records. Never interested in politics—whether those of the minority or of the tobacco factory—Tina eventually withdrew from the Unione, markedly so after the death of her husband. In the years in which I worked in Rovigno, I saw Tina only at one event held at the Comunità Italiana di Rovigno: the 1996 dinner celebrating Rovigno's patron saint, Saint Euphemia.

Not only does Tina rarely frequent the Comunità, she seldom makes the short trip from her home in the New Town to Cittàvecchia. Like many of Istria's elderly Italians who complain about feeling like "strangers in their own home," Tina laments that when she goes to town, she sees only a few people she recognizes. Fortunately, the daily afternoon coffee visits of her friends Norma and Marisa help mitigate Tina's isolation. Every morning, Marisa drinks coffee at the Comunità Italiana (or, in the last few years, a café on the waterfront) with many of the retired Italian women I also frequented. Marisa thus passes on to Tina all the news and gossip of this group, which embodies rovignesi's self-professed love of chattering about others (*chiacchierare* in Italian, *babare* in istro-veneto dialect).

Tina also keeps abreast of happenings through her two children, Irene and Alessandro, both in their midthirties. Irene and Alessandro attended the Italian-language schools in Rovigno, unambiguously identifying themselves as Italians. At the same time, they became much more integrated into the new Istrian reality than did their mother. Admittedly, Tina's work in the tobacco factory exposed her to many Croats, as well as to other South Slavs who moved to Rovigno after the exodus. Tina learned Serbo-Croatian only haltingly, however, never having had formal instruction in school (unlike her children). A limited ability (and often a limited desire) to speak the language of the majority contributed to the isolation of many rimasti who were already young adults or fully grown at the time of the exodus. This strengthened their sense of ethnic solidarity, even among those who were not registered with the Unione, at the same time that it provided a convenient way to distance oneself from the political sphere. As Tina commented one day about the factory, "[I participated in] only cultural activities because when there was some kind of meeting—Madonna! I got permission to go home. . . . It bored me. . . . They spoke in Croatian, and after two minutes they said two words in Italian, and I said, 'Okay, I'm going home.'"

In contrast to Tina, Irene and Alessandro grew up as Yugoslavs who studied Serbo-Croatian in school and, like all Yugoslav children, were inculcated in the ways of "Brotherhood and Unity" by participating in the communist Pioneers, civil defense exercises, and school trips to other parts of Yugoslavia and by learning songs and the folkways of the South Slavs peoples. In many ways, however, Italy remained their primary point of reference. As Irene expressed it in 1999, "I never really felt as if I belonged to Yugoslavia. Now when I read books about the breakup of Yugoslavia, it's as if I'm reading about some faraway place." Through the Unione, Irene received a scholarship to attend the University of Trieste, staying on to teach at a high school level after graduation. After I left the field, Irene returned to Rovigno for one year to teach in the Italian schools there; she has now relocated, permanently it appears, in Italy. Alessandro, in contrast, remained in his hometown for more than a decade after graduating from high school. For many years he worked as a technician and handyman at the Italian-language school. In 1997 he joined his sister in Italy, taking a job in Udine. Tina, Irene, and Alessandro possess dual Italian/Croatian citizenship (made possible, in part, because Tina and Antonio were born in and grew up as citizens of the Italian state), which facilitated these relocations. Despite the fact that Tina and her children never participated in the political life of the Italian minority, their lives are entangled with the social networks, schooling, and patronage (scholarships, employment) of the Unione /Comunità Italiana.

Although many self-described Italians do not enroll officially as members of the various minority associations in Istria (particularly under Yugoslavia, out of continuing fear), it proves difficult, on the practical level, to actively identify as an Italian without some contact with the associations. Paradoxically, the inescapability of the minority organization—reflecting the diverse political conditions in which rimasti and exile identities were shaped after 1945—fractures memory along leadership/association and nonleadership lines even more sharply than among esuli. It also complicates the generational aspects of memory so pronounced among the esuli, though in the last decade many younger Istrian Italians have openly rejected that minority leadership which shaped the position of the Italians under Tito.

Yugoslavia's Italians: "Fifth Column" or "Blood Brothers"?

O dear Istria, oppressed and bleeding,
Even our lives we have given you,
Take up your gun and go to the war,
Defeat the enemy, redeem your land.
Advance united, Croats and Italians,
in the certainty of a better tomorrow.
Fascist dog who serves the oppressors,
For you soon there will be great sorrow.
Our eyes are fixed on victory:
we begin our new history . . .
—"O Istria Cara," *popular partisan song*

In contrast to the exiles, who often resisted the "fascist" label that was applied to them, in the Yugoslav context rimasti largely accepted the appellation "communists." This was necessary in order to deflect lingering suspicions that the rimasti were fascists or irredentists, pointing to the relatively precarious position Istria's Italians occupied in the socialist federation. As Shoup notes in his discussion of Yugoslavia's non-Slavic minorities (including Italians, Hungarians, Albanians, Slovaks and Czechs, Russenes, Bulgarians, and Turks), after the war these populations—who in many cases had collaborated with Yugoslavia's occupiers—were technically "absolved of any collective responsibility for collaboration and were promised recognition as national minorities with the right to receive education in national schools and organize national cultural organizations" (Shoup 1968, 103). Members of the German minority proved the exception and either fled or were expelled (Kosinski 1982,

187–89; Schechtman 1946, 1962; Werner Kupka 1964). In addition to minority-language schools and cultural organizations, minority members were given representation in both the Federal Assembly of Yugoslavia and the parliaments of the individual republics. The Italian minority, for example, had two representatives in the federal assembly (Štojković and Martić 1952).

In practice, "The behavior of the minorities during the war could not simply be forgotten, however, and behind the promises made by the Communists there lurked a deep distrust of the entire minority population" (Shoup 1968, 103). Members of the Italian minority thus found themselves in an ambiguous position and sometimes responded, as a younger minority critic puts it, by becoming "more communist than the communists." In order to erase any doubts that Yugoslavia's Italians were a potentially treacherous "fifth column," Italian minority publications and state propaganda alike emphasized the heroic role Italians played in the partisan war. This inserted Italians into the "new history" forged by the antifascist struggle while simultaneously grounding their experience in an older and alternative trajectory of socialist historiography in Istria. Works such as *Il contributo degli Italiani dell'Istria e di Fiume alla Lotta popolare di Liberazione* (The contribution of the Italians of Istria and Fiume to the People's Liberation fight, Giuricin 1961), *Fratelli nel sangue* (Brothers in blood, Bressan and Giuricin 1964), *Rossa una stella* (A red star, Scotti and Giuricin 1975), *Le armi e la libertà dell'Istria* (The forces and the liberty of Istria, 1981), and *Hrvoji-Kućibreg: Un itinerario per monumenti e lapidi della lotta di liberazione nazionale* (Hrvoji-Kućibreg: An itinerary for the monuments and commemorative plaques of the national liberation struggle, Abram 1984) emplotted the Italian effort into a broader narrative about the Yugoslav struggle.

These works typically detail military actions in which Italian partisans participated and provide biographies of the careers of fallen "martyrs," such as Rovigno's Pino Budicin, who gave his name to a celebrated all-Italian partisan battalion. Narratives of the partisan war often use the religiously charged language of baptism, sacrifice, and redemption. Accounts of the formation of the Pino Budicin battalion at Stanzia Bembo (near the town of Valle), for example, speak of a literal baptism of the fighters; at the ceremony marking the official (if clandestine) birth of the brigade, each participant received a quarter liter of wine (Scotti and Giuricin 1975, 67–72), a gesture redolent of Catholic practices of communion.

Just as fascism had exalted death in war as a means of regenerating Italy through a "baptism of blood" (Gentile 1996), so did communist movements in Italy and Istria (and elsewhere) combine "military and religious imagery by focusing on the symbolism of sacrifice and, in particular, on the ultimate sacrifice, death" (Kertzer 1996, 103). The red of the communist star (*rossa una stella*) thus blurred with the red of the blood spilled for liberty, despite disclaimers that accounts of the partisan war were intended not to create myths or legends but rather to show men as they really were (Scotti and Giuricin 1975, 23). At the emotional funerals held for such fallen heroes, the call of the blood of partisans was said to inspire the living to finish the work begun by these martyrs.

Slain Italians like Pino Budicin, Aldo Rismondo, and Marco Garbin (all from Rovigno)—whose names still grace the streets and Italian cultural circles in Istria—thus became important symbols of the Italian antifascist contribution. These individuals constituted a new pantheon of heroes for an Italian minority seeking to efface the memory of those irredentist "patriots" and "heroes" who had been celebrated in the street names and monuments of fascist Istria (on antifascist monuments, see Abram 1984, and for similar processes by which communist saints were created in the Italian context, see Kertzer 1996, 44–45, 60–61). The way in which such communist memorializations and cults of the dead mirrored (even as they opposed) those of the irredentists/nationalists/fascists—with songs, like the "Inno dei partigiani Italiani" (Hymn of the Italian partisans) demanding the redemption of the nation from the fascists (*a patria redenta dal fascismo*) (Scotti and Giuricin 1975, 560)—underscores the mutual constitution of these discourses in the Julian March.

Other commemorations celebrated events associated with the partisan war, such as the foundation of the Unione degli Italiani dell'Istria e di Fiume (UIIF) in July 1944, by a group of Italians in agreement with the Croatian party leadership.[1] Such ritual practices, together with publications, implicitly stressed the difference between reactionary, chauvinistic Italians—those who had endorsed the fascist cult of irredentist heroes—and "progressive" Italians who embraced the Italo-Slav brotherhood (*fratellanza*). As one author put it in 1945, the Resistance enabled honest Italians in Istria to "redeem" themselves from the taint, "the mark of fascism that weighed like an original sin" (Unione degli Italiani 1945, 9).

In their contribution as partisans, Italians, together with their Croat and Slovene comrades, were seen to have staged a "plebiscite of blood" in the fight to join Istria to Yugoslavia. In a 1945 booklet, Eros Sequi, the first secretary of the Unione degli Italiani (and later professor of Italian literature at the University of Belgrade), called on the Italian government to recognize the annexation of Istria and Fiume to Croatia. "We don't intend to be a pawn in the game of Italian imperialists anymore," declared Sequi. "Rather, we want to be the bridge that will unite Italy and Yugoslavia in a future of liberty and democracy" (in Unione degli Italiani 1945, 48). This choice separated the good Italians from the bad ones (those who fled), as well as from the Germans.

Sequi and other *bravi Italiani* (good Italians) looked ahead to the socialist future—to building a new history, as the partisan song "O Istria Cara" exhorted—while simultaneously privileging an alternative historical narrative about long-standing socialist and workers' movements in Istria (see Martini 1981). This inserted the Italian antifascist participation into a more extensive and organic tradition. Exile accounts either fail to acknowledge or downplay the strength of workers' movements—historically strong in those towns and cities, like Trieste,

Pola, and Rovigno, that benefited from Austrian efforts to create industry (Črno-bori 1979)—instead viewing communism as imposed on Istria after 1945 or as exclusive to Slavic populations.

Alongside the irredentist histories (both Italian and Slav) of national struggle in Istria, however, there existed another corpus of works that interpreted conflict in the peninsula as primarily motivated by class divisions. A 1900 publication by the Socialist party of the Adriatic Region, for example, described Italians as constituting the intellectual and financial class, which controlled both capital and the educational system in the Istrian Peninsula. "The struggle in Istria is one of class, but class is reinforced through racial difference" (Lazzarini 1900, 28–29). Calling for the socialists to direct their propaganda efforts at the educational system, this publication foresees an economic and agrarian "awakening" in Istria. Contemporaneous pamphlets similarly argued, "Our motto must be liberty for Slavs but liberty also for Italians" (Tuntar 1905, 7).

With the close of the Austrian period in Istria and the territory's incorporation into the Italian state, new tactics of struggle came into play as socialist and communist organizations were forced underground by the fascist regime. In leftist historiography, acts of resistance during this period—notably the 1921 workers' rebellion at Albona and the Julian contribution to the Spanish civil war—figure as key moments within a teleological narrative about the eventual triumph of socialism in Yugoslavia (Črnobori 1979; Čulinović 1979). Although the Italian government soon quashed this movement, in Yugoslavia and today in Croatia, the Albona rebellion is remembered as an important precursor of the revolutionary struggle against fascism and Nazism. As one Croatian historian contends, "There are many signs that indicate how the mass adhesion of the Istrian people to the Resistance has its long and profound roots in the movements of the miners and peasants of Albona and nearby Proština" (Čulinović 1979, 2). Similarly, in the socialist historiographical tradition, the proportionately high number of Italian, Slovene, and Croat volunteers from the Julian March who fought for the Spanish Republic comes to signal the deep Istrian commitment to defeating fascism (see Bebler 1978; Furunović 1976; Puppini 1986; and Steffè 1974).

This alternative historical narrative of Italian participation in workers' movements and the Resistance—complete with its own martyrs and sacred calendar—thus offered the Italian minority in Yugoslavia a ready-made means of legitimating itself. Despite this, members of the Italian minority today contend that this legitimation was never complete, not only because of continued suspicion toward Italians but also because of the complicated relationship between antifascism and communism, as well as between the Italian and Yugoslav partisan forces in Istria. Many informants noted that although Italy's capitulation in 1943 was celebrated in Istria, the antifascist struggle did not necessarily prove coterminous with support for a communist regime; thus one previously "submerged" history (the socialist tradition exhumed under Yugoslavia for political purposes) yields to another newly disinterred version of the past.

Antonio Borme, one of the minority's most outspoken activists and a Communist Party member, contends that in contrast to those who falsely hoped for an autonomous region within Yugoslavia, some adherents of the Italian Communist Party did not accept the Yugoslav Communist Party's intention to incorporate Istria into Croatia. During two decades of clandestine activity against the fascist state, Italian communists in Istria had taken their direction and inspiration from the Italian Communist Party. The partisan actions in Istria after September 8, 1943, however, were organized by the Croatian Communist Party. Finding themselves isolated, Italians in Istria generally followed the directives of the Croatian communists. Only after the war did Italians in Istria come to learn of the disagreement between the Italian and Croatian Communist Parties over where to draw the Italo-Yugoslav border (Borme 1995, 63). In addition, during the time of the Cominform split, the continued support shown by many Italians for the PCI (which denounced Tito) and its internationalist line resulted in the imprisonment, expulsion, or flight of many autochthonous Italians, as well as most of those individuals who had come to Istria with the "counter-exodus" (see Thomassen 2001 for the account of one such PCI faithful).

Some skeptical exiles see such protestations by rimasti leaders like Borme as self-serving revisionism, given that antifascists who did not support the Tito regime also left with the exodus (for an interesting memoir by one such "communist victimized by communism," see Budicin 1995). Italians in Istria instead defend choices made out of political idealism and argue that only with Yugoslavia's dissolution has it become possible to articulate and appreciate the complexities and ambiguities of the relationship between antifascism and communism in Istria. Not surprisingly, the theme of the Yugoslavs' betrayal of the antifascist/socialist project figures rimasti accounts in different ways. Antonio Borme described it in a series of interviews given in 1988.

> Repent . . . no, I haven't repented of my choice . . . it was a leftist, humanistic choice. . . . Certainly, it was a utopia. One can't repent of having dreamed: we had under our eyes the example of the Italians of Rovigno and the Slavs of the periphery to whom I taught literature. It was a terrible example: the Slavs were more than ignorant, they were downtrodden. And we didn't know yet about the tragic experiences of the East; the Soviet Union was a myth, Stalin seemed to herald a new social organization that recognized the values of Man and of minorities. All fine, in theory: practice is another thing, but we didn't know that then. . . . We nourished great hopes [for] . . . an autonomous region, predominantly Italian, within the Yugoslav context. We were, certainly, very ingenuous, with our certainty in constructing a better society without even knowing what this society would be. (Borme 1992, 246, 264)

Borme has argued that as a result of the socialism that the Yugoslav regime put into practice, once-ingenuous minority activists were forced to do continual battle for Italians' rights. "We began to fight so that the laws would be enacted. . . . We argued that Istria was a mixed territory and that we didn't want

Italian ghettoes but instead integral bilingualism" (ibid., 247). Activists such as Borme possess what I call a partisan identity, in the sense that they construct their life histories and those of the minority as a series of political and legal struggles. This rhetoric of the battle thus extends the heroic struggle of the war into the postwar period. Similarly, "the symbolic world of Italian Communism relied heavily on a military metaphor (as did the Communist Manifesto). History was portrayed as an ongoing battle" (Kertzer 1996, 44). In the Istrian context, these themes of heroism and battle today paradoxically work in tandem with the trope of victimization to construct rimasti as ingenuous idealists betrayed by the Yugoslav regime for whose foundation they made sacrifices.

As former protagonists like Borme now describe it, in the 1950s the organs of the Italian minority—the Unione degli Italiani dell'Istria e di Fiume and the Gruppo Nazionale Italiano (GNI)—were centralized, state-controlled apparatuses (Borme 1995, 65). In the aftermath of the Cominform split, Italian minority activists found themselves jailed or discredited. The constitutional changes of 1963 and 1971—which signaled wide-ranging shifts throughout Yugoslavia, including expanded self-management, greater republican autonomy, and the recognition of ethnic minorities as "organic entities"—are today heralded for having created a space for the UIIF to expand its role and for Italians to acquire some agency after the difficult postwar years (Borme 1995, 66; see also Radossi 1989). These transformations in the minority association occurred in the general context of the "Croatian Spring," a period in which liberal reformers sought decentralization and nationalists demanded linguistic recognition of Croatian as distinct from Serbian. The Center for Historical Research (Centro di Ricerche Storiche di Rovigno), dedicated to the Italian minority, was established in 1968, providing Italians with a crucial intellectual reference point and greater scholarly exchange with the madrepatria. Giovanni Radossi, founder and director of the center and a teacher at the Italian high school in Rovigno, told me in typical partisan style of the political and financial struggles to realize the proposal for the center, which began full operation only in 1971.[2]

In 1971, the year that the Centro di Ricerche Storiche put out its first publication, the UIIF formed Comunità Italiane, local Italian communities that replaced the older Circoli Italiani (Italian Circles) as organs of Italian self-management. Whereas the Circoli had been largely cultural and folkloristic groups, the Comunità Italiane assumed a much more explicitly political role devoted to advancing the rights and interests of the Italian minority. As the Italian minority began to establish ties with institutions in Italy like the Università Popolare di Trieste—which today provides the Italian minority with textbooks, scholarships, and other educational goods and services—charges of irredentism and nationalism surfaced (Borme 1992, 195).

In the climate of repression and reaction to the "Croatian Spring," Antonio Borme was expelled from the Croatian Communist Party and forced out as UIIF head. Only in 1988 did Italians in Capodistria call for the rehabilitation of

Borme, now seen as a scapegoat who paid for all Italians in Yugoslavia. The timing of this call reflected dramatic political changes within post-Tito Yugoslavia,
as well as a sense of change and self-examination within the Italian minority. As
the economic and political crisis worsened in the late 1980s, a younger generation of Italians in Istria began to both question received orthodoxies and challenge the leadership of the UIIF, the state-sponsored minority organization. In
1988 the deterioration of the Yugoslav economy forced the UIIF to interrupt its
activities when the Slovene and Croatian Republics halted funds for the Italian
association. Proposals for laws to limit bilingualism further threatened the position of the Italian minority. In response, Franco Juri of Capodistria launched
a petition, signed by one thousand Istrians, calling on the Yugoslav government
to recognize the Italians' linguistic and cultural rights. A meeting held in Capodistria and attended by various leaders of the Italian community led to the formation of what became known as Gruppo 88 (Group 88).

At the meeting, prominent figures in the Italian minority denounced the continual erosion of their rights and accused Belgrade of wishing for the disappearance of the Italian minority (Maurizio Tremul, personal communication).
Juri became the leader of Gruppo 88—which also included Roberto Batelli
and Maurizio Tremul, today political representatives of the Italian minority in
Slovenia—seeking to reform the UIIF from within and to foster pluralism
(Lanza 1990, 114–15). Echoing the esuli's discourse, Juri spoke scathingly of
the "ethnocide" endured by the Italian minority under Yugoslavia. At a 1989
roundtable sponsored by Gruppo 88, entitled "The Truth of the Foibe," Borme
similarly reiterated exiles' claims about Italians being killed for the "sole crime
of being Italian" (1995, 74). Borme benefited from Gruppo 88's call for his
rehabilitation, taken up by the UIIF in recognition of his case and of other
Italians victimized by the regime (in Lanza 1990, 122). This constructed a
new set of victims, drawn from the rimasti, alongside those of the foibe and the
exodus.

Although the UIIF voted to formally integrate Gruppo 88, tensions remained
among the groups' respective political leaders, as well as between different em-
phases on the defense of the rights of a national minority and the fostering of a
multiethnic society (ibid., 116). These disagreements manifested not only political shifts but also generational ones, as younger Italians directly challenged
the established power structure of the UIIF. Just as exiles mocked the empty
slogan "The world's most open border," young Italian intellectuals in Istria
such as Silvano Zilli scorned Yugoslav rhetoric about the Italian minority being
a "bridge between peoples." For Zilli—formerly a librarian at the Centro di
Ricerche Storiche and subsequently deputy mayor of Rovigno and a member of
the executive board of the Unione Italiana (UI)—Italians in Istria were instead
the hostages of a regime that used them politically, as well as of a minority leadership that profited from its position and failed to represent the interests of the
Italian ethnic group (Zilli 1990).

Zilli urged Italian leaders to overcome their old-regime mentality by embracing their long history of ethnic *convivenza*, a history from which the minority had been artificially distanced as a result of two ideologically oppressive regimes (Italy and Yugoslavia). With his vision of a multiethnic Istrian identity, Zilli not surprisingly became a powerful voice in the regionalist movement. Whereas the writings of Italian intellectuals such as Zilli and the political initiatives of Gruppo 88 constituted an assault of sorts on the old structures of power, the reformers contained their own divisions. Such differences of opinion became apparent in 1990 at a meeting between Gruppo leaders and exponents of political parties such as the regionalist Istrian Democratic Assembly (DDI-IDS) and the Club Istria (from Capodistria). The existence of these organizations reflected the new multiparty system in Slovenia and Croatia. In preparation for the elections of 1991, Gruppo 88 leaders proposed joining political forces with the DDI-IDS, a suggestion that distressed some supporters. Gruppo 88 eventually faded away, though its call for the reform of the UIIF and ethnic convivenza has borne fruit in the Yugoslav successor states of Slovenia and Croatia.

In 1991 the Unione Italiana, an organization that sought more "democratic" representation for the minority, replaced the Unione degli Italiani dell'Istria e di Fiume and local Comunità Italiane were rechristened Comunità degli Italiani. Several new Italian communities were formed in the Istrian interior—in towns or villages like Grisignana, Montona, and San Lorenzo di Babici—in the effort to give minority members greater representation and autonomy. Within the Unione Italiana, as well as within the local government in both Croatian and Slovenian Istria, a generation of young challengers—individuals such as Elvio Baccarini, Franco and Aurelio Juri, Maurizio Tremul, and Silvano Zilli—have come to power. Locally, in the long-established Comunità many old-timers remain, in contrast to the new communities that are often headed by energetic and (relatively) young individuals.

During my time in Istria, I met with the presidents of three such "new" Italian communities. The creation of these groups has provoked some resentment in long-established communities, which previously represented towns with their own clubs. The multiplication of clubs has, of course, led to a struggle for resources, as the same amount of money must now be divided more ways. The neocommunity heads I spoke with complained bitterly about the lack of support (financial and moral) shown by the older groups. Gianna, a woman in her early forties who heads a club founded in 1993, lamented, "We small communities have very little to work with and have to work hard to get even that." Where once there had been one large association covering a wide district, today there exist two new clubs in addition to the older one. Gianna said that rather than being praised by the old club for her efforts she was rewarded with hostility and jealousy. The large Comunità had invited the folklore section of her club to perform in a nearby community, for example, without informing Gianna, the club's president; she learned of the event only by reading a newspaper blurb about it. When she sent a letter of protest to the big Comunità, Gianna received a rather perfunctory letter informing her that the group would also be giving a show in Italy.

This episode suggests not only possible hostility on the part of the old clubs but also divisions within new associations. I found it rather strange, for example, that members of Gianna's folklore ensemble had not told her of their activities, unless they assumed she already knew. When I asked some of the leadership at the venerable Comunità about how they viewed neocommunities like the one headed by Gianna, they responded that such clubs often are poorly organized and ineffective; dispersing and dividing the already limited money available to the Italian minority, these men argued, would accomplish very little. That such individuals are long-time activists employed by the Comunità, becoming in the process "professional" minority representatives, also suggests the personal stakes involved in such power struggles.

Other Italians I spoke with complained about the two-tiered structure of an Italian minority that privileges not only certain communities but also individuals who enjoy benefits such as paid trips to Italy and university scholarships for their children. Mirella, an employee at the Comunità degli Italiani of Cittanova/Novigrad (in Croatia) and a teacher at Italian schools in Isola and Buie, contended that activists who control the Comunità have profited from their position and built their careers on the backs of humble peasants who rarely received benefits reserved for the Italian minority. Hailing from a peasant family that has lived in Buie for generations, Mirella distinguished two categories of those who remained in ex–Zone B: (1) those who looked on Yugoslavia favorably and (2) those peasants who submitted to the regime in order to stay on their land. The gross distinction that esuli make between themselves and rimasti, the latter seen to have opportunistically profited from the departure of their fellow Italians, is here reinscribed by Mirella as a division internal to the rimasti community. Just as some exiles trace their division to political instrumentalization by opportunistic right-wing exile leaders, so some rimasti believe that they have been betrayed by their own kind. Note that Mirella made such an accusation as an "outsider" despite the fact that she owes her career in part to the Italian community. Although on one hand such charges may work as self-justifications, on the other hand they reflect the complicated relationships many rimasti have with the associations that monopolize Italian-ness at the institutional level.

Many Italian community personnel, including Mirella, draw further distinctions between members who are ethnic "Italians" and Slavic "sympathizers" or supporters, highlighting criteria of authenticity similar to those heard among the exiles. Like those of the esuli, rimasti memory practices emphasize autochthony in various ways, depicting Italians in Istria as both victims and survivors.

Living among the Ruins

Although Italians in Istria once had to either put a good face on their experience or stay silent, today it has become possible for Italians to express the sadness they felt at being left behind. Both Italians who left Istria and those who remained there, then, nurture a nostalgia for a lost "Italian" world whose physical traces remain in Istria. Works on displacement typically have not taken this mirror experience of "emplacement" (Malkki 1995) into account, reflecting the ways in which images of exile often remain predicated upon those of the homeland's destruction or usurpation (for notable exceptions, see Behar 1998; Danforth 1995; and Hart 1999). Even when the destruction of a community is depicted as complete—as in many of the esuli's stories and in their visual representations of the homeland as a ruined landscape—there often remain behind kinfolk, friends, and acquaintances. In the Istrian case, exile accounts of the peninsula's abandonment either silence the fact that many families were divided or downplay the wrenching debates that took place within families about whether to stay or go. Though not physically displaced, Italians in Istria have a sense of an interior displacement, an exile of the heart and mind, if not the body, that has rendered them, like the exiles in the Italian *madrepatria,* "strangers in their own home."

Whereas exiles often preserve idealized memories of the Istria of their childhood, Italians in Istria continue to walk the streets that once echoed with Italian or istro-veneto and whose houses were inhabited by Italian families. Rosanna, a seventy-five-year-old woman from Montona, a hilltop town in the interior of Istria that remains half deserted, lamented her isolation, living as she does in the midst of "strangers" (though she herself married a Croat) and nurturing herself on memories. Like Rosanna and Tina, many older rimasti feel alone, particularly as the already limited number of Italians of the same age group dwindles year by year and as Italian young people move to larger towns or nearby Italy, Austria, and Germany in search of work. Death erodes that community of persons born and raised under Italy just as surely as time wears away the houses where their friends and ancestors once lived. As among the esuli, empty houses (or ones reoccupied by "foreign" peoples like Bosnians) prove powerful metonyms for the exodus, particularly the "destruction" (through division and dispersal) of the Italian "family" in Istria.

Marianna, a former activist in Rovigno's Comunità Italiana and one of the women with whom I regularly drank coffee, recounted the all-too-frequent pang of anguish she experiences when confronted by the physical reminders of the exodus. "Sometimes when I come home," she said, describing her daily walk from the Italian center in the old town to the new suburbs, "I count the windows of the houses. I think of who lived there before, in those houses. There lived so and so, there lived so and so. . . . Everything is changed. And it's not right." When she goes to town, she can easily arrive at the Italian community without "having met anyone [she knows]. . . . Not even one rovignese." Such a reality proves bitter for those who grew up in a small town where "everyone knew everyone." On her daily rambles, perhaps one or two people will greet Marianna in Italian (saying *buon giorno*), and all the rest in Croatian (*dobar dan*). As these comments suggest, those who remained suffer from nostalgia not dissimilar to that of the esuli, missing the once-familiar sights and sounds of their lost world.

Marianna stresses the difference, however, between the rimasti and esuli by contrasting her attitudes to those of her cousin, Roberto. In Marianna's mind, the exiles often have a static and unrealistic view of Istria, whereas those who remained have had to accept the changes, positive and negative, of the last fifty years. Roberto fled Rovigno in a small fishing boat in 1947 after his arrest for burning ("sabotaging") a Russian film. His parents eventually joined him on the second option for Italian citizenship opened in 1952, and the entire family emigrated to Australia. Marianna jokes that Roberto carried away half of Istria (in the form of books and stones from Rovigno) in the process of building his house in Australia. Roberto has returned to Rovigno several times and remains in correspondence with Marianna, though he sometimes "disappoints" her, as when he published an angry letter in an exile journal.

> [This is] the difference between me and my cousin in Australia. He's angry at those who remained here because they've changed Rovigno, because there are these houses [in the new town]. It's not that world anymore, that city that was here fifty years ago. It's a mistaken attitude; I told him that when he came. . . . Everything evolves and changes. . . . Rovigno at that time, before the end of the war, there wasn't even plumbing; you had to go throw it away [chamberpot waste] by hand in the sea. If Italy had remained here, none of these pine trees [referring to the national park] would be here; it would all be hotels, houses, villas, and such. Punta Corrente [the park] wouldn't even exist anymore.

In a heated voice, Marianna added, "You can't expect, those of you who left, that you want to find what was here. You just can't, after fifty years. In another fifty years who knows if these houses will still be here." By addressing "those of *you* who left," Marianna makes explicit the often implicit ways in which rimasti and esuli accounts remain in a constant shadow dialogue with one another.

Marianna's flash of irritation subsides, however, when she distinguishes humble peasants who lost the little that they had from those "privileged" individuals who succeeded in retaining their wealth. In classifying exiles, she adopts the same privileged-versus-peasant distinction that rimasti such as Mirella used to criticize the older generation of minority leadership, which includes Marianna.

> However, these people who went away—not all, many were happy—but those who were peasants and had land where today there are hotels and houses, cry, and they did lose everything. . . . I've seen with my own eyes a peasant who had land around

here who had never been back to see his plot. This was seventeen years ago. He came with his wife; they went to see where his land had been, you see. . . . And I saw him coming back with his wife, tears like this [gestures]; the whole way down the street he was crying, crying. It really moved me. And I said to myself, "But look at this— still!" Because he had seen his land, had seen that on that plot they'd built part of Eden [a hotel complex] or houses . . . crying, crying. To see a man cry like that is really sad. Those who left, who lost [land], were paid with practically nothing. That's really grave. I don't care about those who left with money, however.

Marianna stresses many of the same features—houses and land—that dominate exile understandings and arouse great emotion among esuli, like the returning former peasant. Among the rimasti, then, memory practices prove architectonic in the most literal sense, as Italians inhabit the "ruins of history." Like the exiles, Italians in Istria also play on themes of silence: those evoked by Istria's physical landscape with ghost towns and ruined buildings in the interior and an abandoned countryside no longer under cultivation, as well as those wrought by the long historical denial in former Yugoslavia about the exodus. The survival, persistence, and pragmatic adaptation of Italians in Istria paradoxically break those silences, however, as Italians invest those "ruins" with contemporary meaning (at the same time recognizing that not all of the new structures built on those ruins are bad) and make visible their own existence. Whereas esuli focus on cemeteries as both a literal testimony of their historic presence and a metaphor for Istria's fate, for instance, rimasti honor their dead by attending to cemeteries at the same time that they bring to the monuments of Italian civilization the sounds of life: music, laughter, and children's voices.

The community centers and Italian-language schools that provide the institutional basis for the Italian minority's continued existence often occupy structures dating from the Venetian or Austrian period. Testifying to the Italians' deep roots in the peninsula, these community centers simultaneously evidence the minority's continued existence. At first glance, these community centers resemble those of the exiles in Trieste, serving as social centers for a nostalgic, predominantly elderly population. During the day, the majority of those drinking coffee and chatting at the Italian center in Rovigno, for example, are retirees who reminisce about the past. In contrast to the esuli organizations, however, young Italians ran and operated the bar at Rovigno's center, which was open for most of the day, during my time there.

Young people also frequently attend and participate in activities at the center in much greater numbers than in Trieste. In some cases, these activities consciously preserve tradition, enlisting young people in choirs and dance groups that perform traditional Istrian Italian folklore. In Rovigno, for example, members (young and old) of the Marco Garbin circle keep alive a tradition of acoustic singing (the *bitinada*) peculiar to the city and perform in folkloric programs in both Istria and Italy, as well as in events held at Rovigno's Comunità degli Italiani. At the same time, Italian children also give performances of new songs written in Italian and the traditional dialect. Vlado Benussi, a schoolteacher and musician, has composed many such songs and organizes performances by children; these songs have also been recorded, and tape cassettes circulate in the Italian schools and centers throughout Istria.

I witnessed a performance of such songs at Rovigno's Comunità degli Italiani for the 1996 festival of the city's patron saint, Saint Euphemia. The three-day celebration featured a religious procession and Mass, as well as citywide concerts and fireworks displays, but for the Italian community in Rovigno the group dinner and performance held at the community center was the real highlight of the festival. Here I saw gathered together many of the Italians I came to know during my residence in the town, including schoolchildren and their parents, the retirees with whom I drank my daily coffee, and self-described Italians (like Tina) who almost never set foot in the community center. Both the program and the cross-section of people it attracted underscored the way in which such minority events work to portray the Italian language and culture as neither the last remnants of a dying culture associated with old folks nor the museumlike preserve of folklore performed by young people. The evening's program showcased Rovigno's Italian schoolchildren of varying ages as they sang and danced to Benussi's compositions, as well as contemporary rock songs in Italian and English chosen by the young people themselves.

Events that involve Italian schoolchildren in the life of the Italian community center seek to actively reproduce and reconstitute the Italian minority and its traditions. Under Yugoslavia, such populations were relegated to a largely folkloric role, with Italian groups trotted out for state-sponsored festivals (particularly in the decade after the Second World War) or for tourists' entertainment. In contrast to the territory's abandoned interior, whose desolation told a painful story about exodus, coastal areas that grew dramatically in the 1960s and 1970s reinscribed the space of death and emptiness with tourism. As generally occurs with tourism, folkloric representations of authenticity obscured lived histories (particularly painful ones). For the German, Italian, and Yugoslav tourists who flocked to Istria's coastal resorts and enjoyed performances by Istrian Italian choral and dance groups, the Italian minority of Istria stood not as a painful reminder of war and population transfer but as a quaint cultural survival and a symbol of Yugoslav "Brotherhood and Unity." In places such as Rovigno, the traditional festival on September 16 for Saint Euphemia, for example, was replaced by the folkloric spectacle billed as the Nights of Rovigno (Notti rovignesi), staged in August, at the height of the tourist season.

That the Italian minority participated in such events reflects the ways in which its members at times colluded in silencing preexodus traditions and the history of the exodus, which posed difficult questions for political activists who had remained. Today Italians and others have begun to reclaim traditional memory practices—such as saints' days—together with the history of the exodus while staking powerful claims about the minority's *future*. If any traces of autochthonous Italian culture and language remain in Istria fifty years after the exodus, the rimasti argue, it is only thanks to their continued efforts to carve out a space for the Italian minority despite the hostility of the Yugoslav and Tudjman regimes. In a kind of mirror image of exile accounts, then, the rimasti see themselves as embattled survivors. In the summer of 2000, I attended a meeting at Rovigno's Comunità degli Italiani concerning dual citizenship (Italian and Croatian) for members of the Italian minority. I was struck by the anger with which several older rimasti expressed their sense of having been used and forgotten, by Yugoslavia but particularly by Italy. Some leaders who had once embraced socialism and publicly rejected the "imperialist" and "fascist" Italian state now rewrote history with their claims of having been abandoned utterly by the *madrepatria*. This predictable move did not surprise me; rather, I noted the vehemence with which numerous individuals expressed their sense of being the "real" victims. Such sentiments proved pervasive in the mid-1990s but often were tempered in their public expression, in part because the discursive shift between the active, heroic narrative and the passive, victim account was not yet complete and in part because of the caution imposed by the hostility of the nationalist Tudjman regime. With Tudjman gone, some rimasti now give voice to opinions that perfectly parallel those of esuli in both content and emotional tenor.

Whereas the esuli know that they constitute a dying community with little hope of reproducing itself, however, the rimasti actively worry about the continued survival of the Italian minority in Istria. Indeed, part of the emotion at the meeting on dual citizenship centered on the experience of the rimasti's children, some of whom feel humiliated when treated in Italy as "aliens" (*extra-comunitari*) with the same legal status as Africans and Filipino workers (who presumably are not privy to the same tradition of civiltà as the Istrians). Throughout the 1990s, the difficult economic situation in Croatia led many members of the Italian minority to study or work abroad, typically in Italy, Germany, or Switzerland. Many of those who leave permanently settle elsewhere in a kind of Istrian Italian brain drain. To worried observers, this appears to constitute a second exodus, all the more insidious because it is silent and diffused. If the majority of Istria's young Italians leave the peninsula or are assimilated, the rimasti will become, like the esuli, the "last of the Mohicans": a predominantly elderly population nurtured only on memories of a long-vanished world and tales of that world's betrayal.

In order to prevent this, throughout the 1990s members of the Italian minority in Croatia vigorously protested the Tudjman regime's attacks on bilingualism. Minority leaders appealed to the Italian government, for example, bringing the fate of the Italians in Croatia and Slovenia to wider attention. Many Italians also supported the regionalist party known as the Istrian Democratic Assembly. Narrative practices, or what Portelli has called history-telling—"the combination of the prevalence of the narrative form on the one hand, and the search for a connection between biography and history, between individual experience and the transformations of society, on the other" (1997, 6)—have powerfully underwritten these political efforts.

Rimasti accounts

For fifty years, rimasti and esuli appeared to be telling very different stories about the Second World War, given the discursive constraints imposed by states and ideological divides. Quite possibly, the kinds of accounts rimasti told in private may have been different from the "official" pronouncements of Italian minority leaders; indeed, Italians in Istria I spoke with claim that even though it proved impossible in Yugoslavia to publicly discuss the "trauma" of the exodus, oral histories detailing such violence and suffering were nonetheless preserved within families. This contrasts with the situation of the exiles, where such private memories appear to have been largely shaped in tandem with written representations.

The 1987 novel *La città divisa* (The divided city), written by Claudio Ugussi, was one of the first literary expressions of the rimasti's experience during the exodus. (In the postwar period, rimasti authors had nonetheless produced a large body of poetry and prose works dealing with various aspects of the Istrian experience; see the useful account of both esuli and rimasti literature in Maier 1996; see also Roic 1991, Turconi 1991.) Many other rimasti authors have since followed suit, joining their voices with those of the esuli in denouncing the exodus as a tragedy that was silenced, buried under. Although the accounts of those who left and those who remained continue to describe fascism and the war in very different terms, both stress their autochthony while simultaneously identifying diverse groups as having victimized them. Italians in Istria variously portray their betrayers as including the fascist state, Italians who left, the Yugoslav regime, and/or the successor Slovenian and Croatian regimes of the 1990s. Some individuals describe themselves as having made an idealistic and ingenuous political choice to remain, and others maintain that they had no real say in the decision (made by husbands or other family members) whether to stay or to go. In different ways, these stories—embedded as they are in the context of memory practices and minority politics—work to construct rimasti as victims who have nonetheless persevered.

Implicitly or explicitly, these stories of the Italians' repeated victimization construct Istrians as having suffered as much as or even more than the esuli. The rimasti thus attach their experience to the history of the esuli (and thereby to the other histories of ethnic cleansing discussed in previous chapters) at the same time that they present themselves as having chosen the harder path by deciding to remain during the exodus. That the rimasti have not only lived through the territory's ruination but have also managed to preserve their culture becomes a powerful claim about contemporary Istrian Italians as the most genuine Istrians of all.

In analyzing claims to authenticity encoded by Italian narratives, I draw here on fifty-one formal interviews conducted in Istria. The bulk of these conversations took place in Rovigno, 60 percent of the interviewees being female. Although I did speak with men at Rovigno's Comunità degli Italiani, my interactions with women proved more frequent, in part because of the gender segregation of coffee-drinking groups. I also conducted two group interviews with male friends, one at the Comunità degli Italiani at Umago and the other at Valle. These encounters proved more formal than those with my coffee companions or with Tina and her friends, reflecting not only my much greater familiarity with the women in Rovigno but also the ways in which gender affects autobiographical conventions. The men at Umago and Valle, for example, often discussed events like the war and exodus in broad terms: when they interjected their personal experiences, they focused on work and military service and characterized their families in genealogical terms ("my ancestors came from Venice two hundred years ago"). The women, including those who had been party activists, frequently interspersed their accounts with humor and small details of everyday life.

The preponderance of female interviewees reflects not only questions of access and interest but also the fact that many strong-minded Istrian women serve as Comunità presidents and minority activists. Rovignesi like Tina described a world in which strong females had long been the norm, due in part to the tradition of factory work under Austria. In addition, the prominence of women in my sample manifests the demographics of the exodus, with many (then) young women staying to look after their parents and often remaining unmarried due to a shortage of Italian men. Tina remembered that because of the exodus, women were forced to dance with other women for want of male partners. As a result, a number of Italian women of that generation remained unmarried, and these spinsters (often schoolteachers) often became activists in the Italian community. Although the feminine bias of my data might be seen as influencing my findings about the construction of rimasti as victims (since many women describe themselves as having had a "nonchoice" about staying), male informants—including former partisans and activists—also depict the minority as having been manipulated and persecuted under Yugoslavia in a number of ways.

Whereas Italian exile accounts often portray the period of Italian rule as a lost age of innocence, Italians in Istria tend to see their "golden age" as the Austrian period. Rosanna, the seventy-five-year-old woman from Montona who complained of her isolation, was born during the era of Italian rule and yet waxed enthusiastic about the Hapsburg era as a time of democracy. I heard this theme repeated by many other informants. The secretary of the Comunità in Valle, a man in his thirties, stated his belief that only under Austria did Istria experience "true democracy." The stress on democracy works to delegitimize exile claims and validate those made by Italians in Istria, as well as their political allies in the regionalist movement, to promote a progressive, European, and democratic politics.

This regionalist movement reflects the desire of Istrians, including rimasti, finally to have control over their own destiny after enduring successive totalitarian regimes. Many regionalist supporters see the putative multiculturalism of the Hapsburg Empire as a model and also view this period as one of construction and prosperity, in contrast to the extractive nature of both fascism and communism. Although regime after regime "milked" the Istrian goat (a symbol of Istria and of the regionalist movement), noted the secretary at Valle's Comunità degli Italiani, only Austria gave something back in the form of industry and infrastructure. Bruno Flego, a long-time activist from Pola and an autodidactic historian, also praised Austria, repeating the popular slogan "Austria is an orderly country." Here, the common trope by which fascism is recalled as having brought order and uniformity (Passerini 1987, 129–33) is inverted or displaced onto Austria. Other Istrians cited as positive the Austrian practice of permitting both Slavs and Italians to attend schools in their own languages. These descriptions are contrasted to the fascist period, when Slovenes and Croats were forbidden to speak their native languages in public and forced to take instruction in Italian, as well as to the Tudjman regime and its attacks on bilingualism and Italian-language schools.

Speakers thus depict Italian fascism, as well as Tudjman's Croatian state, as having (willfully) failed to recognize that Istria consisted of what one individual called "a mosaic of peoples" or a "mixture" (mescolanza). Ethnic Croats and Slovenes I interviewed recalled being forced to speak Italian, attend Italian schools, and receive instruction from mainland Italians sent as "missionaries of fascism." Nevin, a cultivator from Rovinj who served as a partisan during the war, spoke of locally born teachers enforcing Italianization policies with zeal; he remembered being slapped on the hands for speaking Croatian by one such schoolteacher, Professoressa D. (The professoressa, who subsequently taught in the Italian schools of socialist Yugoslavia, instead described herself as having been long accustomed to living with Slavs and as having been shocked by the conditions of poverty in which she found her Slavic pupils living in fascist Italy.) Nevin also told of fascists forcing opponents to drink castor oil and referring to Slavs as "schiavoni," a derogatory epithet (derived from the semantic association of slavi with schiavi, or slaves).

Such statements contradict the overall picture painted by esuli of Italian Istria as a harmonious place marked by a general consensus for the regime. Other rimasti detail similar offenses committed under fascism. These tellings recall certain conventions in radical biographies/autobiographies whereby the "conversion" to leftism is often located in formative childhood experiences (Hoogenboom 1996). Marianna recounts, for example, the discrimination some Italians displayed toward Slavs. This chauvinism awoke her social conscience. "I felt bad if a Slav passed by and somebody said 'schiavon'; very offensive. . . . This hurt me, too. From this came [my political principles]; many such things in your youth shape you." Other informants recounted the fascist policy of awarding or denying work on the basis of party membership. Tina, who constructed an autobiography as apolitical as Marianna's is political, remembered, "If men wanted to work in the tobacco factory, they had to have the fascist party card. One joined the fascist party, one went to work. I remember my uncle—he really was an old goat—who would always say to my father: 'Join the party, I'll get you a job in the factory. Just join the party.' My father didn't want to do it."

Tina also remembered being upset as a child because her mother, in opposition to fascism, refused to buy her daughter the compulsory fascist school uniform. At the time, Tina did not appreciate her mother's motives but instead felt bad, since all the other schoolchildren were dressed properly. In her study of fascism and popular memory, Passerini (1987, 130) has noted this literal desire for uniformity as particularly marked among young women. Marianna similarly recalls attending school without the necessary uniform and card. When Minister of Education Giuseppe Bottai visited Rovigno in 1937, Rovigno's schoolchildren came out to greet him in the main square. Marianna lacked the proper uniform and was stuck in the back row.

These petty injustices, coupled with gross discrimination against Slavs and the lack of political freedom, made for strong antifascist feeling in Istria, according to most of my interviewees. These Italians thus rejected the exile vision of widespread support for the Italian regime, as well as the Yugoslav charge that many Italians in Istria were genuine fascist supporters. Marianna, for example, maintained, "Antifascism was very strong in Rovigno; for this the city was called Rovigno La Rossa [the Red]." Although Marianna admitted that the city had its share of fascists, she claims that proportionately more Slavs (from the nearby Villa di Rovigno/Rovinjsko Selo) numbered among the fascists than did Italians. "In fact, the guards who were at Rovigno [during the war] weren't rovignesi," added Marianna, but instead "were from Slav families from the interior and thus were called the 'schiavon' guard." Marianna and others distinguished between fascists, like the guards, who actively embraced the party ideology and "fascists out of need" (*fascisti di bisogno*), who merely joined the party in order to find employment. Note the subtle shift here, with "real fascists" becoming identified with Slavs and real antifascists with autochthonous Istrian Italians, like Marianna.

Marianna was just one of several Italians I knew who had expressed their opposition to fascism by actively participating in the partisan movement. In their life histories, such activists tended to describe the joy they experienced at war's end and the subsequent delusion as the liberation gave way to the exodus and as Slav collaborators, like the fascist guards mentioned by Marianna, switched sides, proclaimed themselves communists, and began to persecute Italians. The accounts of these former partisans contained an inherent tension, as individuals strove to retain the moral capital associated with the *active* heroism of Resistance fighters while depicting themselves as ultimate *victims.*

During my stay in Istria, I came to know many individuals who had participated in the Resistance or whose parents had fought as partisans. Here, I focus on the stories of three individuals in Rovigno who proudly recounted their contributions to the antifascist struggle and lamented what has become of the antifascist legacy. The first of these reiterated the older, standard narrative often heard among members of the Italian minority about the glorious antifascist struggle and Yugoslav "Brotherhood and Unity." Constructing a tale of betrayal in the post-Yugoslav era, this narrative contrasted with the reevaluations of the two other activists from Rovigno, who with Yugoslavia's demise now portray the socialist regime as also having duped and exploited its Italian supporters. All three accounts nonetheless worked to refute (or at least temper) exile claims that these Italian partisans were among the perpetrators of the exodus. Like the esuli, whose martyrs paid the ultimate price to redeem Istria after World War I only to lose it after the Second World War, these rimasti accounts depicted the great sacrifices made to render Istria a just society. These sacrifices have come to naught, leaving rimasti and esuli victims alike.

Nina, an employee at the partisans/veterans' association in Rovigno, told her story in narrative terms associated with an older Yugoslav state-sponsored historiography and those rituals, like the one at Kućibreg, commemorating the antifascist struggle. Not surprisingly, given Nina's frequent participation in such celebrations through her work at the Partisan Association, her life story appeared quite polished, suggesting to me that her narrative was well rehearsed and had been repeated on many occasions in which the antifascist struggle was celebrated. Born in Rovigno in 1922, Nina described her biography as profoundly shaped by the antifascist principles she absorbed from her father. Given that Nina barely knew her father, his opposition to the regime forcing him to emigrate to the United States when she was a small child, her statement implies that she acquired his antifascism in almost biological fashion.

Like many of the Turin workers interviewed by Passerini, Nina and other Istrians thus depicted themselves as born rebels (1987, 23–24). "The theme of almost biological predestination in being Socialist (whether by birth or at heart) recurs often in the subjects' statements when they speak out against Fascism, and about themselves or the groups they identify with" (ibid., 24). This trope also inverts the exile depiction of communism as almost biologically predetermined by the inherent totalitarianism of a putative "Slavic national character."

In narratives like Nina's, Istrian communism/socialism is seen as a deep-rooted, organic (even "pure") movement. This contrasts with fascism, portrayed as having been imposed by outsiders. Whereas exiles depicted Titoists as foreign occupiers, then, antifascists like Nina instead described the fascists as politically illegitimate outsiders with little support among the autochthonous population. She also distinguished between *Italia patria* (Italy as the nation and homeland) and *Italia fascista,* ironically echoing esuli efforts to recuperate a national(ist) tradition distinct from a fascist one.

> When there was Austria we lived well, but when the world war finished and fascism came, our people lived badly because the important positions were all filled by people from Italy, fascists. And they began to imprison our people, to beat them, to give them castor oil, and so on. Thus our people didn't consider Italy highly, not Italy as *madrepatria* but rather the fascist regime. Because of this, in Rovigno there were a lot of partisans, because they were against this fascist Italy.

Nina herself became one such partisan supporter, eventually joining her fiancé, Franco, and his partisan band in the woods. "In the spring, I went into the woods. And I remained there until the liberation in '45. I was a partisan because Franco was secretary of the party for Rovigno and the region. He was also underground, also in the woods." Nina worked primarily in the Women's Antifascist Front (FFA). This group organized a large underground meeting in 1944, the first women's mass meeting in Istria. Nine also labored in the agitprop section of the party, writing articles for the *Voce del Popolo* and distributing pamphlets.

In the autumn of 1944, after the women's conference, Nina and Franco planned to marry. Nina's story reveals the personal sacrifices exacted by the war, as well as the way conventional gender and sexual roles continued to operate within a revolutionary movement. Such dramatic tales also contribute to a heroic tradition about fallen revolutionary fighters and their tragic love stories.

> He wanted to marry me because, he said, "If I die tomorrow, I don't want someone to point their finger at you as if you're a woman of low reputation," . . . and so we decided to get married on September 16, but the 16th was the festival of Saint Euphemia, protectress of Rovigno, and so he said to me, "No, no, let it be . . . we'll marry tomorrow, the 17th." Instead, on the 17th he was wounded, and on the 18th he died. However, before he died, he wanted in front of witnesses—there was the nurse, his cousin, another young person (my relative)—in their presence he wanted us to marry in extremis, and so I got married in extremis. . . . He made me promise him before he died, first, that I would continue that which he taught me, because, he said, "the world must change and you must carry on that which I've taught," and then he wanted me to promise that I would marry again. He told me, "Look, it's useless to remain faithful to a ghost. You can always remember me . . . but you cannot understand political problems and the normal problems of life if you are not a wife and a mother."[3]

Nina kept her dual promise to Franco to marry and to continue her political activities. Nina's two sons by her second husband actively participate in the cultural life of the minority associations, in contrast to their mother's more direct political involvements with the Partisan Association. When I knew her in the mid-1990s, a few years before her death, Nina proudly detailed her various activities to me and did not express any hint of regret or disappointment about Yugoslavia's development. Although highly critical of the Tudjman regime, she forcefully stressed the brotherhood and democracy embodied by the antifascist right and the liberation. Nina did not admit, then, as other Italians in Istria have begun to do, that the exodus may have resulted from a deliberate Yugoslav campaign of hostility.

Nina instead explained the departure of many Italians as resulting from Italian state propaganda, which created fears about a communist regime and manipulated "simple" people. Nina's narrative is typical of an older account that refused to acknowledge either that the exiles may have had "legitimate" reasons for their choice or that the rimasti might have erred in their decision to stay. The vocabulary of ethnic cleansing also anachronistically entered into her description of discourse at the time. This suggests the way in which such rimasti and esuli stories remain, even if but implicitly, in dialogue with one another.

> This was a critical period because, on the one hand, there was the propaganda of De Gasperi, who promised Italians everything and who was saying, "Come [to Italy], because in one month, or two months, you will return to your homes," and these poor people left because they said, "The Croats will run you over and commit ethnic cleansing." . . . Simple people [were vulnerable]. . . . After the liberation the simple people—peasants, fishermen, workers—were victims of this propaganda saying that they would receive everything, that if they left, they'd find everything when they came back and so on. Instead, these poor people were duped because they left not for political reasons but because of a stupid and absurd propaganda.

Nina's narrative and its continued endorsement of Yugoslav socialism contrasted with the opinions expressed by fellow rovignesi Lucio and Marianna. Nina's narrative absolved those Italians who fought as partisans and remained in Istria of any possible guilt by depicting those who left as being in the wrong or as having made a mistake. In contrast, other former Italian activists like Marianna and her colleague Lucio portrayed themselves as having been tricked by "a stupid and absurd propaganda," that of the Yugoslav communists.

Echoing the socialist historiography into which the Istrian Italian antifascist experience was inserted and which Nina's account forcefully validated, in a lengthy interview seventy-five-year-old Lucio emphasized Rovigno's tradition of antifascism. This socialist tradition, together with his eye-opening experience as a soldier in the Italian army, led Lucio to join the partisans after the Italian capitulation in 1943. Making his way home after the Italian army's collapse, Lucio joined up with the celebrated Istrian Italian partisan battalion under Pino Budicin. Despite the groundswell of support from the Italians of Istria for the antifascist cause, contended Lucio, their Yugoslav "comrades" soon fell into the same trap the fascists had: nationalism. After the war, added Lucio, the Yugoslavs also repeated the error of the fascist regime, sending directors and managers from the South who had little feeling for the local culture. These comments parallel Nina's comparison of popular movements to those imposed from without, Nina's distinction between antifascism and fascism here reinscribed as a division between Italian antifascists and Yugoslav communists (*qua* nationalists).

Lucio thus tells a story of long-standing (and autochthonous) Italian antifascists outmaneuvered by those rapidly formed Croatian partisan cells backed by Tito. At a meeting held at Pisino, according to Lucio, these Croat partisans declared Istria's future annexation by Yugoslavia while Italian antifascists like Budicin were excluded from participating in this assembly. Partisans included not only sincere antifascists but also nationalists and opportunists. Despite protests by genuine antifascists, opportunists used the cover of the war to advance their own ends (notably by exacting vendettas through executions in the foibe.) The rebellion of 1943 was therefore characterized by both genuine enthusiasm and a frightening, uncontrollable aspect.

In contrast, the liberation in 1945 appeared orderly and peaceful, but this was a superficial impression.

> The liberation arrived, something you'd never seen before: happy people, crying, those who had already heard the news arrived in Rovigno with flags. . . . There weren't those problems [like in 1943]. No one realized that the same day, that same night that we entered the city the secret police, OZNA, came . . . the same night of the liberation, they began to make arrests, interrogations. . . . One of the relatives of these individuals later told me that they were tried secretly, and all of those who were arrested after the liberation had documents that they had collaborated with the enemy. But there was the liberation, so why didn't they have a public trial? [Instead] they liquidated them in silence. No one knew.

Lucio's statements suggested that slogans about brotherhood and justice chanted during the liberation merely provided the cover under which the party exerted control and eliminated its opponents, though trusting Italians who sincerely believed in the ideals of the antifascist fight did not realize this in the moment of euphoria at the end of the war. As the duplicity of the new regime became clear, Italians began to leave with the exodus. Lucio claimed that he and other antifascist faithful who remained in Rovigno were dismayed by the disbanding of the Communist Party of Rovigno and the creation of the Popular Front. Newly established cooperatives were headed by individuals from Belgrade and Zagreb rather than local rovignesi, further underscoring claims about the regime's lack of a popular base in Istria.

Although Lucio admitted the mistakes that Istrians made (Italians and, especially, Slavs), the narrative resolutely shifted blame to outsiders as having brought about Istria's ills. These South Slav "emissaries" (distinct from Istrians) created a climate of fear and hostility in a number of ways: through summary arrests and the epuration of "fascists" and confiscation of their goods and by forcing children with surnames of Croatian origin who nonetheless identified themselves as Italians to attend Croatian schools. For Lucio, then, the promise of the socialist revolution for the Italians of Istria was quickly extinguished. Critical of the Yugoslav regime that betrayed its Italian supporters, Lucio also condemned the Croatian state headed by Tudjman. Stating that "many people say they lived better under Italian fascism than they do today [in 1996]", Lucio added that as Croatia's first president, Tudjman derived much political and military support from neofascists. The juxtaposing of these comments posits Tudjman's regime as worse than Italian fascism, as well as Yugoslav socialism. At the same time, it constructs a narrative of Istrians' repeated victimization by regimes imposed from without.

In a manner similar to Lucio's, Marianna rendered her personal story, that of an idealist who saw the revolution for social justice repeatedly betrayed by nationalism and the hunger for power, symbolic of the larger tragedy of the Italian minority. Born in 1929 and the eldest in her family, Marianna became an enthusiastic member of the Antifascist Youth Front. "I participated during the war in the antifascist section from 1944 on. I was a young girl, but I understood something. I saw certain injustices, certain things that marked me." Marianna stated that she had always been a leftist (reiterating the "born rebel" theme), though she had never belonged to any party. (Others in Rovigno, however, remembered her as a faithful communist who now sought to distance herself from that tainted past.) Such a claim worked to reinforce the sense that Marianna and other Italians gave expression to an "organic" antifascist sentiment rather than one inculcated by a party (either Italian or Yugoslav).

During and after the war, Marianna worked in the Antifascist Youth sections urging Italians not to leave Istria. Even within her own family, Marianna had to persuade her mother to remain in Rovigno. Marianna suggested that her mother, like many Italians in Istria, was ready to follow the crowd. "The majority of people were like my mother, who when she came home from work would say, 'You know, everyone is leaving; we should go too.' I would say, 'But where would we go?' . . . I was in the youth section, and we put out propaganda urging people not to leave."

At the time, Marianna felt betrayed by relatives and friends who left in spite of her exhortations to remain, just as esuli often feel betrayed by those who remained. By leaving, Italians allowed Istria to be repopulated by South Slavs and rendered the rimasti "strangers in their home."

The exodus did much harm. At that time I was very young; in '47 I was eighteen years old. And I was so sorry to see everyone go. In fact, I experienced it as a trauma when I saw all those people leaving. Rovigno, from the Old City with almost ten thousand inhabitants, eight thousand left. It's like having a disease that drains your blood. I've always said it, and I continue to say it today that if they'd remained, things would have been very different, because we would have been the majority here, not a minority—at least in Rovigno. . . . They left all these houses empty, and thus the regime sent new people. . . . I don't want to say that if they'd remained, other people wouldn't have come, but it would have been much less for the simple fact of the houses. Here, instead, these new arrivals found Rovigno almost totally empty. All they had to do was walk in, nothing else. This was another trauma.

[As a result,] I almost forgot or wanted to forget certain friendships, certain acquaintances, because I felt betrayed. On the other hand, the esuli say, "If you would have gone, too . . ." But if we'd all left, who would have remained to carry forward that which we're now doing? No one would have been left. They [the esuli] didn't have to do anything, only cry for what they'd lost.

Only much later, recounted Marianna, did her anger at being left behind diminish. Just as Marianna has softened toward the esuli over the years, she has also come to understand and acknowledge the motives for their departure. As many exiles do (both Istrians and other displaced peoples; see Hirschon 1998, 30), Marianna blames the Great Powers for disregarding the wishes of the Istrian people. "See, already in '45 when there was the liberation, they duped people. . . . The Great Powers said, 'The people chose [Yugoslavia]." But who chose? The Great Powers chose and then they said, 'You leave because here will be this, there will be that.'" Such statements point to the ways in which the rimasti are redefining their self-understandings, from those positing them as active *subjects* of history—the triumphalist, heroic narrative put forward under socialism—to those depicting them as *objects* of history, repeatedly victimized by broader forces (processes of state building and wars).

Italian idealists like Marianna and Lucio describe themselves as victims of global forces, but they also single out those Yugoslav Communist Party activists who encouraged Italians to leave. In the 1990s, Marianna admitted what seemed unthinkable to her at the time: the Yugoslavs specifically targeted Italians in order to drive them out and "ethnically cleanse" Istria. Marianna described the long process by which she reached this conclusion as one marked by various encounters with former agents of this de-Italianization policy. Such an account works to deflect exile charges that such rimasti revisionism merely follows out of old communists' having suddenly changed their tune.

Marianna depicted her painful enlightenment about the true nature of the exodus as sparked by a chance encounter with an individual who had been part of the secret police at Rovigno after the war. This man told Marianna that she did not realize what a "twisted politics" existed at that time, with many Croat "infiltrators" sent from the outside. While Marianna and others were urging their fellow Italians to remain, then, these Croat agents were telling Istrian Italians to leave. Marianna later met other Croatian activists who revealed their treachery in promoting an anti-Italian campaign. In 1977, for instance, she saw an old acquaintance at a meeting in Zagreb.

[He said to me], "Oh, we finally liberated Rovigno from those Italians." I was dumbstruck. "Look, I guess not, if nothing else because my family remained. And it has grown and flourished." I had a lump in my throat. When I came to Rovigno I told everyone this. [we were] instrumentalized. . . . I felt exploited, used. . . . Either I was ingenuous or too idealistic. I was an idealist. And little by little I opened my eyes.

As Marianna became aware of the reality of Italians' position in Yugoslavia, she fought for their rights in her capacity as former president of the Comunità Italiana in Rovigno and as vice mayor of Rovigno. Marianna, like many other minority activists I spoke with, described life under Yugoslavia as a series of political battles, important and trifling. In 1969, for instance, she attended an anniversary commemoration for the underground antifascist meeting of the women's section held in Istria in 1944. At the 1944 gathering, there had been Italian and Yugoslav flags and placards written in diverse languages as symbols of *fratellanza,* or brotherhood. By contrast, at the anniversary celebration Marianna saw only Croatian flags and signs in Serbo-Croatian.

Fifty years ago there was this atmosphere of brotherhood, of faith, all this that today I don't see. . . . I pointed out [to an organizer] that there were no Italian flags, and an organizer returned with a flag. This man went to talk to the head of the organizers and turned his back on me. "What does this Marianna want? The chorus is going to sing "Bandiera rossa" [Red flag] in Italian, and this should be sufficient for the Italians." I was behind him and I said [in a sarcastic tone], "Thank you, thank you for what you've done for the Italians. Good-bye." . . . It's always a fight for rights, a continual battle.

Although the Yugoslav postwar regime compares negatively with the antifascist movement during the war, Marianna nonetheless admitted that minority activists succeeded in winning a modicum of rights for Istria's Italians. This contrasts with the situation of Croatia in the 1990s, described by Marianna and the other former partisans discussed here as even worse than that prevailing under Yugoslavia. In his nine years as president, Tudjman repeatedly denounced the Italian minority as irredentists, remnants of a population settled under Italian fascism. In refuting such claims, Marianna forcefully stressed the minority's deep roots in the peninsula and the ways in which Istrian Italians in the 1990s had to submit to another campaign of ethnic hatred similar to the one during the exodus.

Today when the regime is far worse than the previous one . . . a battle still remains. *We're here, we didn't just arrive, we were born here.* . . . I am neither an irredentist nor a nationalist. It's just that seeing how we are treated, it seems to me that we should say, "This is mine, this is yours." I want to defend my dignity. Honestly, today we've lost our economic dignity and also that dignity which is ours by right and which we once had, because we weren't gentlemen [*signori*] but we also weren't beggars. Today we're almost beggars, shall we say. *My identity, I already lost it once—with the exodus—and now I've lost it yet again* after everything we'd achieved. . . . Under Yugoslavia, we had a little something—some Italian schools, some Italian day-care centers, some Italian communities that carried out their activities—we were financed; the Commune gave us money. And then came 1990 and everything collapsed, that little bit that we had collapsed; now we don't have anything. We've lost everything.

Marianna thus constructed an image of Istria as a landscape that had been repeatedly ruined. Whereas under socialism the minority managed to build something out of those ruins, in the Croatia of the 1990s those achievements were in grave danger. Together with their pride in the tenacity that Istria's Italians displayed, elderly Istrians like Marianna also express the bitter sense of defeat in those who gave their lives to the antifascist and the socialist cause, only to see its achievements betrayed. Many other informants sounded this theme of defeat, whether or not they had stayed expressly because of their political convictions. During my time in Istria, I heard a wide range of reasons given for why people stayed. In many instances, the choice was primarily political, as the "partisan tales" of activists like Marianna suggested. But, as one would expect, individuals often had several different and even contradictory motives. Marianna, for example, maintained that she made a political decision, but she also cited her father's death, the fear of going into the unknown, and her attachment to the land (testifying to such Italians' "rootedness"). "My father died in '46. Where could we go? I was the oldest . . . eighteen years old, my brother was twelve, the other one was thirteen, and my sister was four. In short, where could we go? To a refugee camp, and then we would end up like my uncles, emigrating abroad. Instead, I like Rovigno, I love it. If I left it, where would I find my caverns, my sea?"

Many other informants cited only personal reasons for their decisions. Several said that they could not leave because they had to look after elderly parents. This task, not surprisingly, fell disproportionately to women. I spoke with several women who were young (and often unmarried) at the time of the exodus and whose siblings had already left. Rosanna from Montona was one of many such women who had stayed with elderly parents. Other individuals explained that because of their age and/or gender, they had very little say in the decision to remain or leave, contrary to the image of rimasti making deliberate, ideological choices. Tina noted that her father made the decision to remain.

Look, my mother died when I was ten years old. Then my father took up with someone else, and she worked in the tobacco factory. Thus it wasn't difficult to leave because whoever worked in the tobacco factory when they went to Italy also found work in tobacco factories there; there were jobs for them. But my father didn't have a profession; he was a fisherman. Since she [his girlfriend] was half crazy, she said, "How can we go to Italy and live there on just one salary?" Little to do about it. But still, my father waited in the line at the option office. And then the police came and began to beat up the people in line, to create problems, and he came home and said, "I'm not going anymore." I was a minor and so [I remained]. . . . How many tears. Friends, relatives left.

Another woman whose partner forced her to stay in Rovigno expressed great bitterness toward both her current situation and her husband. Indeed, she seemed barely able to tolerate her husband's presence and mocked him in front of me. Now elderly, this man suffers from hearing loss and shouts to his wife, only occasionally hearing what she says in reply. This selective hearing seems sadly symbolic of the decision the husband made at the time of the exodus. Then a faithful communist, he disregarded his wife's desire to join the rest of her family in Italy. This woman's sisters and most of her other close relatives left. Today, this woman feels abandoned and angry; she told me that things would have been much better had they gone to Italy.

In most cases, families were divided; only rarely did I meet an Istrian without relatives abroad in Italy, the United States, Canada, Argentina, Brazil, or Australia. Numerous people described to me this division of families and friends as "the greatest tragedy" of the exodus. Such a description makes a claim for the suffering of the rimasti—one half of these divided families—as equal to and bound with that of the esuli. Again and again, individuals recounted their emotion upon seeing their friends depart and their classmates diminish in number, thereby providing a counterpart to the exiles' dramatic tales of leaving Istria.

Whereas exiles described the sadness with which they left their homes and departed to an uncertain future, rimasti stressed the desolation of being left behind. The memories of rimasti often focus on those material traces of exodus which symbolize their internal desolation. One woman from the suburbs of Pola recalled the eerie silence of the deserted city and the desperation of departing esuli, who carried away vials of seawater and chiseled pieces from the Roman Arena. Informants in Rovigno who were schoolchildren at the time spoke of seeing one more chair left empty each day by departing classmates. Italians who were teachers during the exodus similarly remembered colleagues and pupils leaving, absence becoming an all-too-painful presence. Other speakers focused on the emotions felt at the moment of departure, contending that those remaining behind in Istria's ruins suffered just as much as did those who left. Grazia, a former president of the Comunità Italiana, remembered going to the station to accompany those who were leaving for Italy. "We sang and danced to say good-bye to those who were leaving and thus the trauma [for us] was greater," she said.

In contrast to older rimasti accounts, which stressed the active heroism and agency of the minority, justifying choices made and thereby refuting the accusations of esuli, contemporary Istrian stories increasingly refute exile charges by stressing the minority's status as political object and thereby joining up the rimasti's history with that of the exiles. Divisions internal to Italian communities in contemporary Istria, however, appear to yield much more heterogeneous accounts about the exodus than in the case of those who left Istria. The greatest variation in such accounts comes from the motives given for staying (faith in antifascism/socialism or other, "nonpolitical" reasons) and the characterization of the Yugoslav regime, which reflects a marked distinction between the leaders and more humble members of the rimasti community.

Yet regardless of whether Italians look back to Tito with nostalgia, regardless of whether individuals perceive themselves as having enthusiastically chosen to remain or having been forced by circumstances, the stories discussed here do share a basic structure. These life histories generally depict a lost era of democracy and mutual tolerance for diverse ethnic groups (under Austria), an age disrupted by the nationalistic policies of fascism and/or Yugoslav communism, and an aftermath in which Italians remain isolated, divided, and threatened in Yugoslavia's successor states. The variations within this basic structure find parallels in exile accounts: some rimasti stress deliberate political decisions and others privilege their "nonchoice"; some esuli posit firsthand persecution as prompting them to leave, and others merely say that they left with the mass of individuals. In both cases, the diverse experiences of individuals are emplotted into fairly unitary narratives of victimhood that have been shaped in particular political and institutional contexts. Rimasti do not merely attempt to symbolically align the narratives discussed here with exile histories, however, but also have actively sought at both the institutional/political level and the interpersonal one to establish a dialogue with their alienated kin.

Reaching out to the Diaspora and Other Border Crossings

Though exiles and rimasti are linked by ties of kinship, language, and culture, any rapprochement between the two groups still proves delicate at the official level, despite openings provided by Yugoslavia's dissolution. Some local Italian communities and exile circles from particular towns (Rovigno, for instance) have been more successful than others in establishing collaboration. The prominence of the Italian minority in the Istrian regionalist movement has also created new political possibilities, together with new reasons for caution (including a reading of a hybrid history that many esuli cannot countenance).

As Yugoslavia began to unravel in 1989–90, the Istrian Democratic Assembly emerged as an important opposition movement to Tudjman's Croatian Democratic Union (HDZ). The idea of a hybrid, Latin-Slav Istrian identity and a transstate borderland entity (an autonomous Istrian region) giving expression to this multiethnic and multicultural Istrianism lay at the heart of the regionalist project. Winning local majorities in the elections of 1993, 1995, 1997, 1999, and 2001,[4] the DDI-IDS reflected Istrians' rejection of purist visions—explicitly those of the HDZ, implicitly those of the esuli. More practically, regionalism also reflected the desire to address the problems created by the peninsula's division between Croatia and Slovenia, as well as between these two states and Italy.

Loredana Bogliun Debeljuh, one of the DDI-IDS's intellectual formulators, a member of the Italian minority of Dignano, and a sociology instructor at the

University of Fiume, lays particular stress on reconciling Istrians with their far-flung family members and reconstituting the social fabric destroyed during and after the Second World War. At the same time, Debeljuh endorses the view of *all* Istrians as victims, urging exiles "[t]o understand that this Istria has no winners" (1990, 29). Such statements, like the partisan accounts discussed earlier, invert the communist narrative about Italians' finally becoming agents of their own history. Debeljuh and others contend that only today may Istrians become active political subjects.

The subject envisioned by Debeljuh—as well as other rimasti intellectuals and DDI-IDS activists such as Fulvio Šuran and Silvano Zilli—proves autochthonous, territorially and historically rooted. Debeljuh writes, for example, of Istria's "peculiar kind of authenticity, which is Slavic and Italian" (ibid.). That members of the hard-pressed Italian minority (on the defensive against the Tudjman regime throughout the 1990s) were among the DDI-IDS's intellectual architects may explain the shared conceptual basis for identity, although both rimasti and regionalist understandings also issue from a common discursive matrix bound up with the region's various state-building projects. Rimasti intellectuals, not surprisingly, emphasize the crucial significance of the Italian minority as a key "third" term (linking Istria and Croatia to Europe), in a way that can sometimes irk fellow Istrians (as well as non-Istrian Croats). Furio Radin, the representative of the Italian minority in the Croatian Sabor, or parliament, outlines the important role to be played by the Italian national group in Istria as "that of catalyst and mediator for the development of a new climate of dialogue and comprehension, [the role] of 'crossers' . . . between Croatia and Slovenia toward Europe" (Radin in Giuricin 1994, 9; also Šuran 1994).

Putting the rimasti in the front and center raises the question of how to understand and deal with the history of the exodus. From the DDI-IDS's inception, Debeljuh urged the regionalists to actively promote the reintegration of the Istrian diaspora (and thereby heal the exodus's wound) into contemporary Istrian life (in *Istranova*, September 1990). For Debeljuh, the label Istrian is broad enough to accompany both those who left and those who remain. "I maintain that we are all Istrians. Istrianita is like a cloak that protects all of us" (1995, 4). Bringing together members of the diaspora with their Istrian counterparts was thus one of the explicit aims of the First World Congress of Istrians, held at Pola/Pula (Croatia) in April 1995. As Debeljuh described it,

The Congress is conceived as a model for the ideal recomposition of the Istrian people. It is a very important initiative. It is an invitation launched from Istria, in keeping with the new logics of political action in the Region, and it opens a completely new line of communication, of openness, first of all toward our people, toward the Istrians dispersed in the world, and, in my opinion, it's the first small step of a process which is evolving that opened up when in Istria we also had this situation of cultural movement, of recovery of regional identity. I maintain that the organization, the Congress itself, is a pillar (and not the most important one) of the action carried out by the Istrian Region during this mandate. (Ibid., 3)

This gathering promised to bring Istrians from around the world together, as well as display the DDI-IDS's commitment to ethnic tolerance (*convivenza*), pluralism, and democracy. In Debeljuh's estimation, the primary significance of the Congress was to be social and cultural—with a pan-Istrian folklore spectacular, concerts, and art shows—rather than political. Held in a large hotel complex just outside Pola/Pula, the congress led to high expectations. Many members of the Italian minority attended and participated in the proceedings.

Given the event's stress on overcoming the past and working toward the future, young people were welcomed. I had lunch, for example, with members of the Istrian clubs composed of Istrian university students in Trieste, Fiume, and Zagreb. In our lunchtime meeting, as well as in a series of sessions they ran at the congress, these students discussed particular problems—including unemployment and the challenge of maintaining multiethnic identities—that Istrian young people currently face. Like my lunch with these students, much of the "real" business of the congress took place outside such sessions. The hotel bars, for example, became primary meeting points where participants gathered to swap gossip and make new acquaintances. This probably satisfied Debeljuh's hope that the congress would serve as a social event, bringing diverse people together. The cultural aspect that Debeljuh similarly stressed, however, remained largely unrealized. With the exception of a well-received folkloric performance, which staked claims about Istria's autochthonous and hybrid Latin-Slav culture, many of the cultural events were poorly attended.

The attendance at concurrent sessions dedicated to politics, culture, economics, and youth also proved uneven, with most people crowding into the political discussions. Although a few representatives spoke at these political panels, the debate largely consisted of polemics between the DDI-IDS and supporters of the ruling Croatian Democratic Union. As one of the organizers and a DDI-IDS deputy to the Croatian Sabor explained, "When we say we're Istrians, the state institutions say we can't be." In line with this state opposition to regionalism, HDZ supporters reserved two hundred of the eight hundred places at the congress and made a consistent effort to disrupt the proceedings. Throughout, HDZ speakers asserted that Istria is Croatian and that Italian remains a foreign language in Istria; DDI-IDS leaders responded by saying that their tolerance of HDZ dissent at the congress reflected the regionalists' commitment to democracy. At the closing of the congress, these nationalists tried to drown out the chant "Istra, Istra" with shouts for "Hrvatska, Hrvatska" (Croatia, Croatia). Staging their own counterdemonstration, they hoisted a Croatian flag, and one man held aloft a crucifix in one hand and a photo of the pope in the other. Some participants feared that this incident might turn ugly; indeed, one of the students I knew tried to whisk me away, in case any trouble started.

Although such political confrontations confirmed Istrian unity and opposition to a homogenizing center (Zagreb) bent on denying Istrian hybridity, they did little to bring rimasti and esuli together. Rather, the way in which Croatian domestic politics defined the congress confirmed exiles' fears that they had been largely ignored in the planning of the event. Many esuli had stayed away and in the months preceding the conference sent letters of official protest to *Il Piccolo* of Trieste expressing their dissatisfaction with the congress's organization.

Some esuli I spoke with who had initially been enthusiastic about the congress expressed their disappointment. One man who had traveled from France had shown great excitement about the initiative when I made his acquaintance on the congress's opening day. As the event proceeded, however, he registered his discontent. "If they have another such congress, I won't bother to come," he said. Several exile representatives, including those from the Istituto Regionale per la Cultura Istriana, stayed only for a few hours on the congress's first day. After taking in the opening ceremonies, these men quickly headed back to Trieste, apparently unimpressed by what they saw.

Exile representatives often display the same indifference or skepticism at similar events sponsored solely by the Italian minority. One such program consisted of a weeklong series of events, conferences, and cultural gatherings organized by the Italian minority and held in Trieste almost exactly a year after the World Congress. Entitled "Italiani da sempre" (Italians forever), this "Week of Istrian Culture" was designed as another step toward reintegrating the esuli and rimasti, thereby playing a role analogous to the Congress's. As Trieste's mayor put it, the event's aim was to "reconstruct the natural economic and cultural relationship between Istria and Trieste and to make Trieste a reference point for Istrians."

Like the World Congress, "Italiani da sempre" placed great emphasis on cultural events, including exhibits of Istrian Italian art, seminars with Istrian Italian writers, and a folkloric performance by different Italian groups (including one from Rovigno performing the *bitinada,* the acoustic singing style particular to Rovigno) in Trieste's principal piazza. As occurred at Pola, these cultural events were poorly attended overall, and in some cases participants almost outnumbered audience members. Although conferences dedicated to more political topics, such as the history and current state of the Unione Italiana and the activities of the Centro di Ricerche Storiche di Rovigno, attracted more interest, the general lack of enthusiasm confirmed for many participants the exiles' resistance to their overtures.

When I suggested that the "Week of Istrian Culture" had also suffered from a lack of publicity and poor weather (I was one of the few, for example, who endured a heavy rainstorm to watch the folkloric spectacle in Piazza Unità), one of my Istrian acquaintances shot back, "The exiles resent us for stressing our culture and reminding them that we have persisted and survived." Another friend suggested that Trieste in general proved a hostile climate for rimasti; anticipating a poor reception, she had refused to travel to the city and participate in the folkloric spectacle on the grounds that "in Trieste, they treat us like dirt. They look down on us, as if we were *schiavi*. Why do I need to subject myself to that?" Certainly, I would not dispute that calling the whole program "Italiani da sempre" irritated those exiles who worked to construct themselves as the only *Istriani d.o.c.*, or authentic Istrians. Such events may actually work to reinforce the divisions exiles draw between themselves and those who remained behind.

Both the congress and "Italiani da sempre" saw Istrian exile representatives, for example, who put in perfunctory appearances and probably had their pre-formed opinion of the rimasti's hypocrisy confirmed. In both cases, however, I also encountered individual esuli who appeared to be willing to consider that the Italians of Istria had likewise paid a heavy price for the exodus and who maintained that collaboration was possible. My experiences of coming to the Istrian World Congress with the director and president of IRCI and returning by car with Marino Vocci and Livio Dorigo of the Circolo di Istria, for example, could not have been more different. The two experiences symbolize the wide range of relationships exiles have with their lost land and its contemporary inhabitants.

In both cases, traveling to Istrian territory became a kind of "memory trip," my companions' recollections triggered by the scenery around us. While driving to Pola, for example, Arturo Vigini, the president of IRCI, talked about his memories of Istria during the war, when partisans patrolled the countryside and Italians in small towns like his remained shut up in their houses, feeling isolated and fearful. Although my companions of that day occasionally return to Istria, they feel ambivalent and, I would venture to say, somewhat uneasy. Other exiles I spoke with in Trieste have rarely (if ever) returned to Istria, despite its absurd proximity.

Whereas my companions from IRCI drove from Trieste to Pola for three hours without stopping (and then returned to Italy the same evening), my return trip to Trieste several days later, with Marino Vocci and Livio Dorigo of the Circolo di Istria, was an all-day affair, with frequent visits and side trips. The various stops we made to see acquaintances indicate the numerous ties Vocci and Dorigo have with both contemporary Istria and Istrians. Whereas the Circolo di Istria and its leaders seek to cross and break down the political borders that continue to divide "Istrians" of various stripes, other exiles I spoke with have chosen to reforge ties with their native land in a more individual manner. Despite the official distance between the esuli and rimasti, then, ties of kinship and friendship did survive the exodus or were remade in the succeeding decades.

Throughout Istria, for example, one finds many "returnees" or "commuters" (*pendolari*), as locals call them, who have made their own personal reconciliations. These commuters are exiles who regularly return to Istria for the summer or live a good part of the year in their former birthplace. In Rovigno, I interviewed and socialized with various exiles who now spend at least part of the year there. One such man, Alfonso, the retired engineer whose family resettled in Bari (see chapter 6), relocated to Udine several years ago. Today, he divides his time between Udine and Rovigno, where he teaches physics at the local Italian high school on the invitation of an old high school chum. Tina hosts her friend Anita (who left for Florence during the exodus) for several months each year. Now retired, Anita has no problems or rancor about returning to Istria or maintaining friendships with those who stayed behind.

Interestingly, Anita and Tina were not close friends in preexodus Rovigno. "Tina knew my sister," explained Anita, "though in Rovigno everyone more or less knew everyone. However, those two went to school together. My sister was better friends with Tina. I really don't remember much about Tina [before the exodus]". Although Anita's family emigrated to Florence, where she and her mother quickly found work in a tobacco factory not dissimilar to that of Rovigno, Anita felt great nostalgia for her hometown and continued to visit. She frequented friends like Norma, who worked with Tina in the tobacco factory. In the decades following the exodus, Tina and Anita became fast friends, demonstrating how friendships may not only survive such displacement but may also be created anew.

The circle of friends that regularly gathers at Tina's house—and that expands and contracts to include nonregulars like Alfonso (and myself)—epitomizes the different ways in which such personal (and local) ties may challenge the divisions imposed by states and ideologies. On any given afternoon when Anita is staying in Rovigno, for example, she can be found at Tina's house drinking coffee and chatting with Norma and Marisa. Norma married a man who left with the exodus in 1948 and spent many years in Italy. After his first wife died in 1980, Luigi visited Rovigno and renewed his acquaintance with Norma. Until Luigi's death a few years ago, he and Norma divided their time between Italy and Istria. Tina, now a widow, also married a "returnee," albeit of a different sort. Antonio, the man who became her husband, had left Istria with the second option, working for ten years in Italy. When Antonio's first marriage dissolved, he visited his hometown (where his mother still lived) and fell in love with Tina. Although he originally asked Tina to make a life with him in Italy, Tina refused because her elderly father remained in Rovigno. As a result, Antonio returned definitively to Istria and started a second family with Tina. As noted earlier, their children, Irene and Alessandro, now are "returnees" of an altogether different sort: they have found work in Italy and visit Rovigno on weekends and holidays.

For Irene, making the hour-and-a-half drive between Trieste and Rovigno has become routine. After more than ten years in Trieste, the city is "home" in a different way from Rovigno, and Irene has a startlingly wide range of acquaintances there. This reflects Irene's gregarious nature but also the fact that Istrian students in Italy typically live in dormitories, often together with foreign students and other nonlocals; in contrast to the United States, the Italian university system is not residentially based, and, whenever possible, students attend universities in their home cities and live with their families. Ironically, then, students from small towns in Istria may have the opportunity to develop a more cosmopolitan range of friends than many of their Italian counterparts. They also may get to know other Italians from outside their hometown in Istria, suggesting yet another way in which diasporic processes shape a rimasto identity.

Domenica, who hails from a small town near Pola, first met Irene in the dormitory (casa dello studente) at the University of Trieste. For many years Domenica resided in Trieste, first as a student and then as a researcher (thanks to a fellowship). In contrast to Irene, several years ago she moved back to Istria in what appears to be a permanent move. Domenica hesitated, however, to let her right to residency (permesso di soggiorno) in Italy expire. Not only does this residency offer a sense of security, it also symbolizes her assiduous construction of a life encompassing both Italy and Istria; Domenica does not want to feel as if Italy has become a "closed chapter" of her life. Many Italians who actually reside in Istria maintain this permesso di soggiorno in Italy. (See Kavanagh 1994 for another case of "strategic use" of the border for things like visas and pensions along the Spanish-Portuguese frontier.)

Despite the physical borders and political rhetoric that ostensibly divide them, then, the lives of those Italians who stayed in Istria and those who left are often deeply intertwined. In their relationships, for instance, individuals like Tina, Anita, and Norma treat one another as fellow rovignesi, not as members of abstract categories like esuli and rimasti. These women, their children, and their friends regularly cross borders (of Slovenia, Croatia, and Italy) just as they transgress the boundaries of clearly defined groups. Although ideologies and institutions continue to separate esuli and rimasti, some people—as well as groups such as the Circolo di Istria and DDI-IDS—challenge those distinctions, just as others in Trieste reinscribe them.

Only by considering practices together with narratives do we understand how groups on all sides of the borders have experienced the displacement of state making and state breaking. Furthermore, only by examining the voices of those who stayed or were "emplaced" in Istria do we acknowledge the absence that paradoxically remains a presence at the heart of many exile narratives. Attention to narratives of physical displacement together with those of interior displacement, of those who became a minority within a new state, reveals the ways in which such discourses often mirror each other in justifying and legitimating the choices made. At the same time, the experiences of exiles and rimasti parallel and (at least implicitly) address one another, even when they do not acknowledge their affinity. As Teresa Marrero writes of the Cuban experience, "I had the distinct impression that we have led parallel existences, or you know, like when a limb is amputated and the person still feels like it's there: miembros fantasmas" (1995, 45).

CHAPTER EIGHT

Balkan Shadows, Balkan Mirrors:
Paradoxes of "Authentic Hybridity"

> Latin, Illyrian, Slav, Italian names. The vain search for ethnic purity
> reaches down to the most ancient roots, brawling over etymologies and
> writing systems, in a fever to establish the racial origin of the foot that
> first stepped on the white beach and grazed itself on the thorns of the
> thick Mediterranean vegetation, as though this were proof of greater
> authenticity and guaranteed the right to possess these turquoise waters
> and these perfumes in the wind.
>
> The journey down never reaches a point of arrival or departure, the
> Origin is never identified. Scratch an Italianized surname and out
> comes the Slav layer, a Bussani is a Bussanich, but if one continues
> then sometimes an even more ancient layer appears, a name from the
> other side of the Adriatic or elsewhere; the names bounce from one
> shore and from one writing system to another, the ground gives way,
> the waters of life are a yielding, promiscuous swamp.
> —Claudio Magris, *Microcosms*

ATTENTION to the complex dialogues between Italians who
left Istria and those who remained reveals the ways in which a language of autochthony—whether envisioned as pure or hybrid—serves as common political currency throughout the Julian March. This vocabulary of rootedness works
in tandem with the subterranean and illuminist imagery—of historical truths
buried and brought to light again—that simultaneously informs the esuli and
rimasti identities as such, that is, specifically as victims of displacement and historical silencing. Taken together, these symbolic languages evoke paradoxically
complementary images of fluidity and solidity, of hidden wellsprings of history
and genealogy that course through grounded territory (much like the subterranean streams that characterize the karstic terrain of the Julian March) and
eventually empty into the life-giving sea.

Esule writer Fulvio Tomizza nicely captures the interpenetration of these vocabularies in his novel *Materada*. Reflecting on the changes wrought by the communist regime in Istria, Tomizza's protagonist Francesco envisions one kind of disinterment of the past and the bringing to light of a hidden history (presumably that of Istria's Slavic populations and its economic underclass), a process here imagined in specifically vegetative terms. "Now, like when you plow, the earth had been dug up and what was underneath before had suddenly been brought to the surface and was lying there enjoying the sunlight, ready to accept the new seed and make it grow" (1999, 58–59). This seed, however, is later understood to be sterile and the sunlight scorching. Francisco finds himself cheated, in different ways, of his cultivation plot—personal land standing as metonym for the larger territory of Istria—by both the new communist authorities and his own kinsman.

Francesco's embittered farewell to his homeland centers on its most literal properties as land, as organic matter capable of both sustaining and denying life. In his spiteful wish for hail to fall on the crops, Francisco seeks to deprive the terrain the water it so desperately needs and thereby make manifest the ways in which deeply rooted lineages and genealogies have been truncated and fragmented by exodus.

> And there, at the door open to all the countryside below, under the oak that made the sky still darker and the night still blacker, I stood alone and cursed that land forever. . . . I pictured every field one by one, every hedge, every plant, every furrow, and I cursed them, cursed them all. May they never more give fruit or seed; may hail fall on them year after year; may they wither like the hands of the dead. (Ibid., 72)

Tomizza's words, together with those of other exiles and rimasti, highlight the ways in which a rhizomic language of roots and vines (together with a liquid one, water either threatening inundation or giving life) powerfully constructs organic images of territory and kinship. These, in turn, underwrite both groups' claims of being genuine (*patocchi, verace*) and autochthonous populations, as *Italians of Istria* (although the groups generally disagree as to the historic character of Istrian culture). At times, these identities as specific victims (and thereby bearers of a novel identity), on the one hand, and as part of the larger Italian world, on the other, exist in a kind of dramatic tension. Only the narrative shifts between the tropes of submersion and rootedness, which make for a story of the violent uprooting of an autochthonous culture, mediate these contradictions. Though once a part of the mainstream of Italian history, esuli and rimasti have been rendered populations apart as a result of the exodus and its aftermath; one of the aims of each group's storytelling practices is to reinsert their specific histories into broader national histories, as well as wider histories of violence and genocide. These dual themes of submersion and rootedness powerfully reinforce, then, demands for justice (the disinterring of the past) and reparations / minority protection (the recognition of each group, respectively, as rightfully belonging to the soil of Istria). They also encode the dilemmas of kin divided by ideological and physical boundaries and thereby point to the hidden problematics of blood and race (that is, genealogy) which underwrite forms of identity even in an area in which "racism" has frequently been disavowed.

The "politics of submersion" characteristic of the region refers not only to a belief that the past has been obscured, of course, but also to the fear of being buried under and rendered obsolete. As we have seen, esuli and rimasti alike (together with Slovenes in Trieste) express real anxiety over their potential obsolescence as well as pride in their tenacity. The image of remaining a cultural, linguistic, or ethnic island within a hostile sea has proven commonplace in the region, and exiles frequently point to both the infoibamenti and literal drownings carried out by partisans (see chapters 2 and 5) as horrific concretizations of their metaphorical fears of submersion. In drawing a contrast between ideas of submersion by water and subversion by blood, Uli Linke concludes that "[d]espite this opposition of symbolic codes, the same logic is operative in both cases" (1999, xii); the German "spatial metaphor of *Unterwanderung*, literally 'subversive foray from under ground'" (ibid.), captures this dual sense of subversion and submersion. Thus Linke's further observation that "metaphors of water might well be circumlocutions for blood" and hence fears of blood pollution (ibid.: xi) proves useful here.[1] She adds, "It has been suggested elsewhere that *blood*, once taboo in some contexts, finds expression in terms of other fluids or liquid substances: foam, sweat, whirlpool, river, stream" (ibid.).

Though Linke focuses on the German and northern European context and the eastern Adriatic possesses its own specific histories of race, it does not seem at all improbable that such images were conveyed historically to the Julian March through Pan-German nationalism or a more general European "aesthetics of race." In her genealogy of these aesthetics, Linke notes the prevalence in various Indo-European languages of symbolic associations between blood and "vegetative" images such as flowers and trees: "The iconography of blood, earth, and tree (as a metaphor of human genesis) survived in modern European depictions of kinship. . . . Through blood and tree metaphors—as graphic representations of descent—relational systems like kinship, heredity, and lineage are placed into the semantic field of nature" (ibid., 59, 62). In the Istrian case, naturalized images of genealogy and rootedness form the logical counterparts to the architectonic markers of culture and civiltà explored in previous chapters, just as purity and hybridity are two sides of the same coin rather than different specie altogether.

Emerging from a regional political field marked for a half century by these "politics of submersion," as well as an even longer-standing "politics of rootedness," the concept of a multiethnic Istrian identity today promoted by the regionalist movement and briefly discussed in the previous chapter owes much to rimasti claims to both autochthony and "European-ness." Given that rimasti understandings operate in extensive (if sometimes implicit) dialogue with those of the esuli, it does not prove surprising, then, that the seemingly "new" and multicultural regionalist model of identity finds points of convergence with those exclusionary nationalist discourses it opposes. This similarity reflects not only a structural consequence of the dialogic process of mirroring between the two sides of a divided community—which emerges in the close reading of exile and rimasti narratives—but also the mutual constitution of these discourses through multiple moments of state making and dissolution.

As I have demonstrated for various historical moments, languages of purity or homogeneity (typically associated with nation-states) and hybridity (common to multinational empires) have historically competed with one another in an area of problematic state formation like the Julian March (as in the Balkans more generally). At the same time, however, they have quite obviously informed one another, for the notion of hybridity rests on the myth of pure wholes whose intersection generates intermixture.[2] The articulation of a socialist, autonomist alternative to nationalist irredentisms in the Julian March (around the times of both world wars) reveals this shared logic. The history of the South Slav or Yugoslav concept nicely, if tragically, further demonstrates this necessary tension, with the same literary works (such as Prince Njegos's *The Mountain Wreath*) or folkloric traditions (like the Kosovo cycle) marshaled to demonstrate either the purity of a particular ethnic group (such as the Serbs) or the affinity and brotherhood of various South Slav peoples (Wachtel 1998, 19–127).

Contrary to those who have seen in the failed Yugoslav concept (or its subsets, like an autonomous Julian March or Free Territory of Trieste) the *alternative* to exclusive ethno-nationalist identifications, then, a close reading of the history of this idea indicates that it remained inherently bound up with more narrow understandings of identity ("Serb," "Croat," "Slovene," and so on) and proved readily convertible to these ethnic understandings in moments of crisis and reconfiguration of the state. Furthermore, the relatively inclusive notion of a South Slav identity, whether understood in supranational or synthetic/hybrid terms, raised serious questions in both the First (1919–41) and Second Yugoslavia (1944–91) about the place of the many autochthonous non-Slavic peoples (Shoup 1968; Wachtel 1998). Many members of these populations faced expulsion or fled from Yugoslavia after World War II, as in the case of the Italians, Germans, and Hungarians whose association with wartime occupiers rendered them vulnerable targets. Those who remained in Tito's Yugoslavia received minority guarantees and rights, which nonetheless inscribed them as different from the federation's constitutive, South Slav peoples. This suggests that in the multiethnic Yugoslav federation, some peoples appeared to be more "authentic," more rooted, or more equal than others (a complaint, of course, that nationalist elites readily instrumentalized in the 1980s and 1990s). In this chapter, I explore similar paradoxes of identity—what I deem the notion of "authentic hybridity"—for the contemporary Istrian case, situating a hybrid identity in a field marked by competing claims of submersion and rootedness.

This raises the question of the degree to which Istria remains in the shadows of or overshadowed by the Balkans (and its identity politics) and the extent to which Istria instead mirrors and exemplifies the paradoxes of identity common throughout the wider region.[3] On the one hand, I have argued that exile discourse more *explicitly* resembles that of nationalists in various Yugoslav republics than does that of the Istrian regionalists and their Italian minority supporters. Yet on the other hand, as with the example of the broader Yugoslav concept, discourses of a "multiethnic" Istrian identity and their operative logics must be understood critically in light of the multiple processes of state reconfiguration and contestation detailed in this book. Doing this prompts the question whether the regionalist movement represents, as many scholars would have it, a novel political strategy reflecting the way nation-states and their homogenizing logics are being superseded in an increasingly hybrid, deterritorialized, global world (Appadurai 1996). Or does contemporary "Istrianism" instead signal a reinscription of the region's long-standing purity-hybridity dialectic, with the latter term remaining captive to the nationalist imaginary? Has a nostalgia for the region's previous experiments in multinationalism—including the Hapsburg Empire and Yugoslavism—merely been given expression in a new form, namely, Istrian regionalism?

To some extent building on older, local ideas of autonomous or supranational entities, contemporary Istrian regionalism nonetheless partakes of a thoroughly contemporary language of multiculturalism and tolerance. Simultaneously, it reverberates with the older rhetoric of Yugoslavism (leading critics to accuse Istrians of a dreaded "Yugonostalgia") at the same time that it condemns the violent methods whereby "Brotherhood and Unity" was imposed on regions such as Istria. Regionalists often pose Istrianism as a movement from the ground up (characterized by genuine *convivenza*, or ethnic cohabitation), in opposition to the artificial creation of a Yugoslav identity and the attendant violence of the exodus. Not surprisingly, then, Istrians often express more explicit nostalgia for the Austro-Hungarian Empire—seen to have equitably balanced the rights of competing ethnic groups—than for Tito's Yugoslavia. This fondness for Austria (both its hybridity and European-ness) resonates in the eloquent revitalizations of the literary myth of *Mitteleuropa* by Triestine intellectuals such as Claudio Magris (1986; see also Ara 1990, Tassin 1993). Yet it should be recalled here that the diversity of Hapsburg Trieste and its hinterland, lauded today by scholars and political activists alike, was the direct consequence of a centralizing state and its policy of awarding corporate recognition to those religious minorities which "served" and furthered the interests of that state (Dubin 1999, 201–14). Just as those cosmopolitan visions demanded critical interrogation vis-à-vis irredentist and purist formulations (see chapter 1), so too do present-day celebrations of hybridity by both rimasti and their regionalist allies.

Authentic Hybridity

In the summer of 2000, I paid a brief return visit to Istria and found that the broader national political context had changed dramatically with Franjo Tudjman's death that January and the subsequent election of a democratic coalition in February 2000. Among the new parties of power was the Istrian Democratic Assembly, which had governed Istria throughout the Tudjman era. Long defined in opposition to an oppressive center—one that many Istrians viewed as merely the latest in a long line of state powers desiring to create ethno-national purity out of Istria's historically hybrid population—the DDI-IDS suddenly faced the challenge of rebuilding the economic and political system, not just in Istria but in all of Croatia. DDI-IDS president Ivan Nino Jakovčić became Croatia's minister for European integration, announcing as his ambitious goals European integration by 2006 and political recognition (in the form of a "Euroregion") of Istria's unique Latin-Slav cultural and ethnic mix (*Il Piccolo* 2000; P. R. 2000).

The first head of a foreign government received by the new Croatian regime, Italy's then prime minister Massimo D'Alema, pledged Italy's full support in the economic and political spheres and help in facilitating European integration. D'Alema's visit was followed in early summer by that of Romano Prodi, president of the European Commission, and Vittorio Sgarbi, a member of parliament, both of whom toured Istria and visited the Italian communities there. During the honeymoon period of the new governing coalition, the rimasti had much to smile about not only with these shows of interest from the "mother country" but also as the intransigence of the Tudjman regime on questions of bilingualism gave way to support for "integral bilingualism," permitting the use of Italian in the Istrian county government, regional tribunals, and state offices. Furthermore, the new government made attendance at minority-language schools open to all Croatian citizens, regardless of whether they belonged to the specific ethnic group (a possibility Tudjman's minister of education, Vokić, had sought to restrict only to "pure" members of the ethnic group). These measures revealed seemingly sharp and sudden changes in Croatian politics. Istrians in general, and the rimasti in particular, had gone from being cast as irritating or even subversive to being praised as "a national resource" that would facilitate Croatia's entry into the European Union.

Indeed, in the days following the February elections, Jakovčić triumphantly deemed the DDI-IDS as having constituted the "most coherent opposition" force against the Tudjman regime and as having shown the way to Europe. In doing so, Jakovčić reiterated those themes—Istrian autonomy, European integration—which had brought the regionalist party consistent and widespread support in Istria throughout the 1990s and had made it so popular among rimasti. At the same time, many of the same tensions within that political program remain, creating divisions within the DDI-IDS and with their erstwhile political allies.

Questions about the degree of autonomy and privilege accorded a future Istrian region linger, echoing initial disagreements about what autonomy meant in regards to the DDI-IDS's founding manifesto and its demand for an Istrian "Euroregion" cutting across Slovenia, Croatia, and Italy (Debeljuh 1993, 24–25). Notwithstanding regionalist self-portrayals of their aims as liberal and progressive, Tudjman and his supporters repeatedly denounced the regionalists as secessionists, pointing to the Italian minority's prominent role within the DDI-IDS as "evidence" of the party's links with Italian irredentists. The Croatian Right, now the opposition, has continued to attack Jakovčić on his "intentional" vagueness about autonomy and has seen in earlier proposals for a separate constitutional law for the region a dangerous example of separatism (Čurić 2000).

Even the DDI-IDS's political allies became alarmed and irritated when, in March 2000, Jakovčić threatened to resign his ministerial post and lead an autonomous Istria if the central government failed to intervene in the financial crisis that had temporarily shut down the Istrian Bank (Istarska Banka). Although Jakovčić later apologized for his rash statements, they fed opponents' depictions of the Istrian region as a potentially separatist and destabilizing force within Croatia. Similarly, in May 2000, the proposal to redesign the Istrian region to include the islands of Lussino/Losinj and Cherso/Kres, as well as the area around Abbazia/Opatija—an idea that had been discussed for several years on the basis of those areas' historic provenance within an "Istrian reality"—struck both HDZ supporters and the DDI-IDS's allies in the Kvarner Region as inappropriate, in part because it would reconstitute the region that existed under fascist Italy. In the summer of 2001, the prospect of local representatives of the relevant areas in Italy, Slovenia, and Croatia signing an agreement to establish a Euroregion embracing "Istria-Carso-Mare" prompted similar denunciations by former DDI-IDS allies, including Social Democrat and vice president of the Croatian Sabor, or parliament, Mato Arlović (*Il Piccolo* 2001).

Arlović comments reflected not only long-standing concern over the consequences of an Istrian Euroregion but also the political falling out between the DDI-IDS and the governing coalition. In February 2001, Jakovčić resigned his ministerial post and the DDI-IDS withdrew from the coalition. A dispute over the Istrian statute had led critics of the DDI-IDS to claim that the regionalists had arrogated the power—to propose and institute bilingualism (Italian-Croat) at a regional level—requiring a constitutional act. Furthermore, the prospect of such widespread bilingualism revived fears (pervasive in Tudjman's time) that such a practice would set a dangerous precedent for other minorities, specifically the Serbs. Once again, the regionalists stood in opposition to the national center.

A year earlier, regionalists and rimasti leaders had sought to discourage the drawing of any such parallels between themselves and the Serbian minority with their negative reaction to a request by the Serbian community in Istria for special recognition as an autochthonous minority. The response highlights the ways that Istrians do, indeed, reconsider themselves a "special" case. Rimasto leader Maurizio Tremul declared the comparison of the Serb and Italian minorities unfounded, stating of the Italians, "We are autochthonous." Petar Janko, a DDI-IDS deputy in the regional parliament, similarly noted that Italians had lived in Istria for two thousand years, whereas Serbs came to Istria only under Tito's Yugoslavia (after the exodus). Declaring that he had no rancor against the Serbs, Janko nonetheless pointed out that they had much more protection than in other parts of Croatia. (His words echoed those of the Yugoslav activist who asked Marianna, "What does this Marianna want? The chorus is going to sing "Bandiera rossa" in Italian, that should be sufficient".) Janko characterized the Serbs' excessive demands as akin to wanting "to have their cake and eat it too" (*pane sopra la focaccia;* Ljuština 2000).

This controversy about which minorities are really autochthonous and thereby deserve special rights points to the paradox at the heart of Istrian regionalism, as well as rimasti discourse: the vision of Istrian hybridity said to merit a special political recognition and an autonomous region privileges an autochthonous or "authentic hybrid," seen to be rooted in the territory by genealogies and ancestors. This rather exclusive understanding of hybridity does not contradict the Istrian stress on Europeanism; rather it follows out of a sense of Istria's inherent European history and character (which, in turn, further sets apart those Balkan peoples, like the Serbs, who move to the peninsula but remain distinct from Istrians). The "new" oppositional stance taken by the DDI-IDS against the democratic coalition stresses the European character of a special Euroregion and bilingualism proposed for the regional entity, with the implication that other Croatian parties do not prove so enlightened; the recent flap over the Euroregion led DDI-IDS vice president Damir Kajin to accuse the Social Democrats of employing tactics akin to those that Tudjman's HDZ had used when in power, whereas Jakovčić deemed the Istrian statute a "modern and European document" (I. B. 2001a).

Given the regionalists' celebration of their antinational, antiessential alternative, then, it proves ironic (if not altogether surprising) that the authentic hybrid of istrianità shows clear parallels with the autochthonous subject privileged by Italian exiles in Trieste. Where esuli view this subject as "purely" Italian and point to markers such as names, Roman and Venetian architecture, and cemeteries as irrefutable proof of the peninsula's Italian character, supporters of the regionalist project read these same signs as evidence of Istria's historical hybridity, a hybridity no less grounded in territory and no less bound up with state-making projects. Esuli and regionalists/rimasti thus emphasize, albeit in different ways, the autochthony and cultural superiority of Istria vis-à-vis the Balkans.

Both discursive configurations reflect long-standing notions of civiltà (dating from the Venetian and Hapsburg periods) specific to the region. Though the pertinent axis of differentiation here is a West/East one, this understanding of civilization resonates with broader notions of Italian identity—centered around a North/South divide—that came to the fore with the project of building a unitary state. Since at least the nineteenth century, southern Italians, or *meridionali*, have been imagined by some foreigners, northern Italians, and southern reformers in terms not dissimilar to those of the demi-Orientalism described by Wolff for the peoples of Dalmatia and Eastern Europe: as picturesque, backward savages defined by their "proximity to Africa and Orient" (Moe 2001, 121).

Such North/South orientalizing rhetorics continue to hold salience in contemporary Italy (Schneider 1998), just as the symbolic pairing of the West with Europe and the East with the Orient proves commonplace in the political discourse of the new states of Central and Eastern Europe. In the area of former Yugoslavia, looking toward Europe typically means differentiating oneself from the Balkans, depicted in the negative terms associated with Orientalism. Defined by Edward Said as both an academic tradition and "a style of thought based upon an ontological and epistemological distinction made between 'the Orient' and (most of the time) 'the Occident'" (1979, 2; see also Kabbani 1986), the Orientalist tradition has also created internal hierarchies and alterity—as demonstrated in both the Italian and Yugoslav contexts—within the Occident.[4]

Istrian attempts to distinguish themselves from non-Istrian Croats (as Europeans versus Balkanic peoples) thus echo those that Croatian nationalists (among the regionalists' opponents) make in setting themselves apart from "Oriental," "Byzantine," and "Ottoman" Serbs. Whereas Slovenia and Croatia can make claims to European culture on the basis of their long political subjection to Austria-Hungary, Istrians boast an additional autochthonous "Italian" heritage, irrefutable proof for them (and, ironically, the exiles) of their essential European-ness. Indeed, if regionalists posit mixed marriages as a key to Istrian *convivenza*, it must implicitly be the European (that is, Italian) character of the mixture which explains why convivenza has succeeded in Istria, in contrast to Bosnia (and Yugoslavia more generally), where mixed marriages likewise proved common. These pervasive logics of exclusion reflect what scholars have deemed "nesting Orientalisms" (Bakić-Hayden and Hayden 1992; Bakić-Hayden 1995). Alternatively, we can imagine a mobile border or symbolic axis between "European" and "non-European," with Croats declaring themselves Europeans in contrast to Serbs, Istrians declaring themselves Europeans in contrast to other Croats, and Italian exiles from Istria in turn declaring themselves European in opposition to Istrians.

Throughout the 1990s, the DDI-IDS leadership did not remain content to merely stress its European (that is, Venetian and Hapsburg) heritage, however, but also forged ties with European institutions such as the Council of Europe and the European parliament. The Istrian Region, for example, became the first

Croatian region to enter the Council of Europe's Assembly of European Regions. At a 1996 conference held in Istria to promote and encourage other regional associations in Croatia, Jakovčić warned that should Croatia turn away from Europe, the only alternative lay in some sort of "Balkan association." Of this possibility, he exclaimed, "Istrians don't want to remain quagmired in the 'Balkan bog'!" Jakovčić expressed a view of Istrian difference shared by much of the DDI-IDS leadership. Even before Yugoslavia's bloody dissolution, DDI-IDS vice president Loredana Bogliun Debeljuh differentiated Istrians from their bellicose, "Balkanic" neighbors. "I don't know how far we could succumb to the *nationalistic logics of Balkanic Yugoslavia*, certainly we are somewhat outside of these logics . . . *our cultural trajectories are European*" (Debeljuh 1990, 30–31; my italics).

Many Istrians I know expressed views similar to those of Jakovčić and Debeljuh. The same individuals who stressed their tolerance by proudly noting, "We can't distinguish ourselves as Croat or Slovene or Italian—rather, we are Istrians," nonetheless readily differentiated themselves from non-Istrians. They contrasted the peace-loving, hardworking, orderly (read "Austrian") Istrian to the dirty, warlike, and disorderly Balkan type. This raises the question of how understandings of Istrian hybridity—which in its intellectual formulations shares tensions with its purist antinomy—operate in everyday life.

"Istriani d.o.c.": Discourses of "Authentic Hybridity"

While regionalists in the 1990s rightly denounced the external threat posed by centralization and Croatization, an underlying narrative on the ground marked out the presence of Albanians and Bosnian refugees (particularly Muslims) as threats to the unique fabric of Istrian life. (Many of these refugees have subsequently been returned, where possible, to their homes.) The Tudjman government claimed that Istria was targeted for such refugee resettlement solely because the region contained many hotels and lodgings that could conveniently house the victims of displacement. Many Istrians instead interpreted this as a plan to "de-Istrianize" the peninsula, by introducing populations belonging to different cultural, linguistic, and religious traditions.

Ivan Pauletta, a prominent figure in the DDI-IDS, described Istria as "colonized" through a policy of forced immigration by Zagreb; this description rendered Istrians victims rather than (potential) victimizers of unwelcome immigrants. Istria's forced colonization (like the one carried out by the Yugoslav state after World War II) involved a double-pronged approach of refugee resettlement and the importation of directors and managers.

In regards to forced immigration, it is symptomatic that no one, not even the mass media, gets to the heart of the question, that is to those who are truly responsible for the tragedy, but on the contrary, prefer to put Istrians on the bench of the accused with the charge of being inhospitable and of not wanting to accommodate these poor people . . . the cultural and social aftereffects of the phenomenon will emerge, sooner or later, in all their gravity. . . . [There exists] a disproportionate influx of Croats from central Bosnia, who, *removed from their proper roots, are submitted to a double violence.* (1994, 9; my italics)

One of these transplanted Bosnian Croats resident on the Istrian coast supposedly confessed to the DDI-IDS leader that "when the sea is rough he can't sleep because he is afraid of the unfamiliar crashing of the waves" (ibid.). Pauletta's statement reiterates the coastal/interior, town/country division that has long figured in nationalist understandings in the area. All Istrians, regardless of whether they actually live along the coast or not, are now seen as bearers of the associated urban values, in contrast to "rough and rude" Bosnian country bumpkins. At the same time, Pauletta's anecdote implied a territorialized notion of identity that verges on the ecological, the idea that each people belongs to its own environmental niche. This picks up on common stereotypes, reflected by classifications enshrined in Yugoslav ethnography, about Dinaric (mountain) peoples, maritime populations, and so on (Cvijić 1929–31). In the language of regionalist supporters like Franco Juri, from Slovenian Istria, this territorial imagery becomes wedded to environmentalist concerns about a shared environment or "bio-region" and the need for the state to guarantee the "autonomous development of the peoples within their rightful habitats [*proprio habitat*]" (1990, 9).

In the Istrian context, these notions of peoples as belonging to specific environments resonated in the fear that the peninsula was subject to a forced "transplantation" directed from Zagreb, a policy threatening the delicate balance obtained over the centuries by the hybrid but deeply rooted Istrian population. The native hybrid plant appears in danger of being choked out by Bosnian weeds. This vegetative imagery finds its equally naturalized counterpart in the fear about inundation of cultural islands, a metaphor that invokes "isolated gene pools, divergent evolutionary patterns and closed ecosystems . . . [as well as the] self-sustaining social system" (Eriksen 1993, 1).

In its horticultural and organic qualities, such language reminds us that the notion of hybridity has its origins in discourses of race and genetics. Notions of Istrian cultural mixture, like Anzaldúa's (1987) influential image of the *mestiza* formed at the Mexico-U.S. border, are often seen as grounded in nature and biology through mixed unions. The interpenetration of cultural and biological meanings in metaphors of identity further underscores the horticultural meaning originally attached to culture—that of cultivation (Williams 1976; see the extended discussion of notions of rootedness in Malkki 1992). Istrian exiles across the border share such an understanding of culture, as evidenced by their laments over the Istrian countryside's reversion to wilderness after centuries of cultivation, thereby highlighting the connection between cultivation of land and cultivation as refinement.[5] The opposition "urban is to rural as civilized is to uncivilized" continues to figure powerfully in both exile and contemporary Istrian understandings of identity, as we have seen.

The differences between self-described Istrians and the peninsula's new arrivals are also perceived or coded in spatial terms, at least in Rovigno/Rovinj. The Old Town, predominantly Venetian in architectural style, has become home to many such newcomers, who often live in the expropriated vacation apartments of Serbs (apartments that, in turn, belonged to Italians prior to the exodus). According to rovignesi, these immigrants make no effort to learn the Istrian dialect, whether in its Italian or Croatian variants, or to integrate into Istrian life. Echoing the comments of rimasti like Marianna, who feels displaced in her hometown, "native" rovignesi sometimes joked bitterly that when they walked the streets of the Old Town and heard Bosnian speech, they felt as if they were in Sarajevo or Mostar, not their birthplace. Several Istrians similarly complained to me about their Albanian neighbors, believed to belong to large clans that operate in Mafia-like fashion, dominating businesses such as filigree jewelry shops and *burek*, or pastry, stands. The sense of Albanian otherness appeared heightened when I visited the town in the summer of 1999. As a result of the war in Kosovo, some Kosovars had come to join their relatives in Rovigno/Rovinj, many of whom had arrived several decades earlier under Yugoslavia, and jokes and comments about "Shiptari" (Albanians) were circulating in the town to a much higher degree than on my previous stays.

"Genuine" Istrians often lamented the state into which the Old Town, inhabited by these suspect groups, had fallen into: trash was casually tossed out windows, dirty urchinlike children screeched through the narrow streets, and the "unpleasant" odor of Bosnian cooking filled the air. As one woman put it, "Many of these people have never had indoor plumbing, so for them this is like paradise. They don't know how to behave when they enter a civilized home or how to take care of it." Such comments encode a sense that real Istrians, especially members of the Italian minority, have seen this all before. A character in Tomizza's *Materada* comments on the newcomers who came after World War II, "'They're already here. See them? Sitting at that table, with the long hair. From the hinterland, the mountains, to see their new home. They'll have their pick of houses. They've been living in chicken coops like animals, and now they may even take Nando's place'" (1999, 122).

As the "peasants" and "wildmen" arrive to fill abandoned homes, the traditional rural/urban division appears, then, to be inverted: the "barbarians" have not only arrived at the gates of the city but have also occupied the center and let it fall into a state of degradation. One of my acquaintances put it succinctly, "The Balkans start after the arch [leading into Rovigno's Old Town]"; he then added, in English, "That is the immigrant town, the ghetto." For such *Istriani d.o.c.,* that is, self-described "genuine Istrians," these new arrivals—usually compared unfavorably with those who arrived in the immediate post–World War II period and made some effort to assimilate to the Istrian reality—threaten to destroy those very markers of an authentic hybridity which have survived in spite of repeated state-sponsored violence: bilingualism, Latin-Slav cultural fusion, and a cultural patrimony partly conceived in architectonic terms. This emphasis on Istria's architecture as an expression of a historic civiltà echoes statements by exiles, who read the landscape as evidence of Istria's Roman and Venetian (that is, "Italian") settlement. Not surprisingly, contemporary Istrians often use the same cultivation metaphor, particularly of wine (and the label d.o.c., *di origine controllata*), to confer authenticity (of both culture and nature, whose fusion is symbolized by the wine-making process).

Whereas Istrians may perceive Bosnian newcomers as a threat, however, the kind of violence toward ethnic Others shown in Croatia and Croatian Bosnia has not appeared in Istria. Indeed, the regionalist emphasis on autochthony reflects real and significant concerns about the protection of minorities and bilingualism, rights that remained under critical attack throughout the 1990s. If the controversies over the Serbs in Istria and the Istrian statute offer any indication, in the post-Tudjman era a privileged sense of "authentic hybridity" and rootedness will nonetheless remain key to an Istrian identity, grounded as it is in concerns about territory.

Old Rhetorics, New Boundaries?

Not only has the emphasis on autochthony and territory opened the movement up (from within and without) to doubts about what regional autonomy implies (and who has membership in such an autonomist entity), this descending logic of exclusion also manifested itself in another boundary (of pure/authentic hybridity) being drawn within the regionalist camp between *regionalisti d.o.c.* and "old communists." When I left the field in 1996, the DDI-IDS was fracturing into two parties, one led by President Jakovčić and the other headed by Luciano Delbianco, former president of the Istrian Region, and Ivan Pauletta (*Il Piccolo* 1996b). This split had roots in the expulsions of DDI-IDS party members that began in 1994. At the base of such contests were diverse interpretations of regionalism, disagreements over the regional council, personal antagonisms, and presumed connivance on the part of some representatives with the HDZ (Forza 1994, 7).

The internal tensions that led to these expulsions eventually gave rise to a major political row in 1996 over Igor Štoković, the mayor of Pola/Pula, Istria's unofficial capital and its major city. When several DDI-IDS leaders expressed their loss of confidence in Štoković, who was on the DDI-IDS ticket but was said to be "intriguing" with the HDZ, the mayor refused to resign. The DDI-IDS then chose another candidate, who claimed the position that Štoković had refused to cede. Delbianco and his Pola-based faction supported Štoković against Jakovčić, president of the party. In an open letter, Damir Kajin, vice president of the region, questioned the Delbianco group's legitimacy. Noting that in 1993 numerous members of Delbianco's group had passed into the DDI-IDS from the Social Democratic Party (that is, reformed communists), Kajin contended that these communist wolves in regionalist sheep's clothing "had never accepted the line, the fundamental conception, the mode of thinking of the DDI" (Gasparini 1996, 5). The "old communist" mentality attributed by some Istrian critics to the DDI-IDS and its local leaders was thus reinscribed in this formulation as a characteristic of the Delbianco clique, now positioned as "outsiders" who never really understood istrianità. (Despite this supposed comprehension, Delbianco and his party took the prize of Pola/Pula in the elections of May 2001.)

At the time of Delbianco's defection, one observer described the DDI-IDS as an important "organic" movement that, having gotten rid of its diseased elements, would subsequently flourish. An article in the popular Italian-language Istrian weekly *Panorama,* for example, implicitly highlighted the DDI-IDS's role as representative of Istriani d.o.c. Likening the DDI-IDS to a tree (hence rooted in the soil and territory of Istria), the journalist played on the common themes of autochthony, at the same time that the tree metaphor underscored the "ecological" or naturalized aspects of Istrian formulations of hybridity.

> In its development from regionalist movement to party on the national level, the DDI made gigantic steps in changing directions by making old alliances and stipulating new ones of major weight on the political scene. The DDI has every reason, then, to knock off, in the Istrian home, the branches that disturb the harmonious foliage of the DDI tree and to cut those that are old, to directly prune the roots in order to regulate growth. (Gasparini 1996, 7)

A process of political purging here acquires an air of natural necessity, even desirability. As Linke has noted in the German context, "The genealogical tree . . . thus evokes both continuity of essence and territorial rootedness" (1999, 62).

In a 1994 interview, Ivan Pauletta, one of the "rebels" who subsequently sided with Delbianco, similarly questioned the authenticity or organic nature of his political rivals. Positing the existence of internal divisions and orientations within the DDI-IDS, Pauletta contended, "In the first are those who have Istria in their hearts and are motivated by the idea to do something positive for it. *In the second are ranged certain personalities who don't trouble themselves too much with the destiny of the peninsula but rather with their own interests and prestige"* (Pauletta 1994, 8; my italics). Two years later, Kajin would employ the same notion of authentic istrianità in order to delegitimate Pauletta and the leadership of the Istrian Democratic Forum. Critics of the forum insinuated that Delbianco had gone over to the other side, namely to the HDZ, and had powerful financial motives for doing so (Gasparini 1996, 6).

Frequent comments about personal gain and graft hint at the ways in which regional (and regionalist) politics intersect with a postsocialist economic transition. DDI-IDS members' descriptions of opponents as corrupt (both as taking money on the side and as impure or insincere regionalists) may work to deflect charges of wrongdoing away from the regionalist party. A good number of the claims about the "abuse" of power, whether by DDI-IDS members or their opponents, revolve around charges that politicians profit from their position by purchasing formerly state-owned land or enterprises cheaply. In Rovigno/Rovinj, local gossip often dwells on local officials said to be lining their pockets. New luxury cars or sending one's children on exchange programs to Florida were variously cited as signs of obvious opportunism. In the nearby town of Dignano/Vodnjan, several local officials from the regionalist party currently face prosecution on charges of abuse of power. Furthermore, in August 2001 the DDI-IDS's internal policy of having top leaders disclose their personal assets led to the revelation that Jakovčić owned a small real estate empire, which included the entire Istrian village of San Giorgio. Critics immediately accused the regionalist leader of having abused his power by directing public works money for infrastructural development in the village (*Il Piccolo* 2001a; I.B. 2001b).

Not surprisingly, many Istrians seemed resigned to the fact that in the end politicians ultimately behave in a similar manner, whether they are of the party of opposition or of the one in power. Yet some who claimed to have originally expressed enthusiasm for the DDI-IDS now appeared disillusioned, despite (or perhaps because of) the DDI-IDS's triumphant arrival on the national stage. In the summer of 2000, for instance, many in Rovigno/Rovinj predicted that DDI-IDS leaders would face defeat in the next local elections of May 2001. Though the DDI-IDS ultimately retained power in Istria, it lost some key areas (such as the city of Pola/Pula); in places like Rovigno/Rovinj, the "old guard" of the DDI-IDS who had exercised power for a decade found themselves forced out as a result of power struggles largely internal to the party. Some of my informants remained skeptical that these political newcomers would behave differently from their predecessors.

In considering the conceptual limits of istrianità and its consequences for actual political and lived practice, then, my analysis here suggests that this view of identity raises serious questions about the regionalist party's ultimate potential to constitute either a radically different model of inclusion or a new way of doing politics. The troubling tensions inherent to the "authentic hybrid" reflect not only the dialogic nature of pure-hybrid understandings in the Julian March but also the exclusive-inclusive model (a select inclusion) emerging out of that new European order to which Istrians have looked so eagerly. Writing of the European Union, Juan Moreira Delgado has raised questions that speak to the conceptual dilemmas reflected in miniature in Istrian regionalism. "How can a supranational institution find legitimation in a concept of culture which originally refers to small groups or nations? How can the protection of culture be construed to promote European integration?" (2000, 2). For Istria, we might ask: How can a regional, supranational model of Istrian identity find legitimation in a sense of autochthony and rootedness bound up historically in this area with nation-state projects? How can an emphasis on European-ness, in exclusion of Balkan-ness, promote a new European order (of democracy, civil society, and so on)?

In the EU case, Delgado notes that although the Commission of the European Union promotes a vision of a high, pan-European culture, the Committee of Regions stresses the locality of culture, multiculturalism, and protection of minority rights. In effect, this grounds the vision of a "cosmopolitan" European culture in particular, territorially rooted and autochthonous cultures. Not surprisingly, perhaps, the EU Treaty on Union uses a horticultural language to describe the means through which the "flowering of the cultures of the member states" may be achieved (Holmes 2000, 32). Architects of these EU cultural policies explicitly reject U.S. multicultural models, which in theory make everyone the same in their difference. This European vision of multiculturalism begs the question, of course, of the space occupied by non-European immigrants. Though potentially given equal rights as citizens, these newcomers can never be autochthonous Europeans, just as Bosnians can never truly be Istrians.

All this suggests that in Europe generally, as in Istria, we may be witnessing the emergence of two-tiered regimes in which some citizens are more authentic (though not more equal, at least in law) than others. The EU's pronouncements on culture and Europeanism serve to "obscure the EU's own administrative practices—its praxis of exclusion (Stolcke 1995). . . . Its insipid declarations to the contrary, full legal recognition of the right to cultural difference is, in fact, treated with intense suspicion by the leadership of the EU" (ibid., 31–32), a situation that shows many parallels with the Istrian case. The aspiration of the DDI-IDS to Europeanism of the EU brand makes painfully clear the contradictions inherent in that broader project. More generally, the possibility that Istrianism replicates the very exclusive logics it opposes also suggests the potential limits to current political and conceptual vocabularies of identity.

Navigating Identity

Historically locating discourses of purity and hybridity for the case of the Julian March acquires particular significance in light of the ways in which certain paradigmatic cases have often stood in for general theories of related phenomena such as hybridity, borderlands, and diaspora. The specific genealogies of key "cases"—the U.S.-Mexico border for borderland studies, South Asian flows and the Jewish dispersal for theories of diaspora—may not speak to the experience of other places like southeastern Europe.

Though the vogue for such topics in anthropology is recent, purity and intermixture are issues of long-standing and critical significance for the populations of southeastern Europe, as well as questions of emerging concern for states like Italy making the transition from a nation of emigration to a nation of immigration (Carter 1997; Cole 1997). The entangled histories of purity and hybridity in places like the Julian March thus put into question one common view of hybridity as a novel strategy reflecting an increasingly globalized world with porous state boundaries (Appadurai 1996; Waters 1995).

This presentist view also typically celebrates hybridity as a positive antidote to essentialist notions of identity. Yet as recent events in former Yugoslavia or the experience of Istria after World War II suggest, all too often these debates about purity and hybridity—bound up as they are with questions of autochthony and territory—have had dramatic and historically tragic consequences for local populations whose displacement proves to be the consequence of nationalism's homogenizing impulse (Gellner 1987). The striking absence of discussion about former Yugoslavia in the hybridity and borderlands literature points up the limitations of much of the Anglo-American analysis of these phenomena. This lacuna in the hybridity literature contrasts with the way in which some thinking about diasporic politics has taken account of the important role played by displaced communities in fueling interethnic antagonism in various parts of the Balkans (Brubaker 1996, 55–76; Danforth 1995; Karakasidou 1997).

As anthropologists have rejected or challenged once-common views of territorially circumscribed fieldwork sites, as well as unitary identities, they have increasingly become interested in areas in which stable boundaries are challenged and a mestizo consciousness is produced, the realm of both the hybrid and the transnational.[6] The borderlands that attract these scholars may be literal or metaphorical, ranging from the interstices of political borders to the global city, the locale in which the Third World irrupts in the First. Rarely, however, are postsocialist areas such as the Balkans or former Yugoslavia discussed in this anthropological literature on borderlands, despite the fact that the region has been profoundly shaped by its interstitial position between competing empires, states, religions, and political ideologies. Anthropologists who do find the region a fruitful site from which to investigate such questions—as evinced, for instance, by the work of Danforth (1995) and Karakasidou (1997) on diverse aspects of "transnational" identity formation among Macedonians in Australia and Greece, respectively—may arguably be said to belong more to an emergent literature exploring "the anthropology of borders" rather than to the borderland literature per se. The former field stresses the relationships of actual frontier dwellers to distant centers of state power, though, as Donnan and Wilson note, "anthropologists in general have had much more to say about the cultural and symbolic boundaries between groups, than about the concrete, physical borders between them" (1999, 4).

The surprising paucity of dialogue between scholars of the "anthropology of borders" and those of "borderlands anthropology" may help explain what initially seems to be a puzzle: the general neglect of the former Yugoslavia in the borderlands and hybridity literature. Could it be that the spectacular and re-peated failures of the supranational, hybrid Yugoslav concept over the course of this century make it an embarrassing example for those scholars heralding hy-bridity as the progressive alternative to essentialized identities? Celebrated as "sites of creative cultural creolizations, places where criss-crossed identities are forged out of the debris of corroded, formerly (would-be) homogeneous identities," border zones are seen to give rise to hybrids who, as Lavie and Swedenburg put it, "often subversively appropriate and creolize master codes, decentering, desta-bilizing, and carnivalizing dominant forms through 'strategic inflections' and 're-accentuations'" (1996, 15, 9). Instead, the bloody decentering and destabi-lizing effects of the recent Yugoslav wars, with the world turned tragically up-side down, raise the uncomfortable possibility that hybridity—not only in its common-language usage but also in its intellectual formulations (like that of Yugoslavism and Istrianism)—does not necessarily challenge essentialist logics but may actually share those same logics. This example thus poses yet another challenge to a popular view of hybridity (particularly when conceived as a thing, rather than as a strategy or process à la Gupta [1998]) as necessarily of-fering either a novel or radical alternative to purist understandings.[7]

The case of former Yugoslavia, together with the related example of Istria, brings into sharp focus the ways in which some current theoretical formula-tions of both borderlands and hybridity draw heavily not only on linguistic models, whether the carnivalesque one entailed by Bakhtin's concept of het-eroglossia or the syncretism informing creolization, but also on organic or racial models, with mixture opposed to (though created out of) purity. In his book *Colonial Desire*, Robert Young details specifically British genealogies of the hy-brid concept, locating them in racist fears of miscegenation and degeneration. Young reminds us that from the 1840s onward, questions about species and hy-brids proved central to British debates over science, art, and colonial adminis-tration. Young's partial history thus sounds an important cautionary note for those who uncritically embrace hybridity as a novel and "liberatory" strategy of political and cultural practice.

> Hybridity in particular shows the connections between the racial categories of the past and contemporary cultural discourse: it may be used in different ways, given differ-ent inflections and apparently discrete references, but it always reiterates and rein-forces the dynamics of the same conflictual economy whose tensions and divisions it re-enacts in its own antithetical structure. (Young 1995, 27)

Given this, does Anzaldúa's influential 1987 description of the mestiza, the hybrid offspring of the Mexican-U.S. frontier, challenge these older, problem-atic notions of hybridity or merely invert and subvert the values attached to them, leaving in place the assumptions about stable wholes whose fusion gen-erates *la frontera*? As Anzaldúa puts it, the consciousness of the borderlands is forged "[a]t the confluence of two or more genetic streams, with chromosomes constantly 'crossing over,' this mixture of races, rather than resulting in an inferior being, provides hybrid progeny, a mutable, more malleable species with a rich gene pool" (1987, 77). Even if we accept the essentialist resonance of Anzaldúa's language as what Spivak would call a "strategic essentialism" (1990, 11–12),[8] usefully employed for political struggle by the subaltern, we need to inquire whether the means used may ultimately subvert the ends. What are the theoretical, as well as political, consequences of leaving the language of purity in place through an emphasis on impurity and mixture?

Although hybridity is often theoretically opposed to ethnic absolutism, the term's varied histories reveal its embeddedness in specific "essentialist" frameworks, ones often bound up with state-building projects of various sorts. As with ideologies of *mestizaje* used to politically delegitimize "native" groups like Mayans (Hale 1994, 1999) or the Istrian notion of hybridity that works to exclude recent immigrants to the peninsula, the paradoxical notion of "authentic hybridity" may become yet another indigenizing, exclusivist strategy. Mirzoeff similarly maintains, "Thus the claim to hybridity that may seem to be the mark of resistance in former colonial powers can be the sign of political authority in some former colonies" (2000, 9). The continued salience of states in such instances further underscores some of the selective vision of theorists of the contemporary world who proclaim the decline—rather than the reconfiguration—of state power.

As I have demonstrated throughout this book, many contemporary ethnonational movements—whether those of the Istrian exiles in Trieste or those of the Italian minority supporters of a hybrid Istrian identity—continue to draw on well-established rhetorics of identity and history associated with the nation-state. This may occur even when, as in the case of the Istrians supporting a regionalist project, those rhetorics employ seemingly novel terms such as *hybridity* and appear to radically challenge currently existing state forms. Such contemporary movements may be said to employ fairly conventional "repertoires of contention" (Tilly 1986, 1989) even as the state formations within which those repertoires developed are undergoing transformation. In Istria (and elsewhere), the rhetoric of purity and the concomitant discourse of hybridity have proven among well-established repertoires of contention, as well as those involved in the exercise of power (depending on the shifting space of center and periphery). Sinfield's judgment proves apt: "To say this is not to deny resistance [that is, any possibility for it]; only to doubt how far it may be advanced by cultural hybridity" (2000, 105).

Situating such understandings in time and in projects of multiple state building thus offers one answer to the (apparent) riddle presented by contemporary state formation (in the Balkans and beyond), as well as by the theoretical literature on identity formation: Why have borders been celebrated, on one hand, as places of transgression, hybridity, and heterodoxy and, on the other, as sites of defensive discourses of purity and orthodoxy? This question echoes the broader paradox of contemporary life in which transnational movements and border crossings of all sorts appear to be heralding the demise of states (particularly nation-states) at the same time that claims about "pure" identities and polities (including nation-states) also seem to be on the increase. Precisely because borders are such intense sites of ideological labor, they sharpen our vision of how competing claims to purity and hybridity are neither mere reactions to the world's increasing globalization and the weakening of sovereignty (the presentist thesis) nor proof that things have not really changed after all.

Rather, the current unbundling and rebundling of claims about sovereignty and identity reflect ongoing dynamics of state building that have been revitalized by the Cold War's end, as much as they reflect globalization per se. The Cold War made for many instances of divided populations; Germany (Borneman 1992), the Greek-Albanian border (Hart 1999), Korea, and Cuba-Miami are just a few cases that resonate with that of the Julian March. Such Cold War divisions often constituted a particular kind of diaspora: exiles who are geographically close to, yet ideologically closed against, the homeland (and who thereby relocate the "genuine" homeland in their reconstituted communities). Resident in Trieste, a city that has been politically and economically severed from its traditional hinterland, some esuli may rarely or never return to visit their lost homes, in contrast to those diasporic populations elsewhere who maintain extensive ties with their place of origin. In the Julian March, Cold War ideology reinforced the nationalist partitions that over the two world wars had effected large-scale violence and population transfers, as well as economic and political closure. The demise of the bipolar order that rigidified those divisions has made for the reconfiguration of all sorts of boundaries. The most recent changes of government in Croatia remind us that such transformations may occur extremely rapidly (sometimes surprising scholars, just as the Cold War's end caught many of them unawares). At the same time the frameworks by which nonstate actors understand their challenges to given various boundaries often remain indebted to long-standing rhetorics forged in the processes of (nation-)state formation.

Since I left the field in 1996, the political positions of the esuli and rimasti associations have shifted somewhat, partly in response to the changed political realities of their respective states. Some observers (for example, Giampaolo Valdevit) saw the 1996 electoral defeat of Italy's Berlusconi government, which held up Slovenia's EU admission on the grounds of the *beni abbandonati* issue, as perhaps signaling the "end" of the Cold War in Trieste; what the return of Berlusconi to power in 2001 means in these terms is not yet clear, though his government does seem willing to promote the cause of the *beni abbandonati* more than its predecessor did. Regardless, I suspect that the Cold War may have ended for some, but not all, individuals among the esuli. As we have seen, many members of the older generations with whom I worked do not necessarily view the establishment of democracies in Slovenia and Croatia as erasing the boundary between esuli and those currently living in Istria (rimasti and Slavs).

Questions about how average citizens made sense of the Cold War, assimilated it into longer-standing narratives, and date (if they do) the "end" of that conflict—issues rendered most poignant perhaps among families literally divided by its borders and sometimes internally divided by the intersection of generational and political differences—offer anthropologists rich but still underexploited avenues of research. Despite notable exceptions (for example, Borneman 1992), anthropologists have generally proven somewhat amnesiac about the Cold War itself, focusing for the most part on issues of anthropologists' role in the Cold War (Borneman 1998, 3; Nader 1997; Price 1997).

Admittedly, one might argue that the areas in which anthropologists recently have gone to work in significant numbers (Eastern Europe, the former Soviet Union) and topics that currently dominate much anthropological research and theorizing—globalization, deterritorialization, diaspora, hybridity, and refugee flows—demonstrate the discipline's attention to the new realities presented by the post–Cold War era. Yet all too infrequently do analysts sufficiently ground these issues in specific Cold War histories, including particular histories of states. Although some anthropologists have recently declared that even the "transition" out of state socialism in Eastern Europe is over and that we should turn our attention to new phenomena, there remain many important stories to be told about the Cold War and how different groups lived it. In doing this, scholars will illuminate further the contemporary realities of the post–Cold War and take seriously the struggles of groups such as the esuli and rimasti to come to terms with the enduring consequences of that conflict, as well as those of the violent "hot" wars that preceded it.

"Good-bye, Homeland"

I didn't think like poor Nando who, when he saw them going by, on
May third of '45, stroked his chin and said, "Good-bye homeland." . . .
I said, "This isn't the same old joke, this is the start of something new;
there's something behind this, and it's our job to keep our eye on it."
—Fulvio Tomizza, *Materada*

In "keeping an eye" on the reconfigurations of memory and
identity in the contemporary Julian March, I have recovered and juxtaposed not
only distinct theoretical literatures—including those exploring memory, identity, hybridity, displacement, and the legacies of World War II—but also diverse
histories in order to go beyond what much of contemporary theory could easily lead one to conclude for the Julian March: that exile or "diasporic" politics
in Trieste merely reflect changes in the political economy during the last decade
or that the multiculturalism, hybridity, and transborder arrangements celebrated in contemporary Istria are simply examples of new transnational phenomena articulated in the borderlands and interstices of nations. An alternative
formulation (and one I initially went into the field with) might counterpoise the
more narrowly nationalist visions of "backward-looking," politically conserva-
tive exile groups to those of forward-looking, "progressive," tolerant Istrians
embracing hybridity; this view of "bad identity politics" versus "good identity
politics" would read exile concerns with "purity" as products of outdated national ideologies while praising the "novel" political and conceptual alternatives
offered by hybridity-loving Istrians. As I have demonstrated, neither of these
perspectives adequately conveys how the (non)dialogue between exile politics
in Trieste and hybrid multiculturalism in Istria reflects a shared history of contestation over purity and diversity, with the latter having often restated fairly exclusive notions in an autonomist or regionalist guise.

Just as one reading of contemporary theory could have led me to construct
a facile dichotomy between retrograde and progressive identity politics in Trieste and Istria, respectively, so too might I have followed in the mode of more
traditional Mediterranean ethnographies in framing my project as merely a
comparison between two communities rather than a critical rethinking of place
making (both by anthropologists and informants) as suggested by Gupta and

Ferguson (1997a, 1997b), Marcus (1998), and others. Laying the groundwork for what would become known as the "anthropology of frontiers," for example, Cole and Wolf's book on two Tyrolean villages addresses many of the same issues I have explored here—ethnic differentiation and relations between neighbors in an area of competing states and moving borders—and offers an early precedent of a work dealing, at least in part, with the construction of a regional identity. This pathbreaking ethnography also reveals the efforts made during the 1960s and 1970s by anthropologists of the Mediterranean and elsewhere to bring history into their analyses. As its authors put it, "In other words, we needed to think in historical terms, to visualize the relations of St. Felix and Tret to the Anaunia, the Tyrol, Italy, Germany, and Europe as a whole in historical perspective" (Cole and Wolf 1974, 21).

Yet for Cole and Wolf such a historical perspective proves more a question of adding in a time dimension than of exploring historical consciousness or the construction of the region as an *idea* by scholars and informants alike. Their investigation of identity formation in the Italian Alps operates largely within the framework of political economy, treating the relationship between village and nation as "dialectical" and "transformations of local ecological patterns and political alignments in relation to the promptings of market and nation-building" (1974, 4). In their conclusion, the scholars speak of similarities and differences between the villages, highlighting the fundamentally comparative nature of their ethnography. In choosing seemingly incommensurate field sites (at least within the terms of an older anthropological project) and taking them as nodes from which to trace broader processes, my book is thus indebted to the pioneering work of Cole and Wolf, among others, at the same time that its departure in its conceptualization of the object of analysis reveals and contributes to more recent directions in anthropology.

From a number of angles, for instance, scholars have refined and critiqued the notion of core and periphery that animated many important anthropological contributions, including key ethnographies of communities along the Mediterranean and in Europe (Schneider and Schneider 1972, 1976; Schweizer 1988; Verdery 1983; Wolf 1982). My use of the language of center and margins, rather than core and periphery, reflects a rejection of the assumption of a straightforward or one-way relationship of domination and dependence exercised by the core. Furthermore, I use the term *center* to signal specific state systems, as well as the economic markets implied by the term *core* in its classical usage. I have thus underlined various forms of agency, as well as complicity with power (including that of the ethnographer), in state-building processes in the Julian March. These complex relationships—not just "a matter of dialectics between 'bottom' and 'top,' as well as among diverse groups 'at the bottom'" (Donnan and Wilson 1994, 2)—prove perhaps most discernible in frontier spaces.

In articulating a new descriptive vocabulary for the contemporary scene—one in which former assumptions about top and bottom, core and periphery, center and frontier, Left and Right, field and home, and so on have been put into question—many observers have employed a watery language of flows and circulation in the effort to capture the fluidity of the new "globalscape" (see Maurer 2000; Tsing 2000). This slippery discursive configuration owes much to Braudel's innovative work on the Mediterranean, attendant debates about the imprecision of the sea's boundaries, and related conceptualizations of globality in the form of a "world economy" structured around relationships between core and periphery. It proves fitting, then, that a scholarly inquiry navigating the concerns of both a classic and a newer Mediterranean anthropology offers a critical optic (to return from watery metaphors to illuminist ones) on this "fluid" theory.

In an incisive critique of scholars' failure to either examine their own metaphors of movement or to effectively understand the mobility of contemporary capital, Maurer (2000) turns to another aquatic analogy: the killifish, whose embryonic formation confounds schemes of unilinear development. Maurer sees the killifish as making manifest Gilles Deleuze and Felix Guattari's poststructuralist rejection of arborescent logics, that is, the assumptions embedded in the imagery of evolutionary trees and genealogy, in favor of "rhizomics." Reconceptualizing financial flows as akin to "amoeboid cells in a killifish embryo, sliding and sloshing, oozing in the much," Maurer thus offers an antidote to both a narrative of the "rising phoenix" of late-twentieth-century global capital and "the image of contemporary capitalism as hard, penetrating, and all-encompassing" (2000, 672). In a parallel move, my analysis of the historical processes whereby forms and narratives of identity in the Julian March have been fashioned and spread "by subterranean stems and flows" (Deleuze and Guattari in Maurer 2000, 687) interrupts, even as it brings into focus the assumptions underlying them, esuli's and rimasti's own grounded (and *underground*-ed) logics of arboresence (and those of their scholarly proponents), in which lie their moral claims of right to territory.

Just as teleological accounts of capitalism and globalization's progressive march forward through time wrongly assume that the objects of these processes are "given in advance of relationships that produce and reproduce them" (Maurer 2000, 690), so does the belief in a fixed but submerged past, waiting to be exhumed, imply both a given history and a preconstituted community that is the subject and bearer of that past. "The problem with this dual assumption is that the constructed past itself is constitutive of the collectivity" (Trouillot 1995, 16). In making this dual assumption an object of analysis, I have instead evidenced how particular collectivities (andati and rimasti, Italians and Slavs, Left and Right) have been continually (re)constituted through practices of remembrance and contests over history which actors phrase in terms of singular and exclusive historical truths. I have thus insisted throughout this book on the ways that the parameters of historical production are both shaped and delimited by power and through time (the emphasis of part 1) at the same time that I recognized the constructivist nature of both memory and history (the focus of part 2), which operate within those "limits of invention." The killifish may occupy a discursive swamp that troubles "fictions of clear origins, orderly progressions, and neat relationships of relatedness" (Maurer 2000, 690)—akin perhaps to the "promiscuous swamp" of ethnic impurity that Magris (1999: 208) envisions for the Adriatic—but they are also limited to three stages of developmental arrest, or diapause, before the commencement of embryonic development.

Whereas Maurer uses his specific research site in the British Virgin Islands as a starting point from which to critically interrogate contemporary theorizing about capital flows, I have drawn on the histories of displacement in Istria in order to urge a rethinking of scholarly conceptualizations of fluid or "deterritorialized" identities (Appadurai 1996), such as those of the hybrid and the borderland mestizo/a. In doing this, I have navigated between broader concerns of contemporary social theory, on the one hand, and the precise questions about the Istrian exodus that motivate a rich body of regional scholarship, on the other. I have thus heeded historian Glenda Sluga's admonition "[I]f, in the post–Cold War, we are to take advantage of the possibilities for renegotiating communities and citizenship, historians [as well as anthropologists] of twentieth-century Europe need to be attentive to how they represent difference, identity, and sovereignty in the histories that they write" (Sluga 2001, 178).

In her own book on the multiple territorial wranglings over Trieste, Sluga neither fully fleshes out the field of contemporary historians working in the Julian March and exploring questions of difference and identity nor locates herself within that terrain. Part of my contribution to both debates in anthropological theory and scholarship dealing specifically with the Julian March, then, lies in the contextualization of how and under what conditions these scholars have put together their accounts and on which narrative configurations their interpretations draw. Furthermore, I have understood history making in its broadest sense, to include firsthand "witnesses to history," memoir writers, and history-producing "artisans of different kinds," attention to whom enables a "richer view of historical production than most theorists acknowledge" (Trouillot 1995, 25). These various artisans of the past, professional and otherwise, form not just the objects of my ethnographic study but also intellectual interlocutors who read, guided, and challenged my thinking and with whom my analysis remains in dialogue (see Kuper 1994; for an outstanding example of a work in dialogue with that of "local" intellectuals, consult Verdery 1991).

Within this charged field of historical interpretation and in keeping with Sluga's call to pay attention to my own practices of representation, I had per force to confront my own ambiguous position as an outsider (with neither kin nor personal ties to any of the parties involved in the multiple contests detailed here), a young woman, a perceived representative of one of Trieste's post–World War II occupiers (or liberators, depending on one's viewpoint), and an anthropologist. In recent years, regional historians such as Valdevit (1997) have underlined the need for specifically *anthropological* understandings of phenomena like the foibe and the exodus. Social historians in the region, such as Nemec (1998), have begun to answer this call, although anthropological analysis here seems to be understood largely as transcribing oral histories or reconstructing *mentalités,* values and norms, as well as in detailing mythical thinking and folk practices associated with the foibe. In contrast, my anthropological take on the exodus has highlighted the historical, political, and institutional conditions in which scholars, esuli, and rimasti fashion and deploy narratives of exile, as well as the different levels and moments (local, regional, national, and international) of reception for those narratives.

In grounding my study in a history of state violence, rather than a putative "folk" past, I have also moved beyond one kind of solidary ethnographic approach (which rests on the dichotomization of high and low, the powerful and the powerless) to probe multiple levels—textual, interpersonal, and moral—of complicity. I have thus considered esuli and rimasti accounts as forms of illicit discourse in the sense that both "scavenge the detritus of decaying politics, probing areas of deceit and deception. By doing so they invoke displaced histories and reveal deformed moralities" (Holmes 1993, 258). Yet I have also traced these discourses' many shifts between "licitude" and "illicitude" as their speakers have renegotiated and reinhabited the moving interstices between states, as well as between center and margin.

Critical awareness of these various forms of complicity in the ethnographic enterprise offers an advantage over the dialogic model advanced by some of anthropology's postmodern critics, who often do not take account of the darkest possibilities of "collaboration" and who leave in place the "faith in being able to probe the 'inside' of a culture" (Marcus 1998, 188). Despite the indeterminacy stressed by postmodern and poststructuralist critiques, anthropologists at heart still usually want to be on the side of the "good guys" (or at least to be able to identify definitively the heroes and the villains). One result of the postmodernist emphasis on the play of voices and texts has been an effort to bring into the text the oppressed/righteous (rephrased as "voices from the margin") through a variety of innovative textual strategies. The most straightforward means is to let these long-suppressed voices speak, the idea being that anthropologists merely provide the "frame" for such stories (see Abu-Lughod 1993 for a representative example).

A tale by Trieste's own Italo Svevo underscores the various perils of this assumption. Svevo tells a story in which his elderly protagonist Zeno buys one of his son's paintings in the hopes of understanding him and drawing nearer to him. Having bought the painting, Zeno frames it.

> The frame, certainly, served as a kind of commentary. I believe that whenever a thing is framed it acquires a new value. A thing only has to be isolated to become something

in its own right—without its frame it is overshadowed by whatever there is around it. Even Alfio's painting became something when framed. I looked at it first with anger; then, as I began to see what he had tried to do, with pleasure; and finally with admiration, when I suddenly discovered that he had actually done something. . . . And studying it, I had the pleasant feeling of actively collaborating with Alfio. I was painting, myself! (1969, 43).

The arrogance of Zeno's statement "I suddenly discovered that he had *actually done* something," which takes Zeno's own vision for that of Alfio, reminds us (as the postmodernist critique did, though postmodernist anthropologists have not always heeded their own warnings) that placing an ethnographic frame inevitably imposes the anthropologist's theoretical framework on informants' already selective, constructed accounts. We can never merely "let voices speak." Nor can ethnographers exempt themselves from the story told.

In place of the dialogic model, Nelson (1999) has advocated a much more sophisticated reworking of the solidarity-rapport model in her account of "body politics" in Guatemala. Though in a very different context from that of Istrians, Nelson's informants used similar metaphors—a "finger in the wound"—to talk about the unresolved traumas created by both state- and guerrilla-sponsored violence, as well as the complicated relationships between the country's Mayan and ladino populations (one figured in part by notions of purity of blood). Making clear her own place in the field as a *gringa* anthropologist initially imbued with romantic notions of solidarity with a victimized population, Nelson admits that such a position rested on troublesome "fables of rapport" between anthropologist and informant.

In lieu of solidarity, then, Nelson offers a "fluidary analysis" cognizant of "the possibility that the motivations of everyone involved are more complex and that perhaps we cannot account for them . . . [we must reject] the demand that other identities be stable and solid so that we can lean on them (as in saving a victim from a victimizer)" (1999, 69). Though similar to and sympathetic with the project of a complicit ethnography I have undertaken, Nelson ultimately cannot fully abandon the solidarity model. She acknowledges, "I don't want to lose the ways in which solidarity is politically productive and the fact that the antagonisms do exist" (ibid., 50). Nelson's ambivalence toward embracing a fully fluidary position, and mine toward fully realizing the full implications of an ethnography of complicity, signal the degree to which contemporary ethnographies still rely on classic methods and modes of exposition—in the case of my book, those of Mediterraneanist and European ethnographies—even as innovations are forged in changing conditions of fieldwork and writing.

It does not prove coincidental that Nelson and I find ourselves struggling with the inadequacies of older models of solidarity most acutely in situations where a modern "body politics" centers on state-sponsored violence and charges of genocide. Unlike in traditional Greek Orthodox practice, where the ritual ex-humation of the body after a fixed period terminates an ongoing conversation with the dead (Danforth 1982), today we are witnessing the ways in which ex-humations—literal and metaphoric—of "dead bodies" often serve as the start-ing points for political contests and identity (re)formation.

In the case of the Julian March, the more recent incarnations of long-standing discourses of purity and hybridity have been phrased in terms of a vocabulary of traumatic memory, genocide, victims, and victimizers. The power and preva-lence of this language reflect a privileging of the "experiential," particularly ex-periences of violence. "Increasingly, memory worth talking about—worth re-membering—is memory of trauma" (Antze and Lambek 1996, xii), whether it is the trauma of individual sexual abuse or of collective war crimes. This atten-tion to trauma links up with contemporary concerns with accountability and justice (ibid., xxv), as well as related issues of "working through" and healing. In the Julian context, as in much of Europe, the theme of accountability remains bound up with politically charged questions about complicity with fascism and communism. As we have seen, the legacies of World War II and the Cold War are increasingly read through a narrative of genocide privileging ethno-national identities over other identifications (like those of class or other political ide-ologies). In an age that has supposedly witnessed the destruction of metanar-ratives (Lyotard 1984), an account of World War II privileging the Holocaust of Jews has become the ultimate reference point and source of moral capital for many political actors, such as the esuli and rimasti, contesting power. The iden-tification with the suffering of the Jews, for instance, figured in media repre-sentations on all sides of the Yugoslav wars (Živković 2000; see also Novick 1999), which in turn contributed the phrase "ethnic cleansing" to the seman-tic arsenal for discussing violence, retribution, and redress.

As noted again and again, various actors in the Julian March state the need to work through the region's recent traumatic history in order to build a new future. Undoubtedly, considerable differences of opinion exist in how to inter-pret that history, as well as in how to best work through it (legal claims? truth telling? apologies? monuments?). This archaeological impulse to disinter or ex-hume the past, however, echoes the widespread imagining of Trieste as a "dead" place in need of revival. This label has multiple significations, denoting the city's economic decline and its division from Istria, its predominantly aging popula-tion, and its obsession with the recent past and its "unacknowledged" dead. Is-tria's ruined landscape of Italian ghost towns mirrors Trieste's funereal aspects.

This necromantic imagery brings to mind Feeley-Harnik's discussion of an-cestor cults and royal tombs in Madagascar. Upon arriving at her field site, a place characterized (like Trieste and Istria) by economic stagnation, the local people demanded, "'Why do you want to live here? This place is dead!'" (1991, 1), words that referred to a "complex domain, including moral and social as well as narrow 'economic' concerns" (ibid., 15). In Trieste the cult of national ancestors centered on the foibe proves one of the key sites at which the city's political past and present are contested and constructed. In nearby Istria, the history of the foibe uneasily informs claims by members of the Italian minority (as well as Istrians in general) to have suffered a violence whose roots lay in the hatred engendered by warfare. Many of Trieste's young people (including some descendants of esuli), as well as its business people, complain that these various forms of nostalgia and the attendant lack of a vision of the future—deemed by some a neurotic or pathological identity (Ara and Magris 1982, 114; Cary 1993, 23)—have "killed" the city and the region. They might agree, then, with Italo Svevo's assessment of old age as consisting of a bleak acknowledgment of this lack of a future: "the amputation, whereby life is deprived of what it never had—the future—makes life simpler, but also so senseless" (1969, 17). Yet as this book has shown, people in the Julian March, such as Eleonora and Gino, with whose understandings of identity I began reject such a negative vision by drawing on the past (in ways that are themselves historically delimited) in order to narrate their present and future.

The futures of Trieste, Istria, the Julian March, and their inhabitants remain hotly contested at this historical juncture and may follow paths that I would not dare to predict. Nonetheless the controversial meeting of Gianfranco Fini and Luciano Violante held in Trieste in 1998 did signal the "nationalization" of a certain vision of the city's future (and past), one that calls for reintegrating Trieste into the Italian mainstream, as well as returning it to its prominence as a Central European entrepôt. Fini, for example, promoted a vision of the city as both a temporal and a spatial bridge between the Mediterranean and eastern spheres, suggesting that the city's awareness of the difficulty of interethnic *convivenza* rendered it a kind of sentinel against discord (Rumiz 1998a). As one commentator noted at the time, initiatives like the Fini-Violante encounter, signal that in Trieste "[t]here is more future and less past. There is less 'periphery' and more 'centrality'" (Weber 1998). Hedging his bets, he added, "Perhaps."

NOTES

Introduction
In the Shadow of the Balkans, on the Shores of the Mediterranean

1. The precise number of refugees, as well as their ethnic composition (Italian, Slovene, or Croat) remains in dispute. The standard statistical work endorsed by Istrian Italian exiles gives a figure of 350,000 ethnic Italians (Colella 1958). More recent Italian works (Donato 1997; Nodari 1997) have argued for a number closer to 200,000. Raoul Pupo (1995) gives an estimate of 300,000 individuals. Antonio Miculian (1990–91) offers a summary of various estimates, as well as a bibliographic synthesis of works on the exodus.

2. When using a place-name for the first time, I give both the Italian and Slavic variants (Croatian or Slovene). I subsequently employ the version appropriate to the particular context; for example, I give the Italian name when discussing Italian claims. I use the English term *Julian March* to designate the broad region that includes territory in present-day Italy, Slovenia and Croatia. All names of informants have been changed in order to respect their privacy; I use only actual names when writing about public figures and/or events in the Istrian Italian community. Unless otherwise indicated, translations from Italian are mine.

3. Among the exiles, I interviewed more men than women (roughly 65 percent of the informants were male). My informants ranged in age from thirty-four to ninety-one, and most of the individuals questioned were in their late fifties or sixties. The class backgrounds of speakers varied, ranging from the daughter of Capodistrian "nobles" to educated, middle-class teachers and pharmacists to the descendants of humble cultivators and fishermen. I spoke with leaders and members of the exile organizations, as well as with individuals who did not participate in the associations.

As with esuli, in Istria I sought to speak with activists and leaders, as well as individuals who did not actively participate in the associational life of the Comunità Italiana. The gender ratio of Istrian interviewees was almost the inverse of that among the exiles: 60 percent were women and 40 percent men. The ages of informants ranged from twenty-one to eighty-six. The occupations of informants ranged from factory workers to bank employees to schoolteachers and principals. Though my interviews were concentrated in the town of Rovigno, I also conducted interviews in a variety of other locales in both Croatian and Slovenian Istria: Abbazia/Opatija, Buie/Buje, Capodistria/Koper, Cittanova/Novigrad, Dignano/Vodnjan, Grisignana/Grožnjan, Isola/Izola, Montona/Motovun, Pola/Pula, Salvore/Savudrija, Bàbici/Babiči, Sissano/Šišan, Umago/Umag, Valle/Bale, and Verteneglio/Brtonigla.

I consulted the documentation of the Comitato Nazionale dell'Istria e Trieste on deposit at the Istituto Regionale per la Cultura Istriana in Trieste, esuli testimonies and newspapers from the period of the exodus at the Istituto Regionale per la Storia della

Liberazione nel Friuli–Venezia Giulia, documents on the "option" for Italian citizenship and exile journals at the Centro di Ricerche Storiche, material related to the "Julian Question" at both the Archivio Centrale dello Stato and the Archivio del Ministero degli Affari Esteri in Rome, and the files concerning the Allied Military Government in Trieste at the U.S. National Archives.

4. Although I had studied Croatian and had a smattering of Slovene before my sojourn in Istria, I was not as fluent in those languages as I was in Italian. It took time to understand the dialects of Italian spoken in the region—divided into two main branches, *istrioto* (derived from Latin variants stemming from the period of ancient Roman colonization) and *istro-veneto* (dating from the epoch of Venetian control and becoming the lingua franca of Istria under the Italian state, gradually supplanting older local forms like *ruvignese*)—let alone begin to comprehend the dialects of Croatian heard in Istria. Widespread bilingualism (Italian-Croat and Italian-Slovene) in Istria nonetheless permitted me to speak with many ethnic Croats and Slovenes in addition to the Italians who constituted my principal informants. Furthermore, the exodus from Istria, whose memory I set out to study, has been largely defined as an Italian phenomenon, despite the significant numbers of Croats and Slovenes who left Istria during the same period.

5. The Venetians never exercised complete dominion, however, over the entire interior of Istria. The area around Pisino/Pazin (the heart of the peninsula) had come under Hapsburg control by 1374. Here, feudal relationships prevailed, in contrast to the autonomous communes that made up Venetian Istria (Darovec 1993, 39–40). For the different situations prevailing in various parts of Venetian Istrian, see Apollonio 1998. Populations speaking Italian variants and identifying themselves with *civiltà italiana* inhabited compact towns and cities along the coast, as well as interior hill towns such as Montona/Motovun. Ethnic Slovenes and Croats tended to live in dispersed rural settlements. Other ethnic groups in Istria included the rumeni (speakers of a Latin-derived language), the Serbs, and the Montenegrins concentrated at Peroj.

6. I thank Donald Carter for this phrasing.

Chapter One
Mapping the Terrain of Memory

1. Trieste's socialist tradition is often associated with its ethnic Slovene minority, though historically there also existed vibrant Italian socialist and communist movements.

2. There has grown up a vast body of work exploring the social meanings attached to monuments. On war memorials of various sorts, see Hartman 1986; Mosse 1990; Perlman 1988; Winter 1995; Yoneyama 1999; Young 1993. There also exists a considerable literature in Italian devoted to the memorializations of the Risorgimento and the two world wars. For a sampling of this, consult Isnenghi 1997; Matta 1996; Tobia 1991, 1998.

3. During the 1920s antifascist organizations such as the League of Yugoslav Refugees from Venezia Giulia came into existence alongside clandestine groups like ORJUNA and TIGR (Trst-Istria-Gorica-Rijeka). In 1930, members of Tigr engaged in acts of arson and dynamiting in Italy. The subsequent repression by the fascist regume resulted in a new emphasis during the 1930s on "cultural resistance." Slovenes in Trieste, for example,

challenged the ban on the public use of Slovene by organizing language courses, theatrical performances, and other activities in their mother tongue. During World War II, Slovene partisans built on this well-developed network of underground activities by establishing secret schools, hospitals, and a daily newspaper (*Primorski Partisanski*).

4. In the not-too-distant past, however, dialects served as a sign of class distinctions. When the Istrian Peninsula came under Italian control in the 1920s, standard Italian became compulsory in all schools, and a general istro-veneto dialect became the lingua franca of daily life. Istro-veneto, much closer to standard Italian, became more desirable socially than extremely localized dialects, such as ruvignese.

5. Ironically, although things Venetian (gondolas, the Piazza San Marco, the Bridge of Sighs) are quintessential Italian symbols, Venetian architecture and art (like the Venetian Empire) were unmistakably hybrid products, celebrated by a generation of observers such as John Ruskin. For a somewhat different case of reading the Venetian past as European (here in contrast to Ottoman Turks, rather than Slavs), see Herzfeld 1991.

6. On *civiltà italiana*, see Gabaccia (2000, 28) and Silverman (1975, 7–9); for the importance of urban values more generally in the Mediterranean, consult Kenny and Kertzer (1983). Dante also figures prominently in the iconography of nationalist groups like the National League, established in Trieste in 1891. The league has issued numerous cards featuring images of the bard, and its members invoke Dante as their protector. Alongside the Lega Nazionale grew up the Società Dante Alighieri, founded in Trieste in 1895.

7. In turn, increasingly assertive Slavic national associations replicated such initiatives. Throughout the Julian March, private organizations, including the Lega Nazionale and the Cyril and Methodius Society, established Italian- and Slavic-language schools, respectively (for a pro-Lega history, see Secco 1995). The first Slovene elementary school in Trieste opened in 1888, and the National House (Narodni Dom) followed a decade later (Apih 1988, 61–79).

8. In her recent analysis of questions of difference and sovereignty in Trieste, historian Glenda Sluga (2001) follows a similar line of interpretation. She tends, however, to see alternatives (particularly socialist ones) to nationalist conceptions as missed opportunities, rather than as bound up with the same conceptual logics. That said, she offers evidence of the inextricable relationship between notions of purity and hybridity and also reveals the limits of the socialist alternative, particularly in relation to gender. In contrast to my account here, Sluga limits her analysis to Trieste, explicitly excluding from her book territories that came under Yugoslav control after May 1945.

9. In the case of Svevo (whose last name was chosen to indicate his Swabian or German identification), it should be noted that the Jewish community that flourished with Trieste's free port status under the Hapsburgs remained predominantly Italian in origin and identification (Dubin 1999, 20–21). Svevo's wife testifies to his unfailing support for the irredentist/nationalist cause, as well as to his solid Triestine identity. "Ettore's long periods abroad had not made him at all cosmopolitan. He always remained proudly Triestian [sic] and Italian" (Svevo 1990, 71).

10. Slovene historians such as Darko Darovec and Nevenka Troha have finally taken up the question of the Istrian exodus, though their interpretations do not significantly depart from an older view of the exodus that attributes the departure of Italians to their anticommunist and anti-Slavic sentiment rather than to a nationalist campaign on the part of the Yugoslav authorities (Verginella 1997).

Chapter Two
Geographies of Violence: Remembering War

1. For many of those who lived through the Holocaust and defined the *shoah* as a peculiarly Jewish tragedy, a strong sense of continuity with the Jews' history of persecution and suffering prevailed. At the most general level, the theme of exile and diaspora offered an overarching framework, as well as providing more precise notions of witness and testimony. Thus, "The Book of Exodus emerges not only as a paradigm for the myths of exile, freedom, and return, but also as a textual prototype for subsequent 'documentary narrative'—the quintessential *sifrut ha'edut* or 'literature of testimony'" (Young 1988, 20).

2. During the twenty years of Italy's participation in the Triple Alliance with Austro-Hungary and Germany, the Italian government attempted to silence the celebration of Oberdan and other martyrs. Del Vecchio et al. (1928), Favetta (n.d.), and Gentille (1928) provide a picture of the commemorations of Oberdan common in the period of Trieste's union with Italy. At that time, such memorializations no longer earned the disapprobation of the state but rather its active approval, reflecting the transformed relationship of the nation's periphery to its center. For a critical account of the creation of the Oberdan myth, see Alexander (1977).

3. For a sampling of the treatment of Oberdan's life as a teleological movement toward his "apotheosis," consult Busetto 1932; Calcaprina 1935; and Coceani et al. 1918.

4. Examples of works in this genre include Almerigogna et al. 1936; Morano 1922; Oliveri 1921; Palin 1931; Piccoli 1935; Pozzi 1934; Stringari 1926.

5. See, for example, Bencovich 1935; Consiglio 1941; Dainielli et al. 1915; De Santi 1919; Dompieri 1941; Dudan and Teja 1991; Federzoni 1941; Foscari 1921; Giglioli 1920; Missoni 1942; Rambaldi 1919; Salvi 1919; Sartorio 1935; Scarpelli 1933; Smiric 1920; and Tamaro 1918.

6. On the Luxardo family, for instance, see Coceani 1968; De Franchi 1992; Luxardo and Pagnacco 1971.

Chapter Three
Constructing the "Trieste Question," Silencing the Exodus

1. Triestine historian Giampaolo Valdevit has noted that accounts of the Trieste question usually treat single aspects and circumscribed phases of the conflict (1987, 7). Although his *La questione di Trieste, 1941–1954: Politica internazionale e contesto locale* considers the complicated interplay between local and international politics, he does not devote much attention to the problem of Istria. His work, treating Trieste as a test case of U.S. intervention abroad, remains firmly within a historiographical tradition that focuses on Trieste as a diplomatic issue. Utilizing material unavailable to a previous generation of scholars, Valdevit's book thus builds on and expands Diego De Castro's monumental *La questione di Trieste: L'azione politica e diplomatica Italiana dal 1943 al 1954* (1981), as well as Jean-Baptiste Duroselle's *Le conflit de Trieste, 1943–1954* (1966) and Bogdan Novak's (1970) *Trieste, 1941–1954: The Ethnic, Political, and Ideological Struggle*. These works, originally published in Italian, French, and English, respectively, represent the "classic" expositions of the Trieste Crisis. Valdevit also contributes to an Italian tra-

dition of works on diplomatic negotiations over the eastern border. For a sampling of works in this tradition, see Cervani 1977; de'Robertis 1981; Pittioni 1989; Rossi 1972; and Valussi 1972.

Of the classic diplomatic histories, De Castro's massive two-volume work admittedly displays the greatest attention to the fate of Italians in Istria. This reflects De Castro's own identity as an exile from Istria, as well as the work's publication two years prior to the diplomatic resolution of the territorial question. The book repeatedly refers to events in the Istrian Peninsula that affected developments in Trieste. The focus of the one-thousand-page book remains, however, on the diplomatic twists and turns in the dispute.

2. Census results and population statistics were particularly contested, each side claiming that the data supported its arguments. For a pro-Yugoslav take, see the *Cadastre National de l'Istrie* (Institut Adriatique 1946). Perselli (1993) offers a detailed study of censuses between 1850 and 1936.

3. Events in the Julian March also reflected, even as they differed in some key respects, a more specific Anglo-American approach to Italy. For diverse perspectives on the Allied (and particularly the American) role in Italy and the Allied Military Government, see Ellwood 1985; Faenza and Fini 1976; Ginsborg 1990; Harper 1986; Harris 1957; and Quintero 1989.

4. The 1947 Italo-Yugoslav Peace Treaty definitively awarded much of Istria to Yugoslavia. Trieste and its surroundings, however, were to become an international territory under the protection of the newly formed United Nations. It was envisioned that a permanent governor for the FTT answerable to the UN Security Council would be appointed after a period of transitional military administration (Novak 1970, 273). Not surprisingly, the Great Powers (and in particular the United States and the USSR) could not agree on a candidate for governor, and thus the FTT remained stillborn.

5. As of July 1, 1947, the International Refugee Organization assumed responsibility from the United Nations Refugee and Relief Administration (UNRRA) for certain refugees located in Italy; on UNRRA in Italy, consult Woodbridge 1950a, 257–94; 1950b, 422–23. The Italian government pledged its assistance in a variety of sectors, including assuming the expenses for the transport of refugees and their property (see *Accordo fra il Governo Italiano ed il comitato preparatorio per l'organizzazione Internazionale dei Profughi* 1947). IRO ceased operation in Italy in 1950 and the UN High Commission on Refugees assumed some of its responsibilities.

6. See memos VG/AMG/240/6 of 1/16/47, VG/PL/D/32 of 3/12/47, VG/PL/D/35 of 3/13/47, and AHQ/TRI/S/441 of 3/24/47, U.S. National Archives.

7. To prevent a much-feared victory by the Italian Communist Party in the Italian elections of 1948, the Western powers backed the Christian Democrats' demands for Trieste. On March 18, 1948, the U.S., Great Britain, and France issued the "Tripartite Proposal," suggesting that the FTT be awarded to Italy (Novak 1970, 281).

Chapter Four
Revisiting the History of World War II

1. During the war, some members of the CLN of both Trieste and Istria worked with Nazi collaborators such as Bruno Coceani in the belief that the *slavo-comunisti* repre-

sented a greater threat; CLN members such as Carlo Schiffrer, who positioned themselves as heirs to the democratic Mazzinian tradition, instead rejected any such collaboration (Sluga 2001, 81). Members of both groups nonetheless disagreed with the umbrella Italian resistance organization, the Comitato di Liberazione Nazionale di Alta Italia
(CLNAI), refusing to work together with the Slovene Front for the Liberation of the
Slovene Nation (OF).

2. On changes in the Italian political scene, consult Gilbert 1995; Gundle and Parker
1996; Haycraft 1987; Katz and Ignazi 1996; McCarthy 1995; and Mershon and Pasquino
1994.

3. Slovene historiographers of the Titoist period showed considerable continuity with
their predecessors, focusing on the national history of the Slovenes. After 1945, new dimensions of this history—including industrialization, working-class movements, the
formation of a Slovene bourgeoisie, and peasant revolts—received emphasis (Verginella
1999, 14). Nonetheless, Slovene historiography followed its own trajectory, separate
from that devoted to the experiences of Serbs and Croats. In the 1980s and especially
after 1991, Slovene historians began to take up long-neglected questions of World War
II collaborators (Vodopivec 1996a, 128–29, 136–37; 1996b, 267–68); much of the
focus has been on the *domobranci* (home guard), rather than other victims such as the
esuli.

4. On the numbers game, see Boban 1990, 1992; Djilas 1992; Hayden 1994, 1996;
and Kočović 1985.

5. This historiographical tradition includes firsthand accounts (Pesce 1972), books
on the antifascist press (Dal Pont, Leoneth, and Massara 1964; Tarizzo 1969), and detailed studies of specific partisan brigades (Gestro 1982). Many of the works focus on
the local contexts in which the Resistance was waged (see, for instance, Calamandrei
1994). For different takes on the martyrology of Venezia Giulia in the Resistance, see
Bartoli 1948; Lojk 1989; Ventura 1963.

6. Quazza's 1976 study of the "civil war" in the North offered an important precedent
for the debates that emerged in the following decade, as did literary treatments of the
war by novelists such as Calvino and Pavese (Morgan 1999).

7. The first book on Salò, Perticone's *La Repubblica di Salò*, came out in 1946. A long
period with relatively little serious historiographical work followed, leaving the field to
nostalgic memoirs (for a review of this literature, see Bolla 1982, 23–24). The 1970s
saw the beginnings of a more sustained historiographical interest. The steady stream of
publications over the last decade includes both memoirs and historical analyses. These
works include Artieri 1995; Bertoldi 1985, 1994, 1995; Bonvicini 1988; Borsani 1995;
Cervi 1995; Garibaldi 1995; Innocenti 1996; Lazzero 1982, 1983, 1984, 1994; Petacco
1987, 1995; Speroni 1994; and Venè 1989.

8. On the Italian rescue campaign in southern France, see Bierman 1989; Leboucher
1969; and Steinberg 1990. Works exploring the efforts to save Jews within Italy include
Leone 1983; Ramati 1978; and Sorani 1983. Recent historical research has also uncovered the lesser-known history of Allied prisoners of war, many of whom escaped during
the collapse of the army and government in September 1943 and found refuge with Italian peasant families (Absalom 1995).

9. Such toilet stall vandalism appears to have been common under fascism. In her
book on memories of fascism, Passerini notes that the regime viewed lavatories as "seed-
beds of crime" (1987, 95). Italian fascism had a deeply scatological aspect, with the ad-

ministration of castor oil to opponents being one of the fascist squads' favorite punishments; thus it is not surprising that some opposition to the regime also centered around bodily functions. In a quite different context, Aretxaga (1997) and Feldman (1991) detail the use of bodies and bodily waste in the "dirty" protests that male and female IRA prisoners waged in northern Ireland.

10. As in *Kaputt,* Curzio Malaparte's account of the fascist and Nazi war front, "A familiar strategy of the writer, however, to reinforce his identity as a mere observer is to avoid any sense of personal responsibility by accusing others" (Burdett 1999, 113).

Chapter Five
The Politics of Submersion: The Foibe

1. Article 2 of the 1948 Genocide Convention stipulates that genocide encompasses a range of acts "committed with intent to destroy, in whole or in part, a national, ethnical, racial or religious group" (in Andreopoulos 1994, 230).

2. The 1996 resolution of the Italo-Slovene negotiations, with Italy voting in favor of Slovenia's entrance into the EU, nonetheless reveals the fragility of the exiles' bargaining power. With the redefinition of Italian and U.S. state interests, efforts to link Slovenian membership in the EU with a resolution of esuli claims for compensation were explicitly overruled by Italian state officials. This followed out of the electoral defeat of the exiles' political sponsors in the Berlusconi government in April 1995. Though a coalition led by Berlusconi has returned to power, as of this writing Berlusconi has affirmed his support for Slovenia's entrance into the EU as long as it accompanies a satisfactory resolution of the exiles' property issue.

3. Pahor founded Edinost (Unity) as a protest movement in 1990. The name is intended to provoke, referring as it does to a Slovene nationalist group founded in 1875. This strategy finds little sympathy among many of the Slovenes who are leaders in the official minority associations.

4. Exiles' estimates of *infoibati* range anywhere from 5,000 to 50,000 reflecting a numbers game that became intensely politicized in Trieste early on and around which the most bitter debates have centered (Pupo 1997: 36; Spazzali 1997: 98–99; Valdevit 1997: 8). Slovene researcher Pavel Stranj has suggested a figure closer to 4,000 (1992: 89), one echoed in the recent estimates of 4,000–5,000 given by Raoul Pupo (1997: 37).

5. In 1965 the Italian goverment deemed the Risiera a national monument as the result of lobbying by Slovenes and the Istituto Regionale per la Storia del Movimento di Liberazione (see Sluga 1996, 403). The camp was then transformed into a didactic museum. Historian Glenda Sluga has written of the debates about the Risiera, and in particular the trials of war criminals, as having failed "to deal with the role of Italian Fascist forces and Fascist sympathizers in the camp's operation, the anti-Slavism (and anti-Communism) evidenced in its proceedings" (ibid., 408). The trials, for example, found individuals not guilty of crimes against "noninnocent victims," including Yugoslav partisans viewed as instruments of a "belligerent state" (ibid., 407). Sluga thus sees the Risiera as having been understood primarily in terms of a metanarrative about Italian civiltà threatened by barbaric Slavs. This may be true at the local level. From the perspective of the early 2000s, and judging by subsequent historiographical accounts, the museum established at the monument, and the ceremonies held there, however, the

Risiera appears to have been successfully inserted into a broader national narrative about the Holocaust and the Resistance.

6. Only in the late 1950s did the English term *holocaust,* redolent with images of sacrifice, come to be associated almost exclusively with the destruction of European Jewry. James Young (1988) notes that in contrast to other terms locating this destruction in a long narrative of Jewish persecution, *holocaust* conveyed a sense of the events in World War II as unprecedented and unique. At the same time, however, *shoah* and *churban* constructed the events in uniquely Jewish ways, in contrast to the more generalized term *holocaust.* The foibe possess their own terminology, the speleological term foibe acquiring a gruesome connotation in the Italian context. Victims are referred to as *infoibati,* perpetrators as *infoibatori* (Rocchi 1990, 16).

7. Together with irredentist narratives, a host of folk religious practices and beliefs remembering Christian persecution also informed such understandings (Radole 1997, 74).

8. Ronald Reagan's 1985 joint visit to the Bitburg cemetery and to Dachau sparked a series of debates over the meanings of "forgiveness" and the "ownership" of Holocaust victimhood in both Western Europe and the United States (Hartman 1986). Reagan's initial plan had been to remember ordinary German soldiers buried at Bitburg as "victims" of the Nazi regime together with the Jews. The already controversial move became a public relations nightmare when it was revealed that Bitburg also contained the graves of SS men. Saul Friedländer maintains: "Bitburg came to symbolize all the dilemmas of forgetting and remembering, for Germany and its victims, for the victorious allies and the vanquished enemy, for those who lived through the war and those born after 1945: the second generation and, by now, the third" (1986, 27).

9. Scholarly accounts of the foibe that refute or complicate the "ethnic cleansing" thesis fall into two general categories. The first views the foibe as the explosive expression of pent-up hatreds after twenty years of fascism; this violence is attributed to the chaos and brutality engendered by war, as well as to personal vendettas. This interpretation is often, though not always, used to minimize (by "justifying" in a certain sense) the foibe as a spontaneous and brief response to systematic and prolonged (Italian) state-sponsored violence.

Another range of opinions views the foibe as a method of installing a new regime. This interpretation focuses on the executions in the foibe and associated deportations from Trieste and Gorizia as a means of eliminating the personnel of the Italian state and any potential opposition to the new Titoist regime. Scant documentation exists on the executions in the foibe in Istria in 1943, which in some cases appear to have a more "spontaneous" nature than the violence carried out in 1945 (Pupo 1997, 43). Valdevit contends that, in contrast, in 1945 the foibe represented neither "ethnic cleansing" nor "popular furor" but rather a programmatic effort to eliminate all that represented the Italian state. The apparent indiscriminateness of such violence and deportations (which lends itself to the reading of an ethnic targeting of Italians), claims Valdevit, in fact was designed to send a chilling message to the Italians of Venezia Giulia that they must assume a subaltern position in the new "Seventh Republic" of Yugoslavia (Valdevit 1997).

Pupo (1997) echoes this view, suggesting that the immediate postwar violence in the Julian March resembled that occurring elsewhere in Yugoslavia (with the wholesale elimination of the regime's opponents) more than the "popular justice" common to Emilia Romagna (the Italian "triangle of death"). In his view, the Yugoslavs carried out a "preventive epuration" (*epurazione preventativa*) designed to disarm its opposition; for this reason, CLN activists were targeted much more than officials of the RSI, who had already lost legitimacy (ibid., 47–48). Pupo agrees with Valdevit that the Yugoslav policy reflected a precise strategy combined with indiscriminate repression aimed at inculcating fear and insecurity in the local population.

10. Questions of purity—central to the ethnic interpretations privileged today—did enter more obliquely into older understandings of the war as entailing a clash of political ideologies (Left versus Right). On the one hand, fascism and Nazism were cast by their enemies as ideologies obsessed with nationalist purity, in contrast to the internationalist solidarity and "cosmopolitanism" of communism. On the other hand, narratives of Italian antifascism frequently portrayed the fascist as a cosmopolite (urban, "foreign," sexually deviant) and the true antifascist as a pure or autochthonous Italian coming from the people (whether a peasant or of the working class) (Ben-Ghiat 1999, 84, 96; Ward 1999, 67).

11. For a sampling of works exploring the nexus between gender and nationalism in Europe and the Mediterranean, consult Aretxaga 1997; Borneman 1998; Delaney 1991; Linke 1999; and Mosse 1985.

12. On April 23, 2000, the Italian newspaper *Il Manifesto* published an article discussing the Central Register of War Criminals and Security Suspects, compiled by the British and the United Nations at the end of World War II, which had more than one thousand suspected Italian war criminals (few of whom ever faced trial). Italo Sauro, thought to be one of the sons of Nazario Sauro and a captain of the Italian navy at Bickovo in 1942, ranks among these presumed criminals.

13. INPS (Istituto Nazionale per la Providenza Sociale), the Italian pension agency, estimates that six hundred thousand conationals abroad receive such pensions. Of these, 42 percent are paid out to Italians resident in other countries of the European Union, 18.9 percent in Switzerland, 11.6 percent in Argentina, 7.1 percent in Canada, 5.7 percent in Australia, and only 5.3 percent in the territories of former Yugoslavia (Spirito 1996c).

Chapter Six
Narrating Exodus: The Shapes of Memory

1. This custom is common among the displaced more generally; see Brown 2002 and Loizos 1981, 144–45.

2. After a visit to a grave, Istrians typically lit candles in their homes for the recently deceased. Leaving their homes unlocked that evening, the families of victims would make water available for the thirsty spirits believed to walk on the earth that night. In some locales, the bells of death tolled throughout the night (Radole 1997, 156–57). Mortuary practices included a nightlong vigil by the deceased's family (still observed by some Italians in Istria, as I found in Rovigno) and a funeral in which at least one member of each family in the community participated.

3. Writing of the Cuban exile shrine of Ermita de la Caridad in Miami, Tweed notes of the faithful, "They come as a dispersed nation to construct collective identity before a shared national symbol" (1997, 79).

4. For a useful introduction to the complicated relationship between the socialist

regime and the various churches of Yugoslavia, consult Alexander 1979. The partisan movement during the war included both Catholic and Orthodox priests, who wore partisan uniforms and caps with a cross on top of the communist red star (Alexander 1979, 50), but tensions soon developed at war's end as the state sought to control lower clergy through state-sponsored priests' associations. Well into the 1950s, the regime had a difficult relationship with the Catholic Church, many of whose high personnel (such as Archbishop Stepinac) were tried for wartime complicity with the Ustaša in the forced conversions and massacres of Orthodox Serbs.

In Istria the situation was complicated by the overall support shown by lower Slavic clergy for the Yugoslav resistance movement and the fact that higher officials were typically Italian. The territorial struggle between Yugoslavia and Italy over the Julian March resulted in frequent assaults on priests, as well as accusations of espionage and conspiratorial activities with "imperialists"—the Vatican, Italy, the United States, and after 1948 the USSR (ibid., 133–36). The nationalization of properties also crippled the church's traditional financial base. In the 1960s relations between Yugoslavia and the Holy See were regularized at a time when Catholicism increasingly came to be seen as part of a Croatian identity and unity. The expressions of Croatian nationalism that came to the fore and were condemned in 1971 led to new criticisms of the Catholic Church (ibid., 291). The successor states of Croatia and Slovenia, which emerged in the 1990s, have embraced Catholicism as a key element of national identity.

Chapter Seven
Remaking Memory: The View from Istria

1. The leadership had launched an appeal that year, stating as its purpose: "The Unione degli Italiani must mobilize all Italian antifascists in Istria in the fight against the occupier, enemy of our liberty and or our rights. . . . The Unione will work to resolve political, cultural, economic and social problems and will be the political platform for the Italian representatives of the organs of the Popular Power" (in Borme 1995, 64–65). Committees and an assembly were formed the following year as part of the effort to mobilize Italians.

Il Nostro Giornale, a clandestine newspaper, appeared in 1944 and contained the first articles in which Italians were defined as a minority in Istria, as well as within the broader "brotherly community of the peoples of Yugoslavia" (in Debeljuh 1994, 126).That year La Voce del Popolo also appeared and remains to this day the paper of the Italian minority in Istria, distributed as a supplement to the Istrian version of the Triestine paper, Il Piccolo. The journal Fratellanza (Brotherhood) appeared in 1948. In 1952, Edit (the minority publishing house) was established at Fiume. The cultural and news magazine Panorama and the children's journal Pioniere also began publication in Yugoslavia that year. The minority also enjoyed Italian-language radio and TV programming. Radio Capodistria began broadcasting in Italian in 1949, and in 1971 TeleCapodistria came into being, continuing today to offer shows on topics of local cultural, historical, and political interest. In Croatia, Radio-Fiume and Radio-Pola have also offered some Italian-language programming since 1945 and 1968, respectively (Milani-Kruljac 1990, 24–25).

2. The center hosts a considerable library (more than eighty thousand volumes at this date) devoted to local and regional history, with an emphasis on the Italian experience

in Istria, and has various full- and part-time researchers (members of the Italian minority) attached to it. The center also puts out a series of books and volumes, including the *Atti, Collana degli Atti, Fonti, Quaderni,* and *Acta Historica Nova* (Milani-Kruljac 1990, 27).

3. In his oral history of the Spanish anarchists of Casas Viejas, Jerome Mintz discusses similar tensions between revolutionary ideals on one hand and traditional understandings of gender, sexuality, and family forms on the other (1982, 91–99).

4. In contrast, the DDI-IDS has had virtually no success in the small part of Istrian territory under Slovene sovereignty, whose inhabitants seek to maintain a healthy distance from the problems of Croatian Istria. In 1996 the DDI-IDS disappeared altogether from the Slovene electoral lists, replaced by the Littoral League. Given this, my discussion here will focus almost exclusively on the Croatian context.

Chapter Eight
Balkan Shadows, Balkan Mirrors: Paradoxes of "Authentic Hybridity"

1. Triestine lawyer and writer Giorgio Bevilacqua offers an extreme example of the desire to protect the boundaries of Italian national identity from the polluting threat of the Slovene "race." He writes that "the Slavic peoples constitute an immense tide [*marea*] that, permeated by a constant ferment, is marching toward the west" (1991, 11).

2. Evidencing the historical tension between roots and routes, Gilroy (1996) has traced a dialectic between visions of cultural authenticity and purity rooted in a (mythical) African past and the syncretic processes of creolization and hybridity that define a Black Atlantic space crisscrossed by movements of peoples, ships, ideas, and cultural forms. Although Gilroy stresses hybridity, or *métissage,* as an alternative to the privileging of an African or black essence, his work implicitly reveals the complex and interpenetrated nature of notions of mixture and purity.

3. Although the effects of the wars in Croatia and Bosnia were felt in Istria in economic terms (as well as in the presence of refugees), fortunately the peninsula was spared physical violence. Perhaps because of this and despite the plethora of books published in the last decade about the former Yugoslavia, Istria and its history have remained virtually unknown to the English-speaking world (see Bianchini and Shoup 1995 and Thompson 1992 for notable exceptions). A much earlier account of postwar reduction of interethnic tensions in the Julian Region (Gross 1978) instead emphasized the necessary forgetting of genocide and massacres. As far as I know, Moro (1988) offers the only published scholarly work in English dedicated specifically to the topic of the Istrian exodus.

4. For various perspectives on the construction of the Balkans, see Bracewell 1994; Hayden 1996; Herzfeld 1987 and 1997; Razsa and Lindstrom 2001; Todorova 1994 and 1997; and Wolff 1994. In regard to representations of both the Balkans and the Mediterranean within Croatia, there are useful discussions in Čapo Žmegač 1999; Ravnik 1999; and Rihtman-Auguštin 1999. Baskar (1999) offers an interesting reading of Istrian exile understandings of Mediterranean identities versus Balkan ones.

5. See Bauman (1987) and Elias (1978) on the notion of the "civilizing process," cultivation becoming synonymous with (good) manners. Young describes the symbolic cooptation of the "cultivating" metaphor by urbanites: "The city people became the cultivated ones, and the hunters defined by their lack of culture" (1995, 31).

286 NOTES TO CHAPTER EIGHT

6. For a sampling of this theoretical conversation, see Gupta and Ferguson 1997a; Kearney 1991; and Marcus 1998.

7. The developing critique of the literature celebrating the "consciousness of the borderlands" has assumed different directions. Some critics wonder about the limits of hybridity and the concept's precise linkages to a politics of antiracism (Werbner 1997). Another line of analysis charges that hybridity has become yet another commodity in the global market of "difference," particularly in the context of phenomena such as world music and world music festivals (Hutnyk 1997; Werbner 1997). Some analysts, such as van der Veer (1997), instead single out for criticism those who, like Homi Bhabha, both privilege textuality and proclaim the novelty of hybridity. This underlines the need for more historicized conceptualizations of hybridity and diaspora (see also Clifford 1994), as well as borderlands, a task that scholars such as Papastergiadis (1997) and Young (1995) have begun to undertake.

8. Offering one of the most articulate defenses of Anzaldúa against the charges of essentialism, Norma Alarcón argues for a view of "Anzaldúa's work as doubly located on the 'border of meaning'" (1994, 130) and suggests that Anzaldúa "acknowledges the impossibility of regaining a pure origin" (ibid., 131). In Alarcón's estimation, the mestiza consciousness proves tolerant of paradox and breaks down unitary subject positions, suggesting instead a "subject in process." Although Alarcón contends that this subject in process "cannot be unified without double binds and contradications" (ibid.), she never addresses the fact that an essentialist subject position may prove capable of embracing double binds and contradictions. Indeed, this may be a largely overlooked reason for the resilience of essentializing identities, which are as much in a process of becoming as of being.

GLOSSARY

andati — Those who leave/left.

beni abbandonati — Lost properties; in the Istrian context this term refers to homes and land left behind by exiles and ongoing debates about restitution/compensation.

Bitinada — A form of acoustic singing peculiar to Rovigno/Rovinj in Croatian Istria.

bravo italiano/brava gente — The notion of Italians as fundamentally humane and good people, usually in contrast to Nazis (the bad Germans).

Carso/Karst — The rocky plateau overlooking the city of Trieste.

civiltà — Civilization; in the Venetian and Italian contexts, it is typically associated with urban(e) values and, in the form of *civiltà italiana,* a presumed "genius" associated with Italian art and culture and yet communicable through a "civilizing process."

convivenza — Living together; in Istria, it is used to signify ethnic tolerance and cohabitation.

dopo esodo — The period after the exodus, often applied to the generation of exiles' children raised in Italy.

esodo — Exodus; in the Istrian context, the term *l'esodo istriano* refers to the mass migration of ethnic Italians from the Istrian Peninsula between 1943 and 1955.

esuli — Exiles.

foibe — Pits in the karstic terrain around Trieste and Istria in which communist partisans executed soldiers and civilians between 1943 and 1945.

infoibamento — Death by execution in a foibe, or karstic pit.

infoibato/i — Victim(s) executed by being thrown into foibe.

infoibatori — Those who carried out executions in the foibe.

irredentism — A political movement or ideology desiring the territorial joining (or redemption) of areas believed to belong to a nation; from the term *irredenta,* meaning unredeemed.

istrianità — Istrian-ness.

italianità — Italian-ness; often associated but not synonymous with Italian nationalist claims.

madrepatria/patria — Homeland, nation.

missini — Neofascists; derived from the name of the Italian neofascist party, Movimento Sociale Italiano; today it is often used to refer to hard-core supporters who reject the more centrist position of the Alleanza Nazionale party.

profughi — Refugees.

radici — Roots.

razza — Race, as understood in terms of modern biology and "scientific racism."

rimasti — Those who stayed, those who remain.

rovignese/i — Person(s) from Rovigno/Rovinj, Istria.

scomparsi — The "disappeared."

slavo-comunista — A derogatory term assuming a natural affinity between Slavic ethnicity and communist beliefs.

stirpe — Stock or lineage.

Tangentopoli — A massive corruption scandal centered on Milan, involving the worlds of both business and government.

BIBLIOGRAPHY

Books and Scholarly Journals

Abou-El-Haj, Barbara. 1994. *The Medieval Cult of Saints: Formations and Transformations.* Cambridge: Cambridge University Press.

Abram, Mario. 1984. *Hrvoji-Kućibreg: Un itinerario per monumenti e lapidi della lotta di liberazione nazionale, 1944–1984.* Rijeka: Tipograf.

Absalom, Roger. 1995. "Hiding History: The Allies, the Resistance, and the Others in Occupied Italy, 1943–1945." *The Historical Journal* 38 (1): 111–31.

Abu-Lughod, Lila. 1993. *Writing Women's Worlds: Bedouin Stories.* Berkeley: University of California Press.

Adelman, Howard. 1998. "The Aesthetics of Genocide." Paper presented at conference entitled "Slaughter of the Innocents: Understanding Political Killing, Including Limited Terror but Especially Large-Scale Killing and Genocide." Stanford University, March 1998.

Adriacus. 1919. *From Trieste to Valona: The Adriatic Problem and Italy's Aspirations.* Milan: Alfieri and Lacroix.

Alarcón, Norma. 1994. "Conjugating Subjects: The Heteroglossia of Essence and Resistance." In *An Other Tongue: Nation and Ethnicity in the Linguistic Borderlands,* ed. Alfred Arteaga, pp. 125–38. Durham: Duke University Press.

Alberti, Mario, et al. 1917. *Italy's Great War and Her National Aspirations.* Milan: Alfieri and Lacroix.

Alexander, Alfred. 1977. *The Hanging of Wilhelm Oberdank.* London: London Magazine Editions.

Alexander, Stella. 1979. *Church and State in Yugoslavia since 1945.* Cambridge: Cambridge University Press.

Alexich, Nicolò. 1919. *Fiat iustitia!* Rome: Tip. Sociale Polizzi–Valentini.

Allied Military Government (Trieste). 1947a. *Birth of a Free Territory.* Trieste: Public Relations BETFOR.

———. 1947b. "Political Demonstrations." U.S. National Archives, Box 71 (Misc. 122.71).

———. 1947c. *A Political History of Zone A of Venezia Giulia under Allied Military Government (12 June 1945 to 10 February 1947).* U.S. National Archives, Box 71 (Misc. 122.72).

———. 1947d. Untitled report on Pola. U.S. National Archives, Box 71 (Misc. 122.73).

———. 1950. "Trieste Handbook." U.S. National Archives, Box 80 (RG 331, 19).

Almerigogna, Piero, et al. [1916] 1936. *Nazario Sauro e l'Istria.* Trieste: Studio Col.

Anderson, Benedict. 1995. *Imagined Communities.* London: Verso.

Andreopoulos, George J., ed. 1994. *Genocide: Conceptual and Historical Dimensions.* Philadelphia: University of Pennsylvania Press.

Angeli, Antonio. n.d. *Marine istriane: Versi.* Trieste: Arti Grafiche Villaggio del Fanciullo.

Anonimo Giuliano. 1986. *Radici.* Trieste: Italo Svevo.

Anonymous. 1915. *Il diritto d'Italia su Trieste e l'Istria: Documenti.* Milan: Fratelli Bocca Ed.
————. 1943. *Dalla fossa di Katyn alle 'foibe' istriane.* Edizioni Erre 4.
Antze, Paul, and Michael Lambek, eds. 1996. *Tense Past: Cultural Essays in Trauma and Memory.* New York: Routledge.
Anzaldúa, Gloria. 1987. *Borderlands/La Frontera: The New Mestiza.* San Francisco: Aunt Lute.
Anzellotti, Fulvio. 1990. *Zara, addio.* Gorizia: Editrice Goriziana.
Apih, Elio. 1988. *Trieste.* Bari: Editori Laterzi.
Apollonio, Almerigo. 1998. *L'Istria veneta.* Gorizia: Libreria Editrice Goriziana (Istituto Regionale per la Cultura Istriana).
Appadurai, Arjun. 1996. *Modernity at Large: Cultural Dimensions of Globalization.* Minneapolis: University of Minnesota Press.
Ara, Angelo. 1990. *"Mitteleuropa: Recovering a Historical Identity."* In *Comuni radici storiche e socio-culturali nell'area centro-europea: Atti del forum dei intellettuali dei paesi della Pentagonale,* pp. 157–58. Rome: Presidenza del Consiglio dei Ministri, Dipartimento per l'informazione e l'Editoria.
Ara, Angelo, and Claudio Magris. 1982. *Trieste: Un'identità di frontiera.* Turin: Giulio Einaudi.
Aretxaga, Begoña. 1997. *Shattering Silence: Women, Nationalism, and Political Subjectivity in Northern Ireland.* Princeton: Princeton University Press.
Artieri, Giovanni. 1995. *Le guerre dimenticate di Mussolini.* Milan: Arnoldo Mondadori.
Ash, Timothy Garton. 1990. *The Magic Lantern.* New York: Random House.
Bahloul, Joëlle. 1996. *The Architecture of Memory: A Jewish-Muslim Household in Colonial Algeria, 1937–1962.* Translated by Catherine du Peloux Ménagé. Cambridge: Cambridge University Press.
Baily, Samuel. 1990. "Cross-Cultural Comparison and the Writing of Migration History: Some Thoughts on How to Study Italians in the New World." In *Immigration Reconsidered: History, Sociology, and Politics,* ed. Virginia Yans-McLaughlin, pp. 241–53. New York: Oxford University Press.
Bakhtin, M. M. 1981. *The Dialogic Imagination: Four Essays by M. M. Bakhtin.* Edited by Michael Holquist. Translated by C. Emerson and M. Holquist. Austin: University of Texas Press.
Bakić-Hayden, Milica. 1995. "Nesting Orientalisms: The Case of Former Yugoslavia. *Slavic Review* 54 (4): 917–31.
Bakić-Hayden, Milica, and Robert Hayden. 1992. "Orientalist Variations on the Theme 'Balkans': Symbolic Geography in Recent Yugoslav Cultural Politics." *Slavic Review* 51 (1): 1–15.
Baldi, G. 1914. *Guglielmo Oberdan: Il Martire di Trieste.* Florence: Casa Ed. Nerbini.
Ballinger, Pamela. 1994. "Italian Pentecost: The Development of Nationalist Ritual at Fiume." In *Proceedings of the International Congress on Nationalism in Europe, Past and Present,* ed. Justo G. Beramendi, Ramón Máiz, and Xosé M. Núñez, pp. 623–49. Santiago: University of Santiago Press.
Bambara, Gino. 1994. *Zara: Uno zaratino racconta la sua città.* Brescia: Vannini Editrice.
Banac, Ivo. 1988. *With Stalin against Tito: Cominformist Splits in Yugoslav Communism.* Ithaca: Cornell University Press.
————. 1992. "Historiography of the Countries of Eastern Europe: Yugoslavia." *American Historical Review* 97 (4): 1084–1104.

Bandiera, M., and E. Bonetti. 1946. *Venezia Giulia and the Problem of the Italian Eastern Boundary.* Trieste: Typography Lithography Moderna.

Banfield, E. C. 1958. *The Moral Basis of a Backward Society.* New York: Free Press.

BAR. [1915?]. *Guglielmo Oberdan.* Venice: Stab. G. Scarbellin.

Barbiera, Raffaello. 1918. *Ricordi delle terre dolorose.* Milan: Fratelli Treves.

Baroni, Francesco. 1939. *Memorie di un internato triestino: Storia di martiri e d'ignorati eroi nella Grande Guerra, 1915–1918.* Milan: Società Anonima Editrice Dante Aligheri.

Bartoli, Gianni. 1948. *Paolo Reti: Martire della Resistenza 7 Aprile 1945.* Trieste: La Editoriale Libraria.

———. 1960. "Trieste d'Oggi. 'Afflizioni e speranze.' Conferenza tenuta all'Ateneo di Venezia il 15 maggio 1960 nella celebrazione annuale della giornata della società nazionale 'Dante Alighieri.'" n.p.

Baskar, Bojan. 1999. "Made in Trieste. Geopolitical Fears of an Istrianist Discourse on the Mediterranean." *Croatian Journal of Ethnology and Folklore Research* 36 (1): 121–34.

Bauman, Zygmunt. 1987. *Legislators and Interpreters.* Ithaca: Cornell University Press.

Bebler, Anton, ed. 1978. *Naši Spanči.* Ljubljana: Gorenki tisk Kranj.

Behar, Ruth. 1998. *Bridges to Cuba/Puentes a Cuba.* Ann Arbor: University of Michigan Press.

Bencovich, Anna. 1935. *Adriatico in fiamme: La tragedia dell'italianità in Dalmazia.* Milan: Casa Editrice "Oltre Mare."

Ben-Ghiat, Ruth. 1999. "Liberation: Italian Cinema and the Fascist Past, 1945–50." In *Italian Fascism: History, Memory, and Representation,* ed. R.J.B. Bosworth and Patrizia Dogliani, pp. 83–101. New York: St. Martin's Press.

Benson, Susan. 2000. "Inscriptions of the Self: Reflections on Tattooing and Piercing in Contemporary Euro-America." In *Written on the Body,* ed. Jane Caplan, pp. 234–54. Princeton: Princeton University Press.

Benussi, Andrea. 1951. *Ricordi di un combattente istriano.* Zagreb: Državno Izdavačko Poduzeće hrvatske (Biblioteca Italiana 2).

Bertoldi, Silvio. 1985. *Vincitori e Vinti.* Milan: Bompiani.

———. 1994. *Camicia Nera.* Milan: Rizzoli.

———. 1995. *Soldati a Salò.* Milan: Rizzoli.

Bevilacqua, Giorgio. 1991. *Verità scomode.* Trieste: Edizioni Lint.

Bianchini, Stefano, and Paul Shoup, eds. 1995. *The Yugoslav War, Europe, and the Balkans: How to Achieve Security?* Ravenna: Longo Editore.

Biber, Dusan. 1985. "La politica anglo-americana sul problema del confine Italo-Jugoslavo durante la Seconda Guerra Mondiale." In *Trst 1945,* pp. 29–44. Trieste: Narodna in studijska knjisnica.

Bidussa, David. 1994. *Il mito del bravo Italiano.* Milan: Il Saggiatore.

Bierman, John. 1989. "How Italy Protected the Jews in the Occupied South of France, 1942–1943." In *The Italian Refuge: Rescue of Jews During the Holocaust,* ed. Ivo Herzer, Klaus Voight, and James Burgwyn, pp. 218–30. Washington, D.C.: Catholic University of America Press.

Bisharat, George. 1997. "Exile to Compatriot: Transformations in the Social Identity of Palestinian Refugees in the West Bank." In *Culture, Power, Place,* ed. Akhil Gupta and James Ferguson, pp. 203–33. Durham: Duke University Press.

Blažević, Zrinka. 2000. "'Miserrima facies Croatiae': Perception of the Natural Environment of the Triple Border in the Poem 'Plorantis Croatiae saeculae duo' by Pavao Ritter Vitezovic." Paper presented at the conference "Eco-History of the Triplex Confinium." Zadar, Croatia, May 2000.

Boban, Ljubo. 1990. "Jasenovac and the Manipulation of History." *East European Politics and Societies* 4 (3): 580–93.

———. 1992. "Still More Balance on Jasenovac and the Manipulation of History." *East European Politics and Societies* 6 (2): 213–17.

Bocca, Giorgio. 1995. "Vorrei che la destra smettese di prendere per buoni i rottami della Repubblica di Salò." *Espresso* (12 May): 5.

———. 1996a. "Prima o poi si scoprirà che la Resistenza è un'invenzione del PCI." *Espresso* (22 March): 9.

———. 1996b. "Capire i vinti di Salò? On. Violante, c'è da capire." *Espresso* (23 May): 5.

Bogneri, Marcello. 1994. *Così si cantava in Istria: Raccolta di testi di canzonette popolari.* Trieste: Unione degli Istriani.

———. n.d. *Il culto di Dante a Pola nell'ultimo secolo.* Trieste: Unione degli Istriani (Litografia Zenit).

Bolla, Luigi. 1982. *Perché a Salò: Diario dalla Repubblica Sociale Italiana.* Edited by Giordano Bruno Guerri. Milan: Bompiani.

Bon Gherardi, Silva. 1972. *La persecuzione antiebraica a Trieste (1938–1945).* Udine: Del Bianco.

Bonvicini, Guido. 1988. *Decima marinai! Decima comandante!* Milan: Mursia.

Borme, Antonio. 1992. *La minoranza italiana in Istria e a Fiume: Scritti e interventi dal 1964 al 1990 in difesa della sua identità e della sua dignità civile.* Fiume: Unione Italiana.

———. 1995. *Nuovi contributi sulla comunità Italiana in Istria e a Fiume (1967–1990).* Edited by Ezio Giuricin. Fiume: Unione Italiana.

Borneman, John. 1992. *Belonging in the Two Berlins: Kin, State, Nation.* Cambridge: Cambridge University Press.

———. 1997. *Settling Accounts: Violence, Justice, and Accountability in Postsocialist Europe.* Princeton: Princeton University Press.

———. 1998. *Subversions of International Order: Studies in the Political Anthropology of Culture.* Albany: State University of New York Press.

Borsani, Carlo, Jr. 1995. *Carlo Borsani: Una vita per un sogno.* Milan: Mursia.

Bosworth, R. J. B. 1998. *The Italian Dictatorship: Problems and Perspectives in the Interpretation of Mussolini and Fascism.* London: Arnold.

———. 1999. "Film Memories of Fascism." In *Italian Fascism: History, Memory and Representation,* ed. R.J.B. Bosworth and Patrizia Dogliani, pp. 102–23. New York: St. Martin's Press.

Bowman, Alfred Connor. 1982. *Zones of Strain: A Memoir of the Early Cold War.* Stanford: Hoover Institution Press.

Bowman, Glenn. 1993. "Tales of the Lost Land: Palestinian Identity and the Formation of Nationalist Consciousness." In *Space and Place: Theories of Identity and Location,* ed. Erica Carter, James Donald, and Judith Squires, pp. 73–99. London: Lawrence and Wishart.

———. 1995. "Terror, Pain, and the Impossibility of Community." Paper given at conference entitled "War, Exile, and Everyday Life." Zagreb, March 1995.

Bracewell, Wendy. 1994. "'Europeanism,' 'Orientalism,' and National Myths in Yugoslavia." Unpublished article.

Brands, H. W. 1989. *The Specter of Neutralism: The United States and the Emergence of the Third World, 1947–1960.* New York: Columbia University Press.

Braudel, Fernand. 1972a. *The Mediterranean and the Mediterranean World in the Age of Phillip II.* Vol. 1. New York: Harper & Row.

——. 1972b. *The Mediterranean and the Mediterranean World in the Age of Phillip II.* Vol. 2. New York: Harper & Row.

Bressan, Aldo, and Luciano Giuricin. 1964. *Fratelli nel sangue: Contributi per una storia della partecipazione degli Italiani alla guerra.* Fiume: Edit.

Brettell, Caroline. 2000. "Theorizing Migration in Anthropology." In *Migration Theory: Talking Across Disciplines,* ed. Caroline Brettell and James Hollifield, pp. 97–136. New York: Routledge.

Brown, Keith. 2002. *Child-Grandfathers: The Politics of Memory and Experience of Forced Migration in Macedonia, 1948–1998.* Donald W. Treadgold Paper Series 37. Seattle: University of Washington.

Brubaker, Rogers. 1996. *Nationalism Reframed: Nationhood and the National Question in the New Europe.* Cambridge: Cambridge University Press.

Budicin, Antonio. 1995. *Nemico del popolo.* Trieste: Italo Svevo.

Burdett, Charles. 1999. "Changing Identities through Memory: Malaparte's Self-figurations in *Kaputt.*" In *European Memories of the Second World War,* ed. Helmut Peitsch, Charles Burdett, and Clàire Gorrara, pp. 110–19. New York: Berghahn Books.

Buruma, Ian. 1995. *The Wages of Guilt: Memories of War in Germany and Japan.* New York: Meridian.

Busetto, Andrea. 1932. *Oberdan.* Milan: Gruppo Rionale Fascista Guglielmo Oberdan.

Calamandrei, Piero. 1994. *Uomini e città della Resistenza.* Milan: Linea d'Ombra Ed.

Calcaprina, Ugo. 1935. *Oberdan.* Trieste: Casa Ed. Moscheni and Co.

Calestani, Emilia. 1978. *Memorie: Zara, 1937–1944.* Sanremo: Libero Comune di Zara in Esilio e Associazione Nazionale Dalmata.

Campbell, David. 1992. *Writing Security: United States Foreign Policy and the Politics of Identity.* Minneapolis: University of Minnesota Press.

Campbell, John, ed. 1976. *Successful Negotiation: Trieste 1954.* Princeton: Princeton University Press.

Čapo Žmegač, Jasna. 1999. "Ethnology, Mediterranean Studies, and Political Reticence in Croatia." *Croatian Journal of Folklore and Ethnology* 36 (1): 33–52.

Caracciolo, Nicola. 1986. *Gli ebrei e l'Italia durante la guerra, 1940–45.* Rome: Bonacci Editore.

Carrier, James G. 1987. "History and Self-Conception in Ponam Society." *Man* 22:111–31.

Carruthers, Mary J. 1990. *The Book of Memory.* Cambridge: Cambridge University Press.

Carter, Donald. 1997. *States of Grace: Senegalese in Italy and the New European Immigration.* Minneapolis: University of Minnesota Press.

Carter, Erica, James Donald, and Judith Squires, eds. 1993. *Space and Place: Theories of Identity and Location.* London: Lawrence and Wishart.

Cary, Joseph. 1993. *A Ghost in Trieste.* Chicago: University of Chicago Press.

Cascardi, A. J. 1984. "Remembering." *Review of Metaphysics* 38:275–302.

Cattaruzza, Marina. 1995. *Trieste nell'Ottocento: Le trasformazioni di una società civile.* Udine: Del Bianco.

Cernigoi, Claudia. 1997. *Operazione foibe a Trieste.* Udine: Edizioni Kappa Vu.

Cervani, G. 1977. *La storia d'Italia ed il concetto del confine orientale nel pensiero di Fabio Cusin.* Trieste: Edizioni LINT.

Cervi, Mario, ed. 1995. *Salò: Album della Repubblica di Mussolini.* Milan: Rizzoli.

Chalk, Frank. 1994. "Redefining Genocide." In *Genocide: Conceptual and Historical Dimensions*, ed. G. J. Andreopoulos, pp. 47–63. Philadelphia: University of Pennsylvania Press.

Cherin, Ita. 1971. "Testimonianze di rovignesi sfollati a Wagna (1915–1918)." *Atti del Centro di Ricerche Storiche* 2:347–78.

———. 1977–78. "L'esodo degli abitanti di Rovigno nel periodo di guerra, 1915–1918." *Atti del Centro di Ricerche Storiche* 8:368–90.

Chersi, Ettore. 1938. *Le deportazioni degli italiani irredenti in Austria nella guerra di liberazione*. Trieste: Tip. Giuliana.

Ciccarelli, Andrea. 2001. "Dante and the Culture of Risorgimento: Literary, Political, or Ideological Icon?" In *Making and Remaking Italy: The Cultivation of National Identity around the Risorgimento*, ed. Albert Russell Ascoli and Krystyna von Henneberg, pp. 77–102. Oxford: Berg.

Clifford, James. 1994. "Diasporas." *Cultural Anthropology* 9 (3): 302–38.

Clifford, James, and George Marcus, eds. 1986. *Writing Culture: The Poetics and Politics of Ethnography*. Berkeley: University of California Press.

Coból, Nicolò. 1924. *Memorie del mio esilio*. Milan: Caddeo Editore.

Coceani, Bruno. 1938. *L'opera della commissione centrale di patronato tra i fuorusciti adriatici e trentini durante la Guerra Grande*. Trieste: Off. Graf. della Editoriale Libreria.

Coceani, Bruno, et al. 1918. *Guglielmo Oberdan, 1 Febbraio 1858–20 Dicembre 1882*. Trieste: Fascio Nazionale [Tip. Lloyd].

———. 1968. *Nicolò Luxardo: Vita di un uomo*. Padua: Società Cooperativa Tipografica.

Cohen, Gary B. 1981. *The Politics of Ethnic Survival: Germans in Prague, 1861–1914*. Princeton: Princeton University Press.

Cole, Jeffrey. 1997. *The New Racism in Europe: A Sicilian Ethnography*. Cambridge: Cambridge University Press.

Cole, John, and Eric Wolf. 1974. *The Hidden Frontier: Ecology and Ethnicity in an Alpine Valley*. New York: Academic Press.

Colella, Amedeo, ed. 1958. *L'esodo dalle terre adriatiche: Rilevazioni statistiche*. Rome: Stab. Tip. Julia.

Colummi, Cristiana, Liliana Ferrari, Gianna Nassisi, and Germano Trani. 1980. *Storia di un esodo: Istria, 1945–1956*. Trieste: Istituto Regionale per la Storia del Movimento di Liberazione nel Friuli–Venezia Giulia.

Combi, C. A. 1878. *Della rivendicazione dell'Istria agli studi italiani*. Venice: Tip. di G. Antonelli.

Committee for the Defense of the Italian Character of Trieste and Istria. 1953. *Trieste 1953: Facts and Documents*. Trieste: Committee for the Defense of the Italian Character of Trieste and Istria.

Comune di Trieste. 1932. *Il comune di Trieste nel primo decennio fascista*. Trieste: Officine Grafiche della Editoriale Libraria S.A.

Consiglio, Alberto, ed. 1941. *Dalmazia Veneta e Romana*. Roma: Tip. "Europa."

Coon, Lynda L. 1997. *Sacred Fictions: Holy Women and Hagiography in Late Antiquity*. Philadelphia: University of Pennsylvania Press.

Cotta, Sergio. 1977. *Quale Resistenza? Aspetti e problemi della guerra di liberazione in Italia*. Milan: Rusconi.

Cox, Geoffrey. 1977. *The Race for Trieste*. London: William Kimber.

Crainz, Guido. 1999. "The Representation of Fascism and the Resistance in the Documentaries of Italian State Television." In *Italian Fascism: History, Memory, and Representation*, ed. R.J.B. Bosworth and Patrizia Dogliani, pp. 124–43. New York: St. Martin's Press.

Crapanzano, Vincent. 1986. *Waiting: The Whites of South Africa*. New York: Vintage Books.

Črnobori, Tone. 1979. "Le prime società operaie in Istria." In *La Repubblica di Albona nell'anno 1921*, pp. 39–63. Rijeka: Tipograf.

Croce, Benedetto. 1963. *Scritti e discorsi politici, 1943–1947*. Bari: Laterza.

Cuccu, Giovanni. 1991. *Ivo e le stelle: Un partigiano sardo in Jugoslavia*. Cagliari: CUEC Editrice.

Čulinović, Ferdo. 1979. "La Repubblica di Albona: Analisi del movimento rivoluzionario in Istria nel 1921." In *La Repubblica di Albona nell'anno 1921*, ed. Jazu (Jugoslavenske Akademije Znanosti i umjetnosti Rijeka). pp. 1–25. Rijeka: Tipograf.

Curi, Umberto. 1989. *La politica sommersa: Per un'analisi del sistema politico italiano*. Milan: Franco Angeli.

Cuttin, Vittorio. n.d. *Guglielmo Oberdan*. Florence: R. Bemporad e Figlio.

Cvijić, Jovan. 1929–31. *La peninsule balkanique (Balkansko Poluostrvo i juznoslovenske zemlje: osnove antropogeografije)*. Zagreb: Hrvatski Stamparski Zavod.

Dainelli, G., T. de Bacci, et al. 1915. *La Dalmazia: Sua italianità. Suo valore per la libertà d'Italia nell'Adriatico*. Genoa: A. F. Formiggini.

Dal Pont, Adriano, Alfonso Leonetti, and Massimo Massara. 1964. *Giornali fuori legge: La stampa clandestina antifascista, 1922–1943*. Rome: Associazione Nazionale Perseguitati Politici Italiani Antifascisti.

Danforth, Loring. 1982. *The Death Rituals of Rural Greece*. Princeton: Princeton University Press.

———. 1995. *The Macedonian Conflict*. Princeton: Princeton University Press.

Daniel, E. Valentine. 1996. *Charred Lullabies: Chapters in an Anthropography of Violence*. Princeton: Princeton University Press.

Darovec, Darko. 1993. "Rassegna di storia istriana." *Biblioteca Annales* 5.

Davis, Colin. 1999. "Reviewing Memory: Wiesel, Testimony, and Self-Reading." In *European Memories of the Second World War*, ed. Helmut Peitsch, Charles Burdett, and Claire Gorrara, pp. 122–30. New York: Berghahn Books.

Debeljuh, Loredana Bogliun. 1990. "Essere italiani in Istria: 'Il Territorio' e il tentativo difficile di ricucire il tessuto umano di queste terre." *Il Territorio* 27/28:28–31.

———. 1992. "Proposta di realizzazione graduale del bilinguismo nell'area regionale istriana." *Annales* 2:329–32.

———. 1993. "Comments on Istria." *Vita Italiana* 2:20–25.

———. 1994. *L'identità etnica: Gli italiani dell'area Istro-Quarnerina*. Fiume: Unione Italiana.

De Castro, Diego. 1981. *La questione di Trieste: L'azione politica e diplomatica italiana dal 1943 al 1954*. Vols. 1 and 2. Trieste: Edizioni Lint.

De Franchi, Nicolò Luxardo. 1992. *Dietro gli scogli di Zara*. Gorizia: Editrice Goriziana.

De Grazia, Victoria. 1981. *The Culture of Consent*. Cambridge: Cambridge University Press.

Delaney, Carol. 1991. *The Seed and the Soil: Gender and Cosmology in Turkish Village Society*. Berkeley: University of California Press.

Del Boca, Angelo. 1969. *The Ethiopian War, 1935–1941*. Translated by P. D. Cummings. Chicago: University of Chicago Press.

Delbello, Piero. 1992. *Arredi domestici, documenti, strumenti di lavoro dei profughi istriani depositati a Trieste*. Trieste: Edi. Italo Svevo.

De Leonardis, Massimo. 1992. *La 'Diplomazia Atlantica' e la soluzione del problema di Trieste (1952–1954)*. Rome: Edizioni Scientifiche Italiane.

De los Angeles Torres, Maria. 1995. "Beyond the Rupture: Reconciling with Our Enemies, Reconciling with Ourselves." In *Bridges to Cuba/Puentes a Cuba*, ed. Ruth Behar, pp. 25–43. Ann Arbor: University of Michigan Press.

Del Vecchio, Giorgio, et al. 1928. *Per Guglielmo Oberdan e Francesco Rismondi*. Rome: Tip. Ditta Fratelli Pallotta.

Denich, Bette. 1994. "Dismembering Yugoslavia: Nationalist Ideologies and the Symbolic Revival of Genocide." *American Ethnologist* 21 (2): 367–90.

De' Robertis, Antonio Giulio M. 1981. *La frontiera orientale nella diplomazia della Seconda Guerra Mondiale*. Rome: Edizioni Scientifiche Italiane.

De Santi, Raimondi. 1919. *Alcuni particolari sul martirio della Dalmazia*. Zara: Stab. Tipografico E. De Schönfeld.

De Simone, Anna Borsi, et al., eds. 1992. *Testimonianze fotografiche sulle Foibe—Diktat—Esodo*. Milan: Associazione Nazionale Venezia Giulia e Dalmazia.

De Zambotti,Remo. 1980. *Guerra in Dalmazia con la 547° Compagnia Mitraglieri G.A.F.* Milan: Editrice Innocenti.

Dinardo, Richard. 1997. "Glimpse of an Old World Order? Reconsidering the Trieste Crisis of 1945." *Diplomatic History* 21 (3): 365–82.

Djilas, Milovan. 1977. *Wartime*. Translated by Michael Petrovich. New York: Harcourt Brace Jovanovich.

Dogliani, Patrizia. 1999. "Constructing Memory and Anti-Memory: The Monumental Representation of Fascism and Its Denial in Republican Italy." In *Italian Fascism: History, Memory, and Representation*, ed. R.J.B. Bosworth and Patrizia Dogliani, pp. 11–30. New York: St. Martin's Press.

Dompieri, Sergio. 1941. *Dalmazia*. Venice: Industria Poligrafiche Venete.

Donato, Carlo. 1997. "Problemi di quantificazione dell'Esodo Istriano." Paper presented at the conference "Compulsory Removals of Populations after the First and Second World Wars: Central-Eastern Europe, the Balkan-Aegean Region, the Istro Dalmatian Region." Trieste, September 1997.

Donnan, Hastings, and Thomas Wilson, ed. 1994. *Border Approaches: Anthropological Perspectives on Frontiers*. Lanham: University Press of America.

Drndić, Ljubo. 1981. *Le armi e la libertà dell'Istria*. Fiume: Edit.

Dubin, Lois. 1999. *The Port Jews of Habsburg Trieste: Absolutist Politics and Enlightenment Culture*. Stanford: Stanford University Press.

Dudan, Alessandro. 1915. "La Dalmazia di oggi." In *La Dalmazia: Sua italianità, suo valore per la libertà d'Italia nell'Adriatico*, ed. G. Dainelli et al., pp. 65–124. Genoa: A. F. Formìggini.

Dudan, Bruno, and Antonio Teja. 1991. *L'italianità della dalmazia negli ordinamenti e statuti cittadini*. Udine: ANVGD/Istituto per gli Studi di Politica Internazionale.

Dunham, Donald. [1954?]. *Political Aspects of Press Reporting of Crisis of Nov. 1953, Trieste, F.T.T.* Trieste: Allied Military Government.

Duroselle, Jean-Baptiste. 1966. *Le conflit de Trieste, 1943–1954*. Brussels: Editions de l'Institut de Sociologie de l'Université Libre de Bruxelles.

Ehrenburg, Ilja. 1944. "Giorni di gloria. Edito della sezione propaganda del Comitato popolare di liberazione per l'Istria e il Litorale Croato." n.p.

Eley, Geoff. 1988. "Nazism, Politics, and the Image of the Past: Thoughts on the West German Historikstreit, 1986–1987." *Past and Present* 121:171–208.

Elias, Norbert. 1978. *The History of Manners*. New York: Pantheon.

Ellwood, David. 1985. *Italy, 1943–1945*. Bath: Leicester University Press.

Eriksen, Thomas Hylland. 1993. "In Which Sense Do Cultural Islands Exist?" *Social Anthropology* 1 (1B): 133–47.

Fabi, Lucio, ed. 1991. *La guerra in casa, 1914–1918: Soldati e popolazioni del Friuli austriaco nella Grande Guerra*. Monfalcone: Edizioni della Laguna.

Faenza, Roberto, and Marco Fini. 1976. *Gli americani in Italia*. Milan: Feltrinelli Editore.

Famiglia Pisinota. 1967. *Pisino attraverso i ricordi dei miei genitori*. Opicina: Arti Grafiche V.d.F.

Farmer, Sarah. 1999. *Martyred Village: Commemorating the 1944 Massacre at Oradour-sur-Glane*. Berkeley: University of California Press.

Favetta, Bianca Maria. n.d. *Oberdan. Atti dei Civici Musei di Storia ed Arte di Trieste, Quaderno XII*. Trieste: Tip. Moderna.

Federzoni, Luigi. 1941. *L'ora della Dalmazia*. Bologna: Nicola Zanichelli Ed.

Feeley-Harnik, Gillian. 1991. *A Green Estate: Restoring Independence in Madagascar*. Washington, D.C.: Smithsonian Institution Press.

Feierman, Steven. 1990. *Peasant Intellectuals: Anthropology and History in Tanzania*. Madison: University of Wisconsin Press.

Fein, Helen. 1994. "Genocide, Terror, Life Integrity, and War Crimes: The Case for Discrimination." In *Genocide: Conceptual and Historical Dimensions*, ed. G. J. Andreopoulos, pp. 95–107. Philadelphia: University of Pennsylvania Press.

Feldman, Allen. 1991. *Formations of Violence*. Chicago: University of Chicago Press.

Fentress, James, and Chris Wickham. 1992. *Social Memory*. Oxford: Blackwell.

Ferrari, Oreste, ed. 1935. *Per l'Italia immortale. Cesare Battisti: La sua terra e la sua gente*. Trent: Legione Trentina.

Fölkel, Ferruccio. 1979. *La Risiera di San Sabba: Trieste e il Litorale Adriatico durante l'occupazione nazista*. Milan: Arnoldo Mondadori Editore.

Forgacs, David. 1999. "Days of Sodom: The Fascism-Perversion Equation in Films of the 1960s and 1970s." In *Italian Fascism: History, Memory, and Representation*, ed. R.J.B. Bosworth and Patrizia Dogliani, pp. 216–36. New York: St. Martin's Press.

Foscari, Piero. 1915. "La Dalmazia e il problema strategico dell'Adriatico e la reintegrazione nazionale dell'Adriatico ed i pericoli d'un irredentismo slavo." In *La Dalmazia: Sua Italianità, suo valore per la libertà d'Italia nell'Adriatico*, ed. G. Dainelli et al., pp. 167–85. Genoa: A. F. Formiggini.

———. 1921. *La Dalmazia e l'ultimo dei suoi martiri*. Rome: Sede Sociale

Foscolo, Ugo. 1970. *Ultime lettere di Jacopo Ortis*. Translated by Douglas Radcliff-Umstead. Chapel Hill: University of North Carolina Press.

Friedländer, Saul. 1986. "Some German Struggles with Memory." In *Bitburg in Moral and Political Perspective*, ed. Geoffrey Hartman, pp. 27–42. Bloomington: Indiana University Press.

Fubini, Federico. 1996. "Quando Fini sognava Istria e Dalmazia." *Limes* 1:289–303.

Furunović, Dragutin, ed. 1976. *Peti Kongres: Jugoslovenskih Dobrovoljaca Spanske Republikanske Vojske.* Split, Yugoslavia: Jugoslovenski Proizvodaci Papira.

Gabaccia, Donna. 2000. *Italy's Many Diasporas.* Seattle: University of Washington Press.

Gabrovšek Francis. 1946. *Jugoslavia's Frontiers with Italy.* New York: Jugoslav Information Center.

Gal, Susan. 1991. "Bartók's Funeral: Representations of Europe in Hungarian Political Rhetoric." *American Ethnologist* 18 (3): 440–58.

Galli della Loggia, Ernesto. 1996. *La morte della patria: La crisi dell'idea di nazione tra Resistenza, antifascismo e Repubblica.* Rome: Laterza.

Garcia, Cristina. 1992. *Dreaming in Cuban.* New York: Ballantine Books.

Garibaldi, Luciano. 1995. *Le soldatesse di Mussolini.* Milan: Mursia.

Gellner, Ernest. 1987. *Nations and Nationalism.* Ithaca: Cornell University Press.

Genovese, Eugene. 1975. *Roll, Jordan, Roll: The World the Slaves Made.* London: Andre Deustch.

Gentile, Emilio. 1996. *The Sacralization of Politics in Fascist Italy.* Translated by Keith Botsford. Cambridge, Mass.: Harvard University Press.

Gentille, Attilio. 1928. *Il busto di Guglielmo Oberdan nel R. Liceo Scientifico 'Guglielmo Oberdan' di Trieste.* Parenzo: Stab. Tip. G. Coana and Figli.

Gestro, Stefano. 1982. *La divisione italiana partigiana Garibaldi: Montenegro, 1943–1945.* Milan: Mursia.

Giglioli, Giulio Quirino. 1920. *Il dovere degli italiani.* Rome: Tip. Sociale.

Gilbert, Mark. 1995. *The Italian Revolution: The End of Politics, Italian Style?* Boulder: Westview.

Gilmore, David. 1982. "The Anthropology of the Mediterranean Area." *Annual Review of Anthropology* 11:175–205.

Gilroy, Paul. 1987. *There Ain't No Black in the Union Jack: The Cultural Politics of Race and Nation.* London: Hutchinson.

———. [1993] 1996. *The Black Atlantic: Modernity and Double Consciousness.* Cambridge, Mass.: Harvard University Press.

Ginsborg, Paul. 1990. *A History of Contemporary Italy: Society and Politics, 1943–1988.* London: Penguin Books.

———. 1996. "Explaining Italy's Crisis." In *The New Italian Republic: From the Fall of the Berlin Wall to Berlusconi,* ed. Stephen Gundle and Simon Parker, pp. 19–39. London: Routledge.

Giuricin, Gianni. 1988. *Trieste: Luci e ombre.* Trieste: Tabographis.

———. 1993. *Se questa è liberazione.* Trieste: Italo Svevo.

Giuricin, Luciano. 1961. *Il contributo degli Italiani dell'Istria e di Fiume alla Lotta Popolare di Liberazione.* Rijeka: Edit.

———. 1997. "L'esodo istriano, fiumano e dalmato nella storiografia croata." Paper presented at the conference "Compulsory Removals of Populations after the First and Second World Wars: Central-Eastern Europe, the Balkan-Aegean Region, the Istro Dalmatian Region." Trieste, September 1997.

Glick Schiller, Nina. 1999. "Transmigrants and Nation-states: Something Old and Something New in the U.S. Immigrant Experience." In *The Handbook of International Migration: The American Experience,* ed. Charles Hirschman, Philip Kasinitz, and Josh DeWind, pp. 94–119. New York: Russell Sage Foundation.

Gobbi, Romolo. 1992. *Il mito della Resistenza*. Milan: Rizzoli.

Godoli, Elio. 1984. *Trieste*. Rome: Editori Laterza.

Gross, Feliks. 1978. *Ethnics in a Borderland: An Inquiry into the Nature of Ethnicity and Reduction of Ethnic Tensions in a One-Time Genocide Area*. Wesport: Greenwood Press.

Gruenwald, Oskar. 1987. "Yugoslav Camp Literature: Rediscovering the Ghost of a Nation's Past-Present-Future." *Slavic Review* 46 (3/4): 513–28.

Guarino, Bruno. 1989. *La guerra continua: testimonianze di un combattente della Repubblica di Salò*. Acireale: Bonanno Editore.

Gundle, Stephen, and Simon Parker. 1996. "Introduction: The New Italian Republic." In *The New Italian Republic: From the Fall of the Berlin Wall to Berlusconi*, ed. Stephen Gundle and Simon Parker, pp. 1–39. London: Routledge.

Gupta, Akhil. 1998. *Postcolonial Developments: Agriculture in the Making of Modern India*. Durham: Duke University Press.

Gupta, Akhil, and James Ferguson, eds. 1997a. *Culture, Power, Place: Explorations in Critical Anthropology*. Durham: Duke University Press.

———. 1997b. *Anthropological Locations*. Berkeley: University of California Press.

Halbwachs, Maurice. 1992. *On Collective Memory*. Translated by Lewis Coser. Chicago: University of Chicago Press.

Hale, Charles. 1994. *Resistance and Contradiction: Miskitu Indians and the Nicaraguan State, 1894–1987*. Stanford: Stanford University Press.

———. 1999. "Travel Warning: Elite Appropriations of Hybridity, Mestizaje, Antiracism, Equality, and Other Progressive-Sounding Discourses in Highland Guatemala." *Journal of American Folklore* 112 (445): 297–315.

Harkin, M. 1988. "History, Narrative, and Temporality: Examples from the Northwest Coast." *Ethnohistory* 35 (2): 99–130.

Harper, John Lamberton. 1986. *America and the Reconstruction of Italy, 1945–1948*. Cambridge: Cambridge University Press.

Harris, C.R.S. 1957. *Allied Military Administration of Italy, 1943–1945*. London: Her Majesty's Stationery Office.

Hart, Laurie Kain. 1999. "Culture, Civilization, and Demarcation at the Northwest Borders of Greece." *American Ethnologist* 26 (1): 196–220.

Hartman, Geoffrey. 1994. "Introduction: Darkness Visible." In *Holocaust Remembrance: The Shapes of Memory*, ed. Geoffrey Hartman, pp. 1–22. Oxford: Blackwell.

———, ed. 1986. *Bitburg in Moral and Political Perspective*. Bloomington: Indiana University Press.

Haycraft, John. 1987. *Italian Labyrinth: Italy in the 1980's*. Harmondsworth, England: Penguin.

Hayden, Robert. 1994. "Recounting the Dead: The Rediscovery and Redefinition of Wartime Massacres in Late- and Post-Communist Yugoslavia." In *Memory, History, and Opposition under State Socialism*, ed. Rubie Watson, pp. 167–84. Santa Fe: School of American Research Press.

———. 1996. "Schindler's Fate: Genocide, Ethnic Cleansing, and Population Transfers." *Slavic Review* 55 (4): 727–48.

Herzfeld, Michael. 1985. *The Poetics of Manhood: Contest and Identity in a Cretan Mountain Village*. Princeton: Princeton University Press.

———. 1987. *Anthropology through the Looking-Glass: Critical Ethnography in the Margins of Europe*. New York: Cambridge University Press.

————. 1991. *A Place in History: Social and Monumental Time in a Cretan Town.* Princeton: Princeton University Press.

————. 1992. *The Social Production of Indifference: Exploring the Symbolic Roots of Western Bureaucracy.* New York: Berg.

————. 1997. *Cultural Intimacy: Social Poetics and the Nation-State.* New York: Routledge.

Heuser, Beatrice. 1989. *Western 'Containment' Policies in the Cold War: The Yugoslav Case, 1948–53.* London: Routledge.

Hill, Jane H., and Ofelia Zepeda. 1993. "Mrs. Patricio's Trouble: The Distribution of Responsibility in an Account of Personal Experience." In *Responsibility and Evidence in Oral Discourse,* ed. Jane Hill and Judith Irvine, pp. 197–225. Cambridge: Cambridge University Press.

Hirschon, Renée. [1989] 1998. *Heirs of the Greek Catastrophe.* New York: Berghahn Books.

Hochschild, Adam. 1994. *The Unquiet Ghost: Russians Remember Stalin.* New York: Penguin Books.

Holmes, Douglas. 1993. "Illicit Discourse." In *Perilous States: Conversations on Culture, Politics, and Nation,* ed. George E. Marcus, pp. 255–82. Chicago: University of Chicago Press.

————. 2000. *Integral Europe: Fast-Capitalism, Multiculturalism, Neofascism.* Princeton: Princeton University Press.

Hoogenboom, Hilde. 1996. "Vera Figner and Revolutionary Autobiographies: The influence of gender on genre." In *Women in Russia and Ukraine,* ed. Rosalind Marsh, pp. 78–93. Cambridge: Cambridge University Press.

Horn, David. 1991. "Constructing the Sterile City: Pronatalism and Social Sciences in Interwar Italy." *American Ethnologist* 18 (3): 581–601.

Host-Venturi, Giovanni. 1976. *L'Impresa Fiumana.* Rome: G. Volpe.

Hrvatski Institut za Povijest Drustvo 'Egzodus Istarskih Hrvata.' 2001. *Talijanska Uprava Na Hrvatskom Prostoru I Egzodus Hrvata.* Zagreb: Zbornik radova s Medunarodnog znanstrenog skupa.

Hutnyk, John. 1997. "Adorno at Womad: South Asian Crossovers and the Limits of Hybridity-Talk." In *Debating Cultural Hybridity,* ed. Pnina Werbner and Tariq Modood, pp. 106–38. London: Zed Books.

Innocenti, Marco. 1996. *Mussolini a Salò: Il tramonto di un uomo.* Milan: Mursia.

Institut Adriatique. 1946. *Cadastre National de l'Istre.* Zagreb: Imprimerie Naklani Zavod Hrvatske.

Isnenghi, Mario. 1997. *I luoghi della memoria: Strutture ed eventi dell'Italia unita.* Rome: Editori Laterza.

Italian Ministry of Defence. 1994. *Redipuglia.* Rome: Commissariato generale per le onoranze ai caduti in guerra [Industria Cartografica Romana].

Ivanov, Tommaso. 1986. *Il cimitero di Zara.* Brescia: Edizioni del Moretto.

Judson, Pieter. 1996."Frontiers, Islands, Forests, Stones: Mapping the Geography of a German Identity in the Habsburg Monarchy, 1848–1900." In *The Geography of Identity,* ed. Patricia Yaeger, pp. 382–407. Ann Arbor: University of Michigan Press.

Juri, Franco. 1990. "La Ragione della regione." *Istranova* 1 (3): 5.

Kabbani, Rana. 1986. *Europe's Myths of Orient.* Bloomington: Indiana University Press.

Kalc, Aleksej. 1983–84. "Attività politica di Ivan Marija Cok, 1919–1945." Thesis, Università di Trieste.

Kapferer, Bruce. 1988. *Legends of People, Myths of State: Violence, Intolerance, and Political Culture in Sri Lanka and Australia*. Washington, D.C. Smithsonian Institution Press.

Karakasidou, Anastasia N. 1997. *Fields of Wheat, Hills of Blood: Passages to Nationhood in Greek Macedonia, 1870–1990*. Chicago: University of Chicago Press.

Kardelj, Edvard. 1946. *Yugoslavia's Claim to Trieste*. New York: United Committee of South Slavic Americans.

————. 1953. *Trieste and Yugoslav-Italian Relations*. New York: Yugoslav Information Center.

Katz, Richard, and Piero Ignazi, eds. 1996. *Italian Politics: The Year of the Tycoon*. Boulder: Westview Press.

Kavanagh, William. 1994. "Symbolic Boundaries and 'Real' Borders on the Portugese-Spanish Frontier." In *Border Approaches: Anthropological Perspectives on Frontiers*, ed. Hastings Donnan and Thomas Wilson, pp. 75–87. Lanham: University Press of America.

Kearney, Michael. 1986. "From the Invisible Hand to Visible Feet: Anthropological Studies of Migration and Development." *Annual Review of Anthropology* 15:331–61.

————. 1991. "Borders and Boundaries of State and Self at the End of Empire." *Journal of Historical Sociology* 4 (1): 52–74.

Keegan, John. 1996. *The Battle for History: Re-Fighting World War II*. New York: Vintage Books.

Keiser, Lincoln. 1991. *Friend by Day, Enemy by Night: Organized Vengeance in a Kohistani Community*. Fort Worth: Holt, Rinehart and Winston.

Kenny, Michael, and David Kertzer, eds. 1983. *Urban Life in Mediterranean Europe: Anthropological Perspectives*. Urbana: University of Illinois Press.

Kersevan, Alessandra. 1995. *Porzûs: Dialoghi sopra un processo da rifare*. Udine: Edizioni Kappa Vu.

Kertzer, David. 1980. *Christians and Comrades*. Prospect Heights: Waveland.

————. 1996. *Politics and Symbols: The Italian Communist Party and the Fall of Communism*. New Haven: Yale University Press.

Kitchen, John. 1998. *Saints' Lives and the Rhetoric of Gender: Male and Female in Merovingian Hagiography*. New York: Oxford University Press.

Kligman, Gail. 1988. *The Wedding of the Dead: Ritual, Poetics, and Popular Culture in Transylvania*. Berkeley: University of California Press.

Kočović, Bogoljub. 1985. *Zreve Drugog Svetskog rata u Jugoslaviji*. London: Nase delo.

Kos, Milko, et al. 1946. *The Julian March: Studies on Its History and Civilization*. Ljubljana: Academy of Sciences and Art.

Kos, Milko. 1946. "Where Does the Slovene Littoral belong by Civilization and Politically." In *The Julian March: Studies on Its History and Civilization*, ed. M. Kos et. al., pp. 13–20. Ljubljana: Academy of Sciences and Art.

Kosinski, Leszek. 1982. "International Migration of Yugoslavs during and Immediately after World War II." *East European Quarterly* 16 (2): 183–98.

Krleža, Miroslav. [1944?]. *Adriatic Theme*. [London?].

Kumar, Romano. n.d. *L'attività rivoluzionaria della gioventù antifascista di Pola durante la guerra popolare di liberazione*. n.p.

Kuper, Adam. 1994. Culture, Identity, and the Project of a Cosmopolitan Anthropology. *Man* 29 (3): 573–54.

Kuris, Maria Grazia. 1999. "Sulle tracce dei 'soci rifondatori' di Trieste." In *Cromatismi e cromosomi di Trieste*, ed. Alberto Gasparini and Antonella Pocecco, pp. 75–109. Gorizia: I.S.I.G.–Università degli Studi di Trieste.

Lamb, Richard. 1993. *War in Italy, 1943–1945: A Brutal Story*. London: John Murray.

Lampe, John. 1996. *Yugoslavia as History: Twice There Was a Country*. Cambridge: Cambridge University Press.

Lane, Ann. 1996. *Britain, the Cold War, and Yugoslav Unity, 1941–1949*. Brighton: Sussex Academic Press.

Langer, Lawrence. 1991. *Holocaust Testimonies: The Ruins of Memory*. New Haven: Yale University Press.

Lanza, Giovanni. 1990. "Il gruppo nazionale in Istria: Evoluzione di una cultura minoritaria nel contesto jugoslavo (1981–1990)." Thesis, Università degli Studi di Venezia.

Lavie, Smadar, and Ted Swedenburg. 1996. "Introduction." In *Displacement, Diaspora, and Geographies of Identities*, ed. Lavie and Swedenburg, pp. 1–25. Durham: Duke University Press.

Layoun, Mary. 1995. "(Mis)Trusting Narratives: Refugee Stories of Post-1922 Greece and Post-1974 Cyprus." In *Mistrusting Refugees*, ed. E. Valentine Daniel and John Chr. Knudsen, pp. 73–86. Berkeley: University of California Press.

Lazzarini, Giuseppe. 1900. *Lotta di classe e lotta di razze in Istria*. Pola: Tip. J. Krmpotic.

Lazzero, Ricciotti. 1982. *Le SS italiane*. Milan: Rizzoli.

———. 1983. *Le brigate nere*. Milan: Rizzoli.

———. 1984. *La Decima Mas*. Milan: Rizzoli.

———. 1994. *Il sacco d'Italia*. Milan: Arnoldo Mondadori.

Leboucher, Fernande. 1969. *Incredible Mission*. Translated by J. F. Bernard. Garden City: Doubleday.

Ledeen, Michael. 1977. *The First Duce: D'Annunzio at Fiume*. Baltimore: Johns Hopkins University Press.

Lees, Lorraine. 1997. *Keeping Tito Afloat: The United States, Yugoslavia, and the Cold War*. University Park: Pennsylvania State University Press.

Lega Nazionale Trieste. n.d. *Le foibe di Basovizza e Monrupino*. Trieste.

Leone, Massimo. 1983. *Le organizzazioni di soccorso ebraiche in età fascista (1918–1945)*. Rome: Carucci Editore.

Lesser, Wendy. 1987. *The Life Below Ground: A Study of the Subterranean in Literature and History*. Boston: Faber and Faber.

Liechty, Mark. 1996. "Kathmandu as Translocality: Multiple Places in a Nepali Space." In *The Geography of Identity*, ed. Patricia Yaeger, pp. 98–130. Ann Arbor: University of Michigan Press.

Linke, Uli. 1999. *Blood and Nation: The European Aesthetics of Race*. Philadelphia: University of Pennsylvania Press.

Loizos, Peter. 1975. *The Greek Gift: Politics in a Cypriot Village*. New York: St. Martin's Press.

———. 1981. *The Heart Grown Bitter: A Chronicle of Cypriot War Refugees*. Cambridge: Cambridge University Press.

Lojk, M., and R. Lojk, eds. 1989. *Lojze Bratuz: 50 anni dopo/Po 50 Letih*. Gorizia: Edizioni dell'Assessorato alla Pubblica Istruzione.

Lorenzini, Marcello. 1991. *Le stragi delle foibe: Francesco Cossiga a Basovizza*. Trieste: Comitato per le Onoranze ai Caduti delle Foibe.

Luraghi, Raimondo. 1995. *Resistenza: Album della guerra di liberazione.* Milan: Rizzoli.

Luxardo, Nicolò, and Federico Pagnacco. 1971. *Pietro Luxardo: 'Iadra ad Cedem.'* Padua: Tip. A. Bolzonella.

Lyotard, Jean-François. 1984. *The Postmodern Condition: A Report on Knowledge.* Translated by Geoff Bennington and Brian Massumi. Minneapolis: University of Minnesota Press.

Macdonald, Ronald. 1987. *The Burial-Places of Memory: Epic Underworlds in Vergil, Dante, and Milton.* Amherst: University of Massachusetts Press.

Madieri, Marisa. 1987. *Verde acqua.* Turin: Giulio Einaudi.

Madrinato Dalmatico. 1986. *Zara nel ricordo del suo cimitero.* Padua: Società Cooperativa Tipografica.

Magri, Lucio. 1995. "The Resistable Rise of the Italian Right." *New Left Review* 214:125–33.

Magris, Claudio. 1986. *Danube: A Sentimental Journey from the Source to the Black Sea.* Translated by Patrick Creagh. London: Harvill.

———. 1999. *Microcosms.* Translated by Iain Halliday. London: Harvill.

Maier, Bruno. 1996. *La letteratura italiana dell'Istria dalle origini al Novecento.* Trieste: Italo Svevo.

Maier, Charles. 1988. *The Unmasterable Past.* Cambridge, Mass.: Harvard University Press.

Malinowski, Bronislaw. 1984. *Argonauts of the Western Pacific.* Prospect Heights: Waveland Press.

Malkki, Liisa. 1992. "National Geographic: The Rooting of Peoples and the Territorialization of National Identity among Scholars and Refugees." *Cultural Anthropology* 7 (1): 24–44.

———. 1995. "Refugees and Exile: From 'Refugee Studies' to the National Order of Things." *Annual Review of Anthropology* 24:495–523.

———. 1996. *Purity and Exile: Violence, Memory, and National Cosmology among Hutu Refugees in Tanzania.* Chicago: University of Chicago Press.

Malni, Paolo. 1998. *Fuggiaschi: Il campo profughi di Wagna, 1915–1918.* San Canzian d'Isonzo: Edizioni del Consorzio Culturale del Monfalconese.

Marchi, Marco, et al., eds. 1983. *Intellettuali di frontiera, Triestini a Firenze (1900–1950).* Florence: Tip. 'Il Sedicesimo.'

Marcus, George. 1995. "Ethnography in/of the World System: The Emergence of Multi-Sited Ethnography." *Annual Review of Anthropology* 24:95–117.

———. 1998. *Ethnography through Thick and Thin.* Princeton: Princeton University Press.

Marjanović, Vladislav. 1996. "L'histoire politisée—l'historiographie Serbe depuis 1989." In *Histoire et pouvoir en Europe mediane,* pp. 283–308. Paris: L'Harmattan.

Markovski, Venko. 1984. *Goli Otok: The Island of Death. A Diary in Letters.* Boulder: Social Science Monographs.

Marrero, Teresa. 1995. "Miembros Fantasmas/Ghost Limbs." In *Bridges to Cuba/Puentes a Cuba,* pp. 44–56. Ann Arbor: University of Michigan Press.

Martini, Lucifero. 1981. "Il gruppo etnico italiano in jugoslavia e la lingua." In *La Metteleuropa nel tempo: Atti del convegno,* pp. 65–70. Gorizia: Tip. Sociale.

Matta, Tristano, ed. 1996. *Un percorso della memoria: Guida ai luoghi della violenza nazista e fascista in Italia.* Trieste: Electa (Istituto regionale per la storia del movimento di liberazione nel Friuli–Venezia Giulia, Trieste).

Matvejević, Predrag. 1999. *Mediterranean: A Cultural Landscape.* Translated by Michael Henry Heim. Berkeley: University of California Press.

Maurer, Bill. 2000. "A Fish Story: Rethinking Globalization on Virgin Gorda, British Virgin Islands." *American Ethnologist* 27 (3): 670–701.

Mazzantini, Carlo. 1992. *In Search of a Glorious Death.* Translated by Simonetta Wenkert. Manchester: Carcanet.

———. 1995. *I Balilla andarono a Salò: L'armata degli adolescenti che pagò il conto della storia.* Venice: Marsilio.

McCarthy, Patrick. 1995. *The Crisis of the Italian State: From the Origins of the Cold War to the Fall of Berlusconi.* New York: St. Martin's Press.

McDonogh, Gary. 1986. *Good Families of Barcelona: A Social History of Power in the Industrial Era.* Princeton: Princeton University Press.

Melik, Anton. 1946a. *Trieste and the Littoral.* Ljubljana: Research Institute, Section for Frontier Questions.

———. 1946b. *Trieste and North Jugoslavia.* Ljubljana: Research Institute, Section for Frontier Questions.

Melonucci, Melonetto. 1980. *Trieste, cinque anni dopo (dopo Osimo, naturalmente).* Trieste: Marino Bolaffio.

Mershon, Carol, and Gianfranco Pasquino, eds. 1994. *Ending the First Republic.* Boulder: Westview Press.

Miceli, Giovanni, ed. 1917. *Guglielmo Oberdan nelle note biografiche di un amico.* Rome, n.p.

Michaelis, Meir. 1978. *Mussolini and the Jews: German-Italian Relations and the Jewish Question in Italy, 1922–1945.* London: Clarendon Press.

Michelozzi, A. 1919. *La prossima pace: La Dalmazia all'Italia.* Pistoia: Stabilmente Grafico Niccolai.

Miculian, Antonio. 1990–91. "Storiografia e pubblicista sull'esodo: Considerazioni critiche." *Quaderni di Centro di Ricerche Storiche* 10:103–10.

Middleton, David, and Derek Edwards, eds. 1990. *Collective Remembering.* London: Sage Publications.

Milani-Kruljac, Nelida. 1990. *La comunità italiana in Istria e a Fiume fra diglossia e bilinguismo.* Rovigno: Centro di Ricerche Storiche.

Ministero degli Affari Esteri. 1946. *Propositions en vue d'un regime international pour les ports de Trieste et de Fiume.* Rome.

———. 1947. *Accordo fra il governo italiano ed il comitato preparatorio per l'Organizzazione Internazionale dei Profughi.* Rome: Tipografia riservata del Ministero degli Affari Esteri.

Mintz, Jerome. 1982. *The Anarchists of Casas Viejas.* Chicago: University of Chicago Press.

Mirabelli, Roberto. 1918. *Oberdan nella olimpiade storica dell'irredentismo italiano.* Milan: Fratelli Treves.

Mirzoeff, Nicholas. 2000. "The Multiple Viewpoint: Diasporic Visual Cultures." In *Diaspora and Visual Cultures: Representing Africans and Jews,* ed. Nicholas Mirzoeff, pp. 1–18. London: Routledge.

Missoni, Luigi. 1942. *L'Italia ritorna in Dalmazia.* Bologna: L. Cappelli Editore.

Moe, Nelson. 2001. "'This Is Africa': Ruling and Representing Southern Italy, 1860–61." In *Making and Remaking Italy: The Cultivation of National Identity around the Risorgimento,* ed. Albert Russell Ascoli and Krystyna von Henneberg, pp. 119–53. Oxford: Berg.

Montanelli, Indro, and Mario Cervi. 1983. *L'Italia della guerra civile (8 Settembre 1943–9 Maggio 1946)*. Milan: Rizzoli.

Moodie, A. E. 1945. *The Italo-Yugoslav Boundary: A Study in Political Geography*. London: George Philip and Son.

Morano, Carlo Pignatti. 1922. *La vita di Nazario Sauro e il martirio dell'eroe*. Milan: Fratelli Treves.

Moreira, Juan M. Delgado. 2000. "Uses of Culture in the European Union Politics of Citizenship." Presented at the conference entitled "Law, Knowledge, and Power in Post-Colonial and Post-Soviet Anthropology," Moscow, June 2000.

Morgan, Sarah. 1999. "War, Civil War, and the Problem of Violence in Calvino and Pavese." In *European Memories of the Second World War*, ed. Helmut Peitsch, Charles Burdett, and Claire Gorrara, pp. 67–77. New York: Berghahn Books.

Moro, Daniele. 1988. "Refugees from the Eastern Provinces of Italy after 1943." In *Refugees in the Age of Total War*, ed. Anna C. Bramwell, pp. 131–51. London: Unwin Hyman.

Mosse, George. 1985. *Nationalism and Sexuality*. Madison: University of Wisconsin Press.

———. 1990. *Fallen Soldiers: Reshaping the Memory of the World Wars*. New York: Oxford University Press.

Mucci, Tina, and Anna Chiarini. 1999. *A chi appartiene l'Adriatico?* Imola: Editrice La Mandragora.

Myerhoff, Barbara. 1978. *Number Our Days*. New York: Simon and Schuster.

Nader, Laura. 1997. "The Phantom Factor: Impact of the Cold War on Anthropology." In *The Cold War and the University*, ed. André Schiffrin, pp. 107–43. New York: New Press.

Nelson, Diane. 1999. *A Finger in the Wound: Body Politics in Quincentennial Guatemala*. Berkeley: University of California Press.

Nemec, Gloria. 1998. *Un paese perfetto. Storia e memoria di una comunità in esilio: Grisignana d'Istria, 1930–1960*. Gorizia:Libreria Editrice Goriziana (Isituto Regionale per la Cultura Istriana).

Nodari, Pio. 1997. "I flussi migratori dalla Venezia Giulia nei due dopoguerra." Paper presented at the conference "Compulsory Removals of Populations after the First and Second World Wars: Central-Eastern Europe, the Balkan-Aegean Region, the Istro Dalmatian Region." Trieste, September 1997.

Nora, Pierre. 1989. "Between Memory and History: Les Lieux de Mémoire." *Representations* 26:7–25.

Novak, Bogdan. 1970. *Trieste, 1941–1954: The Ethnic, Political, and Ideological Struggle*. Chicago: University of Chicago Press.

Novick, Peter. 1999. *The Holocaust in American Life*. Boston: Houghton Mifflin.

Oliveri, Mario. 1921. *Martiri e glorie*. Pola: Tip. Fratelli Niccolini.

Oretti, Laura. 1994. *A caminando che 'l va*. Trieste: Italo Svevo.

Pacor, Mario. 1968. *Italia e Balcani: Risorgimento alla Resistenza*. Milan: Feltrinelli.

Paggi, Leonardo, ed. 1994. "'In Memory': The Themes and Aims of the Conference." Paper presented at the conference entitled "In Memory: Revisiting Nazi Atrocities in Post–Cold War Europe," Arezzo, Italy, June 1994.

———. 1997. *La memoria del Nazismo nell'Europa di Oggi*. Florence: La Nuova Italia Editrice Scandicci.

Pagnotti, Simonetta. 1990. "I fantasmi di Reggio." *Famiglia Cristiana* 37 (September 9): 36–39.

Palin, Antonio. 1931. *In lode di Nazario Sauro.* Capodistria: Associazione Nazionale Volontari di Guerra, Sezione di Capodistria.

Pansa, Giampaolo. 1969. *L'esercito di Salò nei rapporti riservati della Guarda nazionale repubblicana, 1943–1944.* Milan: Istituto Nazionale per la Storia del Movimento di Liberazione.

———. 1991. *Il Gladio e l'alloro : L'esercito di Salò.* Milan: Mondadori.

Papastergiadis, Nikos. 1997. "Tracing Hybridity in Theory." In *Debating Cultural Hybridity,* ed. Pnina Werbner and Tariq Modood, pp. 257–81. London: Zed Books.

Parentin, Luigi. 1992. *Incontri con l'Istria: La sua storia e la sua gente.* Vol. 1. Trieste: Edizioni LINT.

Pasic, Nicholas. 1989. "In Search of the True Number of World War II Victims in Yugoslavia." *Serbian Studies* 5 (1): 65–83.

Passerini, Luisa. 1979. "Work Ideology and Consensus under Italian Fascism." *History Workshop* 8:82–108.

———. 1987. *Fascism in Popular Memory: The Cultural Experience of the Turin Working Class.* Translated by Robert Lumley and Jude Bloomfield. Cambridge: Cambridge University Press.

Patterson, David. 1992. *The Shriek of Silence: A Phenomenology of the Holocaust Novel.* Lexington: University Press of Kentucky.

Pauletta, Ivan. 1994. "Vedo nero: Interview with Aldo Bencina." *Panorama* 2 (31 January): 7–10.

Pavlowitch, Steven. 1988. *The Improbable Survivor: Yugoslavia and Its Problems, 1918–1988.* Columbus: Ohio State University Press.

Peitsch, Helmut. 1999. "Introduction: Studying European Literary Memories." In *European Memories of the Second World War,* ed. Helmut Peitsch, Charles Burdett, and Claire Gorrara, pp. xiii–xxxi. New York: Berghahn Books.

Pellegrini, Ernestina. 1987. *La Trieste di carta: Aspetti della letteratura triestina del Novecento.* Bergamo: P. Lubrina.

Pellico, Silvio. 1850. *Le mie prigioni.* London: Rolandi.

Perlman, Michael. 1988. *Imaginal Memory and the Place of Hiroshima.* Albany: State University of New York Press.

Perselli, Guerrino. 1993. *I censimenti della popolazione dell'Istria, con Fiume e Trieste, e di alcune città della Dalmazia tra il 1850 e il 1936.* Fiume: Unione Italiana.

Pesce, Giovanni. 1972. *And No Quarter: An Italian Partisan in World War II.* Translated by Frederick Shaine. Athens: Ohio University Press.

Petacco, Arrigo. 1987. *I ragazzi del '44.* Milan: Arnoldo Mondadori.

———. 1995. *L'Italia in guerra, 1940–1945.* Milan: Arnoldo Mondadori.

———. 1999. *L'esodo: La tragedia negata degli italiani d'Istria, Dalmazia e Venezia Giulia.* Milan: Oscar Mondadori.

Peteet, Julie. 1998. "Post Partition Palestinian Identities and the Moral Community." *Social Analysis* 42 (1): 63–87.

Piccoli, Valentino. 1935. *Il martirio di Nazario Sauro.* Milan: Mondadori.

Piemontese, Giuseppe. 1946. *Twenty-nine Months of Italian Occupation of the "Province of Ljubljana."* Ljubljana.

Pinkus, Karen. 1995. *Bodily Regimes*. Minneapolis: University of Minnesota Press.

Pintor, Giaime. 1970. "The 'Shock of Recognition': An Unpolitical Youth on the Road to a New Risorgimento." In *Italy from the Risorgimento to Fascism*, ed. William Salòmone, pp. 422–28. Garden City: Doubleday.

Pirina, Marco, and Annamaria D'Antonio. 1994. *Scomparsi*. Pordenone: Centro studi e ricerche storiche (Fagagna Graphis).

Pirjevec, Joze. n.d. "Trieste: Città di frontiera." In *La voce slovena*, pp. 23–59. Trieste: Grafiche CORRA.

Pisanò, G., and P. Pisanò. 1998. *Il triangolo della morte: La politica della strage in Emilia durante e dopo la guerra civile*. Milan: Mursia.

Pittioni, Domenico. 1989. *La guerra fredda ai confini orientali d'Italia*. Udine: Campanotto Editrice.

Pizzi, Katia. 1999. "'Silentes Loquimur': Archetipo e ideologia nelle foibe di Enrico Morovich." *Quaderni del Centro di Ricerche Storiche di Rovigno* 12:91–103.

Portelli, Alessandro. 1997. *The Battle of Valle Giulia: Oral History and the Art of Dialogue*. Madison: University of Wisconsin Press.

Posar-Giuliano, Guido. 1955. "Memorie istriane." *La Porta Orientale* 3–4:113–21.

Pozzi, Arrigo. 1934. *Il vero volto di Nazario Sauro*. Rome: Casa Editrice Pinciana.

Predonzani, Elio. 1950. "Motivi delle leggende istriane." *Pagine istriane* 4:337–39.

Price, David H. 1997. "Cold War Anthropology: Collaborators and Victims of the National Security State." *Identities* 4 (3–4): 389–431.

Pupo, Raoul. 1995. "L'esodo degli Italiani da Zara, da Fiume e dall'Istria, 1943–1956." *Quaderni del Centro Studi 'Ezio Vanoni'* 3–4:127–63.

———. 1997. "Violenza politica tra guerra e dopoguerra: Il caso delle foibe giuliane, 1943–1945." In *Foibe: Il peso del passato*, ed. Giampaolo Valdevit, pp. 35–58. Venice: Marsilio.

Puppini, Marco. 1986. *In Spagna per la libertà: Antifascisti friuliani giuliani e istriani nella guerra civile spagnola 1936/1939*. Udine: Istituto Friulano per la Storia del Movimento di Liberazione.

Pusterla, Gedeone. [1886] 1996. *Il santuario della Beata Vergine delle Grazie di Semedella*. Trieste: Fameia Capodistriana [Stella Arti Grafiche].

Quarantotto, Giovanni. 1930. *Figure del Risorgimento in Istria*. Trieste: Casa Editrice 'La Vedetta Italiana.'

Quintero, Alejandro Pizarroso. 1989. *Stampa, radio e propaganda: Gli alleati in Italia, 1943–1946*. Milan: Franco Angeli.

Rabel, Roberto G. 1988. *Between East and West: Trieste, the United States, and the Cold War, 1941–1954*. Durham: Duke University Press.

Radole, Giuseppe. 1976. *Canti popolari: Raccolti a Materada, Buroli e Visinada in Istria*. Trieste: Italo Svevo.

———. 1997. *Folclore istriano*. Trieste: MGS Press.

Radossi, Alessio. 1989. "L'unione degli Italiani dell'Istria e di Fiume dal 1954 al 1963." Laurea, Università di Trieste.

Ramati, Alexander. 1978. *While the Pope Kept Silent: Assisi and the Nazi Occupation*. London: George Allen and Unwin.

Rambaldi, P. L. 1919. *Dalmazia Nostra!* Rome: Tip. Nazionale Bertero.

Rapetti, Giuseppe. n.d. *Nazario Sauro e la gente istriana*. Como: Lit. Tip (Comm. L. noseda)

Ravnik, Mojca. 1999. "Where Does the Mediterranean Begin? Can This Question Be Answered from the Viewpoint of Slovenian Ethnology?" *Croatian Journal of Folklore and Ethnology* 36 (1): 65–86.

Razsa, Maple, and Nicole Lindstrom. 2001. "Balkan Is Beautiful: The Role of Balkanism in the Constructions of Contemporary Croatian Identity." Forthcoming in *East European Politics and Society.*

Richards, Charles. 1995. *The New Italians.* London: Penguin Books.

Rihtman-Augustin, Dunja. 1999. "A Croatian Controversy: Mediterranean-Danube-Balkans." *Croatian Journal of Folklore and Ethnology* 36 (1): 103–20.

Rivalta, Ercole. [1934?]. *La passione italiana di Nazario Sauro e Felice Venezian.* Rome:Libreria del Littorio.

Robben, Antonius C.G.M. 1995. "The Politics of Truth and Emotion among Victims and Perpetrators of Violence." In *Fieldwork Under Fire: Contemporary Studies of Violence and Survival,* ed. Carolyn Nordstrom and Antonius C.G.M. Robben, pp. 81–103. Berkeley: University of California Press.

Robinson, Paul. 1997. "Is *Aida* an Orientalist Opera?" In *Revisioning Italy,* ed. Beverly Allen and Mary Russo, pp. 156–68. Minneapolis: University of Minnesota Press.

Robotti, Mario. July 16, 1945. *Relazione.* Rome: Archivio Diplomatico del Ministero degli Affari Esteri, AP 1931–1945 (b. 146, f.1).

Rocchi, Flaminio. 1990. *L'esodo dei 350 mila Giuliani Fiumani e Dalmati.* Rome: Difesa Adriatica [La Cartografica].

———, ed. n.d. *Le foibe di Basovizza e Monrupino. Commemorazione degli infoibati 2 Novembre 1959.* Rome: Arti Grafiche Italiane. [Associazone Nazionale Venezia Giuliae Dalmazia].

Roic, Sanja. 1991. "Eros Sequi, impegno e scrittura." In *La letteratura dell'emigrazione: Gli scrittori di lingua italiana nel mondo,* ed. Jean-Jacques Marchand, pp. 395–410. Turin: Edizione della Fondazione Giovanni Agnelli.

Rosenberg, Tina. 1995. *The Haunted Land: Facing Europe's Ghosts after Communism.* London: Vintage.

Rosenfeld, Gavriel. 2000. *Munich and Memory: Architecture, Monuments, and the Legacy of the Third Reich.* Berkeley: University of California Press.

Rossi, Francesco, ed. 1972. "Una nuova frontiera a Est." *Itinerari* 19:176–79.

Rossi, Mario. 1994. "Il fascismo a Rovigno: Un giudizio a quasi mezzo secolo dalla fine." Rovigno: Centro di Ricerche Storiche di Rovigno.

Rousso, Henry. 1991. *The Vichy Syndrome: History and Memory in France since 1944.* Cambridge, Mass.: Harvard University Press.

Rusconi, Gian Enrico. 1995. *Resistenza e postfacismo.* Bologna: Il Mulino.

Rusinow, Dennison. 1969. *Italy's Austrian Heritage, 1919–1946.* Oxford: Clarendon Press.

Russell, Robert Howard. 1896. *The Edge of the Orient.* New York: Charles Scribner's Sons.

Rustia, Giorgio. 2000. *Contro operazione foibe a Trieste.* Trieste: Riva Arti Grafiche (Associazione famiglie e congiunti dei deportati italiani in Jugoslavia e infoibati).

Ruzza, Carlo, and Oliver Schmidtke. 1996. "Towards a Modern Right: Alleanza Nazionale and the 'Italian Revolution.'" In *The New Italian Republic: From the Fall of the Berlin Wall to Berlusconi,* ed. Stephen Gundle and Simon Parker, pp. 147–58. London: Routledge.

Sahlins, Peter. 1989. *Boundaries.* Berkeley: University of California Press.

Said, Edward. 1979. *Orientalism.* New York: Vintage Books.

———. 1994. "Reflections on Exile." In *Altogether Elsewhere,* ed. Marc Robinson, pp. 137–49. Boston: Faber and Faber.

Salecl, Renata. 1993. "National Identity and Socialist Moral Majority." In *Space and Place: Theories of Identity and Location,* ed. Erica Carter, James Donald, and Judith Squires, pp. 101–10. London: Lawrence and Wishart.

Salvatori, Fausto. 1938. *Canzone a Nazario Sauro.* Rome: Edizione della Presidenza Generale della Lega Navale Italiana.

Salvi, Ercolano. 1919. *Per Spalato.* Rome: Tip. Nazionale Bertero.

Sartorio, Aldo, ed. 1935. *Azzuri di Dalmazia.* Venice: Calcografia del "Gazzetino Illustrato."

Scarpelli, Ubaldo. 1933. *Gente di Dalmazia: Rievocazione ed esaltazione storico-biografica dei grandi italiani di Dalmazia.* Trieste: Edizione Delfino.

Schama, Simon. 1995. *Landscape and Memory.* London: Harper Collins.

Schechtman, Joseph. 1946. "The Elimination of German Minorities in Southeastern Europe." *Journal of Central European Affairs* 6:152–66.

———. 1962. *Postwar Population Transfers in Europe, 1945–1955.* Philadelphia: University of Pennsylvania Press.

Schieder, Wolfgang. 1995. "Dalla Germania." In *L'Italia contemporanea e la storiografia internazionale,* ed. Filippo Mazzonis, pp. 63–92. Venice: Marsilio.

Schiffrer, Carlo. 1946. *Historic Glance at the Relations between Italians and Slavs in Venezia Giulia.* Trieste: Stabilmento Tipografico Nazionale.

Schirmer, Jennifer. 1994. "The Claiming of Space and the Body Politic within National-Security States: The Plaza de Mayo Madres and the Greenham Common Women." In *Remapping Memory: The Politics of TimeSpace,* ed. Jonathan Boyarin, pp. 185–220. Minneapolis: University of Minnesota Press.

Schneider, Jane. 1971. "Of Vigilance and Virgins: Honor, Shame, and Access to Resources in Mediterranean Societies." *Ethnology* 1:1–24.

———, ed. 1998. *Italy's 'Southern Question': Orientalism in One Country.* Oxford: Berg.

Schneider, Jane, and Peter Schneider. 1972. "Modernization and Development: The Role of Regional Elites and Non-Corporate Groups in the European Mediterranean." With Edward Hansen. *Comparative Studies in Society and History* 14:328–50.

Schweizer, Peter. 1988. *Shepherds, Workers, Intellectuals: Culture and Centre-Periphery Relationships in a Sardinian Village.* Stockholm: Department of Anthropology, University of Stockholm.

———. 1976. *Culture and Political Economy in Western Sicily.* New York: Academic Press.

Scocchi, Angelo. 1949. *Ispirazione mazziniana della tentata insurrezione di Trieste del 23 Marzo 1848.* Trieste: Libreria Editrice Mazziniana.

Scotti, Giacomo. 1991. *Goli Otok: Ritorno all'Isola Calva.* Trieste: Edizioni LINT.

Scotti, Giacomo, and Luciano Giuricin. 1975. *Rossa una stella.* Rovigo: Centro di Ricerche Storiche [Unione degli Italiani dell'Istria e di Fiume].

Secco, Aldo. 1991. *Pro Lega: Cartoline edite dal sodalizio, 1891–1991.* Trieste: Lega Nazionale.

———. 1995. *In vedetta operosa, 1891–1991: Cento anni di storia della Lega Nazionale.* Trieste: Editoriale Danubio.

Sedmak, V., and J. Mejak. 1953. *Trieste: The Problem Which Agitates the World.* Belgrade: Edition Jugoslavija.

Seltzer, Mark. 1998. *Serial Killers: Death and Life in America's Wound Culture*. New York: Routledge.

Seri, Alfieri. 1982. *Trieste anni trenta: Momenti di vita Triestina e cronaca della trasformazione edilizia*. Trieste: Italo Svevo.

Shelah, Menachem. 1989. "The Italian Rescue of Yugoslav Jews, 1941–1943." In *The Italian Refuge: Rescue of Jews During the Holocaust*, ed. Ivo Herzer et al., pp. 205–17. Washington, D.C.: Catholic University of America Press.

Shoup, Paul. 1968. *Communism and the Yugoslav National Question*. New York: Columbia University Press.

Sillani, Tomaso. n.d. *Mare nostrum*. Milan: Editori Alfieri and Lacroix.

Silverman, Sydel. 1975. *Three Bells of Civilization: The Life of an Italian Hill Town*. New York: Columbia University Press.

Simeone, William E. 1978. "Fascists and Folklorists in Italy." *Journal of American Folklore* 91:543–57.

Sinfield, Alan. 2000. "Diaspora and Hybridity: Queer Identities and the Ethnicity Model." In *Diaspora and Visual Cultures: Representing Africans and Jews*, ed. Nicholas Mirzoeff, pp. 95–114. London: Routledge.

Skerl, France. 1945. *The Struggle of the Slovenes in the Littoral for the People's Authority*. Ljubljana: Univ. tiskarna u Ljubljani.

Sluga, Glenda. 1994a. "No-Man's Land: The Gendered Boundaries of Post-War Trieste." *Gender and History* 6(2): 184–201.

———. 1994b. "Trieste: Ethnicity and the Cold War, 1945–54." *Journal of Contemporary History* 29:285–303.

———. 1996. "The Risiera di San Sabba: Fascism, anti-Fascism, and Italian Nationalism." *Journal of Modern Italian Studies* 1 (3): 401–12.

———. 1999. "Italian National Memory, National Identity, and Fascism." In *Italian Fascism: History, Memory, and Representation*, ed. R.J.B Bosworth and Patrizia Dogliani, pp. 178–94. New York: St. Martin's Press.

———. 2001. *The Problem of Trieste and the Italo-Yugoslav Border: Difference, Identity, and Sovereignty in Twentieth-Century Europe*. Albany: State University of New York Press.

Smiric, E. 1920. *Studio sull'italianità della Dalmazia in base a documenti ufficiali*. Zara: Tip. del Governo.

Soboul, Albert. 1983. "Religious Feeling and Popular Cults During the French Revolution: 'Patriot Saints' and Martyrs for Liberty." In *Saints and Their Cults*, ed. Stephen Wilson, trans. Jane Hodgkin, pp. 217–32. Cambridge: Cambridge University Press.

Sorani, Settimio. 1983. *L'assistenza ai profughi ebrei in Italia (1933–1941)*. Edited by Amedeo Tagliacozzo. Rome: Carucci Editore.

Spackman, Barbara. 1983. "Il Verbo (e) Sangue: Gabriele D'Annunzio and the Ritualization of Violence." *Quaderni d'Italianistica* 4 (2): 218–29.

———. 1990. "The Fascist Rhetoric of Virility." *Stanford Italian Review* 8 (1–2): 81–102.

Spadolini, Giovanni. 1983. *Oberdan nel Centenario del Martirio*. Trieste: Italo Svevo.

Spazzali, Roberto. 1990a. *Foibe: Un dibattito ancora aperto*. Trieste: Editrice Lega Nazionale.

———. 1990b. "Le foibe istriane: Sinestesia di una tragedia." *Quaderni del Centro Studi Economico-Politici 'Ezio Vanoni'* 20–21:53–68.

———. 1997. "Contabilità degli infoibati: Vecchi elenchi e nuove fonti." In *Foibe: Il peso del passato*, ed. Giampaolo Valdevit, pp. 97–127. Venice: Marsilio.

Speroni, Gigi. 1994. *99 passi dalla morte*. Milan: Rusconi.

Spivak, Gayatri Chakravorty. 1990. *The Post-Colonial Critic: Interviews, Strategies, Dialogues*, ed. Sarah Harasym. New York: Routledge.

Springer, Carolyn. 1987. *The Marble Wilderness*. Cambridge: Cambridge University Press.

Stack, Carol. 1996. *Call to Home: African Americans Reclaim the Rural South*. New York: Basic Books.

Starn, Randolph. 1982. *Contrary Commonwealth: The Theme of Exile in Medieval and Renaissance Italy*. Berkeley: University of California Press.

———. 1999. "Memory and Authenticity." *Studies in Twentieth Century Literature* 23 (1): 191–200.

Steffè, Bruno. 1974. *Antifascisti di Trieste, dell'Istria, dell'Isontino e del Friuli in Spagna*. Trieste: Associazione Italiana Combattente Volontari Antifascisti in Spagna.

Steinberg, Jonathan. 1990. *All or Nothing: The Axis and the Holocaust, 1941–1943*. London: Routledge.

Stewart, Kathleen. 1996. *A Space on the Side of the Road: Cultural Poetics in an "Other" America*. Princeton: Princeton University Press.

Štojković, Ljubiša, and Miloš Martić. 1952. *National Minorities in Yugoslavia*. Belgrade: Publishing and Editing Enterprise 'Jugoslavija.'

Stolcke, Verena. 1995. "Talking Culture: New Boundaries, New Rhetorics of Exclusion in Europe." *Current Anthropology* 36 (1): 1–13.

Stranj, Pavel. 1992. *The Submerged Community*. Trieste: Editorale Stamkpa Triestina.

Stringari, Silvio. 1926. *Nazario Sauro*. Marostica: Arti Grafiche M. Bonomo.

Šuran, Fulvio. 1994. "La famiglia mista: L'esempio italiano." Unpublished article.

Svevo, Italo. 1949. *As a Man Grows Older*. Translated by Beryl De Zoete. New York: New Directions.

———. 1967. *Short Sentimental Journey and Other Stories*. Translated by Beryl De Zoete, L. Collison-Morley, and Ben Johnson. Berkeley: University of California Press.

———. 1969. *Further Confessions of Zeno*. Translated by Ben Johnson and P. N. Furbank. Berkeley: University of California Press.

Svevo, Livia Veneziani. 1990. *Memoir of Italo Svevo*. Translated by Isabel Quigly. Evanston: Marlboro Press/Northwestern University Press.

Tamaro, Attilio. 1915. *Le condizioni degli Italiani soggetti all'Austria nella Venezia Giulia e nella Dalmazia*. Rome: Tip. Nazionale di G. Bertero E.C.

———. 1918. *La Dalmazia e il Risorgimento Nazionale*. Rome: Stab. Cromo-Lito-Tip. Evaristo Armani.

Tarizzo, Domenico. 1969. *Come scriveva la Resistenza: Filologia della stampa clandestina, 1943–45*. Florence: La Nuova Italia.

Tassin, Ferruccio, ed. 1993. *Mitteleuropa 25 anni*. Gorizia: Istituto per gli Incontri Culturali Mitteleuropei [Grafica Goriziana].

Taussig, Michael. 1997. *The Magic of the State*. New York: Routledge.

Teja, Antonio. 1949. *La Dalmazia preveneta: Realtà storica e fantasie jugoslave sulla Dalmazia dei sec. VI–XV*. Santa Margherita Ligure: Tip. Dionisio Devoto.

Thomassen, Bjorn. 2001. "The Borders and Boundaries of the Julian Region: Narrating

Self and Nation from the Fringes of the Italo-Slav Border." Ph.D. diss., European University Institute, Florence.

Thompson, Mark. 1992. *A Paper House: The Ending of Yugoslavia*. London: Vintage.

Tilly, Charles. 1986. *The Contentious French*. Cambridge, Mass.: Belknap Press of Harvard University Press.

———. 1989. "Collective Violence in European Perspective." In *Violence in America: Protest, Rebellion, Reform*, ed. Ted Robert Gurr, pp. 62–100. Newbury Park: Sage Publications.

Tobia, Bruno, et al., 1991. *Una patria per gli italiani: Spazi, itinerari, monumenti nell'Italia unita (1870–1900)*. Rome: Laterza.

———. 1998. *La memoria perduta: I monumenti ai caduti della Grande Guerra a Roma e nel Lazio*. Rome: Nuovo Argos.

Todorova, Maria. 1993. *Balkan Family Structure and the European Pattern: Demographic Developments in Ottoman Bulgaria*. Washington, D.C.: American University Press.

———. 1994. "The Balkans from Discovery to Invention." *Slavic Review* 53 (2): 453–82.

———. 1997. *Imagining the Balkans*. New York: Oxford University Press.

Tolstoy, Nikolai. 1986. *The Minister and the Massacres*. London: Century Hutchinson.

Tomasevich, Jozo. 1969. "Yugoslavia During the Second World War." In *Contemporary Yugoslavia: Twenty Years of Socialist Experiment*, ed. Wayne Vucinich, pp. 59–118. Berkeley: University of California Press.

Tomizza, Fulvio. 1999. *Materada*. Translated by Russell Scott Valentino. Evanston: Northwestern University Press.

Tonel, Claudio, ed. 1991. *Dossier sul neofascismo a Trieste, 1945–1983*. Udine: Arti Grafiche Friulane.

Troha, Nevenka. 1997. "Fra liquidazione del passato e costruzione del future: Le foibe e l'occupazione jugoslava della Venezia Giulia." In *Foibe: Il peso del passato*, ed. Giampaolo Valdevit, pp. 59–98. Venice: Marsilio.

Trouillot, Michel-Rolph. 1991. "Anthropology and the Savage Slot: The Poetics and Politics of Otherness." In *Recapturing Anthropology: Working in the Present*, ed. Richard G. Fox, pp. 17–44. Santa Fe: School of American Research Press.

———. 1995. *Silencing the Past: Power and the Production of History*. Boston: Beacon Press.

Tsing, Anna. 2000. "The Global Situation." *Cultural Anthropology* 15 (3): 327–60.

Tuntar, G. 1905. *Socialismo e questioni nazionali in Istria*. Pola: Ed. la Redazione de 'La Terra d'Istria.'

Turconi, Sergio. 1991. "La letteratura degli Italiani in Jugoslavia e i suoi emigrati." In *La letteratura dell'emigrazione: Gli scrittori di lingua italiana nel mondo*, ed. Jean-Jacques Marchand, pp. 107–21. Turin: Ed. della Fondazione Giovanni Agnelli.

Turner, Terence. 1993. "The Social Skin." In *Reading the Social Body*, ed. Catherine B. Burroughs and Jeffrey David Ehrenreich, pp. 15–39. Iowa City: University of Iowa Press.

Tweed, Thomas. 1997. *Our Lady of the Exile: Diasporic Religion at a Catholic Cuban Shrine in Miami*. New York: Oxford University Press.

Ugussi, Claudio. 1987. *La città divisa: L'altra sponda*. Udine: Campanotto Editore.

Unger, Leonard, and Kristina Šegulja. 1990. *The Trieste Negotiations*. Washington, D.C.: Foreign Policy Institute. Paul H. Nitze School of Advanced International Studies, no. 16.

Unione degli Italiani dell'Istria e di Fiume. 1945. *L'Unione degli Italiani dell'Istria e di Fiume*. Pola: Edizione de 'La Nostra Lotta.'

Valdevit, Giampaolo. 1987. *La questione di Trieste, 1941–1954: Politica internazionale e contesto locale.* Milan: Franco Angeli.

———. 1997. "Foibe: L'eredità della sconfitta." In *Foibe: Il peso del passato,* ed. Giampaolo Valdevit, pp. 15–32. Venice: Marsilio.

Valussi, Giorgio. 1972. *Il confine nordorientale d'Italia.* Trieste: Edizioni LINT.

Van der Veer, Peter. 1997. "'The Enigma of Arrival': Hybridity and Authenticity in the Global Space." In *Debating Cultural Hybridity,* ed. Pnina Werbner and Tariq Modood, pp. 90–105. London: Zed Books.

Venè, Gian Franco. 1989. *Coprifuoco.* Milan: Arnoldo Mondadori.

Ventura, Carlo, ed. 1963. *Mazziniani giulani caduti nella lotta di liberazione.* Udine: Del Bianco.

Verdery, Katherine. 1983. *Transylvanian Villagers.* Berkeley: University of California Press.

———. 1991. *National Ideology under Socialism.* Berkeley: University of California Press.

———. 1996. *What Was Socialism and What Comes Next?* Princeton: Princeton University Press.

———. 1999. *The Political Lives of Dead Bodies.* New York: Columbia University Press.

Verginella, Marta. 1997. "L'esodo istriano nella storiografia slovena." Paper presented at the conference "Compulsory Removals of Populations after the First and Second World Wars: Central-Eastern Europe, the Balkan-Aegean Region, the Istro Dalmatian Region." Trieste, September 1997.

———. 1999. "Il peso della storia." *Qualestoria* 27 (1): 9–34.

Violich, Francis. 1998. *The Bridge to Dalmatia: A Search for the Meaning of Place.* Baltimore: Johns Hopkins University Press.

Vivante, Angelo. [1912] 1984. *Irredentismo Adriatico.* Trieste: Italo Svevo.

Vivoda, Lino. 1998. *Campo profughi Giuliani Caserma Ugo Botti La Spezia.* Imperia: Edizioni Istria Europa.

Vodopivec, Peter. 1996a. "L'historiographie en Slovénie dans les années 80." In *Histoire et pouvoir en Europe Mediane,* pp. 127–37. Paris: L'Harmattan.

———. 1996b. "L'historiographie Slovènie, 1989–1994." In *Histoire et pouvoir en Europe Mediane,* pp. 263–72. Paris: L'Harmattan.

Volk, Sandi. 1999. *Ezulski skrbiniki.* Koper: Knjiznica Annales.

Wachtel, Andrew Baruch. 1998. *Making a Nation, Breaking a Nation.* Stanford: Stanford University Press.

Walston, James. 1997. "History and Memory of the Italian Concentration Camps." *The Historical Journal* 40 (1): 169–83.

Ward, David. 1999. "From Croce to Vico: Carlo Levi's *L'orologio* and Italian Anti-Fascism, 1943–46." In *Italian Fascism: History, Memory, and Representation,* ed. R.J.B. Bosworth and Patrizia Dogliani, pp. 64–82. New York: St. Martin's Press.

Waters, Malcolm. 1995. *Globalization.* London: Routledge.

Weinberg, Florence M. 1986. *The Cave: The Evolution of a Metaphoric Field from Homer to Ariosto.* New York: Peter Lang.

Weldes, Jutta. 1999. "The Cultural Production of Crises: U.S. Identity and Missiles in Cuba." In *Cultures of Insecurity: States, Communities, and the Production of Danger,* ed. Jutta Weldes, Mark Laffey, Hugh Gusterson, and Raymond Duvall, pp. 35–62. Minneapolis: University of Minnesota Press.

Werbner, Pnina. 1997. "Introduction: The Dialectics of Cultural Hybridity." In *Debating*

Cultural Hybridity, ed. Pnina Werbner and Tariq Modood, pp. 1–26. London: Zed Books.

Werner Kupka, Horst. 1964. "The Fate of Yugoslavia's Germans." *Sudeten Bulletin* 12 (12): 358–62.

Wilhelm, Maria. 1988. *The Other Italy.* New York: Norton.

Williams, Raymond. 1976. *Keywords: A Vocabulary of Culture and Society.* New York: Oxford University Press.

Winter, Jay. 1995. *Sites of Memory, Sites of Mourning.* Cambridge: Cambridge University Press.

Wolf, Eric. 1982. *Europe and the People without History.* Berkeley: University of California Press.

Wolff, Larry. 1994. *Inventing Eastern Europe: The Map of Civilization on the Mind of the Enlightenment.* Stanford: Stanford University Press.

————. 2001. *Venice and the Slavs: The Discovery of Dalmatia in the Age of Enlightenment.* Stanford: Stanford University Press.

Woodbridge, George. 1950a. *UNRRA: The History of the United Nations Relief and Rehabilitation Administration.* Vol. 2. New York: Columbia University Press.

————. 1950b. *UNRRA: The History of the United Nations Relief and Rehabilitation Administration.* Vol. 3. New York: Columbia University Press.

Woodward, Susan. 1995. *Balkan Tragedy: Chaos and Dissolution after the Cold War.* Washington, D.C.: Brookings Institution.

Yaeger, Patricia, ed. 1996. *The Geography of Identity.* Ann Arbor: University of Michigan Press.

Yates, Francis A. 1978. *The Art of Memory.* London: Routledge and Kegan Paul.

Yoneyama, Lisa. 1999. *Hiroshima Traces: Time, Space, and the Dialectics of Memory.* Berkeley: University of California Press.

Young, James. 1988. *Writing and Rewriting the Holocaust: Narrative and the Consequences of Interpretation.* Bloomington: Indiana University Press.

————. 1993. *The Texture of Memory: Holocaust Memorials and Meaning.* New Haven: Yale University Press.

Young, Robert J. C. 1995. *Colonial Desire: Hybridity in Theory, Culture, and Race.* London: Routledge.

Yugoslav Government. 1945. "Memorandum of the Government of the Democratic Federative Yugoslavia Concerning the Question of the Julian March and Other Yugoslav Territories under Italy." n.p.

————. 1946. *Trieste and the Julian March.* London: Yugoslav Embassy Information Office [B. Dellagana and Co.].

Yugoslav Institute of International Studies. 1946. *Documents Concerning the Denationalization of Yugoslavs in the Julian March.* Belgrade: Yugoslav Institute of International Studies.

Zelco, Giuliana. 1993. *Vento di terra perduta.* Trieste: Italo Svevo.

Zilli, Silvano. 1989. "Gruppo etnico italiano: Anno zero?" Unpublished article.

————. 1990. "Un passato . . . quale storia?" Unpublished article.

Živković, Marko. 2000. "The Wish to Be a Jew: The Power of the Jewish Trope in the Yugoslav Conflict." *Cahiers de l'URMIS* 6:69–84.

Zuccotti, Susan. 1987. *The Italians and the Holocaust: Persecution, Rescue, and Survival.* New York: Basic Books.

Newspapers and Periodicals

Articles with no obvious authors are listed first. For scholarly journals, see "Books and Scholarly Journals."

PICCOLO, IL

1996a. "Delbianco si fa la sua 'Dieta'" (9 December).
1996b. "Foibe, l'inchiesta arriva oltreconfine" (13 February).
1996c. "Foibe, Lubiana attacca Roma" (23 March).
1997. "Un consiglio dei ministri sulla questione istriana" (19 September).
2000. "La Dieta compie dieci anni" (22 February).
2001a. "È Jakovčić il Paperone dei politici" (August 10).
2001b. "L'Euroregione? È fascista" (24 August).
2001c. "Il regionalismo? È un tabù" (25 August).

EMANCIPAZIONE, L'

1947. "A Trieste i resti di Sauro!" (27 January).
1947b. "Sauro esule con la sua gente" (10 March).

VOCE DEL POPOLO, LA

1996a. "Gli Italiani non fecero pulizie etniche" (28 August).
1996b. "Pensioni italiane revisione improbabile" (29 August).

Aquaro, Angelo. 1996a. "Il pidiessino che ha lanciato l'idea: 'Foibe? Parliamo di cose più serie.'" *Corriere della Sera* (14 August).
———. 1996b. "Messori: Ipocriti, fu genocidio." *Corriere della Sera* (14 August).
A. R. 2000. "La Croazia nell'Ue dal 2006." *Il Piccolo* (9 March).
Bar., G. 1995. "Foibe: 'Cerco testimoni diretti.'" *Il Piccolo* (24 November).
Bolletino D'Informazioni degli Sloveni in Italia. 1980. "Imponente manifestazione unitaria nel cinquantenario della morte dei quattro giovani sloveni, vittimi della barbarie fascista sull'altipiano di Bazovica-Basovizza." September 1–30 (17–18).
———. 1983. "Commemorato a Trieste lo squadrista Giunta." April 1–30 (7–8).
Cavadini, Federica. 1996. "Canfora: No, non fu persecuzione razziale." *Corriere della Sera* (14 August).
Chiarusi, Sofia, and Matteo Moder. 1998. "Violante, Fini e poca storia." *Il Manifesto* (15 March).
Ćurić, Dražen. 2000. "Jakovčić l'insaziabile?" *La Voce del Popolo* (23 February).
Damiani, Alessandro. 1996. "Ennesima polemica sulle foibe: Profanazione." *Panorama* (15 September 1996): 18–19.
Debeljuh, Loredana Bogliun. 1995. "Ricomposizione ideale del popolo istriano: Interview with Rosi Gasparini." *Panorama* 7 (15 April 1995): 3–7.
Derin, Anita. "Considerazioni sull'inaugurazione del Monumento di Martiri delle Foibe." *La Sveglia* 2.
Djilas, Aleksa. 1992. "The Nation That Wasn't." *The New Republic* (21 September): 25–30.

Forza, Silvio. 1994. Lotta per il potere. *Panorama* (28 February): 7–8.

Galli della Loggia, Ernesto. 1996a. "Il tabù storico della sinistra." *Corriere della Sera* (25 August).

———. 1996b. "Un'altra memoria cancellata." *Corriere della Sera* (18 August).

Garau, Giulio. 1998. "Violante-Fini, incontro 'promosso.'" *Il Piccolo* (12 March).

Gasparini, Rosi. 1996. "Lotta per il potere e crisi di partito." *Panorama* 17 (15 September): 4–7.

Giuricin, Ezio. 1994. "Minoranza e opposizione [Interview with Furio Radin]." *Panorama* (15 June) 11: 7–9.

Gruppo Memorandum 88. 1998. "Lettera aperta agli onorevoli Fini e Violante." *Pomeridiano di TriesteOggi* (March 13).

I.B. 2001a. "Il regionalismo? É un tabù." *Il Piccolo* (25 August).

———. 2001b. "San Giorgio: Croazia contro Jakovčić." *Il Piccolo* (24 August).

Kocjan, Miro. 1996. "L'opinione: 'Inopportuna la targe per Nazario Sauro.'" *Il Piccolo* (26 August).

Ljuština, Branko. 2000. "I diritti degli italiani derivano dall'autoctonia." *La Voce del Popolo* (29 May).

Loffredo, Ferdinando. 1939. "La politica della famiglia e della razza." *Difesa della Razza* (November 20, 1930): 29–33.

Manzin, Mauro. 1996. "'Conosciamo 883 criminali italiani.'" *Il Piccolo* (6 March).

———. 1998. "A Trieste per una memoria storica comune." *Il Piccolo* (15 March).

Maranzana, Silvio. 1996. "Ciro, un sergente 'di ferro.'" *Il Piccolo* (23 February).

Maranzana, Silvio, and Riccardo Coretti. 1996. "Sulle tracce dei criminali." *Il Piccolo* (26 March).

Marchesich, Giorgio. 1998. "Abbraccio incestuoso che soffoca la nostra città." *Il Pomeridiano di TriesteOggi* (13 March).

Pagnotti, Simonetta. 1990. "I fantasmi di Reggio." *Famiglia Cristiana* 37:37–39.

Paladini, Giannantonio. 1988. "Jugoslavia: Martiri dimenticati." *Il Gazzettino* (24 March).

Palieri, Armeni. 1998. "Sulle foibe scontro storici-Violante." *Unità* (March 19).

Pansa, Giampaolo. 1996. "Prigioniero di Tito. E del silenzio." *Espresso* (19 September): 20–30.

Radossi, Alessio. 1996. "'Giacca' vuole il passaporto italiano." *Il Piccolo* (15 February).

Ruggiero, Giovanni. 1996. "Foibe, un silenzio che parte da Yalta." *Avvenire* (27 August).

Rumiz, Paolo. 1998a. "É da qui che riparte la coscienza nazionale." *Il Piccolo* (15 March).

———. 1998b. "La seconda repubblica e l'amnistia che nasce dal vizio dell'amnesia." *Il Piccolo* (14 March).

———. 1998c. "Violante e Fini davanti al muro delle memorie." *Il Piccolo* (14 March).

Sabatti, Pier Luigi. 1996. "Sauro ignorato dalla sua città." *Il Piccolo* (19 August).

Sala, Teodoro. 1996. "Italiani, brutta gente." *L'Espresso* (19 September): 26–30.

Sergi, Pantaleone. 1996. "Il giudice denuncia 'Non bloccheranno la verità sulle foibe.'" *La Repubblica* (2 September).

Spadaro, Stelio. 1996. "Foibe, quei silenzi che hanno allontanato Trieste." *L'Unità* (29 August).

Spirito, Pietro. 1995. "Vent'anni all'ombra di Osimo." *Il Piccolo* (10 November).

———. 1996a. "Foibe, Botteghe Oscure dà il via libera." *Il Piccolo* (23 August).

———. 1996b. "Foibe: Fu un sterminio ma il museo non piace." *Il Piccolo* (15 August).

———. 1996c. "Pensioni, timori all'estero." *Il Piccolo* (13 September).

Štorman, Mauro. 1996. "Ferite aperte: Gli infoibamenti in Istria nel periodo, 1943–1946." *Panorama* 6 (31 March): 10–11.

Strada, Vittorio. 1996. "I gulag senza processo." *Avvenire* (28 August).

Tortorella, Maurizio. 1995. "Si scopron le foibe. . ." *Panorama* (17 March): 72.

Valdevit, Giampaolo. 1995. "In questa città il dopoguerra non è mai finito." *Il Piccolo* (10 November).

———. 1996. "Indagini sulle foibe: Dalla giustizia una verità limitata." *Il Piccolo* (20 February).

———. 1998. "Un invito a giocare a carte scoperte il proprio futuro." *Il Piccolo* (15 March).

Weber, Roberto. 1998. "Il dibattito sulla storia? Per i triestini è stato utile." *L'Unità* (March 17).

Zeriali, Paolo. 1998. "Violante si sveglia dopo 50 anni." *Il Pomeridiano di TriesteOggi* (14 March).

INDEX

Printed in Great
Britain
by Amazon